# EUCHARIST AND ESCHATOLOGY

# Eucharist and Eschatology

GEOFFREY WAINWRIGHT

New York
OXFORD UNIVERSITY PRESS
1981

First published in the United States 1981

**Library of Congress Cataloging in Publication Data**

Wainwright, Geoffrey, 1939-
Eucharist and eschatology.

Reprint. Originally published: 2nd ed. London:
Epworth Press, 1978.
Bibliography: p.
Includes index.
1. Lords's Supper. 2. Eschatology. I. Title.
BV825.2.W26 1981    234'.163    81-38348
ISBN 0-19-520248-1      AACR2
ISBN 0-19-520249-X (pbk.)

Printing (last digit): 9 8 7 6 5 4 3 2 1

Printed in the United States of America

# Preface to the American Edition

T HE PUBLICATION of this American edition of *Eucharist and Eschatology* pleases me on two scores. First, it will make more readily available a work which has come to be regarded as a classic treatment of its theme. Second, it is gratifying to find that I still stand by what I wrote more than a decade ago in my theological youth. In *Doxology*, my recent 'systematic theology from a liturgical perspective', I have tried 'on a broader canvas' that 'liturgical way of doing theology' which I first attempted in *Eucharist and Eschatology*. The earlier book, which you now have in hand, may thus be seen as either a cameo or a specially detailed corner of a bigger picture. The eucharist continues to be crucial to my faith, understanding and practice. Eschatology remains the theological horizon in which I live and work.

Eucharist and eschatology are of wider than private interest. In many parts of Catholicism and Protestantism, the eucharist has come freshly alive in ways that vary with the circumstances; and the goal of 'visible unity in one faith and in one eucharistic fellowship', as the constitution of the World Council of Churches envisages it, remains the ecumenical order of the day for the divided confessions whose mutual separation is a counter-testimony to the gospel. The vigorous social and political concerns of the churches and of Christians pose, implicitly or explicitly, questions of eschatology, for it is the nature and realization of 'the kingdom' which is ultimately at stake in them; and, without indulging in cheap apocalypticism yet bearing in mind that the universalization of horizons is a characteristic of biblical apocalyptic, it is permitted to wonder whether, in our global epoch, things may be 'coming to a head' for the entire human race as has never happened before, except proleptically in the life, death and resurrection of Jesus Christ. Eucharist and eschatology are vital to Church and world, and much may depend on their proper linkage.

An appendix contains a kind of annotated bibliography which brings the book up to date. I am grateful to Allen Kelley and Charles Scott at Oxford University Press, New York, for their support of this 'liturgical way of doing theology', which I have now practised on three continents.

*Union Theological Seminary*                    GEOFFREY WAINWRIGHT
*New York City*
*Advent 1980*

# Contents

# *Preface*

THIS BOOK is one man's answer to the call made at Aarhus in 1964 by the World Council of Churches Commission on Faith and Order for a study of the eucharist in the eschatological perspective. The study was substantially complete by the autumn of 1967, when I left Western Europe for Equatorial Africa. Though I have made every effort to keep up with recent publications, it is possible that geographical circumstances have caused me to miss something important. On the other hand, life in Africa has made me less nervous about the liturgical way of doing theology adopted in this book; for in Africa men speak in proverbs, and the mask and the sacred dance allow an experience and expression of deep truth. The publication of a work of dogmatical theology on a liturgical theme ought not, in any case, to bring blushes to its author's cheeks, even at a time when the thick of the theological fighting is taking place on the apologetical front; for unless the thread of worship continues to be woven into the fabric of the church's life and thought, then the defenders of the faith will soon find themselves with nothing left to defend. I must also declare that the experience of Christian worship seems to me to require as a 'model' of God something like that of 'supranaturalistic theism' (which is of course nowhere near so naïve as its 'cultured despisers' sometimes make out); and I simply invite the reader to share this assumption with me, even though another book would be needed nowadays to justify it.

Tribute must be paid to two scholars who at sundry times and in divers manners helped me in my study of the subject of this book: the Rev. A. R. George, M.A., B.D., formerly Principal of Wesley College, Headingley; and Professor N. A. Nissiotis, D.D., Director of the Ecumenical Institute at Bossey, Geneva. My thanks are also due to the Leverhulme trustees, whose award of a European scholarship allowed me to spend the year 1966–67 in Rome working at this study.

Scriptural quotations are usually taken from the Revised Standard Version, copyrighted 1946 and 1952 by the Division of Christian Education of the National Council of the Churches of Christ in the U.S.A. Other translations are my own, unless otherwise stated.

GEOFFREY WAINWRIGHT

*Yaoundé, Advent 1969*

# Abbreviations

| | |
|---|---|
| Brightman | F. E. Brightman, *Liturgies Eastern and Western*, vol. I. |
| *CSEL* | *Corpus Scriptorum Ecclesiasticorum Latinorum.* |
| Denzinger-Schönmetzer | H. Denzinger-A. Schönmetzer, *Enchiridion Symbolorum*, 1965[33]. |
| *EVuB* | E. Käsemann, *Exegetische Versuche und Besinnungen.* |
| *GCS* | *Die griechischen christlichen Schriftsteller der ersten drei Jahrhunderte.* |
| *JTS* | *Journal of Theological Studies.* |
| *NRTh* | *Nouvelle Revue Théologique.* |
| *NTS* | *New Testament Studies.* |
| PG | J. P. Migne, *Patrologia graeca.* |
| PL | J. P. Migne, *Patrologia latina.* |
| Renaudot | E. Renaudot, *Liturgiarum orientalium collectio* 1716. |
| *RHPhR* | *Revue d'Histoire et de Philosophie religieuses.* |
| *TWNT* | *Theologisches Wörterbuch zum Neuen Testament* (ed. G. Kittel). |
| *ZNW* | *Zeitschrift für die neutestamentliche Wissenschaft.* |

# Introduction

A RAPID contrast with the eucharistic treatises of Western theologians of the immediately preceding generations will begin to make clear what is new in the approach to the eucharist adopted in the present study, which bears the title *Eucharist and Eschatology*. The older treatises dealt with the eucharist under three chief aspects. First, they dealt with the *presence* of Christ in or at the sacrament, and particularly with the relation between the bread and wine and that presence. Whether the medieval doctrine of transubstantiation was affirmed or denied, the discussion was conducted in terms that were *ontological* rather than eschatological. Roman theologians were concerned to affirm that the 'substance' of Christ's body displaced the 'substance' of the bread and wine. The Lutheran tendency, basing itself on Luther's understanding of the principle of *communicatio idiomatum* which posited the ubiquity of Christ's humanity in virtue of the ubiquity of His divinity (at the supper this presence is *revealed* by the Word, and particularly through the words 'This is my body' and 'This is my blood'), was to affirm the co-existence of the 'substance' of Christ and the 'substance' of the bread and wine. Zwinglians and Calvinists affirmed that Christ has 'remained in heaven' since His ascension, and that there is a simultaneous but in no wise collocative feeding on Christ as the bread and wine are eaten and drunk.[1] And in all this the notion of an *advent* of the Lord to His people in a visitation of judgement and salvation fared rather badly.

Secondly, the older treatises dealt with the relation between the Cross of Christ and the *sacrificial* nature which classical liturgical tradition has ascribed to the eucharist. Was the eucharist (to borrow the terms of the Anglican Book of Common Prayer) a 'sacrifice of praise and thanksgiving' for the 'full, perfect, and sufficient sacrifice, oblation, and satisfaction' which Christ once made on Calvary, and a responsive offering of 'ourselves, our souls and bodies, to be a reasonable, holy and lively sacrifice'? Or, if the Roman church was right in affirming that 'Christ was offered' at the mass, how was *this* sacrifice to be related to that made on the Cross? In any case, the theologians saw the eucharist as looking back to the *past* event of the Lord's death much more than as looking forward to the *future* event of His coming: they were concerned with the relation between present and past rather than with the relation between present and future.

Thirdly, the treatises dealt with the fruits of communion, and particularly with reference to the *individual* recipient. They were concerned with the communicant's present union with his Lord; in so far as the future eschatological reference entered at all, it was a question of determining the exact type of causal relation between present communion and the future glorious resurrection of the communicant.[2] The treatises were far less concerned with the eucharist as the common meal of the whole churchly people of God in the last days, and with its relation to the messiah's banquet in the kingdom and the abundant feeding that the Bible looked for in the days of the new heavens and the new earth. The ecclesiological and cosmological references of the eucharist found themselves severely curtailed.

It is none of my purpose to denigrate ontology: there are in fact ontological questions raised by the eucharistic presence that are neither unimportant in themselves nor excluded by the eschatological perspective I want to adopt. Equally, the words reported of Jesus over the bread and the cup at the Last Supper, as well as the command 'Do this in remembrance of me', pose questions with regard to sacrifice that are not abolished, but may even rather be illuminated, by the eschatological perspective: the Wine that finally gladdens the heart of man (Ps. 104:15) is also, and first, the Blood of grapes (Gen. 49:11). Likewise the present and future benefits to the individual communicant have their importance given them by such a word of Jesus as 'He who eats my flesh and drinks my blood has eternal life, and I will raise him up at the last day' (John 6:54). I desire rather to examine the eucharist from the perspective set by such texts as those of the so-called 'eschatological prospect' at the Last Supper (Mark 14:25/Matt. 26:29/Luke 22:16, 18, 29f) and the Pauline commentary that the Lord's supper is a proclamation of the Lord's death 'until he come' (I Cor. 11:26). This procedure will bring into prominence certain biblical themes which, though sometimes receiving satisfactory treatment in the liturgies themselves, have not been adequately exploited in much traditional eucharistic theology.

To the reader of Darwell Stone's monumental *History of the Doctrine of the Holy Eucharist* (2 vols., 1909) it may seem that eucharistic theology has throughout the whole history of the church been concerned exclusively with the questions of the presence and the elements, the eucharistic sacrifice, and the benefits to the communicant—with perhaps the added spice of the adoration of the consecrated elements. These questions have indeed loomed large (particularly in Western theology), but the interests of systematic and controversial theology in his own day led the Anglican historian of the eucharist of sixty years ago not only to neglect searching among the eucharistic theologians and liturgies down the centuries for echoes of such eschatological Bible-texts as we have mentioned, but also to miss completely the eschatological emphases in the eucharistic doctrine of (say) Maximus the Confessor's exposition of the liturgy in his *Mystagogia* or that section of the Wesleys' *Hymns on the Lord's Supper* (1745) which is entitled 'The Sacrament a Pledge of Heaven'. The same defect persists in such a recent historical study as the one fascicule on the eucharist that has so far appeared in the massive *Handbuch der Dogmengeschichte* which is being published by Herder: 'Eucharistie in Mittelalter und Neuzeit', by B. Neunheuser (1963).

In the realm of systematic theology, even such a scholar as J. de Baciocchi, who has contributed much to the refreshment of eucharistic theology, continues to give a heavy preponderance to traditionally formulated questions of presence and sacrifice in his manual *L'Eucharistie* (1964).[3] In the often excellent Catholic dictionary of dogmatics, *Handbuch Theologischer Grundbegriffe* (1962–63), the article by J. Betz on the eucharist is entirely absorbed by questions of sacrifice and real presence: in an article of twenty pages the eschatological reference of the eucharist is accorded an incidental mention of seven words. Scarcely better, proportionately, is the otherwise interesting treatise of J. M. Powers, *Eucharistic Theology* (1967).

My aim in the present study is not only to do more justice to the importance of the neglected biblical texts for a doctrine of the eucharist, but also to develop in a systematic way the more or less isolated insights into the eschatological character of the eucharist displayed by the liturgies and the earlier theologians. Eucharistic theology as a whole should benefit from being seen in an eschatological light, and even the habitually controversial questions that have hitherto seemed insoluble may become more tractable.

Now eschatology has been in the theological vogue, thanks to the work of twentieth-century exegetes on the notion of the kingdom of God and its assumption into the writings of the biblical and the systematic theologians. But it would be a mistake to assume that there had been anything like a satisfactory attempt to bring into systematic relation this newly rediscovered eschatology and the theology of the eucharist.

In the first place, it must be recognized that the biblical exegetes have in particular shown sharp divergences as to the relation between present and future in the New Testament texts dealing with the coming of the kingdom, and also that the systematic theologians have differed widely in their ways of interpreting or re-interpreting the relation between 'present' and 'future' which they have drawn from exegesis; yet the liturgical theologians, who usually either write from within the 'catholic' traditions or are themselves 'catholic-minded' theologians, have tended to assume that exegesis and systematic theology offer a fairly standardized picture of eschatology of the *Heilsgeschichte* type, and in consequence they have been willing to consider their duty done once they have said quite simply that the eucharist is not only a memorial of Christ's saving work in the past and a present communion with the Lord but also a (none too closely defined) anticipation of the future messianic banquet in the completed kingdom. Apart from O. Cullmann, who is both the most distinguished exponent of the *Heilsgeschichte* eschatology and also the author of some important contributions to eucharistic theology, critical mention must also be made in this respect of certain other theologians who have otherwise contributed usefully to eucharistic theology, namely: the Jesuit J. Daniélou in his article 'Les repas de la Bible et leur signification' in *La Maison-Dieu* (1949), and in his book *Bible et Liturgie* (1951); the Lutheran G. Delling in his book *Der Gottesdienst im Neuen Testament* (1952); and the Reformed M. Thurian in his book *L'Eucharistie: Mémorial du Seigneur, sacrifice d'action de grâce et d'intercession* (1959).[4]

In the second place, those exegetes and historians of the earliest period who have occupied themselves with the Lord's supper have in this matter of the eschatological dimension worked under the spell (whether succumbed to or struggled against) of H. Lietzmann's theory of the two types of primitive eucharist: the eschatological joy-meal of the Jerusalem church, and the Pauline memorial of the death of Christ (see Lietzmann's *Messe und Herrenmahl*, 1926). They have not made too close reference in this connection to the vexed questions of the general eschatology of the New Testament, let alone to the systematic problems of interpreting 'present' and 'future'. Typical examples here are the articles of O. Cullmann, 'La signification de la Sainte Cène dans le christianisme primitif' in *Revue d'Histoire et de Philosophie Religieuses* (1936); E. Lohmeyer, 'Vom urchristlichen Abendmahl' in *Theologische Rundschau* (1937–38); Y. de Montcheuil, 'Signification eschatologique du repas eucharistique' in *Recherches de Science Religieuse* (1946); and E. Schweizer, 'Das Abendmahl eine Vergegenwärtigung des Todes Jesu oder ein eschatologisches Freudenmahl?' in *Theologische Zeitschrift* (1946); and the books of A. J. B. Higgins, *The Lord's Supper in the New Testament* (1952), and A. B. du Toit, *Der Aspekt der Freude im urchristlichen Abendmahl* (1965).

Thirdly, those properly systematic theologians who have made a detailed study of eschatology have not paid much attention either to the place of the eucharist within their total view of eschatology or to any possible role to be played by the eucharist in the shaping of their eschatology in the first place. In his systematic vein Bultmann, for instance, pays exclusive attention to the preached word as that which confronts man with the need to make ever anew the eschatological decision to live in the freedom which grace makes possible; and since his appreciation of the eucharist is permanently blighted by a notion of the Ignatian 'medicine of immortality' pejoratively interpreted,[5] Bultmann seems forever prevented from seeing the part which the sacrament also might play in his total eschatological vision (see his Gifford Lectures, *History and Eschatology*, 1957).

Three other recent full-dress studies in eschatology pay next to no attention to the eucharist. In his *Die Zukunft des Gekommenen: Grundprobleme der Eschatologie* (1961, 198 pages), W. Kreck mentions the eucharist on page 84 only in order to make a polemical point which in fact depends on a false alternative: 'The sacrament is no "pharmakon athanasias" [*again!*] but rather a seizure (*Beschlagnahmung*) by the present though hidden Lord who can be known and acknowledged only in faith.' In his *Zukunft und Verheissung* (1965, 374 pages), G. Sauter devotes a couple of pages (pp. 267–9) to the way in which worship takes its place among the promises God gives of the future, but the eucharist is not mentioned in particular. J. Moltmann's only reference to the sacraments in his *Theologie der Hoffnung* (1964; 1966⁶, 340 pages) is made in order to disparage the Hellenistic enthusiasts of Corinth who believed that heaven had already been attained with the cultic epiphany of the Lord in the Spirit, and whose belief Paul needed to correct in I Corinthians (pp. 140–50, cf. p. 202).

Nothing in the preceding paragraphs is meant to discredit the work of the exegetes, the liturgical theologians or the systematicians *in their several domains*; and indeed the present study owes many individual insights to the very scholars singled out for critical mention. It was, however, necessary to call attention to a certain mutual unawareness among theologians working in the respective domains of eschatology and eucharistic theology. The present study is an attempt to begin redressing the situation by exploring the relations between the eucharist and eschatology in the latter's various interpretations. As a given phenomenon in the church's life practised from the beginning of Christianity until now, the eucharist should figure among the interests of all the various disciplines of Christian theology: our understanding of the eucharist should be aided by all the theological disciplines as they apply themselves to its study from their own particular angle, and (in the reverse direction) the eucharistic phenomenon itself should help to shape the total outlook of the various theological disciplines.

My own primary concern here will be to show how our understanding of the eucharist may benefit from the rediscovery of eschatology experienced in biblical and systematic theology; secondarily I shall try to indicate how the eucharist itself may, in turn, contribute towards a sound eschatology in theology as a whole and in the total self-understanding and life of the church. The plan is as follows.

It is necessary first of all to set the *eschatological background*, i.e. to indicate the main features of the general recovery of the eschatological perspective in biblical and systematic theology in the present century. The aim is not to proceed with the accuracy of a historian of theology who would give a detailed account of the views of leading scholars: it is rather to distinguish the characteristic positions held; and in so far as personal names are attached to positions, it must be admitted that a certain amount of caricature is involved because the niceties are sometimes sacrificed for the sake of discerning the heart of a position. It will emerge that the key problems in eschatology concern (i) the relation between what in the perspective that predominates in the Bible appear as 'present' and 'future' and (ii) the possible re-interpretations of that relation in systematic terms. At the end of this brief survey we shall know what kind of questions to look for when we come to the central part of the study, namely the examination of the biblical, liturgical and theological evidence for the eschatological content and import of the eucharist.

The central and weightiest three chapters in fact look in turn at the eucharist in terms of *three images*:

first (for this is the dominant image which in some ways includes the
    others), the messianic feast;
second, the advent of Christ;
third, the firstfruits of the kingdom.

I believe that in approaching the sacrament in this frankly pictorial way
we shall be able to keep close to a mode of understanding and experiencing
reality which is particularly characteristic of the Scriptures and of the
liturgies. But stress on the conveyance and apprehension of reality through
images will not be taken as excusing us from the task of trying to discover
in each case what are the most appropriate categories of a somewhat more
abstract nature for conceiving the relation between 'present' and 'future' in
eucharistic eschatology.

In the final chapter we shall draw out the *ecclesiological consequences* of
the eschatological content and import of the eucharist. After indicating
reasons for what will emerge to have been a comparative neglect of the
eschatological perspective over many centuries in the West and a certain
distortion of it in the East, I shall suggest what would be the consequences,
in two particular areas, of a recovery of a healthy eschatological understanding of the eucharist, namely: the consequences for the church's
*mission* as the messenger of the kingdom, and for the church's *unity* as the
body of Christ.

A short conclusion will show how the eucharist, after our understanding
of it has been benefited by the modern rediscovery of eschatology in
general, may itself in turn either challenge or strengthen the various
current styles of eschatological thought.

# I

# *The Eschatological Background*

IN THE twentieth century, Western theology has witnessed a rediscovery of the eschatological dimension of the gospel. It began in German Protestantism, the initial work being done by biblical scholars in their investigation of the New Testament concept of the kingdom of God. The publication which launched the rediscovery was Johannes Weiss's book *Die Predigt Jesu vom Reiche Gottes* (1892; 1900²). Weiss tore to shreds the dominant Ritschlian notion of the kingdom as the moral and spiritual society that was being gradually built up over the years by the followers of Jesus in accordance with the task bequeathed to them by their master; he substituted the notion, which he found in the preaching of Jesus Himself on the kingdom, of the mighty kingly rule of God irrupting finally and decisively into history from beyond. Albert Schweitzer adopted, developed and broadcast Weiss's thesis particularly in his *Von Reimarus zu Wrede* (1906; subsequently entitled *Geschichte der Leben-Jesu-Forschung*). From that date on, New Testament exegetes have made the investigation of Jesus's teaching on the kingdom one of their chief tasks, and systematic theologians have begun the job of turning eschatology from a separate topic treated in an embarrassed final discourse on the last things at the end of a dogmatical system into a theme or perspective which colours the total presentation of a Christian theology. In this chapter we shall survey the work first of the exegetes and then of the systematicians, in order to set the general context of eschatology in which our investigation of the eucharist must take place.

## 1. The work of New Testament scholars

In the New Testament field Albert Schweitzer laid the foundation for the so-called *konsequente Eschatologie* ('thorough-going eschatology').[6] According to Schweitzer, Jesus stood in the tradition of Jewish apocalyptic and proclaimed the imminent irruption of the kingdom of God. He expected the event to take place before the disciples had finished the preaching tour on which He sent them (Schweitzer makes recurrent reference to Matt. 10:23); but when this hope failed, Jesus tried to force God's hand by His own voluntary death, expecting that He would immediately be vindicated and would Himself return on the clouds of heaven to bring in the kingdom. Jesus's eschatological expectations were directed towards the immediate future: and they were disappointed. The tendency to portray Jesus as a deluded fanatic militated against the ready acceptance of what has since been recognized as an irreversible acquisition of the theses of

Weiss and Schweitzer, namely that *the kingdom of God is a final and decisive act of God entering history*.

The acceptance was in time rendered easier by the work of C. H. Dodd in calling attention to sayings and parables of Jesus which seemed to indicate that *the irruption of the divine kingdom into history has already taken place precisely in the person and deeds of Jesus of Nazareth*.[7] Dodd argued that the ἄρα ἔφθασεν ἐφ' ὑμᾶς ἡ βασιλεία τοῦ Θεοῦ of Matt. 12:28 = Luke 11:20 means that the kingdom was already present in the ministry of Jesus, and the ἤγγικεν ἡ βασιλεία τοῦ Θεοῦ of Mark 1:15 and Luke 10:9–11 is interpreted in this light. The parables of crisis were (at least in their original setting) parables of present crisis: confronted by Jesus, men undergo their final judgement by the way in which they respond to Him; either they believe, and enter the kingdom, or else they reject Him and themselves suffer rejection. The parables of growth taught that the 'harvest', 'the divinely ordained climax of history', was *here*. The miracles of healing bring the blessings of the kingdom: the blind see, the deaf hear, the lame walk. Satan has already fallen (Matt. 12:28 = Luke 11:20), the strong man is already bound (Mark 3:27). Dodd went far in re-interpreting those gospel sayings which appear to show that for Jesus the kingdom was a still awaited reality. Continuing Dodd's work, T. F. Glasson demolished the few remaining traces of an expectation on the part of Jesus that He would return in glory to inaugurate the kingdom. In Mark 14:62 and parallels, Jesus is referring to His coming *exaltation*, and the sayings which do speak of a future coming in glory are either misinterpretations of original Jesus-words or else are entirely due to the primitive church or the evangelists themselves. According to Glasson, the hope of the second advent arose in the Christian community largely because the first coming of Christ had not seemed to fulfil the Old Testament prophecies of the Lord's coming *in glory* to judge and to reign.[8]

The positive contribution of Dodd that the kingdom was already present in the person and deeds of Jesus remains. 'Realized eschatology' is an irreversible acquisition of New Testament scholarship provided it is not claimed to be valid in an exclusive way. Most scholars, while fundamentally accepting Dodd's positive thesis, yet believe that there remain some reported sayings of Jesus which speak of the coming of the kingdom as future and which remain untouched either by Dodd's denials of their authenticity or by his sometimes over-subtle re-interpretations of their *prima facie* future reference. Thus J. Jeremias does not find it possible to remove all future reference from the original form of the parables, and he therefore modifies Dodd's initial position to the extent of substituting the tag 'eine sich realisierende Eschatologie' (eschatology that is in process of realization) for the earlier 'realized eschatology': the salvation and judgement already begun in the ministry of Jesus will come to a future climax.[9] Certainly the parables which exhort to vigilance suppose a future coming of the end,[10] and the same is true of the warnings to the disciples of future tribulations.[11] Again there are sayings in which Jesus envisages a future reversal of the present situation: the last shall be first and first last

(Matt. 19:30), the hidden shall be revealed (Matt. 10:26 and pars.), the lowly shall be exalted (Matt. 18:4; cf. Luke 14:11, Matt. 23:12, Luke 18:14), and a whole series of reversals is promised in the Beatitudes and Woes (Luke 6:20–26). The future reference of Mark 9:1 seems inescapable:

Truly, I say to you, there are some standing here who will not taste death before they see the kingdom of God come with power.[12]

Granted then that according to the best critical work the kingdom was both already present and yet still future during the ministry of Jesus,[13] New Testament scholars recognize that their next job is to indicate more precisely the *relation* between the present and the future there. I mention first the thesis put forward by R. H. Fuller in his book *The Mission and Achievement of Jesus* (1954). According to Fuller, the kingdom of God is *proleptically* present in the ministry of Jesus, the impending kingdom is operative in advance; it is actually inaugurated only at Jesus's death. The mighty deeds of Jesus are fore-signs of the great deliverance; it is by the finger of God, not yet his whole hand, that Jesus casts out demons (*op. cit.* pp. 35–43); it is on the Cross that the decisive victory is won. The general position of R. Bultmann is not dissimilar. In Bultmann's view, Jesus preached the kingdom as 'dawning' (*im Anbruch*): its imminence was such that it already pressed in upon the present and forced men to the crisis of decision before the activity of God. For Fuller eschatology is still only partially 'realized' even after Cross, Exaltation and Pentecost (though he does not himself say much about the future final consummation).[14] But for Bultmann there remains, after the Cross and the consequent outpouring of the Holy Spirit, no further mighty act for God to perform in the bringing in of His kingdom.

Others, however, advance detailed arguments in support of their belief that there still remains in 'the time of the church' a future reference in the sayings of Jesus about the kingdom which has not even yet been exhausted. Some of these scholars defend both the authenticity and, apparently, the literal understanding of sayings in which Jesus promises His visible return in glory to inaugurate the definitive kingdom. Here we may mention the following works: G. R. Beasley-Murray, *Jesus and the Future* (1954); O. Cullmann, *Le Retour du Christ* (1943), *Christus und die Zeit* (1946), *Heil als Geschichte* (1965); R. Schnackenburg, *Gottes Herrschaft und Reich* (1959); G. E. Ladd, *Jesus and the Kingdom* (1964); A. L. Moore, *The Parousia in the New Testament* (1966). Others, perceiving that the kingdom is not incontestably here and yet being embarrassed by the thought of a literal second coming, prefer to see the consummation of the kingdom as taking place in some 'trans-historical' way with no return of Christ to earth to inaugurate the consummation. This view is represented in two works by J. A. T. Robinson: *In the End, God* . . . (1950; 1968²), and *Jesus and His Coming* (1957).[15]

Now the difficulties experienced in relating past and future in the sayings of Jesus on the kingdom *as they are reported* may well be due to the existence of differing attempts in the apostolic church to interpret the eschatological phenomenon of Jesus. If (as I consider remains unshaken) Jesus led the disciples to expect His future coming in glory to bring in the kingdom in a way in which it was not already present in His ministry, then the apostolic church was driven to work out an interpretation of what (on the one hand) had already happened and was even then happening, and what (on the other hand), if anything, was still to come. If, as most scholars suppose who allow that He predicted His return in glory at all, Jesus predicted His *imminent* return in glory, then the disappointment of that hope led to different attempts to come to terms with the *Parusie-verzögerung*. Thus Luke–Acts, for instance, offers a solution in terms of a continuing *Heilsgeschichte*.[16] The first coming of Christ is seen not in terms of the absolute *end* of history but rather as the *mid-point* in time. Before the coming of the end there is the continuing work of the Holy Spirit through the missionary preaching of the church. This same view may be found, despite Bultmann's claim of Pauline support for his view that history has already come to an end,[17] in Paul's concern with the church's missionary task in expectation of the return of Christ. In Matthew it becomes clear, even if it were not already so in Paul and in Luke–Acts, that it is not simply a matter of 'mission history' but of '*church* history' in an institutional sense.[18]

Another interpretation emphasizes rather the *present* nature of the end. This is perhaps most characteristic of the Fourth Gospel. It has been claimed that John fills the eschatological vacuum caused by the delay in the parousia by presenting the return of Christ as having already taken place in the coming of the Holy Spirit.[19] According to John final judgement is already a present reality. *Now* is the moment of existential decision: *now* eternal life may be enjoyed.[20]

But neither of these views is held in a pure form even by those New Testament documents of which they are most characteristic. Thus Luke knows that the Spirit-filled mission marks precisely the *last* days (see Acts 2:17 where ἐν ταῖς ἐσχάταις ἡμέραις appears in the quotation from Joel 2:28 though the Hebrew (3:1) and the LXX read 'after this'). The Fourth Gospel *as we have it* presents an eschatology that is not devoid of future reference: it is only by excising a whole string of verses as the work of a later editor (5:28f.; 6:39, 40, 44, 54; 12:48 end) that Bultmann is able to make John a theologian of exclusively *present* eschatology; other scholars, in order to obtain the same result, have regarded the same verses as relics of an earlier eschatology which are really alien to John's own re-interpretation. Nor can the fact be escaped that at every stage of his epistolary career Paul also has both an 'already' and a 'not yet' about his eschatology: christological, kerygmatic and sacramental indicatives in the past and present tenses (Christ has died and is risen: Christ has been preached: You have been baptized: You are in Christ) serve as bases for ethical imperatives and promises of the future; and the Holy Spirit, firstfruits (Rom. 8:23) and earnest (II Cor. 1:22; 5:5; Eph. 1:13f), relates the 'already' and the 'not yet'.

The Letter to the Hebrews offers an interpretation of eschatology over which we may pause a moment because it seems to hold promise for understanding the relation between 'present' and 'future' with reference to the eucharist. That of which the Old Testament offered a shadowing (ὑποδείγματι καὶ σκιᾷ . . . τῶν ἐπουρανίων, 8:5) or fore-shadowing (σκιὰν γὰρ ἔχων ὁ νόμος τῶν μελλόντων ἀγαθῶν, 10:1) has been realized in Jesus Christ, and indeed in His sacrificial death on earth (9:26; 10:12; 12:2) which belongs to the 'reality-filled image (εἰκών, 10:1)' of that heavenly reality into which He has passed through His death (9:11f, 24; 10:12). The heavenly city (11:16; 12:22) and its sanctuary (6:19; 8:2, 5; 9:11f, 24) are eternal and Jesus has entered them. The pilgrim people of God, however, has not yet entered (at least not inamissibly) into its rest (4:1, 9, 11; 10:36; 12:1, 12), has not yet reached the place where its fore-runner (2:10; 6:20; 12:2) is enthroned, has not yet entered the holy place *on high* (1:3; 7:26) with its high-priest (4:14; 9:24), has not yet reached 'the city *which is to come*' (13:14). But because the blood of Jesus has won an eternal redemption (5:9; 9:12, 15) and inaugurated an eternal covenant (13:20), the earthly church may already, as the writer puts it in a liturgic-ally flavoured passage (6:1–6), *taste* 'the *heavenly* gift', 'the powers of the age *to come*', and the earthly church already has access to God (4:16; 9:19–22). Thus the Writer to the Hebrews, in order to convey the eschato-logical position, combines the 'spatial' figure of earth and (an eternal) heaven with the temporal figure of present and future, the whole cohering in the person of Jesus, the forerunner and the same yesterday, today and forever (cf. 13:8).[21]

Thus the New Testament writers themselves had already begun to make their different attempts to interpret 'present' and 'future' with reference to the kingdom of God. When we turn now to the views of modern system-aticians, we shall find that they are largely an elaboration of one emphasis or another to be found among the New Testament writers.

## 2. Work in systematic theology

We must mention, if only summarily to point out its inadequacy, the systematic development of the view that Jesus was a deluded apocalyptist. New Testament *konsequente Eschatologie* becomes systematic *enteschato-logisierte Eschatologie*. To A. Schweitzer's exegetical work M. Werner added a corresponding interpretation of the early history of Christian doctrine: *Die Entstehung des christlichen Dogmas* (1941); and in F. Buri's work of systematic theology (*Die Bedeutung der neutestamentlichen Eschatologie für die neuere protestantische Theologie*, 1935) all that can be salvaged from the disappointed hopes of Jesus and the early Christian attempts at compensation is a 'de-eschatologized eschatology' based (and here Buri elaborates on Schweitzer's maxim of 'reverence for life') on 'the will for absolute life-fulfilment'. According to Buri, eschatology is the triumph of the will in its conflict with knowledge: in face of a man's knowledge of his weakness and the meaninglessness of his existence his will victoriously asserts meaning and purposeful action—and that man is saved from resignation and despair, and for him a new world is born in which misery and death no longer hold sway. All that we in turn can salvage from Buri is his recognition that eschatology does indeed include the full development of human life and personality. For the rest, we must say that his reduction of eschatology to an individualized and psychologized anthropology does not come near doing justice to the biblical picture of a new heaven and a new earth and a people of a new and eternal covenant, all brought into being by the mighty activity of God. Against Buri's interpretation, and those that resemble it in this respect, it must be said at the outset that it is illegitimate to interpret the *universal* scope of biblical talk about new heavens and a new earth as merely a mythological way of talking about what is *ultimately* valid for an individual man; for what is *ultimately* valid will, if God is God, be valid *universally*. (Much later, in *Der Pantokrator* (1969), Buri allows universal eschatology to symbolize the historical and cultural dimensions of 'responsible personal existence'.)

The systematic counterpart to the position of those New Testament scholars who hold that eschatology is during the ministry of Jesus, or at least after Cross, Exaltation and Pentecost, already 'realized' is the position which evacuates 'church history' of any tension towards a consummation at the final advent of Christ and sees simply an unconnected series of present moments, each of which 'laps like a wave on the shore of eternity' (P. Althaus)[22] and is the opportunity for seizing the *eschaton* in an existential decision (R. Bultmann);[23] and here too belongs P. Tillich's transposition of 'the last things' into 'ultimate reality', which is none other than the eternal God Himself who is present as the deep ground of everything and is manifest in so far as we are theonomously transparent to 'the power of being'. At the individualist level, this view becomes *in its extreme forms* either a mysticism which unlike the mysticism of classical tradition experiences a union with God already so perfect that no room for progress is left, or else an existentialism of ever-renewed momentary decisions which allows no growth in sanctification of the continuing Christian person. At the ecclesiological level, this same view becomes that triumphalism not unknown in Roman Catholicism which, following on Augustine's interpretation of the parables of the *kingdom* as parables of the *church*, makes a simple equation between kingdom and church: the church is, by virtue of the divine life coursing through it, a *supernatural* institution amid earthly reality and already so perfect that the *future* reference seems hardly necessary.[24] Now there is some value in this view, both in its 'eternalist' and in its 'existentialist' clothings, both in its individual and in its ecclesiological forms: its value lies in its safeguarding of the 'already' of judgement and salvation. But its approach is so unilateral that it demands correction or completion by an emphasis on the 'not yet' and on church *history*.

It is here that the *Heilsgeschichte* view of eschatology has its contribution to make. Its extreme proponent is, characteristically, as much a biblical theologian as a systematician: I mean O. Cullmann.[25] The presence and futurity of the kingdom are to be taken, quite simply, as purely temporal in reference. Eschatology is 'un concept parfaitement temporel'.[26] Biblical, and therefore real, history is stretched out on a timeline:

creation                    incarnation                    second advent

The time of the church lies in the tension of the 'already now' of the life, death and exaltation of Jesus Christ and the 'not yet' of His final advent. The Holy Spirit is already given as the firstfruits and earnest of the kingdom of the end, but He has not yet done His final work of transforming our bodies at the resurrection for the enjoyment of the kingdom. The significance of the present period of the *Heilsgeschichte* lies in the mission of the church, which exploits God's patient granting of time for the conversion of the world before His incontestable establishment of His rule. For Cullmann Christian worship is a focal instance of the tension between present and future. Worship is the meeting of the congregation with the Lord in the Spirit: with the same Lord who came once and who will come again, in the same Spirit who raised Jesus from the dead and who will raise our mortal bodies at the last. The main weakness of Cullmann's view is illustrated precisely here, in the matter of worship. Cullmann is so concerned to argue for the linear view of time against any notion of 'eternism' that he considers that the 'time' before creation was linear (and that the 'time' after the parousia will be linear); but this threatens the lordship of God over time which Augustine's doctrine of creation *cum tempore* and not *in tempore* was designed to safeguard: and it therefore becomes problematical whether a God deprived of His transcendence over time (His 'eternity') can invade time at the moments of Christian worship and present Himself to the congregation as ever the same God.[27]

A more satisfactory version of *Heilsgeschichte* eschatology may be pieced together from the systematic comments in the works of the Roman Catholic biblical theologian R. Schnackenburg, *Gottes Herrschaft und Reich* (1959) and *Die Kirche im Neuen Testament* (1961). Schnackenburg's strongest emphasis undoubtedly falls on the *heilsgeschichtlich* view of eschatology with its tension between the 'already' and the 'not yet', and is therefore a corrective to the ecclesiastico-triumphalist view that long held sway in his denomination; yet he expressly denies (with appeal to II Peter 3:8) that our period of the *Heilsgeschichte* may be measured by the Western notion of time as 'eine kontinuierlich fortlaufende Linie' since it stands under the urgent sign of the end (with appeal to I Cor. 7:29–31 and I Thess. 5:1–11);[28] nor is he averse to gleaning from Hebrews and a few other (all rather late?) New Testament hints (Col. 1:13; Eph. 2:6; II Tim. 4:18; II Pet. 1:11) the more 'spatial' image of an eternal heavenly kingdom *on high*, in order to overcome the difficulties presented by a *purely* linear conception of the relation between present and future in eschatology.[29]

It seems then that eschatology needs both the 'vertical' and the 'horizontal' models. The eternal invades time in a moment, the supernatural breaks into the natural, the heavenly bursts upon the earthly scene, and at each moment the individual may be confronted with final judgement. Yet time goes on: the parousia of Christ is still awaited, we are not yet in our resurrection bodies, the perfect community does not yet rejoice together in the unclouded vision of God. An attempt to hold the 'vertical' and the 'horizontal' together in one picture is made by the Orthodox theologian O. Clément in his book *Transfigurer le Temps: Notes sur le temps à la lumière de la tradition orthodoxe* (1959). Here time, the continuing 'horizontal' line, is seen as the God-given possibility for God's creation, and particularly for man, to learn to *love*, to learn (that is) to participate in the inner-trinitarian life of the eternal Godhead which is perfect love; history is thus given its positive value. But this time is, as it were, enveloped by eternity; eternity may penetrate time, and since the Incarnation the time of the church is 'chalcedonian'; and what man and all creation have learnt in time will be at the last taken up into eternity.[30]

Clément's position, which is true to the best in Eastern Orthodox tradition, bears a striking resemblance to the mature thought of P. Althaus, whose Lutheran allegiance, however, may account for the fact that his total scheme gives greater attention to the disturbing fact of sin which persists even in Christians.[31] Althaus sees the eschatological tension between the 'already' and the 'not yet', between *das Bleiben des Letzten* and *das Kommen des Letzten*, between 'possessing' and 'awaiting', as grounded in the fact that an *eternal* (and righteous and loving) God is dealing with *historical* (and sinful) man. In Jesus Christ the eternity of God is present for us in history; we as sinners may already know in faith the salvation of hidden fellowship with God. But because God is *God*, His glory must in the end be *revealed* and His will *done*, and He will receive in eternity the free worship of a truly sanctified congregation. The purpose of ongoing history in our world is to allow believers, by constantly laying hold of the renewing love of God constantly present, actually to *become* the righteous and true sons who will enjoy unfettered fellowship with God when their, and the world's, histories are brought to an end by eternity.[32]

Eastern Orthodoxy with its time and eternity, Roman Catholicism with its nature and supernature, Protestant existentialism with its eschatological moment and its ultimate reality: these provide us with a conceptual framework for expressing the 'vertical' reference of eschatology and the *presence* of God who is Himself the eternal one, the transcendent ground of all created nature, the reality which is the ultimate criterion of all reality. Yet the 'horizontal' reference of eschatology, i.e. its *futurity*, is also recognized by Orthodoxy and Catholicism (in so far as they recognize that salvation-history has not yet come to an end because the parousia is still to come) and even by Protestant existentialism (in so far as recognition of the *Unverfügbarkeit* of God forces Bultmann and Gogarten, for example, to speak of man's living not from 'this world', but 'living out of the future' or 'living out of God's future').[33] In this last sense eschatology must for ever retain a 'future' dimension, for finite man will never know God fully and the creature will always depend for life on the creator's gracious *Zukunft* to him; but the strictly temporal future reference must also, I would hold in agreement with the proponents of *heilsgeschichtlich* eschatology, be maintained at the present stage of eschatological realization: God's rule over sin is not yet *manifest* and *incontestable* (as we know from our own experience as sinners), and He still holds greater blessings in store than eye has yet seen, or ear heard, or the heart of man conceived (cf. I Cor. 2:9).

'Vertical' categories (such as time and eternity; nature and supernature; ultimate reality) are a necessary aid to expressing the eschatological tension, but they must not be allowed to displace the 'horizontal' from the picture. Returning therefore to the temporal categories of present and future, we end this section by indicating some of the useful ways that have been proposed of viewing the relation of tension between the 'already now' and the 'not yet'. W. Kreck, for instance, talks in *Die Zukunft des Gekommenen* (1961) chiefly in terms of revelation or disclosure (*Enthüllung, Aufdeckung, Offenbarung, Manifestation*). The kingdom of God, though a present reality since the coming of Jesus Christ, is now *hidden*, but it will be made *manifest*. The One who humbled Himself will be revealed in the glory which is really His, the crucified will be seen as the lord of life, the judged as the judge; and for men this will mean no longer walking by faith but by sight (II Cor. 5:7), no longer seeing through a glass darkly but face to face (I Cor. 13:12). This notion of the future revelation of what is now hiddenly true, the future seeing of what is at present only glimpsed, will be worth retaining in our treatment of the eucharist; and we shall be grateful to keep also Kreck's emphasis on the person of Jesus Christ (the One who has come, who continues to come in a hidden manner, who will come) as the personal bond between what already *is* in the present and what *will be* in the future. We shall, however, have to guard against reducing what is still to come to a 'mere revelation' (the expression creeps into Kreck's usage with *no* pejorative nuance). In any case, no revelation of a hidden thing is ever 'mere', for it always means a *fuller knowledge* for the one who sees, and in personal relations this fuller knowledge brings a deeper quality to the relationship between those involved. But more than that, we must leave room for God still to do *new* things, room for the *new* heaven and the *new* earth in which *risen* men and women will drink the wine *new* with Christ.

Apart from the theme of hiddenness and manifestation, there is another pattern which, with certain variations in terminology, is finding favour as a means of expressing the eschatological relation between present and future: it is the pattern of promise, hope and fulfilment. Already the New Testament scholar W. G. Kümmel gave to his book on the kingdom in the teaching of Jesus the title *Verheissung und Erfüllung* (1945). For Kümmel the ministry of Jesus was already the fulfilment, in His own person and activity, of the old promises of eschatological salvation and gave the assurance of a future universal consummation of what had already begun in Him.[34] Similarly G. E. Ladd's *Jesus and the Kingdom* (1964) is constructed on the plan that the *promise* of the kingdom in the Old Testament has been messianically *fulfilled* in Jesus Christ though the *consummation* still tarries; and the same scheme of *Verheissung: Erfüllung: Vollendung* had appeared in R. Schnackenburg's *Gottes Herrschaft und Reich* (1959).

The important books by two younger systematicians already mentioned, J. Moltmann and G. Sauter, take up this terminology but adapt it in an interesting way so as to give a more prominent place to the human response to the divine activity in bringing in the kingdom, namely: *hope*, and a hope indeed that issues in *action*. Both systematicians make use of the work of the theologian of the Old Testament, G. von Rad, on the biblical understanding of *promise*.[35] According to von Rad, the characteristic pattern of promise and fulfilment in the biblical understanding is this: a divine promise is made, some future action of God supervenes in first fulfilment of the promise, and this new deed itself becomes a new promise for a future and greater fulfilment. Moltmann stresses that God is the God of promise (Heb. 10:23; 11:11 etc.). The resurrection of Jesus is seen as the greatest promise of God, which opens up history: men may, indeed should, now order their actions *in hope* of the new creation which God has promised by the resurrection of Jesus. Based on that promise, man may shape his daily life towards the final kingdom, even though the bringing of that kingdom will be God's own work. From Sauter's difficult book it is, I think, fair to extract as its principal idea the following: it is a characteristic of God always to reserve further action for Himself in the future, but He 'throws forward' some part of that future action into the present *as a promise*. Whereas on what Sauter calls a 'philosophical' view of time man seeks to edge his way safely into the uncertain future by basing himself on the *terra firma* of accumulated past experience, in theology it is rather God who throws from the sure ground of His future a promise that will bring those who grasp it in hope safely through. Jesus Christ is the Amen ( = confirmation) of all God's promises (II Cor. 1:20), and His divine presence is the confirmed promise of the fulfilment of the rule of God in the future. Christ's presence is the promise 'im proleptischen Vorschein ihrer Erfüllung' (p. 258), and to this extent we are saved *in hope*, but not *merely* in hope.

In so far as these eschatologies keep a strictly temporal aspect in the relation between the 'presence' and the 'futurity' of the kingdom, they allow room for the significance of history, and therefore for the movement of men and all creation towards a divinely-ordained goal. Biblical eschatology is in fact inescapably teleological. It will be appropriate therefore to include also the categories of *purpose* and *destiny* in our own eschatological considerations: divine purpose for creation, and creaturely destiny in the divine purpose. Not only do these terms permit us to do justice to the reality of time and history; they are also a help towards conceiving the relation between time and eternity: the definitive kingdom is the substance of God's eternal purpose for man and all creation, yet man and all creation will reach this their destiny only through development in time, being drawn on by God's purpose as by a 'final cause'.

After this brief but indispensable survey of positions in the contemporary rediscovery of eschatology in general, we may now turn to the special subject of our investigation, the eucharist. We know that in trying to determine its eschatological content and import we shall be using the categories of present and future, time and eternity, earth and heaven, nature and supernature, ultimate reality; of hiddenness and disclosure, of knowledge through faith and through sight; of promise, hope and fulfilment; of purpose and destiny. More categories will emerge as we proceed, some of them indeed being contributions which the eucharist may make in turn to the conceptual framework of eschatology as a whole.

# II

# *Antepast of Heaven*

PERHAPS the most obvious thing about the eucharist from the New Testament point of view is that it was instituted during the course of a meal, the Last Supper, and that it has to do with food and drink, bread and wine. Yet its nature as a *meal* has hardly been very prominent in the popular conceptions of the eucharist. The Roman high mass, between the early middle ages and the modern liturgical movement, was a propitiatory sacrifice performed by a priest at a distant altar, the congregation's high-point being its glimpse of the consecrated wafer at the elevation. The Orthodox liturgy is still, particularly in the Russian tradition, a mysterious celebration mostly hidden away behind the icon-screen.[36] The Protestant supper, except perhaps in the form it received in Zürich where the stewards brought bread and wine to the seated assembly and in Holland where the communicants sit round a large table to receive the bread and wine, was (despite its name) hardly a whit more like a meal than the others. Any regular liturgical assembly will admittedly require some stylization in the way in which the Lord's supper is eaten, but the liturgies seem to have gone to excess in disguising the fundamental phenomenological feature of the eucharist. Nor have the theologians usually done justice to the theological implications of the fact that the eucharist is a meal. In recent years, however, the liturgical movement has taken a few halting steps towards a practical expression of the nature of the eucharist as a meal. And a few theologians have suggested that here is a fundamental *theological* category for building a whole eucharistic theology. Among Roman Catholics one notes in this connection the work of J. Pascher, *Eucharistia* ([1947], 1953²), and the essay of G. de Broglie, 'Pour une théologie du festin eucharistique' in *Doctor Communis* (1949–50).[37] Among Protestants Markus Barth has shown a similar concern, as is revealed by the very title of his eucharistic study, *Das Abendmahl: Passamahl, Opfermahl, Messiasmahl* (1945). At the same time New Testament scholars have been drawing attention to the great prominence of meal-words and meal-deeds in the whole ministry of Jesus; and E. Lohmeyer in particular has suggested that it is against the full background of meal-parables and meal-activity in the ministry of Jesus that the eucharist is to be seen.[38]

Our investigation will make clear that the sign of the meal is a basic category if the eschatological content and import of the eucharist are to be properly appreciated. After sketching the background in the Old Testament and in inter-testamental Judaism, we shall consider what part the

notion of eating and drinking in the kingdom of God played in the thought
and practice of Jesus. In particular we shall try to ascertain the way in which
Jesus saw the eucharist to be related to eating and drinking in the kingdom
of God. Concurrently (for in any discussion of the gospel material we are
bound to reckon with the part played by the church in the shaping of the
gospel records), we shall try to discover the apostolic church's views on the
relation. Next will follow an indication of the degree and manner in which
the historic liturgies and the eucharistic theologians of the past have
reflected the dominical and apostolic *données* concerning the eucharist and
the feast of the kingdom. The chapter will be brought to an end by a
number of systematic reflections on the importance of the fact that the
eucharist is a *meal* for seeing the relation between it and eschatology.

## 1. The Old Testament preparation

The Old Testament sets the scene for our understanding of the eschatological significance of the eucharistic meal. Israel shared the idea common
to many religions that eating and drinking, especially in a cultic setting,
is a means of appropriating divine blessings.[39] What, we must ask, was the
particular form taken by this idea in Israel? The Old Testament material
may conveniently be arranged under four headings.

### (a) The meal at the making of the covenant on Mount Sinai

Exodus 24 relates that at the making of the covenant Moses threw half the
blood of the sacrifices against the altar and half on the people, 'the blood
of the covenant' (v. 8). Then:

Moses and Aaron, Nadab, and Abihu, and seventy of the elders of Israel went
up, and they saw the God of Israel; and there was under his feet as it were a
pavement of sapphire stone, like the very heaven for clearness. And he did not
lay his hand on the chief men of the people of Israel; they beheld God, and ate
and drank. (vv. 9–11)

The importance of this passage for eucharistic theology is immediately
clear in view of the cup-word at the Last Supper which, whether in its
Marcan or in its Pauline (and Lucan) form, puts the new covenant and
the eucharist in relation with the covenant concluded on Sinai: 'This is
my blood of the covenant' (Mark 14:24),[40] or 'This cup is the new covenant
in my blood' (I Cor. 11:25; cf. Luke 22:20).[41] The Old Testament passage
introduces, at least at the moment of the inauguration of the covenant, the
themes of (i) eating and drinking in the presence of God and (ii) the vision
of God in his glory. These will be themes demanding attention in our
consideration of the meal of the new covenant.[42]

### (b) Sacred meals in places of sacrifice

If the event of Exodus 24 bears certain unique traits due (no doubt) to its
special position as the *inauguration* of the covenant, there is nevertheless
a strong tradition of other sacred meals in places of sacrifice.[43] In Mizpah

'Jacob offered a sacrifice on the mountain and called his kinsmen to eat bread; and they ate bread and tarried all night on the mountain' (Gen. 31:54 = J/E). On hearing from Moses of the Lord's deliverance of the Israelites from Egypt, Jethro offered a burnt offering and sacrifices, and Aaron and the elders ate bread with him 'before God' (Exod. 18:12 = E). Samuel presided at the people's sacrifices 'on the high place' (I Sam. 9:11–14). It is above all Deuteronomy which lays stress on sacred meals in the sanctuary (12:5–7, 17–18; 14:23, 26; 15:20; 27:7): the Lord has chosen a place of habitation, and His people come and eat and drink 'before him' and rejoice. Though God is not seen (as in Exod. 24:9–11), the worshippers eat and drink in His presence, and we notice the accent placed on rejoicing.[44]

### (c) The wisdom literature

Such cultic practice no doubt stood behind the employment of meal imagery in the wisdom literature to express the giving and receiving of divine blessings.[45] I may quote as a first example the invitation which Wisdom offers to enter her house and to feast:

Wisdom has built her house, she has set up her seven pillars.
She has slaughtered her beasts, she has mixed her wine, she has also set her table.
She has sent out her maids to call from the highest places in the town,
'Whoever is simple, let him turn in here!'
To him who is without sense she says,
'Come, eat of my bread and drink of the wine I have mixed.
Leave simpleness, and live, and walk in the way of insight'.  (Prov. 9:1–6)[46]

The psalmist pictures the Lord's unfailing care for him under the image of a meal:

Thou preparest a table before me in the presence of my enemies;
thou anointest my head with oil, my cup overflows.  (Ps. 23:5)

In the Song of Songs the lovers' bliss finds expression in the imagery of food and drink:

I come to my garden, my sister, my bride,
I gather my myrrh with my spice,
I eat my honeycomb with my honey,
I drink my wine with my milk.
Eat, O friends, and drink; drink deeply, O lovers!  (5:1)

### (d) The feeding and feasting in the future salvation

In the examples so far given the feasting in the presence of the Lord and the Lord's feeding of His people take place at a *present* time. Now we turn to passages which look for a similar feeding and feasting in the *future*. Deutero-Isaiah and Ezekiel speak from the historical situation of the exile in Babylon and promise deliverance from captivity and restoration to Palestine: and according to Isaiah the Lord will feed His people on their homeward journey through the desert (49:9f) as He fed the people of old in the wilderness (48:21); while according to Ezekiel the Lord (34:13f) or His servant David (34:23) will feed His people in a restored homeland which He will cause to produce food in plenty (34:25–31); and Second Isaiah characteristically sees the nations as coming to Israel (55:5) to share in the blessings of the 'everlasting covenant' (55:5):

Ho, *every one* who thirsts, come to the waters; and he who has no money, come, buy and eat!
Come, buy wine and milk without money and without price.
Why do you spend your money for that which is not bread, and your labour for that which does not satisfy?
Hearken diligently to me, and eat what is good, and delight yourselves in fatness.
(55:1–2)

In later passages the tone becomes markedly more apocalyptic. There will be, on the one hand, a massive sacrificial slaughter of the Lord's enemies (Isa. 34:6; Jer. 46:10; Zeph. 1:7) which, at least according to Ezek. 39:17–20, will provide a feast for the birds and the beasts; and, on the other hand, faithful Israel will 'on that day' (Zech. 9:16) eat and drink and rejoice:

Grain shall make the young men flourish, and new wine the maidens.
(Zech. 9:17)

\* \* \*

Behold, my servants shall eat,
    but you shall be hungry;
behold, my servants shall drink;
    but you shall be thirsty;
behold, my servants shall rejoice;
    but you shall be put to shame.    (Isa. 65:13)

Finally there is a passage in the late Isaianic apocalypse which is of particular significance for the eucharist; it speaks of a *future* feast for *all peoples*, in a context of *the abolition of death* and *a day of salvation and rejoicing*:

On this mountain the Lord of hosts will make for all peoples a feast of fat things, a feast of wine on the lees, of fat things full of marrow, of wine on the lees well refined. And he will destroy on this mountain the covering that is cast over all peoples, the veil that is spread over all nations. He will swallow up death for ever [cf. 26:19], and the Lord God will wipe away tears from all faces, and the reproach of his people he will take away from all the earth; for the Lord has spoken. It will be said on that day, 'Lo, this is our God; we have waited for him, that he might save us. This is the Lord; we have waited for him; let us be glad and rejoice in his salvation'.    (Isa. 25:6–9)

## 2. The inter-testamental period

In this period, which for our purposes we shall extend to cover also Judaism contemporary with Jesus and even beyond, some of the above

Old Testament themes (and others as well) are taken up and developed in one particular direction. They are given a strong *messianic* and *futurist* colouring, the future usually being seen in apocalyptic terms as the ending of the present world-order and the coming of the new. The material may be grouped under five headings.

### (a) The abundance of food

The age to come will be an age of plenty. In 4 Ezra 8:52–54 there is a modest description of what God has in store for the righteous 'few' (8:1):

It is for you that paradise is opened, the tree of life is planted, the age to come is prepared, plenty is provided, a city is built, rest is appointed, goodness is established and wisdom perfected beforehand . . . Sorrows have passed, and in the end the treasure of immortality is made manifest.

The Apocalypse of Baruch is more exuberant:

The earth also shall yield its fruit tenthousandfold and on each vine there shall be a thousand branches, and each branch shall produce a thousand clusters, and each cluster shall produce a thousand grapes, and each grape shall produce a cor of wine. And those who have hungered shall rejoice. . . . (II Baruch 29:5)[47]

### (b) The new manna

Israel remembered that God had fed His people with manna in the wilderness at the time of the exodus (Exod. 16:4, 15; Ps. 78:24f; Neh. 9:15; Wisd. 16:20; 4 Ezra 1:19),[48] and there is ample evidence that the Jews expected a renewal of the gift in the coming time of salvation. The Syriac Apocalypse of Baruch speaks thus: 'And it shall come to pass at that selfsame time that the treasury of manna shall again descend from on high, and they will eat of it in those years, because these are they who have come to the consummation of time' (II Baruch 29:8).[49] In some places it is the messiah who will be instrumental in calling down the new manna. Thus in the Midrash Rabbah: 'Just as the former deliverer [Moses] made manna descend, . . . so also the latter deliverer [the messiah] will make manna descend' (Midr Qoh I, 9).[50] The importance of the Jewish expectation of a coming messianic distribution of manna for the Christian eucharist is seen in the feeding miracles of Jesus and in the discourse on the heavenly bread of life of John 6 (the eucharistic significance of each of which will be argued later), and in I Cor. 10 (where the manna of the exodus is presented as a type of the eucharistic bread).

### (c) The passover

According to the synoptic presentations the eucharist was instituted during the course of a passover meal, and the Lucan account in particular (as we shall see) seems to suggest that the eucharist was intended to supersede the passover. We may therefore expect the eucharist to take over, and possibly to modify, certain theological themes connected with the Jewish passover.[51] Now it is certain that a strong eschatological expectation, and that messianic, attached to the Jewish passover at the time of Jesus.[52] The high antiquity of the association between passover and messianic expectation may be shown by the fact that the Samaritans also expected their Taheb (Messiah) to come at passover in the same way as orthodox Judaism;[53] but it is in any case clear from Josephus that messianic excitement reached fever-pitch at passover time,[54] and there are hints to the same effect in the New Testament itself: John 6:4 and 15, Matt. 26:5, Luke 23:19, and Luke 13:1–3.[55] We may therefore confidently suppose that in the time of Jesus the Jews looked for the coming of the messiah in the same night as that in which the great deliverance from Egypt had been wrought.[56] This messianic expectation would then mark the meal during which, according to the synoptic gospels, Jesus instituted the eucharist.[57] There is, moreover, considerable evidence that the Christian church carried over from the Jewish passover this messianic eschatological expectation (now transposed to the *return* of Christ), at least in the case of the paschal vigil:

(i) A. Strobel[58] has argued that Luke 17:20f. is a Lucan composition (based on a traditional logion of Jesus reported also at 17:23 = Matt. 24:23 = Mark 13:21) designed to combat, by insisting on the (inaugurated) *presence* of the kingdom ἐντὸς ὑμῶν, both pharisaic and popular Jewish expectations of a still coming messiah in the paschal νὺξ παρατηρήσεως (so 'A, Θ and Sym. at Exod. 12:42; cf. μετὰ παρατηρήσεως at Luke 17:20) and *also popular Christian expectations of an imminent parousia in that night*.

(ii) B. Lohse has argued that the Quartadecimans' paschal festival in the second half of the second century retained a primitive Christian expectation of the parousia.[59]

(iii) Lactantius (early fourth century) shows how the Easter vigil links both the resurrection of Christ and His coming parousia:

> This is the night in which we keep vigil on account of the coming of our king and God. This night has a twofold meaning: in it Christ received life after his death; and in it he will hereafter gain the kingdom over the whole earth.
>
> (*Div. Inst.* VII, 19: *CSEL*, vol. 19, p. 644)

(iv) Jerome ( +420) knew of the Jewish messianic expectation for passover night and believed that a Christian expectation of Christ's final advent during the Easter vigil dated from apostolic times:

> For suddenly as at dead of night, when all are safely abed and deeply asleep, the shouts of angels and the trumpets of the preceding forces will sound out the advent of Christ. Let us say something that may be useful to the reader. There is a Jewish tradition that the messiah will come in the middle of the night, in likeness of what happened in Egypt when the passover was celebrated, and the angel of death came, and the Lord passed over the tents, and the doorposts were consecrated by lamb's blood. Whence I consider also the apostolic tradition to have

been drawn, that it is not lawful to dismiss the people before midnight from the paschal vigil, for we expect the advent of Christ . . .

(Comm. in Matt. IV, in 25:6, PL 26, 184f)

(v) Isidore of Seville ( + 636) testifies to the same hope:

Vigil is kept on this night, on account of the advent of our king and our God, that at the time of his resurrection he may not find us sleeping but vigilant. There is a twofold reason for keeping this night: first because in it he received life after his passion or second because he will hereafter come for the judgment at the same hour as that in which he rose from the dead.

(Etymolog. VI, 17, 12, PL 82, 248)

If an advent hope could remain associated with the Christian Pasch for so long, we shall not be surprised to find a similar hope associated with the sacrament which, according to the synoptic accounts, Jesus instituted in the course of a passover meal.

### (d) The future (messianic) feasting

The most interesting example of the continuation of the notion of a feasting in the future time of salvation is found in Ethiopian Enoch 62:13–16. In this text the messianic figure of the Son of man is present.

[13]And the righteous and elect shall be saved on that day,
And they shall never thenceforward see the face of the sinners and unrighteous.
[14]And the Lord of Spirits will abide over them,
And with that Son of Man shall they eat
And lie down and rise up for ever and ever.
[15]And the righteous and elect shall have risen from the earth,
And ceased to be of downcast countenance.
[16]And they shall have been clothed with garments of glory,
And they shall be the garments of life from the Lord of Spirits:
And your garments shall not grow old,
Nor your glory pass away before the Lord of Spirits.[60]

Apart from Jesus's own teaching (to be examined later), there is a valuable indication in the gospels that the feast in the coming kingdom formed part of the contemporary hope: when Jesus is at table and teaching in meal-parables, it is one of His table-companions who makes the remark:

Blessed is he who shall eat bread in the kingdom of God.   (Luke 14:15)

### (e) Qumran

It is with trepidation that one enters a new field in which there is great divergence of opinion among the cultivators. I note simply two conjectures made by F. M. Cross, Jr, in his book *The Ancient Library of Qumran and Modern Biblical Studies* (1958).

(i) It is possible that a reference to the feast on the mountain of Isa. 25:6 may be found in the Qumran *Interpretation of Ps. 37*, 4QpPs. 37 II, 10–11 (Cross, *op. cit.*, p. 67, n. 81). In the Qumran commentary it is said of the 'congregation of the poor' (by which the sectaries no doubt meant themselves) that they will inherit the mountain of Israel: *hr mrwm yśr*['*l* . . .], and that they will 'take delight' or 'make merry': *yt 'ngw*, on God's holy mountain (reconstructing the depleted text on the basis of Ezekiel 20:40, as: *hr mrwm yśr*['*l bhr*] *qwdšw yt'ngw*). Though the Qumran expositor is commenting on Ps. 37:21f at this point, the term *yt'ngw* comes from Ps. 37:11, a verse apparently brought back into mind by the presence of the notion of 'inheriting the land' in both verses. Cross points out that the verb *'ng* in the hithpael also occurs at Isa. 55:2 in association with the feeding in the future time of salvation. It is therefore feasible that 4QpPs. 37 offers an echo to the feast on Mount Zion as mentioned at Isa. 25:6. But we cannot take this as certain, for another Qumran specialist, J. Carmignac, sees in the reference to the mountain rather a reference to the desire which the sectaries had to celebrate a *purified sacrificial cultus* in the Temple on Mount Zion.[61]

(ii) Cross makes an interesting suggestion (pp. 62–67) about the passage in the *Rule of the Congregation*, 1QSa II, 11–22. The Qumran passage begins (in Cross's translation): '[This is (the order) of the ses]sion of the "Men of Name who are [invited] to the Feast" for the communal council when [God] sends the Messiah to be with them.'[62] It goes on to describe in detail the seating arrangements and the order of procedure with bread and wine at a meal at which the Priest (presumably the Aaronic messiah) and the messiah of Israel (the royal messiah) are the most prominent figures. The concluding rubric runs: 'And they shall act according to this prescription whenever (the meal) [is arr]anged, when as many as ten solemnly meet together.' Cross's argument is this: the final rubric indicates that the arrangements described are those used in the common meal of the sect in current practice; but the presence of the Priest and the messiah of Israel indicates the messianic banquet; therefore the common meal is shown as 'a liturgical anticipation of the Messianic banquet', in which the priestly head and the lay head of the community stand in for the messiahs of Aaron and Israel. For Cross the meal is an instance of a general principle (accepted also by K. Stendhal, *The Scrolls and the New Testament*, New York, 1957, p. 10) that must be used in the elucidation of the Qumran texts, namely that 'the "apocalyptic community" was at once the future congregation of the elect and the "present" sect whose life was conceived as a foreshadowing of the New Age'. As often elsewhere in Qumran studies, there is wide disagreement among the specialists on the significance of 1QSa II, 11–22. It would occupy a disproportionate amount of space if we were to outline the various views. If Cross's theory is correct, it would show one of the possible influences on Jesus's, or on the primitive church's, understanding of the eucharist; it would certainly demonstrate that the notion of an anticipation of the messianic banquet was conceivable in contemporary Jewish thought.

### 3. Feasting in the kingdom of God according to the New Testament

We now try to ascertain the teaching of Jesus on eating and drinking in the kingdom of God, and in particular to discover how He related the eucharist to such eating and drinking (though we shall, to begin with, make abstraction of sayings reported in the explicitly eucharistic context of the Last Supper). Concurrent consideration will be given to the apostolic church's views on the relation between them. (I myself tend to the 'conservative' assumption that a gospel saying should be attributed to Jesus unless there is good reason to the contrary. But 'radical' scholars who make the opposite assumption, and ascribe all gospel sayings to the primitive church unless there is good reason to the contrary, need not be out of sympathy with the *theological* conclusions I draw from the gospels—at least in so far as these scholars accord to the primitive church that primary function in the origination of doctrine which I prefer to give Jesus Himself.)

## (a) The future feeding and feasting

There are several instances in the gospels of Jesus's having pictured the *future* salvation under the image of feasting and feeding:

(i) There is, first, the quite straightforward and explicit saying reported by Matthew and Luke:

I tell you, many will come from east and west and sit at table with Abraham, Isaac, and Jacob in the kingdom of heaven. (Matt. 8:11)

And men will come from east and west, and from north and south, and sit at table in the kingdom of God. (Luke 13:29)

The saying is placed in different contexts in the two gospels, but both make clear that its point is the impending doom of the present generation of the 'sons of the kingdom' and the admittance of the Gentiles to the coming kingdom (Matt. 8:1–13; Luke 13:22–30). Jesus here takes up the Old Testament theme of the 'centripetal' *coming* of the *multitudes* of the nations to share in the salvation when the God of Israel will reveal His glory.[63] The scene of God's saving revelation and the goal of the nations' confluence was to be, according to the Old Testament, Jerusalem and God's holy mountain: according to Jesus the feasting will take place 'in the kingdom of heaven/God', and we are left with a question of interpretation to take up later.[64]

(ii) The Beatitudes provide a second example of a future feeding:

Blessed are you that hunger now, for you shall be satisfied. (Luke 6:21a)

Blessed are those who hunger and thirst for righteousness, for they shall be satisfied. (Matt. 5:6)

In Luke's version (which most modern commentators prefer), the saying could be interpreted of those who are physically hungry, and this interpretation seems to be confirmed by Luke's corresponding woe: 'Woe to you that are full now, for you shall hunger' (Luke 6:25a). The saying would form part of that straightforward reversal of fortunes in the coming age which figures prominently in the teaching of Jesus (Matt. 18:4; 19:30; 23:12; Luke 14:11; 18:14), and which was expected also by the Qumran community (e.g. 4QpPs. 37). But Matthew's interpretation is not excluded, for it is chiefly among the hungry that there will be found those who long for the establishment of God's righteousness in His kingdom.[65] What is important for our purpose is, first, that a contrast is made between the *present* (the 'now' in Luke's version) and the *future*; and second, that the future bliss is pictured as a feeding at the hand of God ('shall be satisfied' being a reverential passive).

* * *

There are two further instances of Jesus's referring to a future feasting, but we must preface our presentation of them with the warning that in their present form the parables in which they occur may be early re-applications to the second advent of parables which Jesus originally applied to the crisis that was already at least inaugurated by His ministry.

(iii) Matt. 25:14–30 (the parable of the talents) seems in its present form and context to be concerned with Christian conduct in the interval before the return of Christ (see also the Lucan version, 19:12–27, and particularly the introductory verse 11). To each of the good and faithful servants the returning master says:

Enter into the joy of your master ($\epsilon$ἴσελθε εἰς τὴν χαρὰν τοῦ κυρίου σου).

(verses 21, 23)

What concerns us here is the likelihood that χαρά means the festive banquet.[66]

(iv) Luke 12:35–38 presents a parabolic exhortation to vigilance. Those servants are commended whom the master finds awake when he comes from the marriage feast:

Truly, I say to you, he will gird himself and have them sit at table, and he will come and serve (διακονήσει) them.                                        (verse 37b)

The Lucan context appears to make it certain that it is the parousia which is in view, and the meal mentioned is therefore (if we may allegorize this part of the parable) the subsequent messianic banquet.[67] In its original setting the parable may rather have had to do with that 'coming' of Jesus which had already begun; for 'the Son of man *came* not to be served but to serve (διακονῆσαι)' (Mark 10:45), Jesus was among His disciples 'as one who serves (ὡς ὁ διακονῶν)' (Luke 22:27), the master washed His disciples' feet during supper (John 13:3–5). These last remarks lead us into our discussion of the significance of the meals of Jesus during the present time of His ministry.

### (b) Meals during the ministry of Jesus

In the preceding paragraph we have seen that Jesus Himself gave a future reference to eating and drinking in the kingdom, and also (though this is not a point which will concern us immediately) that the primitive church understood and applied His teaching in such a way as to suggest that the future reference would not be exhausted before the parousia. Yet some at least of the meals of Jesus during the present time of His ministry were invested with messianic significance, as will be seen from the following considerations.

(i) It is not, I think, an illegitimate piece of pious imagination to suppose that the meals which Jesus must have taken with the apostles throughout His ministry formed a focus for the enjoyment of fellowship between the messiah and the twelve men whom He chose 'to be with him' (Mark 3:14). This seems to be the implication of the dispute about fasting in Mark 2:18–20 (Matt. 9:14f; Luke 5:33–35): as long as they have the messianic bridegroom with them,[68] the disciples of Jesus do not fast but eat and drink.[69]

(ii) Certainly the meals which Jesus deliberately took with publicans and sinners and which earned Him such notoriety (Mark 2:15–17 = Matt. 9:10–13 = Luke 5:29–32; Matt. 11:19 = Luke 7:34; Luke 15:1–2; 19:1–10) were to be seen as embodying the divine offer of salvation for sinners: it was in this context that Jesus declared that He came to call (or invite, $\kappa\alpha\lambda\epsilon\hat{\iota}\nu$!) not the righteous, but sinners (Mark 2:17). Two things are to be noticed here. First, the initiative of Jesus in inviting sinners to eat with Him and to salvation is clear (Matt. 9:13; Mark 2:17; Luke 5:32; cf. Luke 19:5), yet it is equally clear that sinners sought Him out in order to eat with Him (Matt. 9:10; Mark 2:15; Luke 5:29; 15:1–2; cf. Luke 7:37ff). Second, the mere fact of having eaten and drunk with Jesus is not a guarantee of admission to the feast of the kingdom, as Luke makes clear (13:23–30):

. . . When once the householder has risen up and shut the door, you will begin to stand outside and to knock at the door, saying, 'Lord, open to us'. He will answer you, 'I do not know where you come from'. Then you will begin to say, 'We ate and drank in your presence, and you taught in our streets'. But he will say, 'I tell you, I do not know where you come from; depart from me, all you workers of iniquity!' . . . (verses 25–27)

Sinners were invited . . . *to repentance* (Luke 5:32). Both these points may later shed interesting light on eucharistic practice (pp. 129–35, 141).

(iii) In Matt. 11:28 Jesus offers a present feeding in a style which recalls the feast offered by Wisdom in Prov. 9 or the constant divine nourishing pictured in Ps. 23:

Come unto me, all who labour and are heavy laden, and I will refresh you.[70]

(iv) Apart from the Last Supper, the most momentous meal recorded by the evangelists was that of Jesus's feeding of the multitude—or the two feedings if the Marcan-Matthaean presentation is allowed (Mark 6:30–44; 8:1–10; Matt. 14:13–21; 15:32–39; Luke 9:11–17; John 6:3–15). That the feeding(s) had a messianic significance was apparent already to the Johannine crowd, even if they interpreted the messiahship in political terms: 'They tried to make him king' (John 6:15); and the subsequent Johannine discourse on the bread of life makes it clear that Jesus is the new and superior Moses who dispenses or will dispense the manna that was awaited in the time of salvation, the new bread from heaven being Himself (vv. 35, 48, 51a) or His flesh (v. 51c).[71] In the Marcan and Matthaean versions also, the feedings are clearly meant to show the divine largesse in distributing the blessings of salvation through the messiah. Since Augustine it has been traditional to take the feeding of the five thousand as indicating the provision of salvation for the Jews, and the feeding of the four thousand provision of salvation for the Gentiles. G. H. Boobyer has more recently made a plausible case for looking on both feedings as showing the extension of messianic salvation to the Gentiles.[72]

(v) The same theme, and that also in terms of messianic feeding, is present in Jesus's conversation with the Syrophoenician woman (Mark 7:24–30; Matt. 15:21–28). The blessings of messianic ('Son of David', Matt. 15:22) salvation are 'the children's *bread*'—and 'the *crumbs*' extend the blessings to the Gentiles.[73]

(vi) One more possible example of a messianic feeding already during the course of Jesus's ministry may be given. H. Riesenfeld[74] interprets the incident of the disciples' plucking ears of corn as they passed through the cornfields on the sabbath (Mark 2:23–28) as a sign of the 'dawn' of the eschatological sabbath,[75] characterized by the messianic 'bread' or 'feast' (cf. the corn of Mark 2:23). This interpretation finds support in the use in neighbouring sayings of the messianic metaphors of the bridegroom and wedding feast (Mark 2:19) and the new wine (Mark 2:22).[76]

(c) *The relation between present and future in the meal-words and meal-deeds of Jesus's ministry*

We have seen that Jesus still reserved for the future the feast of the kingdom and yet that His meals during His ministry had messianic significance. How are we to understand this relation between present and future? We may find help in two other phenomena which, like Jesus's own practice and teaching in connection with meals, combine action with verbal interpretation, namely: the 'symbolic acts' of the Old Testament prophets, and the characteristic Johannine category of 'signs'.

The symbolic acts of the Old Testament prophets, which recent scholarship has brought into the limelight,[77] announced an impending action of the Lord and could even be seen as unleashing that action, for the Lord Himself (and here lies the distinction from mimetic magic) had committed Himself to executing the deed of which He ordered the prophets to make the dramatic announcement. The action performed by the prophet often bore an imitative or emblematic relation to the act of God which it introduced, as one or two examples will quickly make clear. Thus Jeremiah is ordered to smash an earthen flask and to declare that the Lord will smash Judah and Jerusalem to smithereens because of their apostasy (Jer. 19); again he is ordered to put a yoke on his own neck and to declare to the Palestinian kinglets, including Judah's Zedekiah, that it is the Lord's will that they should bring their necks under the yoke of the king of Babylon into whose hand the Lord has given these lands (Jer. 27:1–15).

Ezekiel is ordered to draw the city of Jerusalem on a brick and build up a siege against it: and 'this is a sign ('ōth, LXX σημεῖον) for the house of Israel' (Ezek. 4:3).[78]

Likewise recent Johannine scholarship has made great play with the Fourth Gospel's category of σημεῖα.[79] During the course of His ministry Jesus performs a series of 'signs' (2:11; 2:23; 3:2; 4:54; 6:2, 14, 26; 7:31; 9:16; 11:47; 12:18, 37; 20:30) which both point forward to the salvation that will follow on the exaltation of Jesus and also, because it is the eternal Word who is revealing His glory through them in history, already themselves participate in the reality (ἀλήθεια) which they show forth. It is a characteristic of the Johannine signs that they are done publicly and lead to controversy (chs. 5, 6, 9, 11), arousing faith in some people (2:11, 23; 3:2; 4:53; 6:14; 7:31; 9:16; 11:45; 20:30) and in others unbelief and opposition (5:18; 9:16; 11:46–53; 12:37–43).

In the light of the Old Testament prophetic acts and the Johannine signs, I may perhaps now suggest another figure to help in the understanding of the present and future references in the meal-deeds and meal-words in Jesus's ministry. The meals of Jesus's ministry that were already invested with messianic significance are like the drawing of an arc which already suggests the full circle to the beholder with eyes to see and commits the draughtsman to completing the full figure of 360° that already exists in his mind as his explanatory words make clear. In some such sense as this the meals of Jesus during His ministry were signs of the coming feast in the kingdom: they were a throwing forward into the present of the first part of the future feast. Now there is some possibility that Jesus taught His disciples to pray precisely for God already to throw this future feast in part or even in whole into the present, for it is on these lines that the most convincing explanation of the perplexing word ἐπιούσιος in the fourth petition of the Lord's prayer is to be found. A rather detailed examination of this fascinating word will be particularly worth while in view of the long-standing use of the Lord's prayer in the eucharistic liturgies, where its most usual position before communion is probably due to this very petition for bread.[80]

(d) Τὸν ἄρτον ἡμῶν τὸν ἐπιούσιον (Matt. 6:11; Luke 11:3)

The rare, if not quite otherwise unknown,[81] word ἐπιούσιος used by Matthew and Luke in the Lord's prayer was already an etymological puzzle to Origen and has had various meanings suggested for it by commentators and translators ancient and modern.[82]

(i) Origen, who believed ἐπιούσιος to be found neither in Greek literature nor in the popular language but to have been a coinage of the evangelists, favoured a rather improbable derivation from ἐπί and οὐσία and arrived at the meaning 'suited to our ("logical") nature'. The petition was a prayer that we might be fed by the Logos. Feeding on the 'bread' of the spiritual teaching of Christ come down from heaven gives health, vigour and strength to the soul—and (here we move in an eschatological direction) this bread which is the Logos 'imparts a share of its own immortality (for the Word of God is immortal) to him who eats of it'.[83] Cyril of Jerusalem retains the meaning of ἐπιούσιος as 'suited to the nature of the soul' and, unlike Origen, applies the petition to the eucharistic bread.[84] Without indulging in etymological speculations on ἐπιούσιος (for his Latin Bible gave him *quotidianum*), Augustine, who also knows the senses of 'material bread' and 'eucharistic bread', prefers to interpret the petition (in a rather Origenistic way) of feeding on the Word in the preached word and in the daily practice of the divine precepts.[85]

(ii) Another patristic interpretation of the fourth petition of the Lord's prayer conflates two closely related notions: our *daily* bread, and the bread *we need*; and arrives at 'the bread we need for the day'. The approach from the angle of *daily* is represented by the Old Latin version of the New Testament, which translates as *panem quotidianum* in both Matthew and Luke,[86] possibly seeing ἐπιούσιος as containing a present participial form of εἶναι, and understanding: ἐπὶ τὴν οὖσαν (sc. ἡμέραν), (bread needed) *for the current* (day). From the other side, one Eastern tradition puts the accent on 'the bread *we need*'.[87] The ancient commentators in this tradition seem to see ἐπιούσιος as containing οὐσία, though they interpret this, unlike Origen, as the bread we need *for our bodily existence*. Their expositions usually include also the notion of *daily* (ἐφήμερος), which may suggest that they felt a flavour of ἐπὶ τὴν οὖσαν ἡμέραν as well, or which may simply be a paraenetic interpretation due to the influence of the dominical injunction to 'take no thought for the morrow' (Matt. 6:34)—for the same commentators often do make the point that in the light of this injunction we are to pray for *no more than we 'need'* (i.e. a day at a time).[88]

(iii) Jerome tries various Latin words in attempting to arrive at the meaning of ἐπιούσιος,[89] but his preference appears to have been for a meaning which emphasizes the excellence of the bread (which he takes as the eucharistic bread). Two notions seem to contribute to this understanding. First, he sees ἐπιούσιος as equivalent to περιούσιος, which runs through the following range of meanings: peculiar—special—excellent.[90] Second, Jerome allows the possibility that ἐπιούσιος may mean '(of a substance) that is above every substance', and this is apparently what he tries to convey by *super-substantialis*.[91] In one passage Jerome expressly states that 'supersubstantial' bread means bread that is from the divine substance:

For unless a man converts his hardness into softness, he cannot receive the food, which is the bread that comes down from heaven, so as to be able to say: Give us this day our supersubstantial bread, that is, *qui est de tua substantia*.[92]

With Jerome we are clearly well on the way towards a vision of the eucharist in terms of an ontological, supernatural, 'vertical' eschatology, though Jerome was not, as we shall see, unaware of the future dimension.

(iv) Another interpretation is 'everlasting bread', which is found in the Armenian tradition. This may derive from an early Syrian tradition of 'constant' or 'continual' bread,[93] originally perhaps in the sense of 'daily' but shifting through an obvious chain of meaning: unfailing, permanent, everlasting.[94] In his Exposition of the Lord's prayer the fifth-century Armenian St Elisha ( + c. 480) takes the fourth petition to mean 'everlasting bread' and interprets it of the eucharist.[95]

(v) The most interesting possibility is 'bread *for the coming day*'. Etymologically this would see ἐπιούσιος as connected with the verb ἐπιέναι; and in fact an expression derived from this verb, ἡ ἐπιοῦσα (sc. ἡμέρα), is an established way of saying *the coming/next day* (Acts 7:26; 16:11; 20:15; 21:18; cf. 23:11, with νύξ).[96] This understanding is supported by the Egyptian versions of the New Testament: the Sahidic has *penoeik etneu* (our coming bread) in both Matt. and Luke, while the Bohairic has *penoik ethneou* in Luke and *penoik nte rasti* (our bread of tomorrow) in Matt. Especially valuable perhaps is Jerome's information that the 'Gospel of the Hebrews' read 'MAHAR (מחר), *quod dicitur crastinum*',[97] for this may retain a Semitic form of the Lord's prayer which had been in continuous use among Jewish Christians since Jesus Himself.[98] Even if the petition referred to our material bread for the coming day,[99] this would not be in flagrant contradiction with Matt. 6:34, for with ἡ ἐπιοῦσα the emphasis falls on the *immediately* following day or even the day just *beginning*.[100] Where, however, the Fathers reckon with 'bread *of the coming day*' as a possible meaning of ἐπιούσιος, they usually see it as giving the fourth petition an *eschatological* significance: 'Give us *already now*[101] the bread of *the future age*.'[102] What is more, the same Fathers usually, though not always, make a eucharistic application of the petition on these lines of 'bread of the future age'. I will set out the patristic evidence for this future-eschatological (and sometimes eucharistic) interpretation:

(α) Origen knows (though rejects) the interpretation of the petition as a prayer for the bread of the coming age to be given already in the present age. He does not say whether this interpretation was understood eucharistically:

Someone will say that ἐπιούσιος is formed from ἐπιέναι, so that we are instructed to pray that God will anticipate (προλαβών) and grant us already the bread belonging to the age to come, so that what is to be given as it were tomorrow should be given us today, 'today' being understood of the present age and 'tomorrow' of the age to come. (*De orat.* 27, PG 11, 517)

(β) In the contestedly Athanasian treatise *On the Incarnation of the Divine Word and against the Arians* the bread of the fourth petition of the Lord's prayer is interpreted as 'heavenly bread' (ἄρτον οὐράνιον) which is both the Lord who is the living bread come down from heaven and also (since what is born of the Spirit is Spirit) the life-giving Holy Spirit. In the present age we pray for the 'future' bread (τὸν ἐπιούσιον ἄρτον, τουτέστι τὸν μέλλοντα) and have the firstfruits of it (ἀπαρχήν) as we receive the flesh of the Lord. The vocabulary and meaning of the passage seem inescapably eucharistic:

Again the Lord says of himself: 'I am the living bread that came down from heaven'. Elsewhere he calls the Holy Spirit the heavenly bread, saying Τὸν ἄρτον ἡμῶν τὸν ἐπιούσιον δὸς ἡμῖν σήμερον. For he taught us in the prayer to ask in the present age for τὸν ἐπιούσιον ἄρτον, that is the bread to come, of which we have the firstfruits in the present life when we partake of the flesh of the Lord, as he himself said: 'The bread which I shall give is my flesh for the life of the world'; and the flesh of the Lord is the life-giving Spirit, for he was conceived of the life-giving Spirit and 'what is born of the Spirit is Spirit'.

(§16, PG 26,1012)

(γ) In two places Jerome sees the fourth petition of the Lord's prayer as praying for a present eucharistic feeding on the one who will be our bread in the future kingdom. First, we note that the sentence quoted above about the 'supersubstantial bread' which is from the substance of God is immediately followed by this: 'The Hebrew Gospel according to Matthew has: Give us today our tomorrow's bread (*crastinum*); that is: The bread which thou wilt give us in thy kingdom, give us today.'[103] Second: in his commentary on Ezekiel, Jerome says that the fourth petition of the Lord's prayer is a prayer 'that we may be worthy to receive daily in the present age the bread which we shall hereafter receive for ever'.[104]

(δ) Cyril of Alexandria, like Origen, knows, if only to reject, the interpretation that some make of the petition for bread as for 'the coming bread that will be given in the future age (τὸν ἥξοντά τε καὶ δοθησόμενον κατὰ τὸν αἰῶνα τὸν μέλλοντα)'. He does not state whether they made a eucharistic application.[105]

(ε) Peter Chrysologus ( +450) makes four brief but interesting comments on *Panem nostrum quotidianum da nobis hodie* in his Sermons 68, 70, 71 and 72.[106] Rejecting a petition for earthly bread as contrary to Matt. 6:25, he interprets the clause eucharistically and brings the sacramental feeding into relation with the coming feast in eternity. *Quotidianus* means *jugis* ('perpetual'), and the *jugis panis* is Christ Himself, the bread come down from heaven. On Him we shall feed *quotidie, id est, jugiter* in eternity. Already 'today' (*hodie* means *in praesenti vita, in praesenti*) we may feed on Him sacramentally at the feast of the altar, we may be strengthened in body and soul on our journey—until we come to the endless day and to the table of Christ, where we shall receive the fulness of the bread (which is the bread of perfect bliss) we have begun by tasting here.[107]

(ζ) 'Peter of Laodicaea' knows the possibility that ἐπιούσιος may be derived from ἐπιέναι and gives the interpretation:

The bread that does not belong to the present age but with which the saints will be rewarded in the age to come, 'give us already now'.[108]

(η) John Damascene[109] applies ἐπιούσιος to the eucharistic bread which is 'the firstfruits of the bread to come' (ἡ ἀπαρχὴ τοῦ μέλλοντος ἄρτου). He considers this application appropriate, no matter which of two possible derivations of ἐπιούσιος is preferred:

*Epiousios* means either the bread to come, that is the bread of the age to come, or else the bread we take for the sustenance of our *ousia* [he has just previously said that the eucharistic body and blood is εἰς σύστασιν τῆς ἡμετέρας ψυχῆς τε καὶ σώματος].

Like Athanasius above, John Damascene mentions in the same context that in eucharistic communion one receives both the flesh of the Lord and His life-giving Spirit.[110]

\*          \*          \*

To understand the fourth petition as a prayer for God to give already now the bread of the future age allows a consistent interpretation of the Lord's prayer. This is one point at which A. Schweitzer's analyses almost ring true:[111] the disciples are taught to pray for the things that make up the kingdom (namely: the hallowing of God's name, the rule of His will on earth, the forgiveness of sins), and for deliverance from the tribulation that precedes the kingdom's coming—and in this context the fourth petition can only mean 'Give us today the bread we are destined to have in the kingdom' and therefore be a prayer for the inbreaking of the kingdom. We would only wish to make the correction of doing more justice to the sense in which the kingdom has already broken in through Jesus's ministry. Even Schweitzer allows that the miraculous feedings, and then the Last Supper, were 'consecrations' (*Weihen*) of the crowds, and then the (remaining) disciples, to be the coming messianic community: but we must go further in recognizing the 'already', and here E. Lohmeyer's interpretation of τὸν ἄρτον ἡμῶν τὸν ἐπιούσιον is helpful.[112] Lohmeyer argues that ἐπιούσιος is an attempt to render a now irretrievable Aramaic original of Jesus which was deliberately ambivalent. The bread for which we pray is *at one and the same time* both earthly bread to meet the hunger and need of the present day, and also the future bread which will satisfy the elect in the eschatological kingdom and is already given to us in anticipation— just as Jesus's meals with His disciples and with sinners as well as His miraculous feedings of the crowds were, in sign and reality, present experiences of the future messianic meal at which those who now hunger will be satisfied.[113] Lohmeyer is prepared to see the church's eucharist, itself likewise standing astride present and future, as 'germinally present' in the ambivalent petition for bread of Jesus's prayer:[114] and this remark brings us to the question of determining the relation between the church's eucharist and the meals of Jesus's ministry at which, as we saw on pp. 27–29, He was already dispensing parabolically the food of the kingdom—food for which He apparently also taught the disciples to pray.

### (e) The relation between the eucharist and the meals of Jesus's ministry

It is necessary first to establish the *fact* of a relation between the eucharist and the meals of Jesus's ministry, and then to discover the more precise nature of that relation as it affects our understanding of the eschatological content and import of the eucharist.

In order to establish the fact of the relation we must look more closely at the Last Supper, which the synoptic evangelists and Paul all portray as the occasion of the institution of the sacrament.[115] The connection between the eucharist as instituted at the Last Supper and the meals of Jesus during His ministry may be established in the following three or four respects.

(i) The Last Supper, passover meal or not, was a fellowship meal between Jesus and His chosen twelve. It was the last of a series of meals which they had taken together over the previous three years. It was the last meal before the bridegroom who had been the reason for their joyous meal-fellowship was to be removed from His friends (Mark 2:19). It was, according to Jesus's reported words, the last time that He would drink the fruit of the vine until He drank it new *with them* (Matt. 26:29), His chosen men, in the kingdom. The Last Supper was apparently intended to be the last of the parabolic meal-signs dispensed by the man who had come eating and drinking, and next would come the full feasting of the kingdom. Their next festive meal together, at any rate, would take place in the kingdom. Yet it was precisely in the context of this 'eschatological prospect' that Jesus, at least according to the belief of the primitive church, instituted the eucharist. Here is raised the question, with which we shall have to deal presently, of the relation between eucharist and kingdom.

(ii) It is true that only Matthew mentions 'the remission of sins' at the cup-word (Matt. 26:28), but all the synoptists and Paul mention the (new) covenant which could in fact only be established on the forgiveness of sins (cf. Jer. 31:34).[116] If the eucharist is received 'for the remission of sins' it must stand in some kind of relation with the meals during Jesus's ministry which manifested the divine forgiveness for publicans and sinners.

(iii) There is a relation in respect of both ($a$) meaning and ($\beta$) form between the eucharist as instituted at the Last Supper and the feedings of the multitudes:

($a$) The feedings of the crowd show the broad scope of the salvation God intends, salvation now offered to the Gentiles. The same thing is emphasized in the discourse which John attaches to his account of the feeding: 'The bread which I shall give for the life of the world is my flesh' (John 6:51c).[117] No different, at the Last Supper, is the meaning of the cup-word's 'for many' (Mark 14:24; Matt. 26:28).[118]

($\beta$) The heaped-up coincidences of terminology between the institution narratives and the accounts of the feeding miracles are such as to prove that for the primitive church at least, the eucharist and the miraculous feedings stood in a close relation.[119] The following table will make clear the extent of the similarity:

1. Jesus took ($\lambda\alpha\beta\omega\nu/\dot{\epsilon}\lambda\alpha\beta\epsilon\nu$): Matt. 14:19; 15:36; 26:26; Mark 6:41; 8:6; 14:22; Luke 9:16; 22:19; John 6:11; I Cor. 11:23.
2. Bread ($\tau o \upsilon s \ \dot{\alpha}\rho\tau o \upsilon s/\dot{\alpha}\rho\tau o \nu$): Matt. 14:19; 15:36; 26:26; Mark 6:41; 8:6; 14:22; Luke 9:16; 22:19; John 6:11; I Cor. 11:23.

3. He looked up to heaven (ἀναβλέψας εἰς τον οὐρανον): Matt. 14:19; Mark 6:41; Luke 9:16.[120]

4. He blessed/gave thanks (εὐλογησεν/εὐλογησας/εὐχαριστησας): Matt. 14:19; 15:36; 26:26; Mark 6:41; 8:6; 14:22; Luke 9:16; 22:19; John 6:11;[121] I Cor. 11:24.

5. He broke (κλασας/ἐκλασεν/κατεκλασεν): Matt. 14:19; 15:36; 26:26; Mark 6:41; 8:6; 14:22; Luke 9:16; 22:19; I Cor. 11:24.

6. He gave (ἐδωκεν/ἐδιδου/δους/διεδωκεν): Matt. 14:19; 15:36; 26:26; Mark 6:41; 8:6; 14:23; Luke 9:16; 22:19; John 6:11.

7. The crowds/the disciples ate (ἐφαγον/φαγετε): Matt. 14:20; 15:37; 26:26; Mark 6:42; 8:8; Luke 9:17; cf. I Cor. 11:26.

A. Heising[122] suggests that this similarity between the accounts of the central actions in the feeding stories and the eucharistic institution narratives is due to the use of the feeding-stories to give instruction at the eucharist already in the pre-Marcan tradition,[123] a use that was continued by the evangelists themselves. Thus Mark 8:16–21 uses the fact that *bread remained over* after the feedings to teach that Christ (cf. 8:14!) remains present to His church in the eucharist (cf. ἄρτους ἔκλασα, 8:19); Matthew's interest is to teach the liturgical role of the eucharistic minister, and this he does by emphasizing the ministerial role of the apostles at the distribution of the bread to the crowds (14:16, 18, 19; 15:36) and by not mentioning the distribution of the fish; neither does Luke mention the distribution of the fish, and a further touch that suggests a eucharistic interest is the occurrence of the expression ἡ δὲ ἡμέρα ἤρξατο κλίνειν (9:12), which Luke also uses at the Emmaus breaking of bread (24:29); for John the feeding of the crowd is an earthly meal with which the heavenly bread may be contrasted (6:22–34), and John's interest is to show that the one who dispensed earthly bread *can* also dispense the bread of heaven (6:35–58). Heising's ingenuity may have led him a little far afield at some points; but enough is established to show that when the patristic church saw a relation between the feedings and the eucharist (see pp. 42f) it was maintaining a relation which had certainly been seen retrospectively by the primitive church from the viewpoint of its own eucharistic experience, and which had indeed (we would judge) already been seen by Jesus. We shall deal more precisely with the nature of that relation presently.

(iv) H. Riesenfeld gives a eucharistic flavour to his theory that the cornfield episode of Mark 2:23–28 and parallels is a sign of the dawn of that eschatological sabbath which is characterized by the messianic 'bread' or 'feast'. When the gospel accounts of Jesus's words about the incident of David eating the shewbread are contrasted with the LXX text at 1 Regn. 21:7,[124] then the differences point to a eucharistic intent in the gospel texts: David, the prototype of the messiah, replaces Abimelech as subject of the action, and the typically eucharistic verbs λαμβάνειν (Luke 6:4), διδόναι (Mark 2:26; Luke 6:4) and φαγεῖν (Mark 2:26; Luke 6:4; Matt.

12:4; cf. Matt. 26:26) appear together in the same context (just as they do in the accounts of the miraculous feedings) in a way which the Old Testament account would not suggest. If Riesenfeld is right, then the evangelists at least, if not Jesus Himself, saw a relation between the eucharist and the cornfield episode.

*    *    *

But we are now bound to ask what is the precise nature of the relation between the parabolic meal-activity of Jesus during His ministry and the church's eucharist. Is the eucharist the *fulfilment* of the parabolic signs of the meal of the kingdom that were given by Jesus in His ministry? Or does the eucharist continue itself to be a *sign pointing towards* the meal of the kingdom?

We may begin our answer by calling attention to a saying of Jesus which, in varying versions (all packed with semitisms) and different positions, all the synoptists agree in placing at the Last Supper. Mark and Matthew place the saying after the institution of the eucharist, and in the following forms (attention is drawn to the differences by italics):

*Truly*, I say to you, I shall not drink again of the fruit of the vine until that day when I drink it new in the kingdom of God. (Mark 14:25)

I say to you, I shall not drink again of *this* fruit of the vine until that day when I drink it new *with you* in *my Father's* kingdom. (Matt. 26:29)

Luke's longer text, which I accept,[125] gives an account of the institution which is similar in structure to those given by Paul, Mark and Matthew (Luke 22:19–20; I Cor. 11:23–25; Mark 14:22–24; Matt. 26:26–28); but he *prefaces* this by what appears to be a twofold variant of the saying we have just quoted from Mark and Matthew:

[14]And when the hour came, he sat at table, and the apostles with him. [15]And he said to them, 'I have earnestly desired to eat this passover with you before I suffer; [16]for I tell you I shall not eat it (*or:* never eat it again)[126] until it is fulfilled in the kingdom of God.' [17]And he took a cup, and when he had given thanks he said, 'Take this, and divide it among yourselves; [18]for I tell you that from now on I shall not drink of the fruit of the vine until the kingdom of God comes.'

A little later Luke gives another saying which appears to be related to both vv. 15–18 and vv. 19–20:

[29]As my Father appointed a kingdom for me, so do I appoint ($\delta\iota\alpha\tau\acute{\iota}\theta\epsilon\mu\alpha\iota$, cf. $\delta\iota\alpha\theta\acute{\eta}\kappa\eta$ at v.20) for you [30]that you may eat and drink at my table in my kingdom, and sit on thrones judging the twelve tribes of Israel.

In the light of these sayings we may now re-formulate our question thus: Does the church's eucharist fulfil the eschatological prospect held out by Jesus at the Last Supper (and therefore fulfil also the parabolic signs of the meal of the kingdom that were given by Jesus in His ministry)? Or does the eucharist continue itself to be a sign pointing towards the meal of the kingdom?

There is a line of interpretation, stretching back from Markus Barth through Euthymius Zigabenus to John Chrysostom and Ephraim the Syrian, which considers that the eschatological prospect held out by Jesus at the Last Supper did not even have to await the church's eucharist for its fulfilment, let alone remain unfulfilled until a coming of the kingdom which has even yet not occurred, but was *already fulfilled in the meals which Jesus took with His disciples immediately after His resurrection.*[127] Though the New Testament makes no mention of Jesus drinking *wine* in the period after the Resurrection, and therefore gives no explicit support to the fulfilment of that feature at least of Mark 14:25 = Matt. 26:29 = Luke 22:18 by the post-Resurrection meals, yet we must certainly recognize the importance attached by New Testament writers, and particularly Luke, to the meals that Jesus took with his disciples during the forty days:

(i) Luke 24:28–35: the meal at Emmaus.
(ii) Luke 24:36–43: the meal on Easter Sunday evening at Jerusalem.
(iii) Acts 10:41: Peter's preaching before Cornelius and his company mentions that God made the risen Jesus manifest 'not to all the people but to us who were chosen by God as witnesses, *who ate and drank with him after he rose from the dead.*'
(iv) In Acts 1:4 συναλιζόμενος is probably to be associated with ἅλς (salt) and understood as a reference to the risen Jesus's *eating with* the apostles—as in fact the Latin, Syriac and Coptic versions translate.[128]
(v) John 21:13: the breakfast with the fishermen disciples by the sea of Tiberias.[129]

Doubtless the theme of anti-docetic apologetic plays a part in some of these accounts (particularly Luke 24:36–43), but O. Cullmann was surely right in calling attention to the importance of the post-Resurrection meals for eucharistic origins and theology.[130] An indication of the primitive church's awareness of the link between the eucharist and these meals is seen in the terminology used in their description: we note particularly the occurrences of κλᾶν ἄρτον or ἡ κλάσις τοῦ ἄρτου at Luke 24:30, 35, and in the Gospel of the Hebrews and the Epiphanius letter-fragment mentioned in note 129; and we then recall that ἡ κλάσις τοῦ ἄρτου was a very early designation of the eucharist (Acts 2:42, 46 and 20:7, 11 in all probability; I Cor. 10:16; Ignatius, *Eph.* 20:2; Didache 14:1).[131] Moreover, the full Emmaus story (Luke 24:13–35) is so suggestive of the twofold pattern of word and eucharistic meal which characterized the Christian liturgical assembly from a very early date (Acts 2:42; 20:7–12; Justin *Apol.* I, 67) that it appears likely that Luke intends the story to give teaching on the meeting with Christ in the church's worship.[132] If then the eucharist is to be seen in some sense as a continuation of the post-Resurrection meals, themselves understood with Chrysostom as fulfilling the eschatological prospect of the meal in the kingdom, then the case is strengthened for the view at present fashionable among Roman Catholic scholars that the eucharist is already the meal of the kingdom.

But it is not with the post-Resurrection meals that these Catholic scholars in fact begin their argument. They rely rather on the exegetical work done by P. Benoit on the Lucan account of the Last Supper in an article published in *Revue Biblique* in 1939: 'Le récit de la Cène dans Lc. XXII, 15–20. Etude de critique textuelle et littéraire'. In verses 15–20 of Luke 22 Benoit sees a 'curiously symmetrical structure': 'deux panneaux parallèles 15–18 et 19–20, composés chacun de deux éléments qui se répondent d'un tableau à l'autre: Pâque de 15–16 et pain de 19; coupe de 17–18 et coupe de 20' (p. 360). Luke has artfully taken the eschatological cup-word of Mark 14:25, doubled it by an eschatological passover saying of his own composition, and placed both of them *before* (vv. 15–18) the account of the eucharistic institution (vv. 19–20) with the intention of showing that the Christian eucharist is the new rite which fulfils and replaces the old Jewish passover and is already the meal of the kingdom—so that in vv. 29–30 the kingdom, the table of Christ and the thrones are 'transparently' the church, the eucharistic banquet and the government of the community. Ignoring Benoit's remark that a future eschatological sense is not excluded by his ecclesiastical interpretation, and forgetting that Benoit claims this ecclesiastical meaning of the 'eschatological prospect' saying only for Luke, some later scholars press forward as the only right relation between the eucharist and the meal of the kingdom the one of total identity. This is true, for instance, of E. J. Kilmartin, *The Eucharist in the Primitive Church* (1965), who concludes his treatment of the question in Luke *and* in Mark/Matthew by saying quite unrestrictedly 'The Eucharist is the Messianic Banquet of the Kingdom' (pp. 49–53). Rather similarly, and apparently in ignorance of Benoit's work, L. Tondelli had arrived at the view that the eucharist in the church is, according to Jesus's revealed intention at the Last Supper, identical with the fulfilment of the new passover in the Father's kingdom (*L'Eucaristia vista da un esegeta*, 1951).

An indirect support for this view may be sought in the story of the miracle of Cana in John 2. Some recent exegetes, and there is a certain amount of support in early tradition for the view, have looked upon the miracle of Cana as a sign of the eucharist.[133] If the fulfilment of the 'sign' (2:11) waited for the 'hour' (2:4) of Jesus (i.e. His death, cf. 7:30; 8:20; 12:23; 13:1; 17:1), then with the coming of His death and the possibility of the Christian eucharist (cf. 6:51–8; 19:34, where the water and blood coming from Christ's pierced side are often[134] taken to refer to baptism and the eucharist) there came the fulfilment of the sign: the wine of the eucharist was the messianic wine of the kingdom, of which the abundant (2:6) and good (2:10) wine of Cana had been a sign.

But in fact the eucharist cannot be understood as the unequivocal fulfilment of Jesus's parabolic signs of the feast of the kingdom, or of the eschatological prospect held out at the Last Supper. Returning to Luke 22 we find H. Schürmann, for instance, making exegetical objections to Benoit's interpretation: Luke's usage in Acts, he argues, is consistently to make βασιλεία refer to the eschatological kingdom, and never to the church (Acts 1:3, cf. vv. 6–8; 8:12; 14:22; 19:8; 20:25; 28:23, 31). This gives pause for thought but is certainly not decisive since 'kingdom' may be used in a special sense in Luke 22:16, 18 and 29f—for (if Schürmann were right) Luke 22:16 would speak for the only time in the New Testament of the fulfilment of an Old Testament type in 'the kingdom' *rather than* in the ministry of Jesus or in the church, and Luke 17:21[135] is evidence for Luke's understanding of an indisputably 'present' kingdom at least in the ministry of Jesus and probably still in the church. Even if, however, John and Luke may be allowed to present the eucharist as a fulfilment of the verbal and acted signs of the meal of the kingdom that were given by Jesus in His ministry, we are prevented by other parts of the New Testament witness from regarding the eucharist as the *complete* fulfilment of those signs. For we notice, first, that the ἕως τῆς ἡμέρας ἐκείνης of the Marcan (14:25) and Matthaean (26:29) versions seems hard to reconcile with anything but that transformed universe of the *new* heaven and the *new* earth when the wine will be drunk *new* (καινόν, Mark 14:25; Matt. 26:29) by Jesus and His men. Second, the saying of Mark 2:20 = Matt. 9:15b = *Luke* 5:35 about the disciples' fasting when the bridegroom is taken away from them shows that some in the primitive church, if not Jesus Himself (for the saying may be a *Gemeindebildung*), considered that the days of fasting were not yet over and therefore that the kingdom could hardly have come in all its fulness. Third, we observe that though the *joy* which according to Luke characterized the primitive eucharist (Acts 2:46; 16:34[136]) was undoubtedly a mark of the kingdom (Rom. 14:17),[137] it was, if we are to credit the weight of recent exegesis, precisely an unrestricted abandonment to the inebriating pleasures of a rather material heavenly banquet among the Corinthian enthusiasts that called forth Paul's reminder that the eucharist was a showing forth of the Lord's *death*, celebrated *until he come* (I Cor. 11:26).[138] Fourth, the Apocalypse reserves the marriage-supper of the Lamb for a consummation still to come (Rev. 19:7–9), even though the Lord appears to make a promise that may be fulfilled in the present at Rev. 3:20:

Behold, I stand at the door and knock; if any one hears my voice and opens the door, I will come in to him and eat with him, and he with me.

It is for these reasons that the more prudent among the supporters of the view that the eucharist is already the meal of the kingdom leave themselves a loophole by admitting, if a little grudgingly, that their view does not exclude a future consummation: so, for instance, P. Benoit, M. Barth, B. Cooke.[139] Two other scholars, O. Cullmann and P. Lebeau, are more positive in stating that the fulfilment of the signs and promises of the meal of the kingdom in the eucharist, though real, is only a *beginning* and that the final fulfilment is *still awaited*.[140]

This last position seems basically true to the biblical record. The question with which we began this section turns out to have been wrongly posed. There is no exclusive alternative between the eucharist as fulfilment of the signs of Jesus's ministry and the eucharist as itself a sign still of the meal of the kingdom. In accordance with the characteristic biblical pattern of promise and fulfilment, the eucharist is a first and partial fulfilment of the promises of the meal of the kingdom that were given by Jesus during His ministry and it is itself the strengthened promise of the total fulfilment in the final consummation. A broader sweep of the arc has now been drawn, but still the 360° is not complete; the perfect form will be achieved only when we feast forever face to face with the Lord. A look at two other points of biblical teaching on the matter will provide confirmation of this view.

First, I draw attention to the polyvalent import of the synoptic meal-parables: Luke 14:16–24 (the great feast) ⌒ Matt. 22:1–10 (the wedding feast given for the king's son); Matt. 22:11–13 (the wedding garment); Matt. 25:1–13 (the virgins and the wedding feast); Luke 15:22–32 (the feast for the returned prodigal). At their original telling by Jesus these parables probably referred to the crisis for Israel which the coming of Jesus had brought into being, and to the divine offer of forgiveness and fellowship to the repentant which Jesus was also enacting in His meals with publicans and sinners. It is clear, however, that the primitive church did not consider that their relevance had already been exhausted by Jesus's ministry—for the form and position in which one of these parables appears in the gospels make of it an exhortation to vigilance in face of a still awaited parousia (Matt. 25:1–13; and cf. Matt. 25:14–30, especially vv. 21, 23, 30), while another appears as part of a perennial offer of forgiveness to the repentant (Luke 15:22–32, among the three parables of repentance and forgiveness of that chapter), another as authorizing the church's mission to invite even Gentiles to the coming feast (Luke 14:16–24, especially verses 22f), and yet another perhaps as a guide to baptismal and eucharistic discipline (Matt. 22:11–13).[141] Thus we find the church extending and applying to its own teaching and practice in the 'time of the church' the parabolic signs and teaching of Jesus concerning the meal of the kingdom: the church was seeing itself as already realizing those signs and parables in mission and meal, and yet was aware that the present realization was only partial because the parousia was still awaited.

Second, I call attention to the importance of the relation between *covenant and kingdom* for understanding the eschatological content and import of the eucharist. In the 1940s three Swiss scholars, E. Gaugler, M. Barth and E. Schweizer, showed how the notion of the (new) covenant, present in the cup-word at the Last Supper, overcame H. Lietzmann's radical distinction between two types of eucharist, the Jerusalemite and the Pauline: the eucharist was from the start a meal of *joy* because it was the meal of the new covenant, but the new covenant had only come into being through the *death* of Jesus. E. Käsemann, agreeing that the notion of covenant was of vital importance for eucharistic doctrine, brought the new covenant into direct relation with the kingdom. Appealing to the use of διατίθεσθαι in connection with βασιλεία at Luke 22:29, Käsemann states that 'the new διαθήκη is nothing other than the form of the βασιλεία τοῦ θεοῦ which Christ has introduced as an already present reality'; and: 'The death of Jesus is the foundation on which the dispensation of the divine rule is erected. . . . The [eucharistic] cup grants participation in this dispensation of divine rule in that it grants participation in the death of Jesus on which the dispensation is founded.' Käsemann is careful to speak of 'the *present* form' of the βασιλεία.[142] I would approve of the way in which R. Schnackenburg describes the relation between new covenant and kingdom: the new covenant has as its *goal* the perfect fellowship with God in the kingdom of the final consummation.[143] The church already has forgiveness of sins (Matt. 26:28; cf. Jer. 31:34c) and 'tastes' of the powers of the world to come (Heb. 6:5), but the church still has to strive against sin in order to keep what is sacramentally its (Rom. 6) and does not yet enjoy that perfect fellowship with God (Jer. 31:33–34ab) which is pictured as the meal of the kingdom. The distinction and relation between new covenant and final kingdom will permit us also (see pp. 119f, 134) to make clear the *representative* role of the church and its eucharist as the *firstfruits* of the perfect society that will enjoy the feast of divine fellowship in a transfigured creation. Our immediate task, however, is to see how far the church has continued to understand the relation between the eucharist and the meal of the kingdom as we have so far discovered the New Testament to present it.

## 4. The evidence of ecclesiastical monuments, liturgies and theologians

The tour begins in the catacombs. We see no reason, despite the challenge of F. J. Dölger, to doubt the strong sacramental motifs which J. Wilpert discovered in the paintings of the Roman catacombs.[144] In these places of burial, where recurrent depictions of Jonah and his whale and of the raising of Lazarus bespeak the hope of resurrection to eternal life, we find also frequent representations of meals which combine eucharistic imagery with allusions to the feeding miracles and (less certainly) the lake-side breakfast of John 21.[145]

In the Cappella Graeca of the catacomb of Priscilla, for instance, there is found the painting entitled by Wilpert *Fractio panis* and dated by him, a trifle optimistically no doubt, before the middle of the second century. It depicts six people (five men and a woman) reclining on a dining-couch; to their left (our right), a bearded president sits and is breaking bread; below are a cup and two plates with two fishes and five loaves; at the outside edges stand seven baskets, four to our left and three to our right. The loaves and fishes and baskets are transparent allusions to the feeding miracles, while the cup makes the eucharistic meaning clear.

Of the so-called chapels of the sacraments in the catacomb of Callixtus the most interesting is one of the two oldest, designated A3 and dating perhaps from the early third century. On the entrance wall at the left side,

Moses is shown striking the rock (an event variously interpreted in the patristic period of baptism and of the eucharist).[146] Then the left-hand wall bears three pictures evoking baptism: a fisherman, an actual baptism, and the healing of the paralytic or of the man at Bethesda. The back wall has three eucharistic pictures: the multiplication of the loaves and fishes, a meal with seven people (which may be the feeding of the crowd rather than the breakfast by lake Tiberias), and the sacrifice of Isaac. The right-hand wall showed the raising of Lazarus. On the left, back and right walls, above the scenes already mentioned, are found pictures of Jonah. The remaining entrance wall shows the Samaritan woman at the well (the well of living water springing up unto eternal life was variously interpreted of baptism and the eucharist).[147]

From the catacomb of St Peter and St Marcellinus we may mention a pair of fourth-century scenes to either side in the vault of an arcosolium: to the right Christ is turning the water into wine at Cana, touching one of the six jars with a rod; to the left Christ is multiplying the loaves; and in the lunette there is a picture of a heavenly banquet. This conjunction of the miracles of the *loaves* and of the *wine*, clearly intended to suggest the eucharist, is often found in another place of Christian hope: the two scenes are sculpted on many sarcophagi. As one example we give the sarcophagus of Adelphia found in the catacomb of S. Giovanni at Syracuse, Sicily.[148] Another interesting case of the same combination of the miracle of the loaves and the miracle at Cana is that of a painting in an Alexandrian catacomb discovered by C. Wescher in 1864 and dated between the third and sixth centuries: on one side of the miracle of the loaves was the miracle at Cana, and on the other side a small group sitting at a meal, with the inscription: *ΤΑΣ ΕΥΛΟΓΙΑΣ ΤΟΥ Χ[ριστο]Υ ΕΣΘΙΟΝΤΕΣ* (and εὐλογία was frequently used, in the singular and in the plural, by Cyril of Alexandria for the consecrated species of bread and wine).[149]

Among the theologians we often find, in the early centuries at any rate, brief phrases which, by their almost incidental character, reveal that the eschatological scope of the eucharist was present to their authors' mind. Pride of place goes to Ignatius of Antioch for his phrase which German Protestant scholars have turned into a swear-word but which in fact simply depends on the biblical use of healing from disease as a figure of salvation from sin (σώζειν!) and on the equally biblical notions that the wages of sin is death but that Christ gives life to those who feed on His flesh and blood: . . . ἕνα ἄρτον κλῶντες, ὅς ἐστιν φάρμακον ἀθανασίας, ἀντίδοτος τοῦ μὴ ἀποθανεῖν, ἀλλὰ ζῆν ἐν Ἰησοῦ Χριστῷ διὰ παντός (*Eph.* 20:2). In his interpretation of the fourth petition of the Lord's prayer Cyprian says that we daily receive the eucharist *ad cibum salutis*, and he appeals to John 6:51, 53 for the view that only those who communicate will live *in aeternum* (*De or. dom.*, 18: PL 4, 531f). In a similar context Chromatius ( +407) calls the eucharistic bread

that heavenly and spiritual bread which we receive daily for the healing of our souls and the hope of eternal salvation (*quem quotidie ad medelam animae et*

*spem aeternae salutis accipimus*), of which the Lord says in the gospel: **The heavenly bread is my flesh which I will give for the life of this world** [Jn. 6:51].
(*Tract. in Ev. Matth.* 14, 5, PL 20, 360f)

On the subject of giving communion to those who are at the point of death while still under ecclesiastical discipline, the thirteenth canon of Nicaea decrees that in accordance with ancient practice they should not be deprived τοῦ τελευταίου καὶ ἀναγκαιοτάτου ἐφοδίου (Denzinger-Schönmetzer, §129).

There is sometimes a marked difference of emphasis among the theologians in the way in which they view the eucharistic meal as a sign of the meal of the kingdom. In the passages from Peter Chrysologus cited in note 107, for instance, the accent falls on the eucharist as *already* the foretaste of the future feast. In Augustine's treatment of the eucharist, on the other hand, there is a deeply ingrained theme that insists on the 'not yet': the eucharist is necessary only 'hunc', 'hoc tempore', 'in hac terra', 'huic vitae'; and that to which the eucharist will yield place in heaven is not too readily pictured by Augustine as a feast. Thus Augustine says to his catechumens:

The faithful know a spiritual food with which you also are about to become acquainted and which you will receive from the altar of God. It will be *daily* bread (*quotidianus*), [in the sense that is] necessary to this life. For shall we still receive the eucharist when we have come to Christ himself and begun to reign with him for ever? (*Serm.* 57, 7, 7, PL 38, 389)

P. Lebeau has interestingly argued that the 'aquarianism' which substituted water for wine at the eucharist and which the Fathers constantly combated between the second and fifth centuries and even beyond was in origin an Ebionite refusal to acknowledge that with the incarnation, death and resurrection of Jesus and the consequent outpouring of the Holy Spirit the messianic era had been, inaugurated and that the wine associated with it might be drunk: and in this matter heterodox Jewish Christianity prolonged the line of Rechabite protest against any too ready suggestion that the time of the fulfilment of divine promises had begun.[150]

The different ways in which the patristic theologians interpreted the saying of Jesus at the Last Supper about the drinking of new wine in the kingdom illustrate the variety of views on the relation between the eucharist and the meal of the kingdom.[151] Apart from the interpretation which sees the fulfilment of the saying in the post-Resurrection meals and which is itself not without eucharistic significance, there are three others that concern us here. First, there is the line of interpretation which places the fulfilment still in the *future*. This is true of Irenaeus in his millenarian mood,[152] and of Augustine who, omitting the millennium, places the drinking of the new wine in the heavenly kingdom (though he sees 'the new wine' as standing for our renewed bodies and does not envisage the 'drinking' as part of a feast).[153] Irenaeus elsewhere speaks in such a way as to suggest that he might have been ready to see the eucharist as *anticipating* this fulfilment;[154] but Augustine seems rather, in the same passage of the *Quaestiones Evangelorum*, to draw a *contrast* between the *old* wine of the eucharist (for at the institution Christ betokened *per vini sacramentum* the blood He was to shed in the death of the body that He took from the old race of Adam) and the *new* wine which stands for our renewed bodies in the kingdom of heaven.

At the other end of the spectrum are those, second, who see the new wine of the kingdom as being drunk already in the wine of the eucharist. Thus Jerome rejects the millenarian interpretation and applies the new-wine saying to the eucharist, going on:

We drink his [Christ's] blood, and without him we cannot drink, and every day in his sacrifices we press fresh red wines from the fruit of the true vine and of the vine Sorec [שֹׂרֵק Isa. 5:2], which means 'chosen', and from these vines *we drink the new wine in the kingdom of the Father*, not in the oldness of the letter but in the newness of the Spirit, singing the new song which no one can sing except *in the kingdom of the Church, which is the kingdom of the Father.*

(*Ep.* 120, 2, PL 22, 985f)

In the fifth century, Eucherius of Lyons gives the following interpretation:

*The kingdom of God* [referring to Matt. 26:29], as the scholars interpret it, is the Church, in which Christ through his saints daily drinks his own blood, as a head drinking through its members; (*Instruct.* I, 2, PL 50, 798)

and a similar interpretation continued to be popular throughout the medieval West and was shared by Philip Melanchthon:

*In the kingdom of my Father*, that is: in the Church, which means: after my resurrection you will drink my blood in the Church.

(*Ann. in Evang. Matth.* c. XXVI; *Werke in Auswahl*, vol. IV, Gütersloh 1963, p. 207)

The third line of interpretation, and the one which seems to accord best with the biblical record, falls between the two already indicated. It sees the fulfilment of the passover and the drinking of the new wine as taking place in the final kingdom still to come, and to this future fulfilment the present eucharist stands in the positive relation of *sign*, being an effective promise, to those who receive it rightly, of participation in the full and final reality of which it is a taste. Some such interpretation seems implied in a passage in Origen's *Exhortation to Martyrdom* in which he issues a warning to those who may be tempted to apostasy in face of persecution:

But if, understanding that word of Jesus: 'Henceforth I will no longer drink of the fruit of this vine until the day when I drink it new in the kingdom of heaven', we wish to be found one day among those who drink with Jesus, then let us take this warning to heart: 'You cannot drink the cup of the Lord and the cup of demons'. (*Exhort. ad mart.* 40)[155]

Drinking the eucharistic 'cup of the Lord' (I Cor. 10:21) in the present seems here to be a condition of drinking the new wine in the future in the 'kingdom of heaven' (we notice that Origen uses ἐν τῇ βασιλείᾳ τῶν οὐρανῶν in his quotation rather than any of the expressions used by the synoptists at this point: an extra indication of the transcendent nature of the future kingdom). A similar connection is seen by Cyprian in his arguments against the aquarians. After citing Matt. 26:28–29, he goes on:

Whence it appears that the blood of Christ is not offered if there is no wine in the cup, and that the Lord's sacrifice is not legitimately celebrated if our oblation and sacrifice does not correspond to his passion. And how shall we drink new wine, of the fruit of the vine, with Christ in the Father's kingdom if in the sacrifice of God the Father and of Christ we do not offer wine and mix the cup of the Lord in accordance with Dominical tradition? (*Ep.* 63, 9, *CSEL*, p. 708)

A little later on, Cyprian shows how by the drinking of 'the blood of the Lord and the cup of salvation' the 'memory of the old man is thrown off, former worldly conversation is forgotten, and the sad and sorrowful heart that was oppressed by the weight of sins is set free by the joy of divine favour' (*ibid.*, 11, p. 710).

In a text attributed to Titus of Bostra ( + between 363 and 378) we meet an interesting triple pattern which corresponds closely to the pattern of promise-fulfilment-consummation we met towards the end of chapter one:

The Saviour, then, ate the typical (τυπικόν) or legal (νομικόν) passover with his own disciples: for he had come to fulfil the Law and put an end to the shadow (πέρας τῇ σκιᾷ δοῦναι), being himself the reality (ἀλήθεια). And he reserved for us the celebrating of the heavenly (ἐπουράνιον) passover. For he, the reality, came, [he ate the passover, he brought the type to an end (κατηνάλωσε τὸν τύπον) so that reality might prevail]. For the type announced beforehand, but he that was announced was awaiting the coming of the right time. And since the type had to be fulfilled, he finally went up to Jerusalem, of his own free will, towards his passion. There the type, here the reality. And he said at that time: 'I tell you, I will never eat of it again until it is fulfilled in the kingdom of God.' He spoke thus, not because he was to suffer a second time for mankind, but because, having suffered once only, he was to transmit to us the mystery (παραδοῦναι ἡμῖν τὸ μυστήριον), which he will fulfil in the kingdom of heaven (ὃ καὶ πληρώσει ἐν τῇ βασιλείᾳ τῶν οὐρανῶν). For as there was first the paschal lamb and secondly 'what the faithful know' [an arcane reference to the eucharistic mystery], so there will also be a third and incorporeal passover and the sharing in that incorporeal passover, which is the kingdom of heaven.[156]

A similar triple pattern is found in Gregory of Nazianzen's *Discourse on Holy Easter* in a passage in which the eucharist, though not expressly mentioned, is certainly implied in virtue of the important place it occupied in the total celebration of Easter:

We are about to share in the πάσχα in a way which is even now still only 'typical' (νῦν μὲν τυπικῶς ἔτι), though less veiled than the old (καὶ εἰ τοῦ παλαιοῦ γυμνότερον): for the 'legal' passover was, I venture to say, the type of a type (τύπου τύπος), and even more obscure. But shortly the πάσχα will be still more perfect and pure, when the Word drinks it new with us in the kingdom of the Father, revealing to us and teaching us at that time those things which at the present time he has simply let us glimpse in part (μετρίως παρέδειξε). (*Or.* 45, 23, PG 36, 653f)

One more example may be given of the eucharist seen as a sign of the future meal in the heavenly kingdom. It comes from a hymn composed by the Syrian chorepiscopus Balai ( +c. 460) for the dedication of a new church:

His altar is ready, and he takes his meal with us; his glory is offered to men, and they take their place at table; we eat with him at our table; one day he will eat with us at his. Let his glory and his majesty be adored! Here he gives us his body; there he will give us his reward. On earth stands the altar which bears his body, and in the heavenly kingdom he will grant us eternal life and glory. The disciples received the bread he had blessed: he named it his body, and the wine his blood. 'In fellowship with you I have enjoyed the sacrament; you will in turn enjoy it with me in the heavenly kingdom.'[157]

\*     \*     \*

Turning from more or less occasional remarks in letters, sermons and biblical commentaries to more sustained treatments of the sacraments in general or of the eucharist alone, we find that the first such documents in the West, the *De sacramentis* and the *De mysteriis* of Ambrose, consider the eucharist as the fulfilment of various Old Testament types: the manna of the Exodus, the table and the cup of Ps. 23, the feast of Cant. 5; and the eucharistic wine causes the joy of the *sobria ebrietas* that comes from drinking of the Spirit. Nor do the heavenly sacraments (*sacramenta caelestia*) exhaust what remains in store for the future.[158] Yet the treatises already manifest an interest in the ontology of the relation between Christ's presence and the elements which presages future developments. As the Middle Ages progress in the West, this interest comes to occupy a large place in eucharistic treatises and, with one or two qualified exceptions,[159] the eschatological perspective is mentioned, where at all, only in rather a fossilized way and calls forth no developed exposition.

The East fared rather better. In his *Mystagogical Catecheses* Cyril of Jerusalem sees the eucharist as fulfilling (i) the table and the cup of Ps. 23, and (ii) the bread eaten with joy and the wine drunk with a merry heart of Eccles. 9:7.[160] His main emphasis falls on what the initiates *already* enjoy, but he is not blind to the fact that there will be an *advance* from glory to glory (IV, 9).

In his *Catechetical Homilies* Theodore of Mopsuestia gives an attractive account of the relation between the eucharistic meal and the blessings of the final kingdom in an eschatological perspective much indebted to Hebrews.[161] Vivified by the same Holy Spirit who gave immortality to Jesus Christ buried in the tomb, the bread and wine become the body and blood of Christ and the living food of immortality (Theodore appeals to Rom. 1:4; 8:11; John 6:48, 51, 63). Just as Christ manifested himself to His disciples individually after His resurrection and announced to them that they would be associated with Him in the great blessings to come, so now in each particle of the broken loaf He approaches each communicant, greets him, manifests His own resurrection and gives the communicant 'the earnest ('āreb) of the good things to come, for the sake of which we approach this holy mystery; and it is in this way that we are fed, by an immortal food, with the gift of immortality' (XVI, 20; cf. 26). Through communion we receive the firstfruits and earnest of the grace of the Holy Spirit, which feeds and keeps us, and at the last we shall receive it entirely and be fed by Him directly. A characteristic expression of Theodore's is that the eucharist is a τύπος of the blessings to come.[162] He also sets the eucharist firmly in a perspective of *hope*, thus allowing both the 'already' and the 'not yet' to emerge:

> By [this spiritual food] we expect to become immortal and to abide for ever in those (blessings) in the hope of which we take this holy food of the mysteries.
> (XV, 8)

> It is in the expectation of receiving [the life which lasts into immortality] that we partake of this sacrament, by which we believe we have a firm hope of those (blessings) to come.   (XV, 9)

And again, this time in the context of the 'not yet' of II Cor. 5:6–8 and I Cor. 13:12:

> It is in hope that we have received this salvation and (this) life.   (XV, 18)

It is Christ our forerunner who holds together the 'vertical' and the 'horizontal' in this eschatology: by the bread and cup (which are His body and blood) He 'is bringing us, in a way that no one can describe, to share in the good things to come' (XVI, 25; cf. 17–19), which are for Him already present reality (XVI, 30). Meanwhile we have to order our actions according to the future reality that we have already received, in hope, in the eucharist. Citing I Cor. 7:29–31, Theodore goes on:

> So since this world in its entirety subsists as mere (šhimā) appearance (σχῆμα), and indeed, according to the word of the apostle, a passing appearance which will surely vanish, whereas we await the (world) to come, which will abide for ever: (since this is so) we must all order (τάξις) our life according to the (realities) of that other world.   (XVI, 33)

We shall see more of Theodore later, when we come to look at the eucharist as a sign of the parousia (p. 73) and as an image of the worship of heaven (p. 118).

In his homilies on the eucharist, the Nestorian Narsai ( + c. 502) puts the following slightly modified words of the Johannine Christ into his account of what Jesus said at the Last Supper:

> Whoso eateth with love of my body and drinketh of my blood liveth for ever, and abideth in me and I in him.[163]

Like Theodore of Mopsuestia, Narsai stresses in Hom. XVII the way in which the mysteries 'typify' the Resurrection of Christ; and again the breaking of the bread into particles for distribution symbolizes the appearances of the risen Lord to His disciples individually, and

... now he appears, in the reception of his Body, to the Sons of the Church; and they believe in him and receive from him the Pledge of life. (*ibid.* p. 24)

The final blessing given by the priest, with arms upstretched, from the door of the altar, symbolizes Christ's final blessing of the twelve at the Ascension, and

with this blessing with which the bright(-robed) priest blesses us he depicts a type (*or* mystery) of that (blessing) which is about to work in us. When we have been raised from the dead and have put on glory we shall be lifted up on high into heaven with the Saviour. There shall all passions cease from our human nature, and we shall delight in desirable good things without end. (*ibid.* pp. 30f)

Homily XXI makes clear that the eucharistic communion has already typified for the communicants these delights of heaven:

In the midst of his secret palace the King has made them to recline; and the table of life immortal he has set before them. A beauteous bridechamber he has fitted on earth for a type of that which is above, that they may delight therein mystically unto the end. (*ibid.* p. 54)

Maximus the Confessor ( + 662) has a similar notion of the eucharist as the reality-filled sign of what is to come. He uses a whole string of characteristic verbs to express the relation between the liturgy and the future: σημαίνειν, προτυποῦν, προδιαγράφειν, προσημαίνειν; and nouns like τύπος, σύμβολον, ἀρχὴ καὶ προοιμιόν. Since, however, Maximus does not dwell particularly on the imagery of the *meal* as such, we will reserve further treatment for a more appropriate place in the next chapter, contenting ourselves here with reproducing Maximus's own summary of the meaning of eucharistic communion:

By the holy communion of the undefiled and life-giving mysteries [we have] fellowship and identity with him, being made like him through participation: and thus man, from being man, is vouchsafed to become divine. We believe that here in the present life we receive by the grace of faith the same gifts of the Holy Spirit that we believe we shall (if we keep the commandments as well as we can) receive in the coming age in very substance, truth and reality, according to the infallible hope of our faith and the solid and inviolable declaration of the promise; for we shall pass from the grace of faith to the grace of sight when our God and Saviour Jesus Christ manifestly transforms us into himself by removing from us the marks of corruption and graciously gives us the 'original' (ἀρχέτυπα) mysteries which have been here displayed (παραδειχθέντα) for us by means of sensible symbols.

(*Myst.* 24, PG 91, 704f)

John Damascene ( + 749) certainly knows the eucharist as a sign of the food of the future age, as we saw above; but in that long chapter of his treatise *On the Orthodox Faith* which deals with the sacrament (IV, 13, PG 94, 1136–53) he is primarily concerned with other questions; and it is

only at the end, as part of a defence of the application of the term 'antitypes' to the bread and wine, that he opens up an eschatological prospect:

And if they are called 'antitypes' of things to come, it is not because they are not
really the body and blood of Christ but because we now partake through them of
the divinity of Christ which we shall then comprehend by sight alone.

The outstanding late Byzantine commentary on the liturgy is that of
Nicholas Cabasilas ( + 1363), *Explanation of the Divine Liturgy*.[164] Neither
here nor in his sacramentally oriented treatise on *The Life in Christ*[165]
does meal imagery as such play a large part. But at two points in particular
Nicholas makes interesting comments in terms of the imagery of the meal.
In chapter 43 of the Commentary he declares that feeding on Christ is the
sole and permanent source of joy, whether for the faithful departed (with
whom Nicholas begins) or for the church on earth or for all the just at the
consummation:

Now the source of all delight and bliss to those who dwell in that place—whether
you call it paradise, or Abraham's bosom, or the place free from sorrow and
pain, which is full of light, and green and cool, or even if you call it the kingdom
itself—is none other than this cup and this bread. For these are the Mediator,
who went before us into the holy place, who alone leads us to the Father, who
alone is the sun of souls, and who now appears and gives himself to us thus [in
the cup and the bread] as he willed, for we are still the prisoners of the flesh;
and after death we shall look on him and partake of him unveiled, when we shall
see him as he is, . . . when he 'shall gird himself, and make them to sit down,
and will come forth and serve them';[166] he will come resplendent upon the clouds,
and will make the just to shine like the sun. Those who have not been joined to
him in the union which his table can create, cannot enjoy any rest in that place,
or receive there any good thing, great or small.[167]

The other passage comes in *The Life in Christ* and brings out both the
continuity and the distinction between the eucharistic feast and the feast of
heaven:

For they will come from one table to another, from the still veiled to the now
open table, from the bread to the body itself. For at the present time, while they
still live a human life, Christ is their bread, and also their passover, for they are
on their way from here below to the heavenly city. But 'when they have renewed
their strength, they shall take wings like eagles', as the admirable Isaiah says
[40:31], and they will gather by the body itself [cf. Mt. 24:28] that will be stripped
of veils. That is what St John also declares when he says, 'We shall see him as he
is' [I Jn. 3:2]. For to those who have finished their life in the flesh Christ is no
longer bread, nor passover, for they have now reached their resting-place. But
he bears many features of a body: wounds in his hands, nailprints in his feet,
spear-thrust in his side.
    The present (eucharistic) supper leads towards that body. Without the euchar-
ist one cannot receive that body, any more than an eyeless man can see the light.
For have they life in them, who do not partake of this supper? And how can he
who is immortal be the head of dead members?

There is, then, the selfsame virtue at the one table as at the other, and the host is the same in the two worlds: the bridegroom himself, whether in the wedding-hall or at the table that is a preparation for the wedding-hall. Those who have departed without these gifts will, therefore, have no part in life. But those to whom it was given to receive the grace and keep it, they have entered into the joy of their Lord, and have gone with the bridegroom into the wedding-hall, and have enjoyed the new delights of the supper-table—not that this was the first time they had come into contact with these delights; but what they had brought with them they were now perceiving more clearly, for it had been completely revealed to them.

That is the sense in which the kingdom of heaven is ἐντὸς ἡμῶν.[168]

\* \* \*

The classical liturgies of both East and West set the eucharist in relation to the meal of the kingdom, and it is thanks to those among them which have continued in use that a certain awareness of the relation has been maintained even when it has not much occupied the attention of the theologians. One frequent and simple way of expressing the relation, especially in the West, is to attach the epithet 'heavenly' to various items or aspects of the eucharistic celebration. The eucharistic table is the heavenly table (*mensa caelestis*) at which is enjoyed the heavenly banquet (*convivium caeleste*) of the heavenly gifts (*dona caelestia*) of the heavenly bread (*panis caelestis*) and the heavenly cup (*poculum caeleste*), the whole being a heavenly mystery (*mysterium caeleste*). In some Eastern traditions the eucharistic table is called the royal table, which suggests both the king and his kingdom.[169] In the East again, the epithets 'mystical' and 'spiritual' are often attached to the things connected with the sacrament.

Sometimes the eucharist is pictured as Christ's banquet, at which He is present not only as food and drink (though this is usually mentioned in the same context) but also as host or participant in the meal. A very early example of this is found in a eucharistic prayer in the *Acts of Thomas*, 49:

Jesus, who hast deemed us worthy to communicate in the eucharist of thy holy body and blood, behold we make bold to approach thy eucharist and to call on thy holy name; ἐλθὲ καὶ κοινώνησον ἡμῖν.[170]

The Mozarabic office for Wednesday in Holy Week contains the benediction:

Today may he sanctify you perfectly, and may he tomorrow allow you to take your place worthily at his banquet (*convivium suum*).

(M. Férotin, ed., *Liber Sacramentorum*, col. 234)

And in fact in the *post pridie* of the Mozarabic Mass of Holy Thursday (*Missa de Cena Domini per Titulos*) Christ is invoked to come Himself and bless the elements:

Come, we pray thee, O Lord Jesus Christ, into the midst of thy servants, thou who art the author of the banquet of this supper . . . (*ibid.*, col. 239)

Christ's eucharistic banquet is sometimes given a nuptial colouring. In the liturgy of *Addai and Mari* the *turgāma* sung before the reading of the Apostle begins:

O ye that have been invited by the great purpose to the living marriage feast of the banquet of the king of those in heaven and those on earth . . .

(Brightman, p. 257)

and later, on communicating from the chalice the priest says:

For the guests at your banquet, heavenly bridegroom, you have prepared the chalice of your precious blood. Of that same you have given me to drink, sinner as I am. Glory be to you for your ineffable love, for ever. Amen.[171]

During communion in the Armenian liturgy the choir sings a hymn apostrophizing the Church and the sanctuary:

Mother of faith, thou shrine of holy espousals, heavenly bridechamber,
Home of thine immortal bridegroom who hath adorned thee for ever,
A marvellous second heaven art thou from glory to glory exalted,
Which by the laver dost regenerate us children radiant like the light,
Thou that dost distribute this spotless bread and givest us to drink this pure
    blood. . . .   (Brightman, p. 452)

Like Cyril of Jerusalem who held that Christ has already bestowed the enjoyment of his body and blood on the children of the bride-chamber, the liturgies just cited look upon the nuptial feast as a present reality. But the liturgy of *St Ignatius* seems to reserve it for the future when it prays:

Join us to thy flock, and number us among the ranks of thy beloved; make us worthy of thy kingdom, and lead us into thy wedding chamber.

(Renaudot II, p. 218)

We find in fact that even, or rather precisely, in those liturgies which are freest in calling the eucharistic meal already a *heavenly* reality, there is a strong awareness that *future* blessings still remain in store. This is particularly clear in prayers for the *fruits* of communion. In the Eastern liturgies it is a recurrent prayer, both in the final part of the epiclesis and after communion, that the communion may be 'for eternal life' and 'for the inheritance of the kingdom'.[172] The Syrian liturgy of *St James*, in its Greek form, asks God to grant 'the heavenly and eternal gifts that eye has not seen, nor ear heard, nor man's heart conceived, which thou hast prepared for them that love thee' (Brightman, p. 53).[173] The Syro-Malabar liturgy calls the altar the Table of Life, and one of the forms used in that liturgy at the communion from the chalice calls it 'a spiritual banquet unto eternal life'.[174] The fragmentary anaphora attributed to St Epiphanius, to which Dom B. Botte has called attention, refers in its institution narrative to the 'cup of immortality'.[175] A similar perspective obtains in the classical Western liturgies. At the priest's communion in the Roman mass the words are 'The body (blood) of our Lord Jesus Christ preserve my soul unto everlasting life'; and a similar form has been retained in the Anglican services of 1549 and 1662, and their derivations, at the people's communion: 'The body (blood) of our Lord Jesus Christ which was given (shed) for thee preserve thy body and soul unto everlasting life.' It is above all in the post-communion prayers that the medieval Western liturgies make the link between the eucharistic meal and the future and eternal kingdom. A post-communion in the *Missale Gothicum* prays quite simply:

Grant us, almighty God, that as we are refreshed in time by the supper of thy Passion, so we may be worthy to be filled by the banquet in eternity.

(ed. Bannister, no. 214)

The sequence of the mass of Corpus Christi (composed by Thomas Aquinas), after lauding the institution of the sacrament as the replacement of the old by the new, of the shadow by the truth, ends by addressing Christ thus:

Thou who knowest all things and canst do all things, who dost feed us here in this mortal life, make us there to be thy table-fellows, and fellow-heirs and fellow-citizens with the saints.

The relation between the eucharistic meal and the future and eternal kingdom is presented in a variety of ways. Perhaps the most common is that which sees the eucharist as a *pledge* (*pignus*) of heaven; as for example:

Make us, O Lord, we pray, who have received the pledge of eternal salvation, so to persevere in this direction that we may finally attain it (*sic tendere congruenter ut ad eam pervenire possimus*).

(*Missale Romanum*, post-communion of Friday after Lent II)[176]

We pray, O Lord our God, that what thou hast willed to be for us a pledge of immortality, thou wilt grant to become an effective help to eternal salvation (*ad salutis aeternae tribuas provenire suffragium*).

(Leonine Sacramentary, ed. Mohlberg, 1956, no. 484)

We have received, O Lord, the pledge of eternal redemption. May it be to us, we pray, by the intercession of thy saints a help both for the present life and for the future. (Leonine Sacramentary, ed. Mohlberg, 1956, no. 741)

The same notion is found in the antiphon of the Magnificat on Corpus Christi, again a composition of Thomas Aquinas:

O sacred banquet in which Christ is received,
the memory of his passion cultivated,
the heart filled with grace,
and the pledge of future glory given us;

and has even left its trace on Trent:

[Our Saviour] willed it to be a pledge of our future glory and perpetual bliss.

(*Decretum de ss. Eucharistia*, 2; Denzinger-Schönmetzer, §1638)

At other times the eucharist is seen also as the present *image* of what will be made *manifest*:

Receiving the pledge of eternal life, we humbly pray that sustained by help of the apostles, what we [now] perform in the image of the sacrament we may [one day] receive openly (*ut . . . quod in imagine gerimus sacramenti, manifesta perceptione sumamus*);

> (Leonine Sacramentary, ed. Mohlberg, 1956, no. 335;
> cf. Gelasian Sacramentary, ed. Mohlberg, 1960, no. 949)

or as the celebration under '*appearances*' of what we shall receive in *reality*:

May thy sacraments accomplish in us, we pray, O Lord, that which they contain; that the things we now perform in appearance we may [one day] receive in the truth of things (*ut quae nunc specie gerimus, rerum veritate capiamus*);

> (*Missale Romanum*, post-communion of Saturday in the autumn ember week)

or as the *prefiguration* of the full and unending enjoyment of Christ's godhead:

Make us, O Lord, we pray, to be filled with the everlasting enjoyment of thy godhead, which the reception of thy precious Body and Blood in time prefigures.

> (*Missale Romanum*, post-communion of Corpus Christi)

Elsewhere the sacrament is seen as the *promise* of heaven:

May the working of thy power increase in us, we pray, O Lord; that being strengthened by thy divine sacraments, we may be prepared by thy gift to receive the things they promise. (*Missale Romanum*, post-communion of Epiphany II)

May the heavenly table, O Lord, at which we have been fed, sanctify us; and may it make us, having been purified of all our errors, to be admitted to the promises on high (*supernis promissionibus reddat acceptos*).

> (*Missale Romanum*, post-communion of Wednesday after Lent III)

As such the eucharist arouses and strengthens our *hope*:

Let us, dearest brethren, in a united prayer ask for the divine mercy, that these salvation-bringing sacraments which our breasts have received may purify our souls and sanctify our bodies, and establish both our bowels and hearts in the hope of heavenly things (*atque in spem caelestium viscera pariter et corda confirment*); (post-communion in *Missale Gothicum*, ed. Bannister, no. 92)

and in this the West is joined by the East, in the prayer for the fruits of communion at the end of the anaphora of the Dêr-Balizeh papyrus:

and may it serve to us thy servants
for the power of the Holy Spirit
for the establishment and increase of faith
for hope of life in the age to come,
through our Lord Jesus Christ;
to thee, the Father, with him and with the Holy Spirit
be the glory for the ages. Amen.[177]

An entry in Moelcaich's hand in the Stowe Missal says that we already possess *in hope* what we shall truly enjoy in heaven:

We believe, O Lord, we believe that by this body broken and this blood out-poured we have been redeemed, and we trust that we have been strengthened by the reception of this sacrament, so that what we here possess meanwhile by hope we may enjoy in its true fruits when we dwell in heaven (*ut quod spe interim hic tenemus mansuri in celestibus veris fructibus perfruamur*).   (ed. Warner, p. 17)

Another characteristic expression says that we already taste the *joy* which will be full in heaven:

Having been filled by the gift of thy salvation, O Lord, we humbly beg that the thing whose taste gladdens us may by its effect renew us (*ut cujus laetamur gustu, renovemur effectu*).   (Gregorian Sacramentary, ed. Lietzmann, no. 39, 3)

May the venerable solemnity of this sacrament, we ask, O Lord, gladden us; may it fertilize both our minds and bodies by a spiritual sanctification, and exercise them for ever in chaste joys.

(Gelasian Sacramentary, ed. Mohlberg, 1960, no. 681)

So also in a prayer which occurs, with minimal variations, in the Leonine Sacramentary (ed. Mohlberg, 1956, nos. 876 *bis* and 1131 *bis*) and in the Bobbio (ed. Lowe, p. 14) and Stowe (ed. Warner, p. 19) Missals:

May this communion, O Lord, purge us of fault and grant us to share in the joy of heaven (*et caelestis gaudii tribuat esse consortes/participes*);

and finally, from the West, in the post-communion of the Wednesday after Pentecost in the Roman Missal (the final clause occurring in the Leonine Sacramentary, ed. Mohlberg, no. 108, and in the Stowe Missal, ed. Warner, p. 21):

Receiving, O Lord, the heavenly sacraments, we pray for thy mercy, that what we perform in time, we may obtain in the joys of eternity (*ut quod temporaliter gerimus, aeternis gaudiis consequamur*).

In the East, the anaphora of *St Xystus* in the Syro-Malankarese rite prays for the fruit of communion thus:

May these mysteries of which we partake make us partakers of your joy, Lord, and we will offer praise and thanksgiving to you and your only Son and your Holy Spirit, now and always and for ever.[178]

The Syriac anaphora of *St Cyril* prays that the coming of the Holy Spirit, by transforming the bread and wine,

may make us, by this divine communion, pure and holy
in thy eternal kingdom, in that blessed intimacy,
in the dwelling-places of thy splendour, in that bright contemplation
of thee, in the *joy* of those who have done thy will,
in that delight which is at thy right hand; and
through all and in all and for all we will render praise and
glory to thee and to thy only Son and to
thy Holy Spirit. (Renaudot, II, p. 279)

The Alexandrian anaphora of *St Mark* prays that the elements may be to the communicants 'for a share of the bliss (μακαριότητος) of eternal life and immortality' (Brightman, p. 134).

*          *          *

It can hardly be said that the Reformers as theologians did much to restore to the theological consciousness the notion of the supper as a sign of the feast of the kingdom, so occupied were they in combating alleged Roman notions of a repeated propitiatory sacrifice, and in fighting their own internal battles on the mode of Christ's presence. What is worse, as liturgists they helped to remove the notion from ecclesiastical consciousness by obliterating it from the service-books, particularly by their abandonment of the rich variety of medieval Western post-communion prayers. The classical Protestant liturgies contain quite often some rather colourless reference to 'spiritual nourishment unto everlasting life'. But rare indeed is Zwingli's insight in one of his prayers replacing the Roman canon, where he asks that communicants may be led, by the light of grace, to partake worthily in 'thy Son's banquet (*convivium*), wherein he himself is both our host and food (*hospes et epulum*)' (*De canone missae epicheiresis*, 1523);[179] and rarer still the thought expressed in the post-communion invitation to thanksgiving in the rite John à Lasco composed for Dutch refugees in England in 1550:

I hope that you all, in sitting down at this Supper, have perceived by the eye of your faith that blessed time in the kingdom of God when you will sit at table with Abraham, Isaac and Jacob; and that you are already, through trust in the righteousness, merit, and victory of Christ the Lord (in the communion of which we have now been sealed), just as sure of sitting down there as we have now surely all sat down together at this table of the Lord.[180]

It was not until the Wesleys' *Hymns on the Lord's Supper* (1745) that the Western church achieved again a rich appreciation of the eucharist as the sign of the future banquet of the heavenly kingdom. The supper is there called 'the *type* of the heavenly marriage feast' (Hymn 107), but the Wesleys' favourite expressions are *pledge* (Hymns 95, 100, 101, 102, 103, 107, 108, 111), *earnest* (94, 97, 103, 108), and the *taste* of the fulness (101, 103, 108). Hymn 97 talks of us

Who here *begin by faith* to eat
   The supper of the Lamb.   (cf. Hymns 96 & 111)

The words *joy* (93, 95, 96, 101, 102, 103, 108, 109, 110, 111, 112, 113, 115) and *hope* (93, 95, 98) abound. It is chiefly as the *nuptial banquet* that the eucharist and the meal of the kingdom are seen (93, 99, 100, 107, 111, 114). A few examples may be given from this one section entitled 'The Sacrament a Pledge of Heaven' (Hymns 93–115), though similar imagery is frequent in other sections as well.[181]

*The Wine which doth His passion show,*
*We soon with Him shall drink it new*
   *In yonder dazzling courts above;*

*Admitted to the heavenly feast,*
*We shall his choicest blessings taste,*
*    And banquet on His richest love.*
*We soon the midnight cry shall hear,*
*Arise, and meet the Bridegroom near,*
*    The marriage of the Lamb is come;*
*Attended by His heavenly friends,*
*The glorious King of Saints descends*
*    To take His bride in triumph home.*

. . . . . . . . . . . . . . . . . . . . . . . . .

*By faith and hope already there,*
*Even now the marriage-feast we share,*
*    Even now we by the Lamb are fed;*
*Our Lord's celestial joy we prove,*
*Led by the Spirit of His love,*
*    To springs of living comfort led.*   (from Hymn 93)

*        *        *

*He hallow'd the cup Which now we receive,*
*The pledge of our hope With Jesus to live,*
*(Where sorrow and sadness Shall never be found,)*
*With glory and gladness Eternally crown'd.*

*The fruit of the vine (The joy it implies)*
*Again we shall join To drink in the skies,*
*Exult in His favour, Our triumph renew;*
*And I, saith the Saviour, Will drink it with you.*   (from Hymn 95)

*        *        *

*To heaven the mystic banquet leads;*
*    Let us to heaven ascend,*
*And bear this joy upon our heads*
*    Till it in glory end.*
*Till all who truly join in this,*
*    The marriage supper share,*
*Enter into their Master's bliss,*
*    And feast for ever there.*   (from Hymn 99)

*        *        *

*For all that joy which now we taste,*
*    Our happy hallow'd souls prepare;*
*O let us hold the earnest fast,*
*    This pledge that we Thy heaven shall share,*
*Shall drink it new with Thee above,*
*    The wine of Thy eternal love.*   (from Hymn 108)

*        *        *

With the Wesleys we may end our survey of the classical liturgies and theologians. I now draw some systematic conclusions from our examination of the biblical and historical use of the verbal and dramatic image of the meal as it illustrates the eschatological content and import of the eucharist.

## 5. Systematic conclusions

Having the form of a meal, the eucharist belongs to that universally known realm of spoken and acted imagery which describes and embodies the relation between God and men in terms of eating and drinking. Within the biblical tradition the eucharist is ranged, and in a pre-eminent place, among those *signs* which announce before men, and inaugurate among them, that reality which is included in the eternal purpose of God and which is to come true for men: it is the sign of the kingdom of God in so far as the kingdom is conceived (and it is perhaps the dominant conception) as a feast for the citizens. One may set out under five heads the relation of the eucharist *as meal* to the kingdom.

First, the eucharistic meal expresses both the continuity and the difference that mark the relation between the present and the future forms of the kingdom, between its earthly and its heavenly forms. The one is a *taste* of the other, a real taste but not the *fulness*. It is *the Lord* who feeds us at His table, but His glory is not directly *apparent* to our eyes; in the Wesleys' words:

*Nourish'd on earth with living bread,*
*We now are at His table fed,*
*    But wait to see our heavenly King;*
*To see the great Invisible*
*Without a sacramental veil,*
*    With all His robes of glory on,*
*In rapturous joy and love and praise*
*Him to behold with open face,*
*    High on His everlasting throne!*[182]

The church on earth feeds at the Lord's table *periodically*, but the feasting in the definitive kingdom is *uninterrupted*.[183] The Lord's supper is the *reality-filled promise* to be eaten in *hope* of the final kingdom. Ultimate reality is glimpsed by the eyes of faith but has not yet permeated and transformed opaque and recalcitrant man.

Second, the eucharistic meal expresses the structure of the reality in which God has chosen to bind Himself together with men. All creation is dependent on the transcendent God for life. In the case of man this is shown by the *necessity* of food and by its divine *provision*. Because the eucharist uses ordinary food and drink, it expresses this fact and allows men to thank God for it. But because it uses the bread and wine as *signs* with a particular significance given to them by the Lord Jesus Christ, the eucharist goes much further: it announces, and begins to effect, God's good pleasure not merely to provide in a rather external way for the vital necessities of His creatures, but also to enter into such a communion of life with mankind that He feeds men on His own being, while yet remaining distinct (so that we may be said to eat and drink 'in His presence') and transcendent (as the one who gives). Christ is food, table-fellow and host. Man acknowledges the kingdom of God to the extent that he acknowledges his dependence on Him with thanksgiving; man enjoys the kingdom of

God to the extent that he allows himself to be fed by God from His very being.[184]

Third, the eucharistic meal expresses the fact that the kingdom has to do with the whole of creation and the whole of man; it expresses the positive value of the material creation and of physical man within it. There is no final opposition between the earthly and the heavenly, between the material and the spiritual, between body and soul. If God destined man for spiritual fellowship with Himself, it was as a physical being that He intended him to enjoy that fellowship; and the material creation, as the scene of that fellowship, was destined to possess spiritual significance. In the eucharistic meal, the material bread and wine eaten and drunk from a table of wood or an altar of stone achieves this spiritual significance as it mediates communion between man in his physical body and God who is spirit. The eucharistic meal is therefore already a sign of the new heaven and the new earth on which risen men and women will enjoy perfect fellowship with God in the consummated kingdom.

Fourth (to develop the same point with a different emphasis), the eucharistic meal also expresses the fact that the material creation has its positive value given to it only by its spiritual destiny of mediating personal communion between God and man.[185] To borrow a Pauline phrase and use it somewhat out of context: The kingdom of God is not meat and drink but righteousness, and peace, and joy in the Holy Ghost (Rom. 14:17). In good Semitic idiom this might mean that eating and drinking have to do with the kingdom of God *only in so far* as they express and embody righteousness, and peace, and joy in the Holy Ghost. The eucharistic meal is the sign of that righteousness, peace, and joy in the Holy Ghost which will be fully experienced in the final kingdom. It is a sign of righteousness, because it shows men sitting at table with God in that 'right relation' which is fellowship no longer marred by sin because God has forgiven the sinner and is making him really righteous. It is a sign of peace, because it shows God establishing the perfect peace which will finally reign between God and men and enfold all relations among men.[186] It is a sign of joy in the Holy Ghost, because the cup conveys a taste of that *sobria ebrietas* which the Spirit gives (cf. Eph. 5:18; Gal. 5:21–23).

Fifth, the eucharistic meal expresses the communal nature of the kingdom. The community of the kingdom shares in the one loaf (cf. I Cor. 10:17), at the one table of the Lord. For men the kingdom of God means being bound together in a common dependence upon the one Lord and in a common enjoyment of Him. We look upon our table-fellows as they are found in Christ.

\*     \*     \*

These conclusions bring to an end our examination of the eucharist *as a meal*, a meal which is the sign and taste of the kingdom of God. The next chapter considers the relation between the eucharist and the final *advent* of Christ.

# III

# *Maranatha*

W HEN PAUL writes to the Corinthians that the Lord's supper is a
proclamation of the Lord's death *until he come* (I Cor. 11:26),
he is not merely giving them a negative warning that the eucharist is not a celebration of unbridled eschatological joy but is under the
banner of the Lord's death until His final advent: he is also opening up
the prospect of the realization of the purposes of God and is setting the
eucharist in that context;[187] and it is highly probable that he is echoing a
cry used in the eucharistic liturgy: *Maranatha!* Our purpose in this chapter
is to let the eucharist be seen in the perspective of the final advent of Christ.
What, we must ask, is the relation between Christ's presence at the eucharistic feast and His final coming?

## 1. In remembrance of Him till He come

That the primitive church understood that Jesus was still to come again at
'the end' is clear from other texts as well as I Cor. 11:26. These texts are
found in every layer of the New Testament documents, and the most
likely explanation of this agreement is the simplest one, namely that Jesus
had led His followers to expect His coming again at the last day.[188]
Yet other dominical sayings promise His presence among His disciples
meanwhile. We have noticed already (note 186) that Narsai appealed to
Matt. 28:20b in connection with Christ's appearance to the communicants at the distribution of the bread. Another promise which has also been
understood eucharistically is that contained in Matt. 18:20:

Where two or three are gathered in my name, there am I in the midst of them.

There is considerable early Syrian evidence for a eucharistic use of this
verse. A sermon by Ephraim puts the following words into Christ's mouth
at the institution of the sacrament: 'When you gather together in my name
as a church, wherever it is, do what I did, in remembrance of me' (*Hymni
et Sermones*, ed. T. J. Lamy, t.I, Mechliniae, 1882, col. 426). In the light of
this it is easy to see the same allusion in three other cases; first, in the
*Demonstratio de Paschate* of Aphraates, which makes Christ say:

Thus do, in remembrance of me, when you gather together;

(Patrologia Syriaca I, 518)

second, in the anaphora of *Theodore*, at the institution narrative and
anamnesis:

Thus do whenever you gather together in remembrance of me . . . and so we
have gathered together . . . ;  (Renaudot II, p. 619)

third, and most notably, in the very ancient anaphora of *Addai and Mari*:

And we also, O my Lord, thy weak and frail and miserable servants who are gathered together in thy name, both stand before thee at this time and have received the example [τύπος] which is from thee delivered unto us . . .
(Brightman, p. 287)[189]

In modern times M. Barth has tentatively proposed a eucharistic understanding of Matt. 18:20;[190] and J. Hamer has made an interesting connection between Matt. 18:20 and I Cor. 11:26. Arguing that the form with εἰς and the accusative (εἰς τὸ ἐμὸν ὄνομα) represents the Aramaic *le shem* which bears 'un sens final clairement accusé', Hamer claims that 'to gather together in my name' means 'to gather together *for* me' and, drawing now a parallel with I Cor. 11:26, suggests that the meaning in Matt. 18:20 is 'gathered together awaiting my final return'—so that 'there am I in the midst of you' is a declaration that the church's expectation has already been rewarded, at least invisibly, in the liturgical assembly.[191] Whether the specifically eucharistic meaning of Matt. 18:20 is allowed to be original or not, we are certainly left with the fact that beside the coming of Christ which the church expected at the end there is also a presence of Christ in the midst of the assembled community which, being clearly more 'definite' (personal) than the 'general' (cosmic) presence which may be ascribed to Christ in virtue of His divinity, may appropriately be said to imply a *coming* of Christ *as He is known among men*.[192]

As far as the eucharist is concerned, it may be through an examination of the notion of *anamnesis* that we shall find a framework for understanding the twofold fact that Christ's coming is still awaited and yet that He comes to His assembled people as they celebrate the Lord's supper. The Pauline text with which we began this chapter is the apostle's own comment on the traditional institution narrative, which he has just repeated for the Corinthians' benefit. The link is made as follows:

[23]For I received from the Lord what I also delivered to you, that the Lord Jesus on the night when he was betrayed took bread, [24]and when he had given thanks, he broke it, and said, 'This is my body which is for you. Do this in remembrance of me (τοῦτο ποιεῖτε εἰς τὴν ἐμὴν ἀνάμνησιν).' [25]In the same way also the cup, after supper, saying, 'This cup is the new covenant in my blood. Do this, as often as you drink it, in remembrance of me.' [26]For as often as you eat this bread and drink the cup, you proclaim the Lord's death until he comes.
(I Cor 11:23–26)

Now scholarly discussion has mainly turned on the way in which the eucharist is a memorial of Christ's death, but the mutual proximity of ἄχρι οὗ ἔλθῃ and εἰς τὴν ἐμὴν ἀνάμνησιν justifies an investigation of a possible connection between the eucharistic memorial of Christ and His final advent.

At any rate the composers of eucharistic prayers have often felt that I Cor. 11:26 with its eschatological prospect was important enough to

merit inclusion in the institution narrative cited in the canon; and they
have sometimes turned the text into a direct first-person saying of Jesus:
so, for instance, the anaphora of *Apostolic Constitutions VIII* ('. . . you
proclaim my death until I come'); the Syriac *St James* ('ye do proclaim
my death and confess my resurrection until I come'; Brightman, p. 87),
and many West Syrian anaphoras; the liturgy of *St Basil*, which already
had in its early Egyptian, apparently pre-Basilican form 'You announce
my death until I come';[193] the Alexandrian *St Mark* ('. . . you proclaim
my death and you confess my resurrection and assumption until I come';
Brightman, p. 133), and the Coptic *St Cyril* ('ye do show my death, ye do
confess my resurrection, ye do make my memorial until I come'; Brightman, p. 177). In North Italy we observe that Ambrose already reproduces
from the liturgy the following form:

As often as you do this, you will make remembrance of me, until I come again;
(*De sacramentis*, IV, 6, 26, ed. Botte, p. 116)

and Maximus of Turin ( + *c.* 420) similarly:

As often as you do these things, you will proclaim my death, until I come.
(*Serm.* 78, PL 57, 690)

In later texts of the Ambrosian liturgy this undergoes an interesting
expansion:

As often as you do these things, you will do them in remembrance of me, you
will preach my death, you will proclaim my resurrection, you will hope for my
coming, until I come again to you from heaven (*adventum meum sperabitis,
donec iterum de caelis veniam ad vos*).[194]

The Mozarabic liturgy also embroiders on the theme 'until he come',
though in a third-person form:

As often as you eat this bread and drink that cup, you will proclaim the Lord's
death until he comes in brightness from heaven (*donec veniat in claritate de celis*).
(M. Férotin, ed., *Liber Sacramentorum*, p. xxv)

The traditional anaphoras usually pick up from the institution narrative
the theme of remembrance and begin that section of the prayer known
to liturgiologists as the anamnesis with some such phrase as *Unde et
memores* (Roman canon) or Μεμνημένοι τοίνυν (Byzantine liturgy of *St
Chrysostom*). The earliest extant example of the technical anamnesis, that
of the *Apostolic Tradition* of Hippolytus, remembers the death and resurrection: *Memores igitur mortis et resurrectionis eius*. . . . Later prayers
elaborate the anamnesis by referring to some or all of the whole series of
major events in Jesus's earthly life from His conception to His ascension.
Some prayers, and this is what particularly interests us, make mention of
the second advent in their anamnesis. In the earliest examples the second
advent is set on the same continuous line with the *past* events of Jesus's
earthly life:

Remembering therefore his passion and death, his resurrection and his ascension into heaven, and his future second *parousia* in which he is coming to judge the quick and the dead and to reward every man according to his works. . . .

(Apost. Const. VIII, Brightman, p. 20)

Remembering therefore . . . and his second glorious and dreadful *parousia* when he will come with glory to judge the quick and the dead, when he will reward every man according to his works . . .

(St James, Brightman, pp. 52f; similarly in the Syriac though<br>addressed to the Son, Brightman, p. 87)

The same thing is found in the Byzantine liturgies of *St Basil*[195] and *St Chrysostom*, though the mention of the 'glorious (and dreadful, *Basil only*) second coming' does not call forth an immediate mention of judgement. But later liturgies often balked at the idea of 'remembering' an event that had not yet taken place and changed the syntactical construction so that another verb, such as 'looking for', became used in connection with the second advent. Thus the West Syrian liturgy of *St Denys of Athens* has:

Obeying therefore thy dominical command, and celebrating in a perpetual mystery the remembrance of thy death and resurrection by this sacrifice, we also look for thy second coming . . . (Renaudot II, p. 205)

The Armenian liturgy has:

We therefore, O Lord, presenting unto thee according to this commandment this saving mystery of the body and blood of thine only-begotten, do remember the saving sufferings he endured for us, his life-giving crucifixion, his burial of three days, his blessed resurrection, his divine ascension and his session at thy right hand, O Father, and we confess and bless his fearful and glorious second coming. (Brightman, pp. 437f)[196]

The English Non-Jurors' Liturgy of 1718, following closely its model in *Apostolic Constitutions VIII*, sets the second coming in line with the other mighty acts:

Wherefore, having in remembrance His passion, death and resurrection from the dead, His ascension into heaven, and second coming with glory and great power to judge . . .[197]

But more recent Anglican revisions which mention the second coming in their anamnesis prefer to 'look for' it (so Scotland 1929, Ceylon 1933[1] and 1935[2], South Africa 1954, Canada 1959 and India 1960).[198] In the Taizé liturgy 'nous attendons et nous implorons son retour'. The importance attached to the mention of the final parousia in the West Syrian liturgies can be gauged by the lengthy descriptions of that dread day which were attached to the anamnesis. I allow myself the luxury of giving just one sample, from the liturgy of *Severus of Antioch*, where the passage begins in Renaudot (II, p. 324): 'Meminimus etiam manifestationis tuae secundae gloriosae et timore plenae', and goes on:

. . . when Thou shalt sit upon Thy lofty and dreadful Throne, and around Thee shall stand thousand thousands of Angels; and a stream of fire shall descend, and consume the wicked without mercy; and all men shall render an account of their works, having no need of accuser or advocate, but the very works which they have done shall be rehearsed, for their thoughts themselves shall accuse or acquit them. When fire shall test the work of every man; when there shall be no opportunity of excuse, even to the wise and learned, in that terrible time; when quaking and fear shall fall upon all reasonable creatures, and every mouth shall be stopped, and confusion shall seize the wicked and foolish; when a brother will not be an aid, and pity will not be of avail, nor will fathers be any protection; when vengeance without mercy will follow those who did not know mercy. In that day, turn not Thy face from us and despise not Thine heritage that it should be delivered to eternal torments. Let us not be heirs of darkness where is no ray of light, nor do Thou make us outcasts from Thy fellowship, O Lord; nor deny us and say to us, 'For I know you not'; place us not on Thy left hand, with those who saw Thee hungry and fed Thee not, sick and visited Thee not; but acknowledge us and number us in the company of those who have done Thy will. Therefore, Thy people and Thine heritage beseech Thee, and through Thee and with Thee, Thy Father.[199]

*          *          *

In order to understand the relation between the eucharistic memorial and the parousia, we must first go rapidly over some ground that has been trodden in recent years in the matter of the liturgical remembrance of *past* events. This will have the incidental advantage of calling attention to a line of approach which is beginning to overcome the opposition between Catholics and Protestants on the controversial question of the eucharistic sacrifice.

Sacramental theologians of Catholic allegiance or inclination have made a bold attempt to wrest the idea of remembrance from the use of the 'mere memorialists' commonly called Zwinglians. The Benedictine Odo Casel and his school turned to the Hellenistic mysteries for guidance and proposed an understanding of the mass as the cultically enacted commemoration of the sacrifice of Christ on the Cross (and the resurrection which is inseparable from it), here made 'really present' not 'historically' but 'in a mystery'; the eucharist is a *Mysteriengedächtnis* of the death-and-resurrection of Christ.[200] Max Thurian has attempted to give a similar notion firmer biblical grounding by setting the eucharist in the broader context of the major scriptural theme of memorial.[201] Since Casel and Thurian lay claim to τοῦτο ποιεῖτε εἰς τὴν ἐμὴν ἀνάμνησιν for dominical support, we must turn to this phrase first, and particularly to J. Jeremias's exegesis of it, which clearly inspires Thurian's basic outlook and which, if correct, would be of great interest for our own investigation of the relation between the eucharist and Christ's final coming.

J. Jeremias put forward his interpretation of εἰς τὴν ἐμὴν ἀνάμνησιν as 'damit Gott meiner gedenke' in the second edition of *Die Abendmahlsworte Jesu* (1949, pp. 115–18) and elaborated on it in the third (1960, pp. 229–46). Briefly, his thesis is that Jesus instituted the celebration of the eucharist not in order to remind the disciples of Him but to remind *God*; but when God remembers, He acts; He is therefore being asked to remember the messiah (i.e. Jesus, who has already begun the work of salvation) by bringing in the kingdom through the parousia. The ἄχρι οὗ ἔλθῃ of I Cor. 11:26 is taken, its temporal sense not being denied, to include also a final sense and be a correct comment on Paul's part. The eucharist is celebrated with a view to imploring the final consummation of the work of salvation.

Now the view of the eucharist as imploring Christ's final coming has not received much attention because Jeremias's critics have never really got beyond his major premise, namely that the eucharist is performed in order to remind *God* of Jesus. Their objections are made on linguistic grounds,[202] and also on various theological grounds: D. R. Jones considers that such an interpretation would place the church in the dogmatically unthinkable position of mediating between Christ and the Father (whereas it seems to me that no more is implied than that the church recalls before God His own gift of Christ and His work and prays for His return and the completion of His work); H. Kosmala holds that it would be foreign to Christianity to pray for God to 'send' Christ because the messiah, at His exaltation, has Himself become Lord and will 'come' (but there is no more a contradiction at the End between 'being sent' and 'coming' than there is at the Incarnation between the Johannine Christ's saying 'The Father sent me' and His saying 'I came'); G. D. Kilpatrick thinks that Jeremias's interpretation, by looking towards the future, contradicts the real nature of the eucharist, which is to be the vehicle of God's *present* activity (but we shall see that there is distinction but no *opposition* between present and future in respect of Christ's coming).[203] But Jeremias's interpretation can be considered thoroughly credible when it is seen against the background of the Old Testament notion of remembrance as this has been explored by Old Testament scholars in recent years.[204]

In particular the notion of remembrance played an important part in Israel's worship.[205] G. von Rad would find a wide measure of agreement among Old Testament scholars for his summary statement: 'Sucht man in der atl. Kultsprache nach einer . . . allgemeinen Formel für die Bedeutung, die der Kultus für Israel hatte, so könnte man sagen, dass er Israel bei Jahwe ins Gedächtnis bringt. Der Ausdruck von dem Gedenken Gottes (זִכָּרוֹן זֵכֶר) begegnet jedenfalls häufig und wird mit sehr verschiedenen kultischen Begehungen in Verbindung gebracht.'[206] In complaint-psalms Yahweh is called upon to remember His covenantal mercies of the past and now to intervene favourably on the ground of what He remembers (Pss. 25:6f; 74:2; 119:49; cf. the intercessory prayer at Exod. 32:13f). In hymns Yahweh is praised for His faithfulness in remembering His covenant (Pss. 98:3; 105:8, 42; 106:45; 115:12; 136:23). In Ps. 132 'Remember unto David all the hardships he endured . . .' (v. 1) is a prayer, grounded in the promise of the Lord (vv. 11f), for David's present anointed successor (v. 10).[207] Various cultic objects and actions serve, to use the terminology of P, 'as a memorial (זכרון) for (ל) the children of Israel before Yahweh' (Exod. 28:12, 29; 30:16; 39:7; Lev. 23:24; Num. 10:9f; 31:54). In the case of the מִנְחָה (cereal-offering), the אַזְכָּרָה is that part of the offering which was burnt probably in order to *bring to God's mind* the total offering and the offerer (Lev. 2:2, 9; 6:15).[208] Outside the cult, the way in which a sign, itself divinely posed, may serve to remind God of His covenant promises is illustrated by the rainbow of Gen. 9:8–17.

Returning to the cult, we find that worship is also the occasion for *Israel to remember*: to remember Yahweh, and the past mercies of their covenant God. In the book of Deuteronomy, whose cultic background has been clearly demonstrated by G. von Rad,[209] Israel's remembering of Yahweh and His deeds is presented as the ground for the people's obedience in the future (5:15; 6:20–25; 8:1–20; 15:15; 16:3; 24:9, 18). Particularly interesting for our purposes, however, is the case of the combined feast of the passover and unleavened bread. In Exodus 13:3–10 the ordinance of unleavened bread is explained thus: 'It shall be to you as a sign on your hand and as a memorial (וּלְזִכָּרוֹן) between your eyes, that the law of the Lord may be in your mouth; for with a strong hand the Lord has brought you out of Egypt' (v. 9). It looks likely that the זִכָּרוֹן here is to serve *Israel's* remembering of the day of the deliverance from Egypt: by 'keeping this service' in the promised land (v. 5) Israel will fulfil Moses's injunction 'Remember (זָכוֹר) this day in which you came out of Egypt . . .' (v. 3). But that we may not restrict the remembering to Israel is clear from Exod. 12:14: besides being לָכֶם לְזִכָּרוֹן (which may mean that Israel will remember, as apparently in Exod. 13:9, or else that the feast will serve as a liturgical memorial 'for your benefit' *in the eyes of God*), passover is also clearly said to be חַג לַיהוה (ἑορτὴν Κυρίῳ); and Exod. 12:42; 13:6, Deut. 16:1–8 and Jub. 49:15 also indicate that passover is a celebration 'to the Lord'. Thus the passover not only serves to remind Israel of the Exodus but is also performed 'for the Lord', and therefore acts, like all Israel's worship, to put Yahweh in mind of His people; and it becomes clear why the later Jews expected God to send them the messiah at passover time.

From the Old Testament we may therefore draw a theology of worship as a *memorial* which not only serves to remind men of the past mercies of God as a ground for their present obedience but also enables men to recall before God His past promises and deeds in thanksgiving and in prayer for new blessings. If it be objected that the notion of God needing to be reminded is too naïvely anthropomorphic, we can only plead, first, that the Old Testament presents the cult and its memorials as an institution ordained *by God* and, second, that by the token of the objection every kind of thanksgiving and intercession would go by the board as well.

Coming back to the eucharist in particular, we find that the idea of memorial is a help to those for whom the relation between the unique sacrifice of Christ on Calvary and the traditionally sacrificial nature of the eucharist has constituted a problem. The eucharist is a dominically instituted memorial-rite which, not only serving to remind men but also being performed before God, is sacrificial at least in so far as it recalls before God with thanksgiving that one sacrifice and prays for the continuing benefits of that sacrifice to be granted now. The notion of memorial was certainly used by some patristic writers in their explanation of the sacrificial nature of the eucharist. Thus Justin, who sees the eucharist to have been prophesied by the 'pure offering' of Mal. 1:10, writes of 'the bread of the eucharist, which the Lord Jesus Christ transmitted to us to celebrate as a memorial of the passion which he suffered for the cleansing of men's souls from all evil, so that we may give thanks to God . . .' (*Dial. con Tryph.*, 41, PG 6, 564). John Chrysostom declares 'we do not make a different sacrifice . . . but always the same, or rather we celebrate a memorial (ἀνάμνησιν ἐργαζόμεθα) of a sacrifice' (*In Heb. hom.* 17, 3, PG 63, 131); and Theodore of Mopsuestia explains similarly that the sacrifice is 'not a new one and one that the priest performs as his, but it is a memorial of that other real sacrifice' (*Hom. Cat.* XV, 15, edd. Tonneau and Devreesse, p. 485).[210]

But we may, I think, broaden our vision so that the memorial of His sacrificial death takes its place within a more comprehensive memorial of Christ Himself. Jesus said: 'Do this in memory of *me*.'[211] It is *Christ Himself* who is commemorated, and Christ is not only clothed with all that He did at His first coming but is also the one who is to come again. It is because the eucharist is a memorial of the one and the same Christ who has come and who is to come that the anamnesis of the anaphoras can *remember* 'all thy saving dispensation for us, from thy conception, birth and holy baptism, thy saving passion, thy life-giving death, thy three days' burial, thy glorious resurrection, thy ascension into heaven and thy sitting at the right hand of God the Father, *and thy dreadful advent*. . . .' (so the Syrian *St Mark*, in Renaudot II, p. 177f). It is because the eucharist is a memorial of the one and the same Christ who has come and who is to come that Theodore of Mopsuestia can say that the celebrant performs sacramentally 'cela même que Notre Seigneur le Christ a effectivement accompli *et accomplira*' (*Hom. Cat.* XV, 19, edd. Tonneau and Devreesse, p. 495).[212] The eucharist is celebrated in the time of *hope* before the second coming of Christ, of which the first coming of Christ was a *promise*. The church recalls before the Father in thanksgiving the first coming of Christ and prays for the second coming of Christ in final fulfilment of that promise. And because the Blessed Trinity is Lord of time, the one Christ who came and who is to come can come even now at the eucharist in answer to the church's prayer, in partial fulfilment of the promise and therefore as its strengthening, even though the moment of the final coming remains a divine secret. At every eucharist the church is in fact praying that the parousia may take place at that very moment, and if the Father 'merely' sends His Son in the sacramental mode we have at least a taste of that future which God reserves for Himself to give one day.

Now what liturgical evidence have we for the view that the eucharist is a recalling of the first coming of Christ in the expectation that that promise will find a partial fulfilment at that very moment, if not indeed its full accomplishment by the immediate final advent? I suggested that the Pauline phrase 'until he come' was probably an echo of the primitive church's cry *Maranatha*, and it is to this that we turn first.

## 2. Maranatha!

The finding of the *Didache* (published in 1883) opened the way for a recovery of the liturgical interpretation of the Aramaic expression *maranatha* which occurs at I Cor. 16:22 and which had become in medieval times a scarcely understood accompaniment of pronouncements of anathema. It is already significant that the other Hebrew or Aramaic words preserved in universal Christian usage are words used in worship: Abba, Amen, Hosanna, Hallelujah. In any case the expression *maranatha* occurs in Didache 10:6 immediately after the prayers which are set out in chapters 9 and 10 for use in connection with a meal in the Christian assembly. In *Messe und Herrenmahl* (pp. 230–38), H. Lietzmann made the extremely plausible suggestion that Didache 10:6 contains a liturgical dialogue between president and people:

> *President:* Let grace come and this world pass away.
> *People:*    Hosanna to the Son of David.[213]
> *President:* If anyone is holy let him come. If any is not, let him repent. Maranatha.
> *People:*    Amen.

Lietzmann argued further that the prayers of 9:2 and 9:3 belonged to a eucharist in which the cup preceded the bread; the eucharist was followed by an agape for which 10:2–5 gives the closing prayers (cf. 10:1: 'After you are filled, give thanks thus'). Our liturgical dialogue of 10:6, displaced by the compiler probably in order not to interrupt the string of prayers which were spoken by the president alone, found its real place immediately after the blessings over the eucharistic elements and before communion. In it the president prays for the end of the world and the parousia of the Lord: 'Let Grace [a christological title, according to Lietzmann] come and this world pass away.' The people greet the approaching Lord: 'Hosanna to the Son of David.' It is as a congregation of sinless saints that the church celebrates the eucharist (cf. 14:1–3), and so the president declares, in a style which recalls the Τὰ ἅγια τοῖς ἁγίοις spoken before the communion in the Eastern liturgies: 'Let the holy come, let the unholy repent.' The *maranatha* is to be understood in a double sense: it is a prayer for the parousia ('Come, Lord!'), and a confession of the Lord's sacramental advent in the eucharist ('The Lord has come!').

Lietzmann's suggestion that Did. 10:6 contains a dialogue between president and people has found wide acceptance; but the dialogue has been assigned to another place in the liturgy by M. Dibelius.[214] According to Dibelius it is not only the prayer of Did. 10:1–4 which belongs to the agape (which it closes)[215] but the prayers of 9:1–4 also belong to the agape (which they introduce). The dialogue of 10:6 occurs in its proper place: it follows the agape and *constitutes the opening of the eucharistic liturgy* (which the Didache does not go on to describe). *Maranatha*, which Dibelius allots to the congregation rather than to the president, is a cry for the Lord who will come at the end of the world and who is at this very moment making His entry into the midst of the congregation: 'Come, Lord!' A rather similar interpretation is given by J. P. Audet, who sees the dialogue of 10:6 as marking the transition from one room of the *domus ecclesiae* where the agape has been celebrated to another where the eucharist will begin.[216]

It has also been proposed that already in I Cor. 16 *maranatha* forms part of the properly eucharistic liturgy which Paul knew would follow the reading of his letter in the service of the word in the Corinthian congregation. G. Bornkamm, following others, suggests that, if abstraction is made of Paul's personal greetings, I Cor. 16:20–24 contains a series of liturgical formulae: (1) The summons to the holy kiss; (2) the anathema upon anyone who does not love the Lord; (3) the *maranatha*; and (4) the assurance of the grace of the Lord Jesus.[217] The intention of the anathema is to exclude the unworthy, at the beginning of the celebration, from participation in the sacrament. The *maranatha*, whether it is understood as an invocation of the coming Lord or as the proclamation of the Lord now present in the congregation (i.e. whether it means 'Lord, come' or 'The Lord has come and is here'; on which see below), is an appeal to the heavenly judge and lends a threatening emphasis to the anathema: it is *divine* judgement which will fall on the offender who participates unworthily. The hearer is therefore being summoned to examine himself.[218]

I think we may take the association of *maranatha* with the eucharistic liturgy in the primitive church as fairly established, even if its exact place has not been settled beyond doubt. What, now, is its importance for the eschatological content and import of the eucharist? We must begin philologically.[219]

In the search for the Aramaic original, μαρανaθά may be acceptably divided in two ways: μαρανα θα or μαραν αθα. In either case the first word means 'our Lord': מָרַנָא and מָרַן are both possible forms. If the former is the one intended in μαρανaθα, then (on the safe assumption that the second part of the Greek represents some part of the verb אתא) θα represents the imperative תָא and the meaning is clear: 'Our Lord, come!' But if מָרַן is intended, then aθa may represent either אֶתָא or אֲתָא. Now אֶתָא is another form of the imperative, and so the meaning would still be 'Our Lord, come!'; but אֲתָא is a perfect, giving the meaning 'Our Lord has come'. The Fathers, who had lost the specifically eucharistic association of the word, took μαραναθα in this last sense and applied it to the incarnation.[220] But it is possible to take אתא as a *present* perfect, with the meaning 'Our Lord has come and is now here, is present', and this could then be understood of the cultic presence of Christ.

The phrase ἔρχου Κύριε 'Ιησοῦ in Rev. 22:20 suggests that *maranatha* was originally understood as an *imperative*. It is a prayer for the advent of Christ: Our Lord, come! There is every likelihood that when this prayer was uttered in the liturgical assembly at Corinth it had a double reference: it prayed for both the final parousia and also the Lord's immediate coming to His people in the eucharist.[221] Little is changed, however, if we take *maranatha* as a present perfect: it is then an acclamation of the presence of the one who is still to come and yet who promised His presence to the two or three gathered in His name: The Lord is here! If *Maranatha* belongs (as is perhaps most likely) at the opening of the eucharistic liturgy proper, it is either an acclamation of the presence of the Lord who has been in the assembly through the service of the word and who will continue to be there in the eucharist, or else (if the fifties of the first century is not too early a date to make a distinction in the church's understanding of Christ's presence in the word-service and His presence in the eucharist) a prayer for the eucharistic presence of Christ as at least a partial anticipation of the parousia.

## 3. Benedictus qui venit

It is curious that *Maranatha* disappeared from the eucharistic liturgy; but its place was perhaps taken by a phrase from Matt. 21:9, the verse from which the Didache no doubt drew the 'Ωσαννὰ τῷ υἱῷ Δαυίδ that it placed before *Maranatha*. The phrase which may have taken the place of *Maranatha* is Εὐλογημένος ὁ ἐρχόμενος ἐν ὀνόματι Κυρίου.[222] In any case this cry is such a constant feature of eucharistic liturgies that it merits our attention as we examine the relation between the coming of Christ at the End and His coming at the eucharist.

In the Western church we know the *Benedictus qui venit* within the canon, following directly on the *Sanctus*;[223] and it occurs in this position also in the classical Eastern liturgies, with the exception of the Egyptian tradition. Its first position in the eucharistic liturgy seems, however, to have been between the great prayer and communion. Thus the *Testamentum Domini* reads at this point:

> After these things the seal of thanksgiving thus: Let the Name of the Lord be blessed for ever.
>
> The people: Amen.
>
> The priest: Blessed is He that hath come [B.: cometh] in the Name of the Lord. Blessed [is] the Name of His praise.
> And let all the people say: So be it, so be it.[224]

And in the liturgy of *Apostolic Constitutions VIII*, 'Hosanna to the Son of David: Blessed is he that cometh in the name of the Lord' appears as part of the response to the priest's Τὰ ἅγια τοῖς ἁγίοις at the elevation of the elements before communion.[225] Two yet other[226] places are accorded to 'Blessed is he that comes' in the Armenian liturgy (which does also include it in the canon after the *Sanctus*): it is said by the celebrant as he takes the gifts from the deacons after the Great Entrance,[227] and it is sung by the choir *after* the people's communion (Brightman, p. 453).[228] In the Ethiopian Anaphora of the Apostles, 'Blessed is he that cometh in the name of the Lord' is said after the invocation of the Holy Spirit upon the bread and the cup to make them the body and blood of the Lord (Brightman, p. 233f).

How are we to understand the eucharistic uses of *Benedictus qui venit*? J. Jeremias has called attention to the Midrashic messianic exegesis of the 'Blessed is he that cometh in the name of the Lord' of Ps. 118:26a.[229] That this exegesis was known in New Testament times is clear from the accounts of Jesus's triumphal entry into Jerusalem. Yet if the church was willing to acknowledge the appropriateness of applying the cry to Jesus the messiah at His first coming, it was also able, in the light of its hope for the parousia, to exploit the present-participial form ὁ ἐρχόμενος as making also a future reference to the one and the same Jesus who was still to come. The first coming of Christ in fulfilment of the Old Testament promise was itself a renewed promise which awaits an even greater fulfilment at the final coming. This understanding is in fact suggested by the form in which the *Benedictus qui venit* characteristically appears in the anaphoras of the West Syrian liturgies: 'Blessed is he that came and cometh . . .'. The West Syrian emphasis on the second coming elsewhere in the anaphora (see above pp. 62–64) makes us sure that the 'cometh' here refers to the second advent;[230] and the fact that the cry is used precisely in the eucharistic liturgy is not without its significance in respect of the sacrament being said to prefigure the final coming.

We find indeed that in the liturgy of *Apostolic Constitutions VIII* another significant expression from the LXX of Ps. 117 (118) follows immediately on the Εὐλογημένος ὁ ἐρχόμενος ἐν ὀνόματι Κυρίου said before communion; it is: Θεὸς Κύριος καὶ ἐπεφάνη ἐν ἡμῖν (*A.C.* VIII, 13, 13, ed. Funk, I, p. 516). The same combination is also found in the same position in the present texts of the Byzantine liturgy of *St Chrysostom* (with the minor variation, exactly as in ψ 117:27, ἐπέφανεν ἡμῖν, Brightman, p. 396). After communion in the Armenian liturgy the same pair of phrases appears, though in reverse order:

Our God and our Lord hath appeared to us:
Blessed is he that cometh in the name of the Lord.   (Brightman, p. 453)

It seems fair to conclude, especially in the light of its use in these three liturgies in combination with Θεὸς Κύριος καὶ ἐπεφάνεν ἡμῖν at the point of the elevation of the *Sancta sanctis* or the communion, that the *Benedictus qui venit* found its place in eucharistic liturgies for the good reason that it can suggest, in a usefully ambiguous way, the present coming of the one who has come and who is still to come. To this extent it may be considered

the legitimate replacement of *Maranatha*. There are in fact various other
liturgical indications that the eucharist has been understood as the coming
of the Lord to His people in a visitation which prefigures the final advent,
and to these we now turn.

## 4. Further liturgical evidence for a eucharistic prefiguration of the final advent

### (a) The Great Entry

In the Greek tradition, the bringing of the bread and wine from the
table of preparation to the altar is decked out as the processional entry of
the divine king invisibly accompanied by the heavenly hosts. He is greeted
in the so-called Cherubic Hymn as 'the king of all'[231] or 'the king of
kings'.[232] The Armenian liturgy, clearly tributary of Byzantium in the
matter of the Great Entry, makes its own rich elaborations.[233] It declares
that 'the body of the Lord and the blood of the Saviour are set forth';
and while He is being greeted by the choir in the Cherubic Hymn as 'the
King of all', the priest and deacon make play with various verses from the
Psalms (and elsewhere) to describe his entry:

In them hath he set a tabernacle for the sun which cometh forth as a bridegroom
out of his chamber and rejoiceth as a giant to run his course.   (Ps. 19:4–5)

Cast up an highway for him that rideth upon the heaven of heavens towards the
east.   (Isa. 62:10b; and Ps. 68(67):33, LXX)

God shall come from the south and the holy one from mount Paran.   (Hab. 3:3a)

Lift up your heads, o ye gates, and be ye lift up, ye everlasting doors, and the
king of glory shall come in . . .   (Ps. 24:7–10)

When the celebrant receives the gifts from the hands of the deacons,
he makes with them the sign of the cross towards the people and says:
'Blessed is he that cometh in the name of the Lord.' Shortly thereafter the
choir can declare: 'Christ hath been manifested among us: God, which is,
hath seated himself here . . .', and the deacon can make the summons:
'Ye who with faith stand before the holy royal table, see the king Christ
sitting and surrounded with the heavenly hosts.' This Christophany is set
in the perspective of the final coming of Christ by the prayer which has
meanwhile accompanied the *lavabo*:

. . . let us stand in prayer before the holy table of God and find the grace of
mercy in the day of his appearing and at the second coming of our Lord and
Saviour Jesus Christ.[234]

### (b) Sursum corda

The precise origin of the very early summons *Sursum corda*, which in one
form or another occurs in the opening dialogue of all classical eucharistic
prayers,[235] is unknown. When the Fathers expound the summons they
dwell on the need to lift one's thoughts from earthly things to heaven,

where our life is hid with Christ in God.[236] The thought of participating in the life of heaven will occupy us later on; but here we may observe that though our citizenship is already in heaven, it is nonetheless true that we still await a Saviour from there (Phil. 3:20). G. P. Wetter suggested that the *Sursum corda* is in fact a summons to go meet the Lord who is about to make His cultic epiphany.[237] T. F. Torrance seems to see the *Sursum corda* as epitomizing his view that the eucharist is 'an eschatological anticipation both of the Advent of the Son of Man and the rapture of the Church'.[238] We ourselves may draw a parallel with the words of the Christ of the Lucan apocalypse: 'Look up and raise your heads, because your redemption is drawing near', a redemption to be brought by 'the Son of man coming in a cloud with power and great glory' (Luke 21:27f).[239]

### (c) Maximus the Confessor

In chapters 14–21 of his *Mystagogia* (PG 91, 692–97), Maximus sees the greater part of the liturgy as a pre-enactment of the final drama of the parousia and the entry into the life of heaven. In particular, the reading of the gospel, the subsequent descent of the priest from the sacerdotal throne, and the expulsion of the catechumens and others who are 'unworthy' by the ministers: these ceremonies signify (σημαίνειν) and prefigure (προτυποῦν), are the image (εἰκών) and type (τύπος) of, the preaching of the gospel which is followed by the End (see Matt. 24:14), at which Christ will descend with His angels to make the great separating judgement. With the great entrance of the holy mysteries heaven is entered, and we shall see more of how the rest of the liturgy, according to Maximus, prefigures the life of heaven later on.

### (d) Theodore of Mopsuestia

Theodore connects particularly the *communion* with the coming of Christ at the last to raise the dead. The communion is a reproduction of the appearances of the risen Lord to His disciples in order to promise them a share in the resurrection, and already the communicants receive 'in hope' that incorruptible life which Christ will give them at the last, and the 'earnest' ('*āreb*) of which He indeed already gives them (see especially *Hom. Cat.* XVI, 17–20, 25–26). A recent edition of the Holy Qurbana from within the West Syrian liturgical family in India comments that a display of the consecrated elements before the people's communion (there was originally a procession with the elements through the church, and the display is still accompanied by lights and incense and fans) is traditionally said to represent Christ's second coming, and the communion is said to be a token of the new life of the resurrection.[240]

### (e) John and Charles Wesley

Without attaching the Lord's coming to any particular point in the liturgy, the Wesleys' hymns make clear that the eucharist 'antedates' His final advent:

[3]*He whom we remember here,*
*Christ shall in the clouds appear;*
*Manifest to every eye,*
*We shall soon behold Him nigh.*

[4]*Faith ascends the mountain's height,*
*Now enjoys the pompous sight,*
*Antedates the final doom,*
*Sees the Judge in glory come.*

[5]*Lo, He comes triumphant down,*
*Seated on His great white throne!*
*Cherubs bear it on their wings,*
*Shouting bear the King of kings.*   (from Hymn 98)

Because the church already has the sacramental pledge of His presence, it prays eagerly for the final coming of the Lord when that pledge will no longer be needed:

[2]*He tasted death for every one:*
  *The Saviour of mankind*
*Out of our sight to heaven is gone,*
  *But left His pledge behind.*

[3]*His sacramental pledge we take,*
  *Nor will we let it go;*
*Till in the clouds our Lord comes back,*
  *We thus His death will show.*

[4]*Come quickly, Lord, for whom we mourn,*
  *And comfort all that grieve;*
*Prepare the bride, and then return,*
  *And to Thyself receive.*

[5]*Now to Thy glorious kingdom come;*
  *(Thou hast a token given;)*
*And while Thy arms receive us home,*
  *Recall Thy pledge in heaven.*   (from Hymn 100)

*          *          *

Turning from consideration of particular words and actions spoken and done in the course of the liturgies, we now examine two matters to do with the setting of the eucharistic celebration in time and space, two matters of calendar and compass, which also show how the sacrament is placed in an eschatological perspective. I refer first to the celebration of the eucharist on *Sunday*, and second to its celebration facing *East*.

## 5. 'On a fixed day'

Through most of Christian history there has been a close connection between eucharist and Sunday, between the Lord's supper and the Lord's day. W. Rordorf indeed suggests that the name Lord's day is derived from the day's connection with the Lord's supper.[241] However that may be (and we may prefer to see each drawing its name directly from its own specific association with the risen Lord), some link between the day and the meal is already made in the New Testament and is of importance for the eschatological content and bearing of the eucharist.

Acts 20:7 reports that the church at Troas, on the occasion of Paul's visit, gathered together on the first day of the week to break bread. It is highly probable that this was a regular weekly assembly; and it may safely be taken that the breaking of bread over which Paul appears to have presided on this occasion refers either to the eucharist itself or to a full meal which included the sacrament as its distinctive feature before the latter had been made (probably on account of such unseemliness as arose at Corinth when it was celebrated in the context of a full meal, I Cor. 11) into a separate observance.[242] Whether the assembly at Troas took place in the evening and night of our Saturday/Sunday or of our Sunday/Monday is uncertain: if Luke is using the Roman system of reckoning the day when he speaks of 'the first day of the week' in Acts 20:7, then the latter is the case; if he is using the Jewish liturgical reckoning, however, the assembly would have started on the evening of Saturday, the beginning of 'the first day of the week'. H. Riesenfeld has suggested that the Christian Sunday began as a prolongation of the Jewish sabbath: Christians kept the sabbath by attending Jewish worship and then, because the sabbath no longer sufficed since it has been fulfilled by Jesus, they assembled in houses for specifically Christian worship as soon as the sabbath was over.[243] If such a Jewish-Christian influence affected the church at Troas, then the assembly of Acts 20:7-12 would have taken place on Saturday/Sunday. On the other hand, *Sunday* evening may have imposed itself on the earliest church as the time for the weekly assembly on account of the memory of the meals which the risen Lord had shared with His disciples on the first Easter Sunday.[244] In any case, as will be seen presently, it was Sunday *morning* (which is the morning both of the Roman Sunday and of the Jewish 'first day of the week') which soon became fixed as the time of the eucharistic assembly.

There are two further hints in the New Testament that Sunday was the day of liturgical assembly. In I Cor. 16:2 Paul directs each person to set something aside on the first day of every week towards his collection for the church at Jerusalem. Even if the phrase παρ' ἑαυτῷ suggests that the contribution was to be put away at home rather than brought to a liturgical assembly, it is more probable that Paul is attaching this act of charity to a day with Christian significance than that he is referring to a suppositious regular pay-day in Corinth. The other indication is to be found in Rev. 1:10: 'I was in the Spirit on the Lord's day (ἐν τῇ κυριακῇ ἡμέρᾳ).' Commentators usually take this as the earliest known occasion on which Sunday is called the Lord's day, an appellation which was soon to become common. The particular day on which John's vision took place is significant in view of the imagery of worship which permeates the Apocalypse, for John's descriptions of the worship of heaven are rooted in the liturgy of the church on earth.

The New Testament evidence for the connection between Sunday and the eucharistic gathering is admittedly scanty, but it seems fair to interpret it in the light of what we find in the second century, where there is in fact an accumulation of testimonies in favour of the connection. First, we note Pliny's letter to Trajan (*Ep.* X, 96). Whatever the other problems of interpretation posed by Pliny's evidence, it is commonly agreed that the 'fixed day' (*status dies*) on which Christians meet can only be Sunday. Some have thought that the *sacramentum* mentioned by Pliny at the meeting before daylight is the eucharist;[245] but even if the *sacramentum* refers to baptism, as some have suggested,[246] W. Rordorf is then surely right to suppose that the eucharist, though not mentioned by Pliny, also took place at the regular gathering before dawn—since it could no longer be held in conjunction with the agape at the second meeting later in the day (. . . *ad capiendum cibum*) which the Christians had given up, and yet it is unthinkable that they should have abandoned the eucharist.[247] Second, the Didache provides sure evidence of a weekly Sunday eucharist: 'Every Lord's day assemble yourselves: break bread and give thanks (κλάσατε ἄρτον καὶ εὐχαριστήσατε), after confessing your transgressions that your sacrifice may be pure' (14:1).[248] Third, Justin Martyr, the first Christian author to use the pagan term *Sun*day, describes the service of word and eucharist which takes place 'on the day called after the sun' (*Apol.* I, 67, PG 6,429). Fourth, when Tertullian reports that Christians were suspected of worshipping the sun because they devoted Sunday (*dies solis*) to rejoicing, the eucharistic implication is not far to seek.[249] But what is the theological significance of the established connection between the eucharist and Sunday?

The *eschatological* significance of Sunday constitutes a recurrent theme in patristic literature. Three or four points are of special importance in connection with the eucharist:

### (a) The day of resurrection

It was very early in the morning of the first day of the week that the women found the empty tomb. It was on the first day of the week that the risen Lord first appeared to His disciples. Sunday is, therefore, to the early Church 'the day of resurrection'.[250] But the resurrection of Jesus is the promise of the general resurrection. It is therefore highly appropriate that on *this* day of the week the church should gather to meet the risen Lord and receive from Him, the conqueror of man's last enemy, the 'medicine of immortality' so that we may have eternal life in Christ Jesus. 'Eusebius of Alexandria' makes the Lord Himself responsible for choosing this day, the memorial of His resurrection, as the day for celebrating His eucharistic memorial. Quoting the eucharistic institution narrative and ending up τοῦτο ποιεῖτε εἰς τὴν ἐμὴν ἀνάμνησιν, Eusebius goes on:

The memorial, therefore, of the Lord is the holy day which is called the Lord's day. . . . On the same day he gave to the world the firstfruits of the resurrection. It was that same day, as we have said, that he also prescribed for the celebration of the memorial of the holy mysteries. This same day became to us, therefore, the source of all goodness. . . . (*Serm.* 16, 1, PG 86, 416)

### (b) The day of the new creation

With the resurrection of Christ the age to come is already inaugurated, creation is in principle renewed—a theme which the Fathers often expressed by the imagery of the 'eighth day' applied to Sunday, the eighth day going beyond the present 'week' into the future age.[251] It is therefore entirely appropriate that it should be on Sunday, the eighth day, that the new race should meet its head[252] and already taste the life of the new creation in the bread and wine of the eucharist.

### (c) The Ascension

There is some evidence that the early church associated the Lord's ascension with Sunday, either because it was held to have taken place on the first Easter Sunday and was later commemorated concomitantly with the resurrection,[253] or because it was linked with the Christian Pentecost which was reckoned to have first fallen on a Sunday and has been celebrated on no other day as far as we know.[254] What is interesting for us is that Acts 1:11 brings parousia and ascension into connection,[255] and it would not be far from the patristic mind to let the $οὕτως$ of that verse include the idea of 'on the same day': Sunday.

### (d) The day of the parousia

If the Lord's resurrection took place on a Sunday, then so might the parousia when the Lord came to raise the dead; if the Lord's ascension occurred on a Sunday, then so might His return in like manner. The belief that Christ's final advent will take place on a Sunday has indeed left a few traces,[256] and in one case it is brought into connection with the church's weekly eucharist. I refer to a Syriac document variously entitled *The Teaching of the Apostles* or *Canons of the Apostles*.[257] The second of the 'ordinances and laws' reads as follows:

The apostles further appointed: On the first day of the week let there be service, and the reading of the Holy Scriptures, and the oblation: because on the first day of the week our Lord rose from the place of the dead, and on the first day of the week he arose upon the world, and on the first day of the week he ascended up to heaven, and on the first day of the week he will appear at last with the angels of heaven [or: his holy angels].

Again we find revealed the suitability of Sunday as the day for celebrating that eucharistic commemoration in which, between His exaltation and His parousia, the Lord meets His church.[258]

\*        \*        \*

Participation in the Sunday eucharist has been the touchstone of faithfulness through most of the history of Christendom. Even when the daily eucharist became widespread in the West, the Sunday mass retained its special place as a mass of obligation. The Reformers singularly failed to make the ancient connection, either in theory or in practice, between Sunday and eucharist.[259] But there are signs in many quarters now of a renewed appreciation of Sunday as the characteristically eucharistic day. The liturgical movement has brought Catholics to concentrate on the *Sunday* mass,[260] and not just as the fulfilment of the individual's canonical obligation but as the parish's chief gathering for worship; it has brought some Protestant parishes to introduce a weekly eucharist instead of a monthly or quarterly celebration. In the Pentecostalist movement (which displays so many of the features that marked the beginning of 'the last days': tongues, healing, prophecy), the congregations assemble every Lord's day for the breaking of bread.

Among the theologians G. Delling has referred, if briefly, to Sunday as the day of Christ's resurrection which points forward to the general resurrection and the eschatological feast beyond it that is already anticipated in the Sunday eucharist.[261] In more detail, J. J. von Allmen has argued for a single weekly eucharist on Sundays:[262] there is a 'protestant' falsification of Sunday which, by neglecting to celebrate the eucharist on that day, puts Sunday into line with the other days of the week, 'the days of this world', and thus denies the presence here and now of the coming kingdom; there is a 'catholic' falsification of Sunday which, by celebrating the eucharist on the other days of the week, puts days which are still of this world into line with Sunday and thus suggests that the future age is definitively here; a single Sunday eucharist, it is von Allmen's argument, would respect the eschatological tension in which the church lives, allowing the eye of faith to see the future kingdom already secretly present in the midst of this transient but still continuing world. The appreciation of Sunday as the characteristically eucharistic day, and that in an eschatological perspective, has never been lost in Orthodoxy: see for instance a recent article by O. Clément, 'Le dimanche et le Jour éternel' in *Verbum Caro*, no. 79 (1966), pp. 99–124.

Having seen the significance of the association between the eucharist and Sunday for the eschatological content and import of the sacrament, we leave the calendar for the compass and look now at the *orientation* of the eucharistic assembly.

## 6. 'Look towards the East!'

When John Damascene lists the reasons why Christians face East for worship he includes several, all of which had in fact been recurrent themes in patristic literature, that are of special interest to our consideration of the eucharist in an eschatological perspective:[263]
(a) The scriptural designations of Christ as 'Sun of righteousness' (so the prophecy of Mal. 4:2, in the Hebrew 3:20) and as Ἀνατολή (Luke

1:78). We note that Christ was called 'Sun of righteousness' usually with reference to His rising at His resurrection,[264] and His resurrection was the promise of the general resurrection at the last day. We remark also that since 'Aνατολή was a messianic title,[265] it could be understood to refer to the messiah's second coming as well as His first.[266]

(b) Christ's ascension into heaven towards the East. The Fathers refer the LXX text of Ps. 67 (68):34 (ψάλατε τῷ Θεῷ τῷ ἐπιβεβηκότι ἐπὶ τὸν οὐρανὸν τοῦ οὐρανοῦ κατὰ ἀνατολάς) to the ascension and use the result to justify orientation in prayer.[267]

(c) Christ's expected return 'in like manner'. Besides Acts 1:11, John Damascene appeals also to Matt. 24:27. The same text inspired a passage which Migne includes among the *spuria* of Hippolytus.[268] The Syriac *Teaching of the Apostles*, to which reference was made on p. 77 above, is explicit:

The apostles therefore appointed: Pray ye towards the east: because, 'as the lightning which lighteneth from the east and is seen even to the west, so shall the coming of the Son of man be'—that by this we might know and understand that He will appear from the east suddenly [*or:* at the last].[269]

(d) The eastward position of Eden (cf. Gen. 2:8; 3:24). Perhaps the most common patristic explanation of orientation in prayer is that it is a reminder of the Paradise from which we were expelled and which we pray, strive and expect to re-enter.[270]

*     *     *

These four themes together make the eschatological connotations of orientation in prayer inescapable. The practice points to Christ who rose from the dead, who ascended into heaven as our forerunner, and who will return at the last to raise us up and take us with Himself into paradise.[271] Orientation for all Christian prayer is a practice for which there is widespread early testimony,[272] but we are particularly interested in a number of *eucharistic* texts which mention orientation and to which must be attached the eschatological associations just mentioned.

When *Apostolic Constitutions* II, 57 gives orders for the disposition of the church building, it begins: 'Let the building be oblong, turned to the east . . .';[273] and in its instructions for the conduct of the liturgy the same chapter directs: 'After this [a series of sermons by the presbyters and the bishop] let all rise up with one accord, and looking towards the east, after the catechumens and penitents have departed, pray to God who ascended up to the heaven of heavens to the east.'[274] In the Egyptian liturgies the deacon formally summoned the worshippers to look towards the East for the great eucharistic prayer. According to the Alexandrian *Canons of Basil* (*circa* 400), the deacon summoned the people to stand, to turn towards the East, and to pay attention to the hallowing.[275] In the text of the Coptic anaphora of *St Basil* we find in fact that the deacon says before the opening dialogue of the great prayer:

Come closer, stand reverently, you men, and look eastward. Let us pay heed;
(Renaudot I, p. 13)

and then, while the priest is leading up to the *Sanctus*, the deacon says again:

You who are sitting, stand up. Look eastward.   (Renaudot I, p. 13)

The same diaconal summons, Εἰς ἀνατολὰς βλέψατε, is found before the *Sanctus* in the Alexandrian Greek liturgy of *St Basil* (Renaudot I, p. 65), in the Greek *St Mark* (Brightman, p. 131) and Coptic *St Cyril* (Brightman, p. 175), and in the Ethiopian *Anaphora of the Apostles* (Brightman, p. 231).

*          *          *

So far in this chapter we have placed most emphasis on the positive side of the parousia: the church longs for Christ to come again to raise the dead and to give life incorruptible. But Christ will come in judgement (Matt. 16:27; John 5:25–29; Acts 17:31; II Cor. 5:10; II Tim. 4:1; I John 2:28, cf. 4:17; Rev. 22:12), and judgement is not unequivocally positive. We must now see what place falls to the eucharist in the perspective of the final judgement.

## 7. The eucharist and judgement

According to the New Testament there is a last assize at which all men will be judged (II Cor. 5:10). It is equally clear that judgement takes place already, according to the way in which a man responds when he is confronted by Christ (John 3:18; 5:24). There is already now 'no condemnation for those who are in Christ Jesus' (Rom. 8:1); if any man is in Christ the new creation is already present (II Cor. 5:17). The expression 'in Christ' points to the fact that it is by baptism εἰς Χριστόν that the final assize is anticipated. It is in baptism that we participate in the death and resurrection of the Representative Man; and because Christ's death was God's condemnation on all human sin, and the Resurrection the divine vindication of Christ's acceptance of the ultimate verdict on sin, the baptized has, *in Christ*, already passed through the death merited by his sin and walks now in newness of life.[276] Yet in the interval between the sacramental anticipation of the final judgement in baptism and the appearance before the last assize itself, it is a regrettable but apparently inevitable fact of the baptized person's life that he *sins* and thereby repudiates in practice his baptismal acceptance of the divine judgement on sin. It is our argument that the eucharist is a repeated projection of the last judgement which each time partly fulfils, and therefore strengthens, the promise of judgement and pardon which we received in hope in our baptism. The Jesus who bore on the Cross the condemnation due to man's sin has been made Lord and appointed by God to be the universal judge at the last day (Acts 10:42), and already the Lord comes in judgement at every eucharist. The most obvious scriptural text to be examined in this connection is I Cor. 11:27–34.[277]

### (a) I Cor. 11:27–34

In I Cor. 11:27–34 Paul reels off a string of juridical and near-juridical terms in connection with the eucharist: δοκιμάζειν, κρίμα, διακρίνειν, κρίνειν, κατακρίνειν, ἀναξίως, ἔνοχος. Examination reveals both (i) that the offence which roused the apostle to this language was incurred in connection with the eucharist, and also (ii) that the eucharist itself was, in Paul's view, the vehicle of dominical judgement on the offence.

(i) More precisely, the Corinthians' offence was both ecclesiological and christological and showed itself when they met together to celebrate the meal of agape and eucharist. This occasion is the supreme instance of Christians' gathering as the church (συνερχομένων ὑμῶν ἐν ἐκκλησίᾳ, verse 18):[278] and yet it was precisely here that the Corinthians displayed the divisions (σχίσματα, v. 18) and factions (αἱρέσεις, v. 19) among themselves. The first arrivals did not wait for the others to come (v. 33), and some were left to go hungry (v. 21). For the rich to 'humiliate those who have nothing' was to 'despise the church of God' (v. 22). This ecclesiological dimension of the Corinthians' offence lends support to the interpretation of 'not discerning the body' in verse 29 as a reference to the churchly body.[279] But since the church is precisely the body of Christ, the Corinthians' sin had a christological dimension. Their selfish behaviour meant that they were turning the Lord's supper into their own supper (v. 20f): but the bread and the cup of the properly sacramental part (vv. 23–26) of the whole meal remained the bread and cup 'of the Lord' (v. 27a); and to eat and drink these unworthily, on account of being in a state of division through selfishness, meant becoming guilty of the body and blood of the Lord (v. 27b). It is here that the interpretation which understands 'not discerning the body' in verse 29 to refer to the sacramental element comes into its own. For although being guilty of the body and blood of the Lord may certainly imply standing alongside those who cried 'Crucify him!' (which is what Heb. 6:6 pictures the apostate as doing), the exact balance in verse 27 between (a) the bread and the cup of the Lord and (b) the body and blood of the Lord indicates that Paul saw sufficient relation between the elements and the body and blood for verse 27 to mean also that guilt is incurred with respect to the eucharistic body and blood—so that when σῶμα occurs again in the next verse but one, we may be justified in taking it once more as referring to the eucharistic element, failure to 'discern the body' being failure to recognize in the bread the vehicle of the Lord's personal presence.[280] However we may resolve the question of 'not discerning the body' in I Cor. 11:29, the case is clear from the complete passage, i.e. verses 17 to 34, that by their selfish and unbrotherly conduct some Corinthians are repudiating the judgement pronounced on sin in the death of Jesus, a judgement whose validity they themselves once acknowledged at their baptism. But the Saviour has also been appointed Judge: and the meal at which he intends to give the benefits of salvation may become the meal at which he executes judgement.

(ii) Paul is quite clear that in the Corinthian church at least, the eucharist has become the vehicle of dominical judgement: eating and drinking 'without discerning the body' is the cause (διὰ τοῦτο, v. 30) of sickness among many and of the death of some. Käsemann notes how Paul's thought moves from the eschatological future (ἔνοχος ἔσται, v. 27) to the fact that the Corinthians are *already* eating and drinking judgement to themselves (vv. 29–30): 'In the sacrament, what is revealed on the Last Day becomes in a certain way already a present reality' ('Anliegen und Eigenart . . .', pp. 23f). Was this eucharistic judgement restricted to the case of the Corinthians or may we draw the conclusion that every eucharist is the occasion of dominical judgement? As we shall see presently, the Fathers and the liturgies clearly took the latter option, and a variety of considerations confirm their choice. Apart from the decretal-like style of the apostle in I Cor. 11:27ff (see Käsemann, *art. cit.*, p. 23), which suggests that Paul is here formulating general rules for the church's approach to the supper, there are also good theological grounds for this interpretation. The foundation of the eucharistic judgement is the fact that every eucharist is the occasion of Christ's coming, and Christ the Lord is both Saviour and Judge. Käsemann expresses it graphically (*art. cit.*, pp. 25f):

When the Lord comes on the scene, it is also the universal Judge who appears. . . . His presence never leaves us unaffected. We do not, by our own disrespect, render his gift ineffective or make the presence of Christ unhappen. We cannot paralyse God's eschatological action. Salvation scorned becomes judgment. . . . Where the Saviour is despised, the universal Judge remains present and shows himself in that very place as the one from whose presence there is no escape. . . . The sacramental coming of the Lord always sets men in the perspective of the Last Day and therefore itself bears the marks of what God will do at the Last Day. It is a kind of anticipation, within the church, of the Last Day.

The reason why the eucharist may turn into a condemnatory judgement is the fact that, despite our baptismal acceptance of the divine judgement on sin, we are still prone to sin. Nor, despite the forgiveness conferred on us sacramentally in our baptism, have we yet heard the final pronouncement of forgiveness at the last assize and entered to take our place at the meal of the kingdom—as perhaps their excessive merriment (ὃς δὲ μεθύει, v. 21) indicates the Corinthians to have believed. The eucharist is celebrated in the interval between our baptism and our appearance before the last assize: by it the Christian is allowed, nay required, to test himself (I Cor. 11:28), to show enough discrimination about himself (v. 31) to know that he is a sinner whose condemnation Jesus has borne—in order that he may not (already now) be judged by the Lord (v. 31), may not eat and drink judgement to himself (v. 29: κρίμα is usually a verdict of guilty, cf. v. 34), may not *finally* be pronounced guilty of the Lord's death (ἔνοχος ἔσται, v. 27) and share the *ultimate* condemnation of 'the world' (ἵνα μὴ σὺν τῷ κόσμῳ κατακριθῶμεν, v. 32). In other words, the Christian is at every eucharist required to renew his baptismal acceptance of the divine condemnation on sin.

But the mention of baptism reminds us of the *saving* purpose of God which was manifested in the death and *resurrection* of Jesus, through participation in which the baptized person is not only dead to sin but walking in *newness of life*. Even in the stern words of I Cor. 11:27–34 the fundamental optimism which is surely grounded in the Christian's baptismal incorporation into Christ breaks through: *present* judgement by the Lord (vv. 29–32a) is a gracious chastisement (παιδευόμεθα, v. 32a), whose purpose is to (bring us to repentance and so) save us from *final* condemnation (v. 32b).

If even a eucharist that is approached unworthily may work at least indirectly for the good of the communicant, then what of a eucharist that is *rightly* approached?

## (b) Matthew 26:28: εἰς ἄφεσιν ἁμαρτιῶν

There is in fact a further judicial aspect of the eucharist that it was not Paul's concern to stress with the Corinthians. St Matthew's account of the institution attaches to the eucharistic cup these words: 'Drink of it, all of you; for this is my blood of the covenant, which is poured out for many *for the remission of sins*' (26:27f). Drinking the sacramental cup therefore serves, like baptism (Acts 2:38), εἰς ἄφεσιν ἁμαρτιῶν—provided (we may add) that as in the case of baptism so also in the case of the eucharist the sacrament is approached with repentance. A judge may acquit as well as condemn! This acquittal is precisely the meaning of God's 'justifying' the believer. The condemnation of sin which the divine justice demands has been carried out in the death of Jesus, in which Father and Son co-operated for the sake of man's *salvation*. It is therefore clearly the will of the Father, and of Jesus the Saviour whom He has now appointed Judge, that men should be acquitted. The only condition is (in Johannine terminology) to believe in the Son and in the One who sent Him (John 3:18; 5:24) —which includes recognition that the death of Jesus was the divine condemnation on all sin, a recognition manifested in repentance for one's own sin. The penitent believer is justified, acquitted; and at every eucharist the divine acquittal is pronounced that will be heard at the last assize.

In the Fathers and in the ancient liturgies of both East and West the dual theme of remission of sins and non-condemnation recurs constantly in connection with the eucharist, and it is often explicitly set in the perspective not only of the death of Christ but also of His final coming to judge both the quick and the dead. To the liturgical and patristic evidence we now turn.

## (c) Eucharistic judgement in the liturgies and the Fathers

We may begin where we left off, with Matt. 26:28. The classical anaphoras all reproduce the phrase εἰς ἄφεσιν ἁμαρτιῶν at the cup-word in their

institution narratives: and this might perhaps be explained by the desire
not to omit any recorded word of Jesus, and by the prominence which
Matthew usually enjoyed among the synoptic gospels. But when the
Eastern anaphoras add the phrase to the word over the bread as well, then
we begin to suspect the importance of the notion to theology and to piety.
This doubling of εἰς ἄφεσιν ἁμαρτιῶν is found already in Serapion's
anaphora[281] and in the anaphora of *Apostolic Constitutions VIII* (Brightman, p. 20). It persisted in the liturgy of *St Basil*, from the Byzantine
form of which it no doubt found its way into the Byzantine form of
*St Chrysostom*.[282] Its continuing presence in the Egyptian liturgy is attested
by the Dêr-Balizeh papyrus (edd. Roberts and Capelle, p. 28), by the
Greek *St Mark* and the Coptic *St Cyril* (Brightman, pp. 132f, 177), and
by the Ethiopian *Anaphora of the Apostles* (Brightman, p. 232). On Syrian
territory it is found in the Greek *St James* (where also the deacons say at
the time of the recital of the institution, Εἰς ἄφεσιν ἁμαρτιῶν καὶ εἰς ζωὴν
αἰώνιον: so Brightman, pp. 51f), in the Syriac *St James* (where the celebrant himself recites the institution with the form 'for the remission of sins
and for eternal life' over both bread and cup: so Brightman, p. 87), in
many West Syrian anaphoras, and even in the newly restored version of
*Addai and Mari* among Indian Uniats.[283] That we have here to do with
more than the well-known stylistic tendency to parallelism between bread-
word and cup-word in liturgical versions of the institution narrative, is
confirmed by the prominence of the connection between communion and
remission of sins made (as we are about to see) at other points in the
course of the eucharistic texts as well.

We saw before (pp. 61–64) that many liturgies make mention of the
parousia and of the final judgement at the end of the institution narrative
and in the anamnesis. This same perspective is maintained when in the
second half of the epiclesis the Eastern liturgies come to pray for the
fruits of communion. When prayer is made at this point that communion
may be for the remission of sins, a present reference is no doubt intended;
but that the *present* remission of sins does not exhaust the desired fruits
of communion is made clear by the accompanying mention of non-
condemnation (in the day of judgement), and of entry into the heavenly
kingdom and eternal life. Three examples may be given in illustration:

And may there come, O my Lord, thine Holy Spirit and rest upon this offering of
thy servants and bless it and hallow it that it be to us, O my Lord, for the pardon
of offences and the remission of sins and for the great hope of resurrection from
the dead and for new life in the kingdom of heaven with all those who have been
well-pleasing in thy sight. (*Addai and Mari*, Brightman, p. 287)[284]

Send down thy Holy Spirit upon us and upon these gifts lying here . . . that they
may be to those who partake of them for the purification of their soul, for the
remission of sins, for the communion of thy Holy Spirit, for the fulness (πλήρωμα)
of the kingdom [of heaven], for boldness (παρρησία) before thee, and not for
judgment (κρίμα) or for condemnation (κατάκριμα).
                              (Byzantine *St Chrysostom*, Brightman, pp. 329f [386f])

Send thy Holy Spirit upon these oblations and show this bread to be the venerable body of our Lord Jesus Christ, and this cup the blood of our Lord Jesus
Christ, that to all who receive of them they may be for life, resurrection, remission of sins, health of soul and body, illumination of mind, and defence
before the dreadful judgment-seat of thy Christ . . .

> (*First Anaphora of the Twelve Apostles*, ed. A. Raes, in *Anaphora
> syriacae*, vol. I, fasc. 2, Roma, 1940, pp. 218–21)

\* \* \*

The same themes recur in Eastern liturgies between the great prayer and
communion. In the liturgy of *Addai and Mari* the priest says as he takes
the bread into his hands before the fraction:

Praise to thine holy name, O our Lord Jesus Christ, and worship to thy sovereignty at all times for ever. Amen. For thou art the living and life-giving bread
which came down from heaven and giveth life to the whole world and they who
eat of it die not and they who receive it are saved and pardoned in it and live
in it for ever; (Brightman, p. 290)

and after the fraction, consignation and intinction he says:

These glorious and holy and life-giving and divine mysteries have been set apart
and consecrated and perfected and fulfilled and united and commingled and
attached and sealed one to the other in the adorable and glorious name of the
glorious Trinity the Father and the Son and the Holy Ghost, that they may be to
us, O my Lord, for the pardon of offences and the forgiveness of sins and the
great hope of the resurrection from the dead and for new life in the kingdom of
heaven, to us and to the holy church of Christ our Lord here and in every place
now and ever and world without end. (Brightman, p. 292)

In the Maronite liturgy the priest prays at the fraction:

Blessed art thou, our Lord Jesus Christ, living bread come down from heaven to
be for those who receive thee life for ever. May every believer who has taken
part with us in this eucharist share, O our God, in thy heavenly kingdom for
ever. At the day of judgement, Lord, may thy body and blood not be for our
confusion and punishment for ever. Grant that I, O Lord Jesus Christ, may have
an open face before thee, when thou appearest with thy angels in thy great glory,
for ever.

> (M. Hayek, *Liturgie maronite*, pp. 277f, cf. p. 316)

The Byzantine *St Basil* contains the following prayer said 'secretly' by the
priest:

. . . Yea, O our God, and make none of us guilty (ἔνοχον) of these thy dreadful
and heavenly mysteries, nor sick (ἀσθενῆ) in soul or body from partaking of them
unworthily (ἀναξίως): but grant us even unto our last breath to receive rightly
(ἀξίως) the hope (τὴν ἐλπίδα; *but modern text:* τὴν μερίδα, share) of thy hallowed
things for (εἰς) a viaticum (ἐφόδιον) of eternal life and an acceptable defence
before the fearful judgment-seat of thy Christ; so that we also, with all the

saints who have pleased thee since the world began, may become partakers of thy eternal blessings which thou hast prepared for them that love thee, O Lord.
(Brightman, pp. 338f, 410)

On the point of communicating, the celebrant in the Greek *St James* prays:

O Lord our God, heavenly bread who art the life of the all, I have sinned before heaven and in thy sight and I am not worthy (ἄξιος) to partake of thy spotless mysteries: but thou who art the compassionate God, make me worthy by thy grace to partake, without condemnation (ἀκατακρίτως), of thy holy body and thy precious blood for the remission of sins and life everlasting. (Brightman, pp. 63f)

As he brings the elements down to give communion to the people, the priest in the Syriac *St James* says:

From thy propitiatory altar let there come down pardon for thy servants, O Son of God, who came for our salvation and shall come for our resurrection and the renewal of our race for ever. (Brightman, p. 103)

Among the communion prayers in the anaphora of *James of Sarugh* is the following:

May the body and blood of thy only Son be for us a leaven of life and the pledge of life in the day of judgment. (Renaudot II, pp. 365f)

\*    \*    \*

The concise formulas at the delivery of the elements tell the same story. I give two examples from among the many possible:

The servant of God N. receives the precious and holy body and blood of our Lord and God and Saviour Jesus Christ for the remission of his sins and eternal life. (Byzantine *St Chrysostom*, Brightman, p. 396)

My brother, this is the body of our Lord Jesus Christ which is given to you for the pardon of faults, the remission of sins and life unto ages of ages.
(M. Hayek, *Liturgie maronite*, p. 281)

\*    \*    \*

After the communion the Eastern liturgies become more expansive again. In the rite of *Apostolic Constitutions VIII* there is the following diaconal summons:

Having received the precious body and the precious blood of Christ, let us give him thanks who has made us worthy to receive his holy mysteries and let us pray they may not be for our condemnation (κρίμα) but for our salvation, for the good of our souls and bodies, for the preservation of our piety, for the remission of sins and for the life of the age to come. (Brightman, p. 25)

In the liturgy of *Addai and Mari* the final blessing runs:

He who hath blessed us with all spiritual blessings in heavenly places in Jesus

Christ our Lord [Eph. 1:3] and hath bidden us to his kingdom and called us and brought us nigh to his longed-for good things which pass not away neither cease nor are destroyed, even as he promised and assured to us in his lifegiving gospel and said to the blessed company of his disciples 'Verily verily I say unto you, whoso eateth my flesh and drinketh my blood dwelleth in me and I in him and I will raise him up at the last day and he shall not come into judgment but is passed from death unto life eternal' [cf. Jn. 6:56, 54b; 5:24b: *an interesting combination!*]: may he then bless our company and guard our congregation and make our people glorious, which have come and had delight in the power of his glorious and holy and lifegiving and divine mysteries. And with the living sign of the cross of our Lord be ye sealed and guarded from all harm hidden or open now and ever and world without end.   (Brightman, pp. 303f)

The Syriac *St James* gives this prayer to the priest at the cleansing of the vessels:

Thy sacred and holy mouth, O my Lord, hath promised and said on this wise 'Whoso eateth my body and drinketh my blood and believeth in me dwelleth in me and I in him and I will raise him up at the last day' [cf. Jn. 6:56, 40]. And to us, O Lord, who have eaten thy holy body and drunk thy propitiatory blood, let it not be for judgment, for vengeance nor for condemnation nor for accusation to me and to thy faithful people but for the pardon of offences and for the remission of sins and for a blessed resurrection from the house of the dead and for boldness before thy fearful judgment seat, O our Lord and our God for ever.
(Brightman, p. 106)

As a last example from the Eastern liturgies I quote a magnificent prayer which, unlike the one just given, does not dwell on the possible shadow-side. It is reported by Narsai as being said 'with love and rejoicing' by the whole congregation after communion:

Our Lord Jesus, King to be adored of all creatures, do away from us all harms by the power of Thy mysteries; and when Thou shinest forth at the end of the times for the redemption of all, may we go forth to meet Thee with confidence with Hosannas. May we confess to Thy name for Thy goodness towards our race, who hast pardoned our debts and blotted them out by Thy Body and Thy Blood. And here and there may we be worthy to send up to Thy Godhead glory and comeliness and confession for ever and ever.   (ed. Connolly, p. 29)

*     *     *

When we turn to the medieval Western liturgy, and particularly the Roman, we find (I think) two important differences of emphasis in comparison with the Eastern liturgies. The first, and indisputable, difference is that there is practically never any reference in the Western texts of the eucharist to the second coming of Christ. The elaboration of the institution narrative on the basis of I Cor. 11:26 which we found in the Ambrosian and Mozarabic rites (see p. 62) is a very rare instance. In Western eucharistic prayers the anamnesis does not make that mention of the second advent and the ensuing judgement which we saw to be common in the East at that point. There is in fact in the old ordinary of the Roman mass not a single reference to the parousia.[285] Even in the variable post-communion prayers, which constitute the most usual occasion in the West of opening up the future prospect, the typical movement of thought is from a present and continuing purification from sin (*purificatio, mundatio, purgatio, absolutio*) to a future enjoyment of the full blessings of heaven, *the point of transition being left unspecified.*[286] When prayer is made, as in the priest's *Perceptio corporis tui* before communion in the Roman rite, that reception may not be for judgement and condemnation, there is no indication that the *final* judgement is in mind: the contrasted benefit which is being prayed for is protection and healing of mind and body, no mention being made here (in distinction to the similar prayers quoted above from the Maronite liturgy, p. 85, the Byzantine *St Basil*, pp. 85f, the liturgy of *Apostolic Constitutions VIII*, p. 86, and the Syriac *St James*, p. 87) of the blessings which we may expect only at and beyond the last judgement.

The second difference, though perhaps not so marked, is that in comparison with the East, the West places more emphasis on prayer that remission of sins may come as a result of the *offering of the sacrifice*, and correspondingly less emphasis on the thought that the remission of sins is one of the blessings given by Christ in *communion*. Certainly the Eastern liturgies consider that the eucharist is a sacrifice offered for the remission of sins; but from the epiclesis onwards it is the thought of the blessings conveyed through the reception of communion, of which remission of sins is one, which predominates. In the Roman mass, on the other hand, the notion of a sacrifice offered gains a dominant hold at the offertory and keeps it right through the canon. The balance is not, I think, redressed by the priest's private prayers before and after communion, nor even by the variable post-communions.

The liturgies of the Reformation can hardly be said to have done much to set the eucharist in the perspective of the final coming of Christ in judgement. Perhaps the Anglican Church did most. The 1549 Book of Common Prayer introduced the following prayer into the canon:

Graunt . . . that, at the day of the generall resurreccion, we and all they which bee of the misticall body of thy sonne, may altogether be set on his right hand, and heare that his most joyfull voyce: Come unto me, O ye that be blessed of my father, and possesse the kingdom, whiche is prepared for you from the begynning of the worlde;

but this disappeared from the transposed intercessions in the 1552 Prayer Book.[287] Cranmer also alluded to I Cor. 11:26 in the canon, but the context makes clear that his interest is not so much in the mention of 'his coming again' as in the establishment (a concern he shared with all the Reformers) of the right relation between the eucharist and the unique sacrifice made by Christ on the Cross:

. . . [Almighty] God [our] heavenly father, which of thy tender mercie diddest geve thine only sonne Jesus Christ to suffre death upon the crosse for our redempcion, who made there (by his one oblacion once offered) a full, perfect, and sufficient sacrifyce, oblacion and satysfaccyon, for the sinnes of the whole worlde, and did institute, and in his holy gospelle commaund us to celebrate [1552 and 1662: continue] a perpetuall memory of that his precious death, untyll his comming again. . . . (1549 [1552, 1662] Book of Common Prayer)

Apart from that, we note the stern warnings in the Exhortations that communion by the impenitent will 'increase their damnation' (1549), and the insistence throughout that the faithful communicant receives remission of his sins. Remission of sins is the most frequently mentioned benefit of faithful communion;[288] but feeding on the 'spiritual food' of the sacrament is also seen by Cranmer as giving the divine assurance that we are 'heirs through hope of thy everlasting kingdom'.

\*     \*     \*

We need spend little time here on the patristic and medieval theologians, since they by and large reflect their respective liturgical traditions on this question of the relation between the eucharist and the coming of Christ in judgement.

It is perhaps surprising, in view of the relative prominence of the second advent in their eucharistic liturgies, that some Eastern writers do not make considerably more direct mention of it in their eucharistic theology. And though they certainly hold that communion is $\epsilon$ἰς ἄφεσιν ἁμαρτιῶν, some of them are inclined to borrow images from medicine and biology which suggest a continuous and continuing process (examples will be given on pp. 111f), rather than the punctiliar imagery of jurisprudence (for example: 'acquittal'), in order to express the saving effect of communion rightly received. Nevertheless, Theodore of Mopsuestia, for instance, is quite certain that communion gives remission of sins to the penitent sinner (*Hom.* XVI, 33ff, edd. Tonneau-Devreesse, pp. 587ff), and we have already noted his insistence that Christ's coming to us in communion is the promise and earnest of His final coming to us for a blessed resurrection (p. 73). Likewise John Damascene and Nicholas Cabasilas know that the gift of Christ to the faithful communicant is remission of sins and eternal life. Thus the Damascene:

. . . The bread of the prothesis, and the wine and water, are by the invocation and coming of the Holy Spirit changed in a supernatural way into the body and blood of Christ. . . . [The body of Christ] is to them that receive it rightly (ἀξίως) and in faith (πίστει), for the remission of sins, for eternal life, and for the protection of soul and body; but to them that receive it unworthily (ἀναξίως) and in unbelief (ἐν ἀπιστίᾳ), it is unto punishment and retribution; just as the Lord's death is, for those who believe, life and incorruption unto the enjoyment of eternal bliss; but to unbelievers and those who killed the Lord, it is unto punishment and eternal retribution.[289]

And Nicholas Cabasilas opens his commentary on the liturgy with the clear statement:

> In the celebration of the holy mysteries the work done is the transformation of the gifts into the divine body and blood, and the aim is the sanctification of the faithful who, through these mysteries, receive the remission of sins and the inheritance of the kingdom of heaven.   (PG 150, 368)

But we note that Cabasilas finds no place for the second advent among the mighty acts of Christ which he sees represented by the various ceremonies in the course of the liturgy, it being rather the most significant events between the Lord's incarnation and Pentecost that are shown forth by the liturgical action. A different interpretation of the liturgical action was, however, also known to Eastern theologians. We noted (p. 73) that Maximus the Confessor interpreted the reading of the gospel, the subsequent descent of the priest from the sacerdotal throne and the expulsion by the ministers of the catechumens and others who are unworthy as the image and type of the preaching of the gospel which is followed by the End (see Matt. 24:14), at which Christ will descend with His angels to make the separating judgement.

In similar style Symeon of Thessalonica ( + 1429) makes the following interpretation. I summarize:

> The lessons signify the missionary preaching of the apostles after the Lord's ascension. The gospel in particular prepares the way for the End which will take place when the good news has been preached throughout the world. At the End the Lord will send His angels to separate out the bad from the good, and this the church already does by the deacons' dismissal of the unbaptized and excommunicate. The entry of the venerable gifts in brilliant procession 'manifests (ἐμφαίνει) the parousia of Christ in which he will come with glory'. The events of the great entry teach that the faithful will inherit the kingdom of God at the appearing of the Saviour: 'but the kingdom of God is Christ himself and the vision of his saving work (οἰκονομία), namely his stooping even unto death, his self-sacrifice for us and his showing his sacrificed, lifegiving and divine body with its wounds, his becoming immortal and awarding us the victory over death by offering us, from his wounds, immortality, life and divinisation, food and drink . . . being himself the bread of life. . . . Therefore the great entry signifies both the parousia of the Saviour and his burial.' And Symeon goes on to give a double interpretation of the rest of the liturgical action: it represents both the past events of the passion, death, resurrection and ascension (here Symeon moves in the same realm of interpretation as Theodore of Andida and Nicholas Cabasilas) and also the life of the kingdom of heaven (here Symeon shares the same realm of interpretation as Maximus the Confessor).[290]

We may regret the confusion in which Symeon lands himself in the detailed application of his principles,[291] but we cannot do other than salute his vision of the liturgy as a dramatic prefiguration of the parousia and the final kingdom made possible by the presence of the one Christ who came once bringing the divine kingdom in His own person and who will come again at the end to establish God's universal kingdom in power and glory.

\* \* \*

In the West the theologians of the eucharist show, as might be expected from their liturgies, a lack of interest in the event of the Lord's second coming in judgement. From Cyprian onwards the typical Western theology was that the eucharist was above all a (commemorative) *sacrifice* which brought to the penitent and faithful communicant remission of sins, communion serving also to ensure his continuing dwelling in Christ through His ecclesial body. As an example of the eucharist as sacrifice for the remission of sins I give the following quotation from Ambrose, interesting also because of its concurrent use of medicinal imagery. Citing the prayer of oblation from the canon (*offerimus tibi hanc immaculatam hostiam . . . et petimus et precamur uti hanc oblationem suscipias . . .*), Ambrose goes on:

So every time you communicate (*accipis*), what does the apostle say to you? 'Every time we communicate we proclaim the Lord's death.' If we proclaim the Lord's death we proclaim the remission of sins. If every time his blood is shed it is shed for the remission of sins, then I must always communicate (*accipere*) so that he may always remit my sins. Since I am always sinning, I must always have a *remedy* (*medicinam*). (*De sacr.* IV, 6, 27f; cf. V, 4, 25; ed. Botte, pp. 116f; 132f)

For an example of the way in which communion was seen as the means of dwelling in Christ through His ecclesial body for ever, I refer the reader to a text from Augustine, *In Evang. Jo. tr.* 26, 11–20 (PL 35, 1611–15). Two particularly unfortunate developments took place in the later Western history. First, an ever-increasing emphasis was placed on the *offering* of the sacrifice as that which availed for the remission of sins, and there was a corresponding recession in the importance of communion as the means of receiving the benefits which Christ Himself gives. And second: though warning against unworthy communion has always been a universal feature of theology, the West developed such a stress on preparatory purification through the sacrament of penance that even the great St Thomas was mildly embarrassed by the fact that remission of sins was ascribed to *communion itself* by the liturgical texts, and the theologians of Trent showed even greater discomfort in face of the Reformers' teaching on this benefit of faithful communion.[292]

## 8. The parousia projected
The contribution of this chapter to our study of the eschatological content and import of the eucharist can be summarized under four heads.

(a) The eucharist is celebrated as the memorial of *Christ Himself*: τοῦτο ποιεῖτε εἰς τὴν ἐμὴν ἀνάμνησιν. The church recalls before the Father, with thanksgiving, the first coming of Christ and the work of salvation which He then began. Understanding that first coming as a promise and earnest of yet greater things, the church also prays the Father, in hope and expectation, that He will complete the bringing in of His kingdom by even now sending the one and the same messiah again, for the accomplishing of His final work. Though the church is impatient, the Father keeps to himself knowledge of the day and the hour when the kingdom will finally come and God's beneficent rule be enjoyed in all its fullness.

(b) But meanwhile the eucharist itself stands under the promise made by Christ at His first coming: 'Where two or three are gathered together in my name, there am I in the midst of them.' The church boldly claims the promise, and hails the Lord when He comes: 'Our Lord, come! Our Lord has come!' The church prays for the final advent of the Lord; but if the moment for that is not yet come, the church may still acclaim the presence of Christ who comes even now to confirm His people's hope.

(c) Because of the sovereignty of the eternal God over time, the one Christ may come to meet His people in the present, clothed with the mighty acts of the incarnation, passion, resurrection and ascension which are the promise of man's final salvation, and already exercising the functions which He will exercise at His final coming. To the penitent He brings assurance of their acquittal, and to the faithful He gives the taste of the life incorruptible which they will receive from Him at the last and will continue to receive from Him in the heavenly kingdom through all eternity. To the no longer penitent and believing and to the not yet penitent and believing the coming of Christ at the eucharist is a threat of condemnation at the last assize and of exclusion from the delights of heaven. Salvation spurned turns into condemnation.

(d) The word *projection*, and that in two (related) senses, may be used to express the relation between the final advent of Christ and His coming at the eucharist:

(i) Christ's coming at the eucharist is a projection in the temporal sense that it is a 'throwing forward' of Christ's final advent into the present. What is part of the final purpose of the eternal God but is still future in the dealings between God and man is, by the divine initiative, thrown forward into man's present experience so that man may order himself according to what he thereby sees the kingdom of God to imply in the way of fellowship between God and man and the extirpation of all that would oppose the divine sovereignty. When the future and universal kingdom is thrown forward into the present it is, necessarily, 'scaled down', and there we come to the second sense of projection.

(ii) Christ's coming at the eucharist is a projection of His final advent in something like the map-maker's sense of projection. That is to say, it is a representation of a large reality by means of a set of comprehensible symbols. Only, the reality represented by the eucharist is not merely large but ultimate, and the relation between symbol and reality is not merely extrinsic and established by human convention but, at least as far as the central and essential symbolism of bread eaten and wine drunk is concerned, was established by the Lord Himself, and with words very much like these: 'Take, eat; this is my body' and 'This cup is the new covenant in my blood'; and this is a fact which—even upon the least 'realistic' interpretation—puts those who eat the bread and drink the wine into a relation with the Lord and the divine kingdom that is more intimate than my relation with the earth when I see it represented on Mercator's projection.[293]

# IV

# *The Firstfruits of the Kingdom*

W E H A V E seen that the eucharist is the meal at which the messiah feeds His people as a sign of the feasting in the coming kingdom, and that it is also the occasion of the Lord's visitation of His people to assure the penitent and believing of the verdict of acquittal they will hear when He returns to hold the last assize. From these points of view the two chief actors in the drama are the Lord Jesus Christ and His church. Now the written apostolic witness calls the risen Christ 'the firstborn of many brethren' (Rom. 8:29; cf. Col. 1:18), 'the firstfruits of them that slept' (I Cor. 15:20); and the church is called 'the firstfruits of God's creatures' (Jas. 1:18). So although the New Testament nowhere uses the words firstborn and firstfruits in direct connection with the eucharist, there is some scriptural justification for making use of these two thoroughly Hebraic images in the elucidation of the relation between the sacrament and the kingdom of God. In this part of our study we shall be led also to see something of the pneumatological scope of the eucharistic celebration, and our hitherto christomonist approach will thereby receive some correction.

## 1. The final kingdom

True to our eschatological perspective, let us start with the final term of the two images: the firstborn of *many brethren*, and the firstfruits of *all God's creatures*. The New Testament presents us with a vision of the consummation in which the whole creation will come under the total rule of God. The Christ who was God's agent in creation (John 1:3; I Cor. 8:6; Col. 1:16f; Heb. 1:2) will also be the agent of the consummation; for all things are 'unto him' ($\epsilon i s$ $a \dot{v} \tau \acute{o} \nu$, Col. 1:16), all things will be summed up in him (Eph. 1:10), and he will deliver the kingdom to God the Father (I Cor. 15:24). And *God will be all in all* (I Cor. 15:28c). The primary meaning of this last statement is, as the Pauline context makes clear, that the whole creation will enjoy that perfect submission to God the Father which the only-begotten Son has enjoyed from all eternity. At the universal level this will mean something that can be described as a global renewal: all things will have been made new (Rev. 21:5; I Cor. 7:31b), and there will be new heavens and a new earth (II Pet. 3:13 and Rev. 21:1, citing Isa. 65:17 and 66:22). For rational creatures it will mean, as Revelation pictures it, perfect worship of the God whose service, in the Prayer Book phrase, is perfect freedom. Risen men and women will join their firstborn brother in complete submission to the Father; and because this complete submission will render us transparent to the divine splendour and fill us with the life of God, we may say in Hebraic language that many sons will have been brought to glory (Heb. 2:10) or, in Hellenistic idiom, that we shall have become partakers of the divine nature (II Pet. 1:4). Our worship of the Father will be through, with and in Christ (*per ipsum, et cum ipso, et in ipso* as the doxology of the Roman canon has it): but the divine Lamb also is in the midst of the throne and will receive our worship (Rev. 5:8–14; 7:9–12; 22:3f), and He it is who will feed us with the life of God at His own marriage-feast (Rev. 19:7–9). Aware that even the kaleidoscopic imagery of the Book of Revelation can do no more than suggest the full splendour of the final kingdom, we must nevertheless try to set the eucharistic celebration of the present time in the light of that heavenly assembly when all the many brethren will together share the divine life, to the perfect praise of God, in a creation totally suffused with His glory.

The path we shall take in the rest of this chapter is therefore this. We shall look first at the fact that the Word and the Spirit, the divine agents of creation and re-creation, are associated with the eucharistic action. In a brief interlude we shall play on the theme of the divine glory, for this theme will bind together much else in this chapter. Next we shall look at the eucharistic elements of bread and wine in the perspective of the finally transfigured creation, tackling here a question which has hitherto been side-stepped in this study, namely the question of the real presence. This will lead into a consideration of the present eucharistic community in the light of the community of the final kingdom. The chapter will be concluded with some remarks showing that though the eucharistic celebration of the present falls short of the final kingdom, it is to be understood above all in the positive sense of a promise of what is to be.

## 2. The Word and the Spirit

We begin in what may seem an unlikely place, namely the long-standing and nowadays surely rather jaded controversy between the Greek and the Latin churches as to the moment and the agent of eucharistic consecration. As is well known, the Latin church, beginning perhaps at the time of Ambrose,[294] placed more and more stress on the recital of the institution narrative, and especially on the Lord's own words spoken by the priest *in persona Christi*—until the position was finally reached when the Council of Florence could define 'Hoc est enim corpus meum' and 'Hic est enim calix sanguinis mei . . .' as the words that consecrate.[295] The Eastern church, on the other hand, makes much of the principle enunciated by Cyril of Jerusalem:

We beseech the merciful God to send forth (ἐξαποστεῖλαι) the Holy Spirit upon the elements, that he may make the bread the body of Christ and the wine the blood of Christ; for whatever the Holy Spirit has touched is sanctified and changed (πάντως γάρ, οὗ ἂν ἐφάψηται τὸ ἅγιον πνεῦμα, τοῦτο ἡγίασται καὶ μεταβέβληται),[296] and does not consider the consecration complete until the Holy Ghost has been invoked in the epiclesis which follows the institution narrative in the classical Eastern anaphoras. To my mind, the desire to fix a precise *moment* of consecration is a perverse departure from the earlier conception that consecration is effected by or in response to the whole eucharistic prayer,[297] perverse because it is a step in the direction of that objectivism into which man's understanding of the sacraments always threatens to fall.[298] As to the *agent* of consecration, it is only a bad theology of the Trinity which can produce arguments tending to play off one Person against another, as for instance when Gregory Dix apparently rejected any role of the Holy Spirit in the eucharistic consecration on the ground that it reduced the Son's part to pure passivity.[299] Though we may distinguish within the divine activity towards the world and ascribe certain functions to one Person by appropriation, we may not *oppose* the roles of the Persons; for there is harmony, not discord, within the Blessed Trinity, and in their activity towards the world the divine Persons actively co-operate.

In the areas that are going to interest us particularly, namely creation and re-creation, we find Scripture suggesting that both the Second and the Third Persons of the Trinity play an active part. In Old Testament terms this is expressed by Ps. 33:6:

By the word of the Lord the heavens were made,
 and all their host by the breath of his mouth.

The Johannine Christ says:

When the Spirit of truth comes, he will guide you into all the truth; for he will not speak on his own authority, but whatever he hears he will speak, and he will declare to you the things that are to come. He will glorify me, for he will take what is mine and declare it to you. All that the Father has is mine; therefore I said that he will take what is mine and declare it to you.   (John 16:13–15)

And Paul writes:

But you are not in the flesh, you are in the Spirit, if the Spirit of God really dwells in you. Any one who does not have the Spirit of Christ does not belong to him. But if Christ is in you, although your bodies are dead because of sin, your spirits are alive because of righteousness. If the Spirit of him who raised Jesus from the dead dwells in you, he who raised Christ Jesus from the dead will give life to your mortal bodies also through his Spirit which dwells in you.
(Rom. 8:9–11)

Without going into the nuances of individual views, I may quote two or three Fathers from the time before the hardening of the controversy between East and West to show that, as one would expect from the biblical picture of the divine activity towards the world and the church, there need be no opposition between the work of Christ and the work of the Holy Spirit in the eucharistic consecration.[300] Gregory the Great stated quite simply:

> Our creator . . . changes the bread and the wine mixed with water . . . into his body and blood . . . by the hallowing of his Spirit.
>
> *(apud* Paul the Deacon, *Vit. Greg.,* 23, PL 75, 53)

John Chrysostom pictures the present Christ as speaking through the priest the words which He spoke at the Last Supper and which retain their creative force:

> Christ is present ($\pi\acute{a}\rho\epsilon\sigma\tau\iota\nu$), and the one who prepared that table [at the Last Supper] prepares also this now. For it is no mere man who makes the gifts become the body and blood of Christ, but Christ himself who was crucified for us. The priest is 'playing a part ($\sigma\chi\hat{\eta}\mu\alpha\,\pi\lambda\eta\rho\hat{\omega}\nu$)' when he pronounces the words, the power and the grace are God's. 'This is my body,' he says. This word transforms ($\mu\epsilon\tau\alpha\rho\rho\upsilon\theta\mu\acute{\iota}\zeta\epsilon\iota$) the gifts; and just as the word 'Be fruitful, and multiply, and fill the earth' was spoken only once and yet gives us the power of procreation throughout all time, so also this word, spoken only once, accomplishes the perfect sacrifice upon every table of the churches until this day and will do so until his coming ($\mu\acute{\epsilon}\chi\rho\iota\,\tau\hat{\eta}s\,\alpha\dot{\upsilon}\tau o\hat{\upsilon}\,\pi\alpha\rho o\upsilon\sigma\acute{\iota}\alpha s$).
>
> *(Hom. de prod. Iudae* I, 6, PG 49, 380)

Elsewhere Chrysostom refers to the work of the Holy Spirit in consecration:

> When the priest stands before the table with hands uplifted to heaven and calls on the Holy Spirit to come and touch the gifts. . . .   *(De cemeterio* 3, PG 49, 397f)

John Damascene pictures the complementary activities of the creative Word and of the Holy Spirit in this way:

> If then the Word of God is living and active [Heb. 4:12] and if whatever the Lord willed he made [Ps. 135:6]; if God said *Let there be light,* and there was light, and *Let there be a firmament,* and it was so [Gen. 1:3, 6]; if by the Word of the Lord the heavens were established, and all their power by the breath of his mouth [Ps. 33:6]; if the heaven and the earth, water, fire and air and all the order of them, as well as man who is the most famous of living creatures, were accomplished by the Word of the Lord; and if God the Word himself willed to become man and assumed flesh from the pure and spotless blood of the holy and ever-virgin Mary, without human seed: can he not make the bread his body and the wine and water his blood? He said in the beginning: *Let the earth put forth vegetation* [Gen. 1:11], and even till now, thanks to the rain, it continues to put forth its produce, impelled and empowered by the divine command. God said: *This is my body* and *This is my blood* and *Do this in memory of me,* and by virtue of his own all-powerful command, it is so until he come (for Paul says: until he come); and rain falls upon this new culture through the epiclesis, the over-shadowing power of the Holy Spirit. For as whatever God made He made by the energy of the Holy Spirit, so now it is the energy of the Spirit which performs ($\dot{\epsilon}\rho\gamma\acute{a}\zeta\epsilon\tau\alpha\iota$) the things that are supernatural ($\tau\grave{a}\,\dot{\upsilon}\pi\grave{\epsilon}\rho\,\phi\acute{\upsilon}\sigma\iota\nu$) which cannot be discerned except by faith.   *(De fid. orth.* IV, 13, PG 94, 1140f)

In the light of good Trinitarian theology and of patristic teaching on the eucharistic consecration, we may therefore now see how the activity of both the Second and the Third Persons of the Godhead sets the eucharist in the perspective of that ultimate condition when God will be all in all.

## (a) The Word

Apart from the notion of the consecratory power of the words spoken by Christ at the Last Supper and repeated by the priest acting *in persona Christi* at the eucharist, there is another way in which the eucharistic consecration has been associated with the Second Person of the Trinity: I refer to the invocation of the Word to come and consecrate the elements which is found in the fourth-century Egyptian anaphora of Serapion and in a few Gallican and Mozarabic eucharistic prayers.[301] Serapion's Logos-epiclesis runs thus:

O God of truth, let thy holy Word come upon this bread (ἐπιδημησάτω . . . ἐπί) that the bread may become body of the Word, and upon this cup that the cup may become blood of the Truth.[302]

That Serapion's view of the epiclesis was shared by Athanasius seems the most natural implication of a fragment preserved from a sermon of the latter's to the newly baptized:

When the great prayers and holy supplications have been sent up, the Word descends into the bread and the cup, and they become his body.[303]

Among the multifarious Gallican and Mozarabic prayers the invoked consecratory agents are various. Here are a couple of instances in which the Word is prayed for:

Send thy Word from heaven, O Lord, to wipe away faults and to hallow the oblations.    (M. Férotin, ed., *Liber Sacramentorum*, col. 200)

May thy holy Word come down, we pray, O almighty God, upon these things which we offer thee; may the Spirit of thine inestimable glory come down; may the gift of thy ancient favour come down, that our (*or* this) oblation may become a spiritual victim, accepted as a sweet-smelling sacrifice.

(*Missale Gallicanum*, PL 72, 342 & 345)[304]

Now what is the eschatological significance of this notion that the agent of eucharistic consecration is the Word or the words of the Word? We have already noticed that the Fathers make use, in connection with eucharistic consecration, of the biblical doctrine that the Second Person of the Trinity was active in creation as the Word: He spoke creation into being, and He therefore has the *power* (for the Fathers are concerned in these contexts to answer the question: how is it *possible* that the bread and wine become the body and blood?) to change the eucharistic elements by His word. I think we may extend this argument and use it in another way. We may direct our thoughts towards the kingdom and say that the Word is also the agent of the *eschatologically new* creation. At the eucharist we may see Jesus Christ as speaking the *re*-creative word which transforms the old creation into the new. The Reformed theologian F. J. Leenhardt, in a study which helped to launch an interesting debate particularly in Roman Catholic circles, sought to interpret 'This is my body' rather along these lines in an attempt to renew, and render more acceptable to Protestants, the Roman doctrine of transubstantiation. When Christ gives the bread with the words *This is my body*, then the bread is no longer, in its deepest constitution, what the baker made it but what the Word has made it. For a thing *is* what it *is in the will and purpose of God*; and if the Word has declared that it is the divine intention that this bread *be* the body of Christ, then that is what the bread henceforth is.[305] For reasons to become apparent (pp. 104–10), I cannot accept Leenhardt quite as he stands;[306] but we may be grateful for his emphasis on the (re-)creative activity of the Word. We shall have to say later that the consecrated bread and wine of the eucharist stands in such a relation to the renewed creation of the end that even in its profoundest constitution *it both is and is not* the body and blood of Christ (and I hope to be able to make that statement into less of a nonsense than it appears at first blush). But that the eucharist is an occasion of the Word's exercising His eschatological activity of re-creation and transformation to bring creation to its ultimate destiny, I would certainly hold.

An interesting variant on the theme of the (re-)creative activity of the Second Person of the Trinity at the eucharist is found in the institution narrative in the Armenian liturgy, which begins thus: 'Then taking the bread in his holy divine immortal immaculate and *creative* hands he blessed . . .' (Brightman, pp. 436f; Hanssens III, p. 415). Again, the reference to the institution in the sixth-century fragment of a Persian anaphora given by Brightman on p. 515 of *Liturgies Eastern and Western* reads: 'He took bread and wine which his own will had made, and he sanctified it . . .'[307] Moving within this thought-pattern, we may say that at the eucharist the creator re-creates his creatures of bread and wine.

So acts the Word. But what of the Spirit?

## (b) The Spirit

There is no competition between the Word and the Spirit. If it was God's Word that said 'Let there be light', then His Spirit was brooding over the face of the waters (Gen. 1:2f). If it was by the Word (דָּבָר) of the Lord that the heavens were made, then all their host came into being by the Breath (רוּחַ) of His mouth (Ps. 33:6).[308] When the Lord sends forth His Spirit, He creates (ברא) and renews (חדשׁ): so Ps. 104:30. The Spirit is active in the rebirth of men (John 3:5–7; Titus 3:5). He is the life-giver (John 6:63; 7:38f; II Cor. 3:6) and through Him we shall be resurrected (cf. Rom. 8:11) in our spiritual bodies (I Cor. 15:44). We shall not be surprised therefore to find the liturgies and the theologians ascribing a part to the Holy Spirit in the eschatological re-creation or transformation which takes place at the eucharist.

It is probable that this thought already lay behind Paul's reference to the Exodus types of the eucharist as πνευματικὸν βρῶμα and πνευματικὸν πόμα:

All ate the same spiritual food and all drank the same spiritual drink. For they drank from the spiritual Rock which followed them, and the Rock was Christ.
(I Cor. 10:3f)

I am aware of the interpretation which takes πνευματικός to mean 'typical' but consider that the first interpretation is supported by I Cor. 12:13c, which I take to be eucharistic in significance.[309] The Pauline expressions in I Cor. 10:3f appear to be the source of patristic and liturgical references to the eucharist as *cibus spiritualis, esca spiritualis* and *potus spiritualis*—though it must be admitted that the usual meaning of these phrases in the Fathers and in the liturgies tends towards 'spiritually assimilable'.[310] Among recent exegetes, I Cor. 10:3f is seen as giving a pneumatological reference to the eucharist by E. Käsemann, J. Betz, P. Lebeau, and J. J. von Allmen.[311]

In what are probably the two most ancient anaphoras extant, that of the *Apostolic Tradition* ascribed to Hippolytus and that of the liturgy of *Addai and Mari*, we find a prayer for the descent of the Holy Spirit into or upon the elements so that those who communicate may receive certain benefits:

Et petimus ut mittas spiritum tuum sanctum in oblationem sanctae ecclesiae: in unum congregans des omnibus qui participiunt sanctis in repletionem spiritus sancti ad confirmationem fidei in veritate, ut te laudemus et glorificemus per . . .
*(Apostolic Tradition, 4)*[312]

And may there come, O my Lord, thine Holy Spirit and rest upon this offering of thy servants and bless it and hallow it that it be to us, O my Lord, for the pardon of offences and the remission of sins and for the great hope of resurrection from the dead and for new life in the kingdom of heaven with all those who have been well-pleasing in thy sight. *(Addai and Mari*, Brightman, p. 287)[313]

In the liturgy of *Apostolic Constitutions VIII* the prayer is that the Holy Spirit may show (ἀποφήνῃ) the bread and wine to be the body and blood of Christ in order that the communicants may receive certain benefits:

. . . that thou wilt send down thy Holy Spirit, the witness of the sufferings of the Lord Jesus, upon this sacrifice, that He may show this bread to be the body of thy Christ and this cup the blood of thy Christ, that all who receive of it may . . .
(Brightman, p. 21)

This remained the typical style of Eastern epiclesis, with the insertion in some cases of *upon us* as in the Byzantine anaphora of *St Chrysostom*:

. . . and we beseech thee to send down thy Holy Spirit *upon us* and upon these gifts lying before Thee and make (ποίησον) this bread the precious body of thy Christ and that which is in this cup the precious blood of thy Christ, changing (μεταβαλών) them by thy Holy Spirit, that they may be to those who receive them for . . . (Brightman, pp. 386f)[314]

In some Eastern liturgies the elements are said to be *filled* with Holy Spirit, and the communion gives the Holy Spirit to the participants. Thus in the institution narratives of the Greek *St James* and of the Alexandrian *St Mark* Christ is said to have filled the cup with Holy Spirit:

Likewise also the cup after supper he took and mixed with wine and water, and, looking up to heaven to thee his own Father and our God and the God of all, He gave thanks [over it], blessed and hallowed it and filled it with Holy Spirit and distributed it to his holy and blessed disciples and apostles, saying . . .

(Alexandrian St Mark, Brightman, p. 133)[315]

In the final part of some prayers of epiclesis 'the communion of the Holy Spirit' is listed among the desired benefits of participation in the sacrament: so, for example, in the Byzantine anaphoras of *St Basil* and *St Chrysostom* (Brightman, pp. 330, 387); compare also the liturgy of *Apostolic Constitutions VIII* (Brightman, p. 21, line 11), and the Ethiopian Anaphora of the Apostles (Brightman, p. 233, lines 20f, 26). Theodore of Mopsuestia explains the priest's cry of 'Holy things for the holy people' at the elevation by saying that 'holy and immortal is this food which is the body and blood of our Lord, and full of holiness, because the Holy Spirit has come down upon it' (*Hom.*, XVI, 22, edd. Tonneau and Devreesse, p. 565). In the Byzantine rite the Holy Spirit is associated with the commixture and with the addition of warm water, the 'zeon', to the cup before communion.[316]

It would be tedious to cite from the many Greek and Syrian authors who, particularly from the later fourth century onwards, assign a prominent role in the eucharist to the Holy Spirit.[317] The Western theologians ascribed, increasingly so, a less prominent role to the Holy Spirit, but never quite quenched Him in total oblivion. From earlier days one may cite Ambrose:

Every time you drink, you receive the remission of sins and are inebriated by the Spirit. That is why the apostle says: *Do not get drunk with wine, but be filled with the Spirit* [Eph. 5:18]. For he who gets drunk with wine totters and reels; he who gets drunk with the Spirit is rooted in Christ. So it is an excellent drunkenness that produces sobriety of mind;   (*De sacramentis* V, 3, 17, ed. Botte, p. 128)

and Augustine:

We eat what has been taken from the fruits of the earth and consecrated by a mystical prayer (*prece mystica consecratum*). . . . That which is brought by the hands of men to the point of being the visible species is not sanctified to be such a great sacrament except by the invisible working of the Spirit of God . . .

(*De trin.* III, 4, 10, PL 42, 874)

Later some Gallican and Mozarabic masses contain petitions for the descent of the Spirit to sanctify the elements or to change them into the body and blood of Christ with a view to profiting the communicants, while in the *Missale Gothicum* the *post-secreta* of the *Missa dominicalis V* reads:

. . . beseeching that thou wouldest deign to pour thy Holy Spirit into us who eat and drink the things that confer eternal life and the everlasting kingdom.

(ed. Bannister, no. 527)

*     *     *

As with the Word, so with the Spirit. The divine Person who is active in creation, in renewal, and in human rebirth and resurrection, is also active in the eucharist. To us is given in the eucharist *the Holy Spirit of promise who is the first instalment of our inheritance* (Eph. 1:14).

Having seen that the re-creative agents of the Word and the Spirit are held to be active in the eucharist, we should now look more precisely at the ways in which (first) the eucharistic elements and (second) the eucharistic community are, by the Word and the Spirit, set in relation to the final kingdom. But since the topic of the eucharistic elements has been a particularly thorny one between Catholics and Protestants as well as within Protestantism, I shall prepare the way for our discussion by a few remarks on the relation between the eucharist and an attribute or quality which is ascribed to the whole Godhead, namely the divine *glory*. I hope that the following pages may shed an incidental ray of relatively fresh light on the age-old question of the mode of the divine presence at the eucharist.

### 3. The divine glory

In the Bible[318] glory is, in its theological sense, first and foremost a permanent attribute of God (Isa. 48:11; 59:19; John 17:5, 24) and is, in God's dealings with men from Old Testament days, the visible mark of His revealed presence (Exod. 16:7, 10; 24:16f; Lev. 9:6, 23; Num. 14:10; 16:19; 20:6; I Kings 8:10f; II Chron. 7:1–3; Ps. 145:11f; Isa. 60:1–3; Ezek. 3:23; 8:4; 9:3; 10:18f; 11:23; 43:2–5; 44:4). In Isaiah's vision, which is particularly interesting to us because of the place that Isa. 6:2f found in the church's eucharistic prayers,[319] the seraphim cry to one another: 'Holy, holy, holy is the Lord of hosts; *the whole earth is full of his glory*.' Second Isaiah expected a universal revelation of the divine glory: 'And the glory of the Lord shall be revealed, and all flesh shall see it together' (Isa. 40:5). In the New Testament Jesus Christ manifested the divine glory to men (Luke 2:32; 9:32; John 1:14), but not yet in a permanent and universal manifestation. According to John, Jesus declared at the Last Supper that He had communicated the divine glory to the disciples (John 17:22);[320] and according to Paul, Christians are already, since they behold or reflect ($\kappa\alpha\tau o\pi\rho\iota\zeta\acute{o}\mu\epsilon\nu o\iota$) the glory of the Lord, being changed into His likeness from glory into glory (II Cor. 3:18). But our divinely derived glory will not be *revealed* until Christ returns with glory and our bodies are raised to be like His glorious body (Rom. 8:17–25; I Cor. 15:42–44; II Cor. 4:16–18; Col. 3:3f; Phil. 3:20f; I Pet. 4:13f, cf. 5:4; I John 3:2) and we enter God's final kingdom and glory (I Thess. 2:12), which the Book of Revelation pictures as the heavenly Jerusalem filled with glory (21:11, 23; cf. 22:5). When men have felt[321] the divine glory among them, then even in this world they have *glorified* God (Luke 2:20); and the use of the verb $\delta o\xi\acute{a}\zeta\epsilon\iota\nu$ for the worship already rendered to God by angels and men points forward to the fact that the life of the final kingdom will be a continual rendering to God of the glory which He will continually bestow. Not only will all God's saints bless Him, but all His works will give Him thanks (Ps. 145:10–13): and in this way the whole creation will share in the liberty of the glory of the children of God (Rom. 8:17–23), a glory that is derived from God and rendered to Him in that service which is perfect freedom. It is on account of this circulation of divine glory that it may be said that 'God will be all in all' in a sense that maintains the distinctness of the transcendent God from His creation and yet will allow the whole of that creation to enjoy the divine life in so far as it is communicable.

The liturgies make disappointingly little use of the notion of glory. God is 'glorified' at the time of the *Sanctus* (in which, for a moment at any rate, the church joins in the unceasing worship of heaven), and also in the doxologies which conclude the great eucharistic prayer and other prayers; but there is not much explicit recognition of the fact that it is only as we receive the glory of God that we are able to render Him glory. We note, however, that the epiclesis of the eucharistic prayer of *Apostolic Tradition*, whatever difficulties it presents in the way of detailed interpretation, clearly prays for the sending of the Holy Spirit upon or into the oblation so that it may be to the communicants *in repletionem spiritus sancti*, and this '*in order that we may praise and glorify thee through thy child Jesus Christ through whom be to thee glory and honour* (*ut te laudemus et glorificemus* . . .)'. When we recall the part played by the Spirit in the communication of divine glory according to II Cor. 3, then this text from *Apostolic Tradition* and a few later texts which I am about to cite suggest how a theology might be elaborated of the eucharist as the sacramental anticipation of a universe totally transfigured by the glory of God, receiving glory from Him and rendering glory to Him. The epiclesis in the Greek liturgy of *St James* prays that the Holy Spirit may come upon the gifts with 'his holy and good and *glorious* presence' to hallow them and (the prayer now continues with a notion that was not expressed in the epiclesis of *Apostolic Tradition* or in that of *Addai and Mari*, our two earliest instances) to make them the body and blood of Christ; and then after communion there is the following hymn of dismissal:

*From glory to glory advancing* we hymn Thee, the Saviour of our souls. *Glory be to the Father and to the Son and to the Holy Ghost, Now and ever and unto the ages.*[322]

In the eucharistic prayer of the Dêr-Balizeh papyrus both 'full' and 'glory' are taken as cue-words to lead from the *Sanctus* into that 'first epiclesis' which is characteristic of Alexandrian anaphoras and which may well be more native to the Egyptian rite than the Syrian-style second epiclesis which follows the institution narrative in *St Mark*:[323]

'Holy, holy, holy, Lord of hosts. The heaven and the earth are full of thy glory.' Fill us also with the glory that is from thee ($\pi\lambda\dot{\eta}\rho\omega\sigma o\nu$ $\kappa a\dot{\iota}$ $\dot{\eta}\mu\hat{a}s$ $\tau\hat{\eta}s$ $\pi a\rho\dot{a}$ $\sigma o\hat{v}$ $\delta\dot{o}\xi\eta s$), and deign to send down thy Holy Spirit upon these creatures and make the bread the body [of the Lord] etc. (edd. Roberts and Capelle, p. 24)[324]

In the present text of *St Mark* the anaphora reads at that point:

'Holy, holy, holy, Lord of hosts. The heaven and the earth are full of thy holy glory.' For full, in very truth, is the heaven and the earth of thy holy glory through the manifestation (ἐπιφάνεια) of our Lord and God and Saviour Jesus Christ. Fill also, O God, this sacrifice with the blessing which is from thee (τῆς παρὰ σοῦ εὐλογίας) through the descent of thy holy Spirit. For our Lord ... [and the prayer goes on to recite the institution narrative];   (Brightman, p. 132)

and the second epiclesis calls for the Holy Spirit to make the bread and the cup the body and blood of Christ 'that they may be to all who partake of them ... for (εἰς) a share in the bliss of eternal life and immortality, for the *glorifying* of thy all-holy name (εἰς δοξολογίαν τοῦ παναγίου σου ὀνόματος), &c.' (Brightman, p. 134). The final blessing in the liturgy of *Addai and Mari* includes these words: 'May the Lord make our people *glorious*, which have come and had delight in the power of his *glorious* and holy and life-giving and divine mysteries' (Brightman, p. 304).

The hints in the traditional liturgies are scarce, but it would seem possible to consider the eucharist as a provisional instance of that glorification of men and nature by God which will mark the new heavens and the new earth, and as the anticipation of that glorification of God by men and all creation which will be the final and complete acknowledgement of His universal kingdom. The eucharist is no more than provisional and anticipatory because God's glory is not yet *visibly* perceived, received and reflected by men and nature—whereas it is of the order of glory to be *seen*; and because men and nature do not yet render God the perfect homage that is His due. The eucharist bears, moreover, the mark of incompleteness in that it is as yet only *part* of mankind and of creation that receives and renders God's glory, and that *not perpetually*. But within these limits the eucharist is a real expression of the divine kingdom, and an expression which contains within itself its own dynamism as the glory strives to become visible and to embrace the whole of nature and humanity. Let us now look more closely at the way in which (first) the eucharistic bread and wine and (second) the eucharistic community are set by the Word and the Spirit into relation to the transfigured creation and the worshipping community of God's final kingdom.

## 4. The bread, the wine and the transfigured creation

It is fairly fashionable among Roman Catholic theologians to bring the consecration of the eucharistic bread and wine into relation with the notion of a transfigured creation; but they do so with only a vague awareness, if indeed they are conscious of it at all, of the problem that is thereby posed for them in connection with their *de fide* doctrine of transubstantiation.[325] If they pursued strictly and consistently the relation they establish between the consecrated elements and the transfigured creation, then they would find themselves in the presence of undesirable results at one end or the other of the relation. For many of them point to the consecrated ele-

ments as a first instance of the transformed creation. Now if one starts
from the eucharistic consecration understood as transubstantiation of the
bread and wine into the body and blood of Christ, then by a simple prolongation of the lines one arrives at a notion of the transfigured final
creation as 'substantially' Christ, with the new heavens and the new earth
as 'accidents'; but this is hard to distinguish from pantheism or from the
total absorption of all things into the Divine.[326] On the other hand, if one
starts with the vision of a transfigured creation in which Christ feeds with
His people at His own table on the abundant fruits of the new earth, then
in coming to the eucharist one arrives at a view of Christ feeding His
people at the holy table on (consecrated) bread and wine; but there is no
transubstantiation of the bread and wine into His body and blood.[327]
A couple of examples will suffice to show how unguardedly Roman
Catholics can write who see the eucharistic consecration as a first instance
of the transfigured creation of the End. (To avoid the risk of misrepresentation in a delicate matter, the texts are here left in their original language.)

We turn first to H. M. Féret: 'Le Christ que nous rejoignons dans le
mystère eucharistique et que nous possédons avec sa gloire et avec sa
puissance dans le mystère eucharistique, c'est le Christ glorieux assumant
la création matérielle tout entière, par la matière même du sacrifice
eucharistique qui ne subsiste plus, selon la doctrine de la transsubstantiation telle qu'elle a été définie au Concile de Trente, que dans la substance
de l'humanité glorieuse du Christ assumant ainsi, par sa charité, toute
l'Eglise et toute la création'; and again: 'Du seul fait de la transsubstantiation, cet univers matériel, partout où il y a une hostie ou un calice con-
sacrés, apparaît comme tout rempli de la présence de Jésus-Christ, non
pas d'une présence quelconque et indéfinissable, mais de sa présence personnelle, corporelle même, de Seigneur ressuscité et glorieux, de Seigneur
attirant désormais irrésistiblement dans la gloire de son Père toute la
création polarisée vers lui.'[328] The other example is taken from P. de Haes:
'Die consecratorische kracht van de glorie breekt door in onze wereld in
elke consecratie van de Heilige Mis. Eens zal heel de wereld en al het
geschapene vervuld zijn van God die alles in alles zal zijn. Deze uiteinde-
lijke nieuwe hemel en nieuwe aarde wordt reeds nu ingezet en aangekon-
digd, geanticipeerd en in onderpand geschonken in de eucharistische
tegenwoordigheid. Onze aarde wordt in de aardse onverheerlijkte werkelijkheid van brood en wijn door de consecratie betrokken in de uiteinde-
lijke verheerlijking van de verrezen Heer.'[329]

Many Protestants will consider that if Roman Catholic theologians find
themselves, within the terms of their own theology, impaled on the horns
of a dilemma when they view the consecration of the eucharistic elements
as a first instance of the final transfiguration of creation, then that dilemma
is in fact a false one in so far as it is due to the mistaken doctrine of transubstantiation. Especially a Protestant who wishes to hold in no form
whatever a doctrine of 'the *real* presence' (that is, a doctrine in which
Christ's presence at the eucharist is in some way associated with the *things*

bread and wine) may be inclined, if once his eyes are opened to the eschatological prospect, to say that the eucharist is rightly, and *adequately*, set into relation with the final kingdom if it is viewed as an (anticipatory) feeding *with* Christ, at His table, on the fruits of the new creation. This view would undoubtedly be true to a strong, indeed the strongest, strand in biblical and dominical teaching on the relation between the eucharist and the final messianic feasting; for not only does it stand in line with the Old Testament notions of eating and drinking in the presence of the Lord and of being fed at the Lord's hand (see pp. 19–21), but also it stands in line with Jesus's meal activity throughout His earthly ministry, and with the eschatological prospect He opened up at the Last Supper (Mark 14:25; Matt. 26:29; Luke 22:15–18, 29f).[330] But it does not seem to do justice to the theme of John 6 and its imagery of *feeding on Christ*. To feed *with* Christ, though undoubtedly an experience of profound joy, is not so intimate a relationship as that which can be described as feeding *on* Christ. If the Christian life, now and for ever, is a feeding on Christ, then the Lord's supper, as the celebration in which Christians *eat* and *drink*, must play *some* role in that feeding on Christ. It is beyond the bounds of credulity that in the Fourth Gospel at any rate (for it must be admitted that John 6 is the only part of the New Testament to speak directly of feeding *on* Christ if we eschew what would be precisely a question-begging appeal to the institution narratives or to I Cor. 10:16–17), there should be *no* connection intended between eating and drinking the eucharistic bread and wine and feeding on Christ.[331] The eschatological perspective may help us to see what view to take of that connection.

Now three things may be said about life in the final kingdom, and, expressed in christological terms, these are they. First, it will be *life in Christ*; for already Christians live 'in Christ' (as is Paul's constant theme), and all things will be summed up 'in Christ' (Eph. 1:10). Second, it will be *life with Christ*; for it will follow the pattern set by the Lord's earthly ministry and the promise He made to the thief on the cross, 'Today you will be with me in Paradise' (see also Phil. 1:23). Third, it will be *Christ living in us*; for it will be a continuation, in an enhanced form no doubt, of the truth which Paul expressed by saying 'It is no longer I who live, but Christ who lives in me' (Gal. 2:20),[332] and which the Fourth Gospel expresses by talk of the divine indwelling ($\mu\acute{\epsilon}\nu\epsilon\iota\nu$) in the believer (John 14–17).[333]

In more general theological terms, these three things correspond respectively to the divine *transcendence* which encompasses all created things, the *distinction* between God and His creature, and the *immanence* of God in all His creation; and in the eschatological condition creation's enjoyment of this threefold fact will be so perfect that the life of the definitive kingdom may be described as the unimpeded circulation of the divine glory (see pp. 102f). In terms of the imagery of the meal, the best single picture to express this final condition is that of feasting in fellowship with Christ, at His table, on the fruits of the creation which has been transfigured through His agency as the mighty Word; for this suggests both the transcendence of the giver on whom all life depends and also an intimate communion with the Godhead ('table-fellowship') which yet respects the distinction between Creator and creature—and there is no doubt that this is the predominant way in which Jesus used meal-signs and meal-parables throughout His ministry, and that it accords with the eschatological prospect opened up by Jesus at the Last Supper.[334] But it stops short of doing full justice to the Johannine imagery of feeding *on* Christ and to the Pauline saying about Christ living *in* me. For this reason it becomes necessary, at the cost of confusing the imagery (for one cannot simultaneously 'picture' Christ as giver and as gift), to admit that Christ is not only the host at the banquet and a table-fellow but also the food: and the confusion of the imagery serves in fact as a salutary reminder that it is a divine mystery how God can give Himself to His creature and yet remain 'outside' as the giver, how God can be 'known' by men and yet remain the unfathomable abyss.[335] If this will remain a mystery in the final kingdom, then so must the meal which the Lord has given us as a *sign* of the kingdom also be characterized by the same mystery.

Theological discussion of the eucharist will never therefore issue in a complete explanation of how Christ may be present as both host and food. But since we are creatures endowed with reason and speech and our worship is in that sense 'logical', we are bound to commit ourselves to some kind of verbal formulations in theology and in the liturgy: and I think the following four considerations may be mentioned for guidance in talk (whether in theology or at the eucharist itself) about the presence of Christ at the meal which is the sign of the kingdom.

(a) God's transcendence is theologically prior to His immanence, for God is prior to His creation.[336] Where, therefore, within theological discourse and liturgical use, the simultaneous employment of two images each of which expresses a truth gives rise to a pictorial incompatibility (as is the case with Christ as host and Christ as food), then we should allow the one to predominate which better safeguards the *transcendence* of God. This means, in the case of the eucharist, giving more prominence to Christ as the *giver* of the banquet; and the feature of intimate communion with the Godhead (which is what the image of Christ as *food* expresses) is not altogether lost because, first, there is a 'personalist' sense in which the giver is 'in' His gift[337] and, second, faithful eating and drinking *in company with Christ* certainly involves being transformed by His presence. It is not unimportant that the weight of the Bible's usage, in both Old and New Testaments, of the imagery of feeding and of the meal should fall in favour of God as the transcendent giver who 'feeds' His people, and of a fellowship between man and God in which the distinction between them is clearly maintained (as when Israel eats 'before the Lord' and when Jesus eats *with* men both in His earthly ministry and, according to the sayings opening up the eschatological prospect at the Last Supper, in the final kingdom).

(b) We should therefore in particular avoid any doctrine of the eucharistic *elements* of bread and wine which threatens to give more prominence to Christ as food than to Christ as host and table-fellow. In his study *L'Eucaristia vista da un esegeta* (1951), L. Tondelli made a bold bid to revive in the awareness of Roman Catholic theologians the notion, which though recognized as orthodox had very much been lost sight of, that Christ is host and table-companion at the eucharistic feast. I can suggest the reason why this notion had been neglected and why such attempts as Tondelli's fail to make much impact on Catholics: the reason is that a doctrine of transubstantiation (which was not, of course, rejected by Tondelli himself) which places such stress on the fact that the whole Christ (*Christus totus et integer*) is present as the 'substance' of the elements of bread and wine makes it psychologically (though the theologians may find ways of getting round the problem, as I am aware)[338] impossible to give much place to the thought of Christ as the host and a table-fellow; yet that is what He most obviously was at the Last Supper which, as Catholics are wont to say,[339] was 'the first mass'.[340]

(c) A greater stress than is customary in the West on the role of the Holy Spirit in the eucharist might have two main benefits:

(i) It should lessen the danger of confining Christ's presence to the elements. We observe that in the oldest extant invocations of the Holy Spirit upon the bread and wine, those of *Apostolic Tradition* and of *Addai and Mari*, it is not *stated* (though we may admit that their framers believed in some kind of identification between the consecrated elements and the body and blood of Christ) that the purpose of the coming of the Holy Spirit was to make the bread and wine the body and blood of Christ; rather the thought moves directly to the eschatologically oriented effects on the communicants:

. . . that we all may be filled with the Holy Spirit . . . that we may praise and glorify thee . . . (*Apostolic Tradition*)

. . . and bless it and hallow it that it be to us . . . for the great hope of resurrection from the dead and for new life in the kingdom of heaven with all those who have been well-pleasing in thy sight. (*Addai and Mari*)[341]

Even when in later examples of the epiclesis the transformation of the elements into the body and blood of Christ is mentioned, the thought does not rest there but moves to the desired effects upon the communicants: and the Byzantine tradition inserts right at the start of the invocation the telling phrase: 'Send down thy Holy Spirit *upon us* and upon these gifts . . .', thereby making clear that the divine presence embraces the whole eucharistic event, both the assembled community and the food which it is gathered to eat.[342]

(ii) The Holy Spirit is the Person who, as it were, 'applies' Christ to the Christian and to the church; or we may say that it is 'in the Holy Spirit' that Christ comes to the church. But if the material means of the spoken and heard word, the printed and read word, and the water poured in baptism, are claimed and used by the Holy Spirit to 'apply Christ' or, to use the other form of expression, are claimed and used by Christ to come to His people 'in the Holy Spirit', then we may wonder why the bread and wine eaten and drunk in the eucharist may not be seen in the same kind of way, without recourse to the numerical identification of the elements with Christ. The difference between the eucharist and the others would not be a difference in kind, but a difference perhaps in degree; for through the sacrament of eating and drinking, Christ may enter into the very marrow of our being, and it may be here that we experience 'His *closest* love' as the Wesleys put it.[343] Provided, for such a proviso is demanded by the whole doctrine of the value of matter as created by God and as the theatre and medium of God's dealings with men: [344] provided we may take Calvin as a 'real instrumentalist' and not as a 'mere parallelist',[345] then (I think) there is much to be learnt from Calvin's refusal to enter the thick of the purely christological fray on the modalities of the real presence, and from his stress on the Holy Spirit as the 'link' between Christ and the church.

(d) But what of the words of Christ as He delivered the bread and the cup to the disciples at the institution of the eucharist? Two broad tendencies are apparent in modern exegesis. The one takes $\sigma\hat{\omega}\mu a$ (or $\sigma\acute{a}\rho\xi$)[346] and $a\hat{\iota}\mu a$ as a correlative pair referring directly to the person of Jesus ($\sigma\hat{\omega}\mu a/\sigma\acute{a}\rho\xi$ being the person in His external presentation, $a\hat{\iota}\mu a$ being the person's 'vital principle'), often with the thought that the two terms together suggest Jesus as given in sacrifice.[347] The other tendency is to stress the word spoken at the delivery of the bread ('This is my body') as indicating that the bread is the sign of Christ's *presence* (His body in that sense)—whereas the word at the cup (and here the Pauline and Lucan form is obviously preferred: 'This cup is the new covenant . . .') is taken as the sign of the new *covenant* (which was, of course, grounded in Christ's blood).[348] Neither of these tendencies, as such, says anything about the nature of the relationship established by Jesus between the bread (and wine) and His own person, and the field is left open for everything between the most crudely realistic and the most anaemically merely-symbolic interpretation.

My own opinion is that the clue lies in a Hebraic notion which Israel probably never defined but to which modern Old Testament scholars have given the name: *extension of personality*.[349] A person's words or his messenger or his servant, for instance, are his own 'extended personality' in that they serve his purpose and effect his will, though clearly there remains also a distinction between the person and such extensions. In accounts of Old Testament 'theophanies' there is often an oscillation which makes us (that is, Western Europeans) unsure as to whether it is the Lord or His angel who has appeared.[350] Within this conceptual pattern the eucharistic elements both *are* and *are not* Christ Himself.[351] That this is the Semitic Christian understanding of the relationship between Christ and the eucharistic bread and wine is suggested by Narsai's comments in expounding the great prayer:

> Our Lord Jesus departed from us to the place above, that at his coming he might lift us up with him to the kingdom of the height, and because he went away to a place that is far from our ken, he was pleased to comfort us by his Body and his Blood until his coming. And because it is not possible that he should give his Body and his Blood to his church, he commanded us to perform this mystery with bread and wine. Happy is the people of the Christians! What does it (not) possess, and what hope is there (not) in keeping for it on high without end?
>
> (*Hom.* XVII, ed. Connolly, p. 16)

And Narsai goes on to ascribe the possibility of this identity/non-identity to the working of the Holy Spirit, putting these words into Christ's mouth in his account of the institution of the sacrament:

> Be ye offering bread and wine, as I have taught you, and I will accomplish and make them the Body and Blood. Body and Blood do I make the bread and wine through the brooding and operation of the Holy Spirit.   (*ibid.*, p. 17)

I would only add that by thus serving perfectly the Lord's purpose and completely effecting His will, the bread and the wine become the first-fruits of that renewed creation which will be so entirely submitted to the divine lordship that it will enjoy total penetration by the divine glory while yet remaining distinct from the transcendent God it worships.[352]

There we may leave for the moment our consideration of the relation in which the eucharistic bread and wine are set to the final kingdom, and turn now to look at the way in which the Word and the Spirit put the *eucharistic community* in relation to that kingdom.

## 5. The eucharistic assembly and the company of heaven

### (a) *The causal connection*

God's goal for men is participation in the heavenly kingdom; and in many of the liturgical texts which have been quoted during the course of our study, prayer is made that the benefits of communion may extend as far as participation in the heavenly kingdom.[353] This is clearly in accord with the outlook of the discourse in John 6:

> Truly, truly, I say to you, unless you eat the flesh of the Son of man and drink his blood, you have no life in you; he who eats my flesh and drinks my blood has eternal life, and I will raise him up at the last day. For my flesh is food indeed, and my blood is drink indeed. He who eats my flesh and drinks my blood abides in me, and I in him. As the living Father sent me, and I live because of the Father, so he who eats me will live because of me. This is the bread which came down from heaven, not such as the fathers ate and died; he who eats this bread will live for ever.   (vv. 53–58)

If we now try to define more precisely this *causal relation* between eucharistic communion and participation in the kingdom of God (or eternal life, in Johannine terms), our discussion stands under the rubric of this

Johannine text and two essential principles expressed in it: first, eternal life or participation in the kingdom is to be understood in personalistic terms as the gift given *by Jesus Christ*; and second, there are two stages in men's enjoyment of the kingdom, in the sense that Christians *already* have eternal life (John 6:54a, 56) and yet *still await* the resurrection (v. 54b) and the life beyond ($\zeta\acute{\eta}\sigma\epsilon\iota$ ($\epsilon\grave{\iota}s$ $\tau\grave{o}\nu$ $\alpha\grave{\iota}\hat{\omega}\nu\alpha$), vv. 57, 58b).

The liturgies by their images, and the theologians by their elaboration of such images, suggest various ways of understanding how eucharistic communion effects the Christian's participation in the divine kingdom which is both present and still to come. One may detect five main approaches:[354]

(i) As food sustains life at the purely natural level, so also the sacramental food of the eucharist is our *food for eternal life*. This theme is found, for instance, in Western post-communion prayers, where it is expressed with an admirable simplicity and concision. So, for instance:

Fed, O Lord, by the heavenly bread, may we be nourished, we pray, unto eternal life; (*Missale Romanum*, May 6)[355]

... that by the same sacrament with which thou dost strengthen us in time, thou mayest make us partakers of everlasting life; (Leonine Sacramentary)[356]

May it be to us, we pray, O Lord, a holy food and the cup of salvation, which both fortifies our temporal life and procures us eternal life.

(Gelasian Sacramentary, Sexagesima)[357]

Among the Wesleys' *Hymns on the Lord's Supper* we note the following example:

*Author of life divine,*
  *Who hast a table spread,*
*Furnished with mystic wine*
  *And everlasting bread,*
*Preserve the life Thyself hast given,*
*And feed and train us up for heaven.* (Hymn No. 40)

An advantage of this approach is that it may express continuity and growth in the eternal life which Christ already gives and which will be perfected in heaven; but it leaves out of account the element of rupture that is represented by human death and by the expected resurrection and judgement at the parousia of Christ.

(ii) Another theme that occurs in Western post-communion prayers is the *medicinal*. Sometimes the words *medela* or *medicina* are used, but far the most frequent expression is *remedium*. Communion cures from sin and restores to health and eternal life. So, for instance:

By thy sanctifying gifts, O almighty God, may our evil inclinations be cured, and may eternal remedies be supplied to us.

(*Missale Romanum*, Ember Saturday in Lent; Tuesday in Holy Week; 17th Sunday after Pentecost)[358]

. . . grant, we pray, that they may provide remedies for us both for our temporal life and for eternal life. (*Missale Romanum*, 28 January, 8 September)[359]

. . . make them be for us both a present remedy and a future.
(*Missale Romanum*, Ember Saturday in Advent)[360]

What we have taken with our mouth, O Lord, may we receive with a pure heart, and from being a temporal gift may it become to us an everlasting remedy.
(*Missale Romanum*, after communion, in the ordinary of the mass)[361]

In the East, Gregory of Nyssa and Cyril of Alexandria develop the medical imagery in a massive way. They see the consecrated elements as the anti-dote to the poison of sin and as the cure of man's corruptibility, man's body being transformed by them into Christ's immortal body. Thus Gregory of Nyssa, for instance:

Those who have been tricked into taking poison counteract its destructive influence with another drug, but the antidote must, like the poison, enter right into a man's entrails for the effect of the remedy to spread through the whole body; so also we who had tasted of that which rots our nature needed that which would undo the decomposition, an antidote (ἀλεξιτήριον) that would enter into us and remove by counteraction the harmful effects of the poison that our body had taken in. What is then this antidote? Nothing other than that body which was shown to be stronger than death and became a source of life for us. Just as a little leaven, as the apostle says, assimilates the whole lump to itself, so also the body which was immortalized by God [*reading* ἀθανατισθέν], once it has entered into our body, changes and translates it totally into itself (ὅλον πρὸς ἑαυτὸ μεταποιεῖ καὶ μετατίθησιν). Just as the addition of a destructive agent to a healthy body reduces it to uselessness, so also the immortal body, once it has entered the man who receives it, changes him totally into its own nature (πρὸς τὴν ἑαυτοῦ φύσιν καὶ τὸ πᾶν μετεποίησεν).[362]

To indicate that the presence of Christ in the communicant's body has already begun its transforming work (though it will not complete its work until the resurrection), Cyril of Alexandria also likens the body received in communion to a 'seed' or 'germ'.[363] We may approve both the seriousness with which this view takes sin, and also the stress on the transformation of the communicant which begins already now but will be completed only through the resurrection; but we must consider the dwelling on medical details grotesque, and the talk of the communicant's being *changed into Christ* dangerous.

(iii) Some post-Tridentine and more recent Roman theologians have tended to look on communion as a merely indirect cause of future glory. In that it provides grace for use to conquer sin and to persevere in good works, the eucharist helps the Christian in the working out of his final salvation. This may perhaps be welcomed as a corrective to the dangers of 'automatism' involved in the use of biological (alimentary and medical) images;[364] but it can hardly be said to do full justice even to the image with which it is often associated and which is so frequent in Latin post-communion prayers, namely that of communion as the *pignus* of eternal life or future glory—let alone to the fact that in communion it is the *glorious Christ* who is received and who begins and continues His transforming work.[365]

(iv) M. Schmaus has developed this last idea in an attractive essay in which he sees eucharistic communion chiefly in terms of a personal encounter with the risen and glorious Christ.[366] Christ's resurrection is the exemplar of the general resurrection and of the final transformation of all creation which He Himself will effect; and already the glorious Christ, in whose person the end is even now present, comes to meet His people, to draw into closer union with Himself those who will freely allow Him to do so and gradually transform them into His own likeness. Eucharistic communion is the privileged place of this encounter with Christ; for as in ordinary human relations bodily proximity has value as *Ausdruckgestalt und Intensivierungsmedium der Begegnung*, similarly in the eucharist '[bietet] die Kommunion, d.h. die Aufnahme des sakramental gegenwärtigen Leibes und Blutes Christi, besondere Chancen für die Christusbegegnung' (p. 274). Schmaus's general approach is strongly reminiscent of Theodore of Mopsuestia (see our p. 73), and also of a passage in Narsai which is particularly valuable for the way in which it stresses the active faith and hope which must reach out to the promise of final renewal for the whole man that Christ freely gives, and begins to fulfil, through communion. I will quote the passage from Narsai extensively because it is interesting also in view of a further point which will be raised later:

They [the communicants] hold it sure that the Body of the King dwells in the visible bread; and in it the resurrection of the dead is preached to him that eats of it. . . . Let us honour them [the bread and wine] as the Body and Blood of the King; that they may conduct us even unto the glorious things that are in the Kingdom. Let us believe that they are able to give life to our mortality; and let us stretch forth our mind to the expectation of the hope that is in them. With the hidden mind let us look in a hidden manner on the visible things; and let us not doubt concerning the renovation that is (wrought) in the things that are manifest. Let the beholder not look upon the bread, nor yet upon the wine, but upon the Power that consecrates the bread and the wine. The bread and the wine are set as a sign before the eyes of the body, that it may take part with the mind in those things that are not apparent. The body cannot with the mind see hidden things, nor can it, like the thoughts, discern things secret. On its account the Gift was given by means of bread, that by outward things it might gain hope toward things hidden. To it and to the soul was promised the enjoyment that is hidden in the mystery; and for its comfort were the manifest things of food and drink. Lo, by visible things it is accustomed to be comforted from its grief; and, that He might not grieve it, its Lord comforted it with the bread and wine. With bread and wine He prepared for it a mark towards the things to come, that it might be aiming at the renovation that is prepared for it.[367]

(v) We noted Gregory of Nyssa's view that the eucharistic body of Christ transforms the individual communicant into its own nature. Leo the Great speaks similarly: 'For the effect of partaking of the body and blood of Christ is nothing other than that we are changed into what we receive (*non enim aliud agit participatio corporis et sanguinis Christi, quam ut in id quod sumimus transeamus*)'—and the pope immediately opens up the final eschatological prospect with a reference to Col. 3:4: 'For when Christ who is your life appears, then you also will appear with him in glory.'[368] Augustine gives an ecclesiological twist to the notion of our being changed into Christ's body through the eucharist, declaring that the effect of eating the (eucharistic) body of Christ is that we are turned into the (ecclesial) body of Christ:

For its effect . . . is unity, that having been made his body and having been made members of him, we may be what we receive (*simus quod accipimus*).
(*Serm.* 57, 7, PL 38, 389)[369]

The ecclesiological reference is no more than subjacent when Cyril of Jerusalem explains to the neophytes that their partaking of the eucharistic bread and wine makes them 'concorporal and consanguinary (σύσσωμοι καὶ σύναιμοι)' with Christ;[370] but Cyril of Alexandria takes the same step in the East as Augustine took in the West and brings out the churchly dimension. Writing on John 17:21 he says:

In order, then, that we ourselves also may come together and be blended into unity with God and with each other, although through the actual difference which exists in each one of us we have a distinct individuality of soul and body, the Only-begotten has contrived a means which his own due wisdom and the counsel of the Father have sought out. For by one body (that is, his own), blessing through the mystery of the Communion those who believe on him, he makes us of the same body (σύσσωμους) with himself and with each other. For who could sunder or divide from their natural union with one another those who are knit together through the one holy body into unity with Christ? For if we all partake of the one bread, we are all made one body; for Christ cannot suffer severance. Therefore also the church is become Christ's body, and we are also individually his members, according to the wisdom of Paul. For we, being all of us united to the one Christ through his holy body, inasmuch as we have received him who is one and indivisible into our own bodies, owe the service of our members to him rather than to ourselves.[371]

This approach by way of the image of the *body of Christ* we may certainly accept as a valuable expression of the truth that it is only as we are in Christ and Christ lives in us that we share in eternal life and shall be raised to share in it;[372] but the image is a dangerous one if it is not balanced by others, for it is easy to stress the *identity* between the body of Christ born of Mary, the eucharistic body of Christ, and the churchly body of Christ, in such a way that the *distinction* between them is lost sight of.[373]

\*        \*        \*

We have so far treated the way in which the *individual communicant* is effectively set in relation to the final kingdom, and the treatment of this theme is justified by John 6:51c–58; but the ecclesiological dimension introduced in point (v) leads us to a discussion of the way in which the whole eucharistic community is, by the Word and the Spirit, corporately set in relation to the kingdom, and here two themes need to be treated: first, the eucharist as *creative of the church's unity*; and second, the eucharist as *participation in the worship of heaven*.

## (b) The eucharist as creative of the church's unity

It is only recently, and Roman Catholic theologians have led the way, that Western theology has come to give prominence again to the theme, eclipsed in the West between the period of high scholasticism and our own century, of the eucharist as *constructive of the church, and particularly of its unity*.[374] The fundamental biblical text is clearly I Cor. 10:16f:

> [16]The cup of blessing which we bless is it not participation (κοινωνία) in the blood of Christ? The bread which we break is it not κοινωνία in the body of Christ? [17]Because there is one bread, we who are many are one body, for we all partake of the one bread.

The interpretation of these two verses is not without its problems, but it is inescapable that Paul here sees eucharistic communion as the source of churchly unity. Some writers have suggested that the eucharistic use of the word *body* is the source of Paul's designation of the church as the body of Christ—which would be a striking illustration indeed of the constitutive role of the sacrament in the life of the church.[375] However that may be, it seems clear that, whereas ecclesiological significance may have earlier been attached especially to common participation in the eucharistic *covenant-cup*,[376] Paul's mention of bread and cup in reverse order in I Cor. 10:16 is due to his own desire to put the stress rather on the element of *bread*, which, by virtue of the dominical word 'This is my body' attached to it, did, to say the least, accord well with the apostle's ecclesiological use of the term body.[377] It seems equally clear that κοινωνία is to be interpreted in the first place as *participation in the sacramental species* (rather than as simple fellowship of Christians one with another in the meal), for that is the sense demanded by Paul's argument against eating food sacrificed to idols which forms the context of our two verses, and it underlines the fact that it is the one Christ Himself, present through the sacramental token, who is the source of that unity among Christians which Paul mentions, rather as an aside, in verse 17.

Another Pauline text that probably speaks of the eucharistic communion as the source of the church's unity is I Cor. 12:12f:

> [12]For just as the body is one and has many members, and all the members of the body, though many, are one body, so it is with Christ. [13]For by one Spirit we were all baptized into one body—Jews or Greeks, slaves or free—*and all were made to drink of one Spirit*.

But though v. 13b is allowed, and in some cases preferentially or even absolutely given, a eucharistic interpretation by Clement of Alexandria, John Chrysostom, Augustine, Thomas Aquinas, Luther, Calvin and

Andreas Osiander ( +1617),[378] it is possible that the text refers rather to baptism. The aorist ἐποτίσθημεν would seem to tell against a eucharistic interpretation, but it may be taken as referring particularly to first communion. It seems likely, in any case, that the epiclesis in the Byzantine liturgy of *St Basil* contains a reminiscence of this text as well as of I Cor. 10:16f:

... and unite all of us who partake of the one bread and the cup to one another in the κοινωνία of the one Holy Spirit ... (Brightman, p. 330)

We have noticed how Cyril of Alexandria and Augustine saw eucharistic communion as the source of unity in one body. In the West the same theme is continued in post-communion prayers, such as the following:

Pour into us, O Lord, the Spirit of thy love, that those whom thou hast fed with the one heavenly bread, thou mayest in thy mercy make to be of one heart and mind. (*Missale Romanum*, Friday after Ash Wednesday)[379]

And for Thomas Aquinas the *res* of the eucharist, its effect, is the church's unity-in-love: 'corpus mysticum est res in eucharistia', 'res huius sacramenti est unitas corporis mystici'.[380] In the East Isidore of Pelusium ( +435) explains the name 'communion' in this way:

The reception of the divine mysteries is called communion (κοινωνία) because it unites us with Christ and makes us sharers (κοινωνούς) in his kingdom;
(*Epp.* I, 228, PG 78, 325)

and John Damascene, though losing the mention of the kingdom, makes it explicit that communion in Christ includes communion *with one another*:

It is called communion, and rightly so, because through it we have communion with Christ and participation in his flesh and in his divinity, and because through it we have communion and are united one with another; for since we partake of one loaf, we all become one body of Christ, and one blood, and members one of another, being made concorporal with Christ. (*De fid. orth.* IV, 13, PG 94, 1153)

I have drawn attention to eucharistic communion as *creative* of unity, and I shall make use of this idea later on (pp. 141–43); but in justice it must be pointed out that communion is also seen as *expressive* of (already existing) unity. This can be seen in the use made of the simile of the many grains of corn having been made into the one loaf, and the many grapes having gone into the wine of the eucharistic cup. If in Didache 9:4 this theme was used as a prayer for the gathering of the church into the final kingdom,[381] it was used by Augustine rather as an illustration of the existing unity of the eucharistic community, a unity which admittedly needed recalling to the mind of fractious church-members. Thus Augustine, though he certainly sees eucharistic communion as creative of unity (see p. 114), also sees the bread (made from many grains) and the wine (made from many grapes) which now stand on the altar as the *mysterium* of the one body which the communicants *have already been made by their baptism*; and on these grounds he summons them to behave peaceably and in love, or else they give the lie to the 'Amen' which they say in response to the words *Corpus Christi* as they receive communion.[382] The need for unity-in-love *before* taking part in the Lord's supper is already made plain by Paul in I Cor. 11, and the theme can be traced among the Fathers as they comment on the kiss of peace in the liturgy.[383] When, therefore, Roman Catholic theologians concisely say that the eucharist both *signifies* and *causes* churchly unity,[384] they are being faithful to the biblical and patristic teaching that communion both presupposes and strengthens the unity of the church. But we shall argue later that there are nevertheless circumstances in which the eucharist's *causative* role must predominate over its *significative*—unless, of course, we take the word 'sign' itself not in the sense of an expression of an existing reality but rather in the sense of a creative action which declares the *purpose* of God and begins to effect its fulfilment. . . .[385]

*(c) The eucharist as participation in the worship of heaven*

Here is a point at which the 'vertical' model of eschatology is clearly needed. Though the great doxologies at the end of the eucharistic prayers remind us that our worship of God will go on *per omnia saecula saeculorum*, νῦν καὶ ἀεὶ καὶ εἰς τοὺς αἰῶνας τῶν αἰώνων; and though Maximus the Confessor (who makes the whole of the liturgy from the great entrance onwards a *pre*figuration of the life of heaven) sees (i) the saying of the creed as *pre*figuring (προσημαίνει) the mystic gratitude which we shall express *in the future age* for our salvation, (ii) the *Sanctus* as intimating that our human nature will learn *in the future age* to celebrate and sanctify the Godhead in union with the incorporeal powers, and (iii) the saying of the Lord's prayer as the symbol of the real adoption by virtue of which all the saints *will* be called sons of God: yet the emphasis of the liturgical texts falls on the fact that at the focal point of the *Sanctus* at any rate, the earthly church actually and already participates in the worship of heaven. In one way or another, the liturgical texts make the eucharistic assembly repeat or join in the cry of the heavenly company: 'Holy, holy, holy, Lord God of hosts, heaven and earth are full of Thy glory!'[386] Three points may be mentioned in particular. First, the introductions to the *Sanctus* make clear that the worship offered by the heavenly company is *unceasing*;[387] whereas we are bound to admit that despite the fact that 'dignum et justum est, aequum et salutare, nos tibi semper et ubique gratias agere', the worship of the earthly church is *not uninterrupted*. Second, the addition made by the liturgical *Sanctus* to the text of Isa. 6:3: '*Heaven and* earth are full of thy glory', stresses *the all-embracing scope of the glory of God* which the church on earth can see only through the eyes of faith but which is pressing towards incontestable manifestation. Third, to the mention of the angelic creatures who offer heavenly worship the Greek liturgy of *St James* adds also the mention of *the earth and sky* and of *the souls of the saints*:

It is truly meet and right, fitting and due, to praise thee, to hymn thee, to bless thee, to worship thee, to glorify thee, to give thee thanks, who art the creator of all things visible and invisible . . . whom heaven and the heaven of heavens hymn, and all their power, the sun, the moon, and the whole choir of stars, earth and sea and all that in them is, Jerusalem the heavenly assembly, the church of the firstborn written in heaven, the spirits of just men and prophets, the souls of martyrs and apostles, angels, archangels, thrones, dominions, principalities, authorities and terrible powers, the many-eyed cherubim and the six-winged seraphim who with twain of their wings cover their faces, with twain cover their feet, and with twain flying cry the one to the other with unresting mouths and unsilenced doxologies the triumphal hymn to the majesty of thy glory, with clear voice singing, shouting, glorifying, crying aloud, and saying: Holy, holy, holy . . .
                                                    (Brightman, p. 50)[388]

We may notice another, rather different but by no means contradictory, approach to the relation between the eucharistic worship of the earthly church and the worship of heaven. Theodore of Mopsuestia sees the eucharist as the present earthly εἰκών and τύπος of the worship which our Precursor offered by His sacrificial death and continues to offer in heaven, and which we shall offer in the age to come. He comments thus on the *Sursum corda*:

The priest prepares the people by saying: Lift up your minds, to show that though it is on earth that we are supposed to perform this dreadful and ineffable liturgy, yet it is upwards, towards heaven, that we must look, and towards God that we must direct the intention of our soul, because we are making a memorial of the sacrifice and death of our Lord Christ, who for us suffered and rose again, was joined to the divine nature, is seated at the right hand of God and is in heaven. It is there that we too, therefore, must direct the gaze of our soul, and there that from this memorial we must transport our heart.
                             (Hom. XVI, 3; edd. Tonneau-Devreesse, pp. 539f)[389]

Not dissimilar is that theme in Western Catholic theology which sees in the mass the earthly church's offering of itself through Christ (or Christ's offering of the church through Himself) to the Father: and this theme, particularly when it is set in the eschatological perspective of the perfect and perpetual submission of the total community to the Father through the Son in the final kingdom, offers one less easily blasphemous way of understanding the traditionally sacrificial nature of the eucharist than to say that the church offers Christ.

For a final indication of the way in which earthly eucharistic worship is related to the worship of heaven we may turn to architecture. There is a monograph by A. Stange, *Das frühchristliche Kirchengebäude als Bild des Himmels* (1950).[390] Here I do no more than call attention, by way of example, to the Syrian style of basilica and its symbolic interpretation:

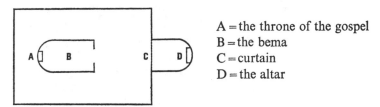

A = the throne of the gospel
B = the bema
C = curtain
D = the altar

The bema, which is the focal point for the first part of the liturgy (the service of the word), is considered to represent Jerusalem standing in the midst of the earth, while the apse, which is the scene of the eucharistic liturgy proper, represents heaven.[391] Narsai gives a twofold interpretation of the sanctuary which illustrates the way in which the resurrection and ascension of Christ open up the way for our resurrection and our entry into heaven; and it is in this place that the earthly church celebrates its eucharist:

> The sanctuary also forms a symbol of the Garden of Joseph, whence flowed life for men and angels. In another order it is a type of that Kingdom which our Lord entered, and into which He will bring with Him all His friends. The adorable altar thereof is a symbol of that throne of the Great and Glorious, upon which He will be seen of watchers and men in the day of His revelation. The apse typifies things below and above: it calls to mind the things that have been, and those that are to be it typifies spiritually.   (Hom. XVII, ed. Connolly, pp. 4f)

## 6. A threefold reflection

After the foregoing examination of the evidence of Bible, liturgies and theologians as to the positive ways in which the bread and the wine and the eucharistic assembly are illumined when set in the perspective of the trans-figured creation and the glorified and glorifying community which will characterize the final kingdom, I shall now conclude this chapter with a threefold reflection on the ways in which the eucharist nevertheless *falls short* of the final kingdom; but it will quickly become clear that this is by no means a negative note on which to end a chapter.

(a) The eucharist falls short of the final kingdom, first, from the point of view of *extension*. Of the whole of mankind it is only the church which celebrates and enjoys the eucharist; and of the whole earth it is only bread and wine, and not even all bread and all wine, which glorify God by serving the purpose of communicating abundant life to the depths of men's being. But this limitation is not to be understood in a negative sense. For it is in the first place *by the grace of God* that this part at least of mankind and of the world receives and renders the divine glory: and then also this part is, by God's grace, *pars pro toto*.[392]

To justify this twofold statement one may invoke the principle of *representative election*. The biblical history of God's dealings with men is marked by this principle. As the opening chapters of Genesis make clear, God's gracious purpose embraces the whole creation, with mankind as its crown; and if, on account of the persistent sin of men, God concentrated

His purpose with ever decreasing extension and ever increasing intensity first on Israel and then on the remnant of Israel and finally on one Jew Jesus Christ, yet the universal scope of God's ultimate purpose remained, and after Jesus Christ and the descent of the Holy Spirit at Pentecost there began the history of God's expansion of the part until finally the whole of mankind and creation will acknowledge His rule and reflect His glory. Even if the form in which I have just expressed it may seem too *heilsgeschichtlich* for the taste of some (though I cannot see how much less would do justice to the general fact that men live 'in time' and to the specific fact that God has chosen to act in and through the one particular historical nation of Israel, the one particular historical man Jesus Christ, and the one particular historical institution of the church), yet the principle itself of representative election cannot be expunged from the faith without denying one or more of the following three things: (i) God has acted, and acts, in and through *some* people; (ii) not *all* people yet enjoy the knowledge of God in which salvation consists; (iii) God's ultimate, and gracious, will is to be all in all. How then does the eucharist fall in with this principle of representative election?

First, and very simply, the eucharist is an instance of *election*. That is to say, *God* chooses this group of people who gather for the celebration in obedience to Jesus's command, and this bread and this wine which they eat and drink in the course of it: chooses them to serve His purpose, and therein to receive and render the glory which is the mark of God's presence and rule.[393]

Second, the eucharist is *representative* of a greater whole. Where the eucharist is celebrated, there at one point at any rate the future age is thrown forward into the present, eternity is seizing time, the creator is raising nature to its highest destiny, ultimate reality is breaking through from the depths to the surface; for there and then at least, God is all in all. And this is a prophetic sign, announcing and inaugurating the final destiny of all that is; for God's kingdom will be total. If a Syrian tradition knows that the red, the green and the white of the altar-spreads on which the sacred vessels are placed symbolize, respectively, the fiery universe, the verdant earth and the holy church, because the Qurbana is at the very centre of God's economy of creation and redemption, then this may provoke a smile on the lips of those Protestant theologians who are devoted only to the spoken and written word; but it will hold good as an expression, in one style and at one level of symbolism, of the truth that the eucharist is the God-given sign of the destiny of all creation.[394]

(b) The eucharist falls short of the final kingdom, second, because it is *a periodic and not a perpetual celebration.* We do not yet glorify God unceasingly, nor open ourselves without interruption to the abundant life and glory which God intends to give us. The fault lies in our continuance in sin; and therefore the Lord's supper remains, until Christ comes, under the banner of His death, which is the divine judgement on all sin. But again this limitation is not to be understood in a negative sense. For, in the first place, the judge comes precisely in the eucharistic celebration and assures the penitent of their acquittal, and the judge is none other than the saviour who by His intimate presence in communion continues His work of transforming men into His own likeness. At every eucharistic celebration the assembly which is gathered in penitence and faith is released from captivity to sin and death, and is liberated for life and the service of the God whose service is perfect freedom.[395] And, in the second place and as a direct consequence of the first point, the periodic eucharist sets a pattern which Christians must learn to reproduce in their daily lives so that the whole of their existence becomes increasingly open to receive and reflect the glory of God and grows closer and closer to becoming in fact the perpetual eucharist of the final kingdom in which we shall receive and adore eternally. The creative sign of the eucharist must be seized in hope, and we must order the whole of our lives according to that of which it is the promise and earnest: an abundant life in God's presence, in joyful and total dependence on Him, and in perfect and adoring submission to His sovereign will.

(c) The eucharist falls short of the final kingdom, third, because *the divine glory is not visibly present in the celebration*. It is of the nature of the divine glory to be visible,[396] but all that need be seen in the eucharist is a small group of people round a wooden table, not many wise, not many mighty, not many noble, and doing no more than eat bread and drink wine with thanksgiving. Yet again, however, this limitation is not to be understood in a negative sense. For in the first place, those gathered round the table perceive the kingdom by faith if not by sight (II Cor. 5:7); they may even see, if only through a glass darkly (I Cor. 13:12).[397] The bread they are eating is the bread of life, and the wine they drink is the cup of salvation; and here we may recall the fine passage from Narsai which we reproduced (p. 113). They are being fed by the Lord who is invisibly present to give them a share in His own life; and here it is the Byzantine liturgy which comes to our aid:

Give heed, O Lord Jesus Christ our God, from thy holy habitation and from the glorious throne of thy kingdom, and come to hallow us, O Thou who sittest on high with the Father and art invisibly present with us here; and vouchsafe to give us by thy own mighty hand thy immaculate body and precious blood, and by us to all the people.[398]

In the second place, we know that nothing is hidden that shall not be revealed (Matt. 10:26; Mark 4:22; Luke 8:17, 12:2). If our life is at present hid with Christ in God, we know that when Christ who is our life appears we also shall appear with Him in glory (Col. 3:3f). If it does not yet appear what we shall be, we know that when He appears we shall be like Him, for we shall see Him as He is (I John 3:2). The hidden presence of the glorious Christ at the eucharist to change us secretly from glory into glory is therefore to be regarded positively as an effective promise of the glory we shall visibly share with Him at His advent and in the final kingdom. May we, I wonder, see the splendid vestments worn at the eucharist in the Eastern traditions and in the Western Catholic tradition as a sign of the glory that is trying to break through into visibility? But there we already approach a third point. For in the third place, the present invisibility of the divine glory is to be understood positively because it is due to God's willingness that men should come *freely* to acknowledge His sovereignty and therefore to *enjoy* His kingdom. The divine glory which is the mark of God's presence and rule must always be on the point of breaking through into visibility, for God is *God*;[399] and if He refrains from the incontestable establishment of His universal rule, it is because He gives men time to hear the gospel of Jesus Christ, to seize its promise in hope, to let their lives be shaped by His transforming presence, and to order their daily actions in the world according to the rule of God.[400]

# V

# *The Ecclesiological Consequences*

WE SAW in the introduction how the eschatological dimension of the eucharist has fared badly in Western theology at least since the Reformation. In fact the neglect reaches much further back. The centre of theological gravity had already shifted to the manner of Christ's presence in the elements by the time of the controversy between Paschasius Radbertus and Ratramnus in the ninth century and the case of Berengar of Tours in the eleventh. Carolingian and later commentaries on the mass were concerned to find in the course of the liturgical action an anecdotal representation of all the details of Christ's life at His first coming;[401] and there was little in the way of a compensating scheme of future-eschatological interpretation such as Maximus the Confessor provided for the liturgical action in the East, which would have kept alive the notion that Christ's first coming was but the promise of His final advent. The medieval understanding as to what was the essential nature of the eucharist became more and more aligned with the image which dominated Western interpretation of Christ's saving work, namely the offering of Himself in propitiatory sacrifice to the Father; so that the mass was seen chiefly as the church's propitiatory offering of Christ in sacrifice to the Father,[402] and it was hardly understood as the meal that is the sign of the feeding and feasting of the kingdom. Moreover, the later Middle Ages largely lost the notion, still present in St Thomas, of the eucharist as constructive of the unity-in-love of the whole church; and thought on the benefits of communion tended to stop at the personal benefits to the soul of the individual communicant.[403]

The main purpose of the present chapter is to show what would be the possible consequences for the church's mission and its unity of a recovered appreciation of the eschatological content and import of the eucharist as the sign of the kingdom; but it will be helpful first to indicate briefly some of the factors that contributed towards the earlier restriction in the church's awareness of the sacrament's eschatological scope.

## 1. Loss . . . and recovery?

First, we note the re-adaptation occasioned by the disappointment of the church's expectation of an early parousia. It is probable that the theme of the *Parusieverzögerung* has been overworked by some recent scholars in their interpretation of the primitive and early church;[404] and it may well be that what appear in the Pauline writings and the synoptic gospels and even perhaps in authentic words of Jesus as temporal delimitations of the parousia are not to be interpreted principally in a chronological sense but are rather due to the conviction of the imminence of God's rule which is pressing urgently in upon a world that does not yet acknowledge it:[405] but it is impossible to escape the fact that at a certain moment after the death and resurrection of Jesus, if not from the time of Jesus's own preaching, the primitive church expected a temporally imminent advent of Christ in glory (Mark 9:1 (cf. 8:38) = Matt. 16:27f = Luke 9:26f; Mark 13:26–30 = Matt. 24:30–34 = Luke 21:27–32; Mark 13:33–37 = Matt. 24:42–44 = Luke 12:35–40; Matt. 10:23; 25:13; Rom. 13:11f; I Cor. 15:51; Eph. 5:16; Phil. 3:20f; 4:5; Col. 3:4; I Thess. 2:19; 3:13; 4:13–17; II Thess. 2:1–12; II Tim. 3:1; Heb. 9:28; 10:25, 37; Jas. 5:7–9; I Pet. 1:13; I John 2:18, 28; 3:2; Rev. 1:1; 3:11, 22:7, 10, 12, 20). As long as this expectation was alive, the eucharist must have been celebrated with eyes turned towards the return of Christ and the messianic feasting in the final kingdom. Once the urgent sense of temporal proximity was lost, it is psychologically understandable, but nonetheless theologically regrettable, that the church should have relaxed its awareness of the nature of the eucharist as the sign of the final advent of Christ and of the banquet of the kingdom.

Second, we may suppose that even when the expectation of the first generation or two had been disappointed, the eschatological dimension of the eucharist retained a fair degree of prominence at least as long as the church was exposed to persecution and martyrdom. For the persecutions could be read as the prelude of the fast approaching End (Matt. 24; Mark 13); and certainly those threatened with martyrdom could not do without the eucharist (*Sine dominico non possumus* was the watchword of the martyrs of Abitinae during the persecution of Diocletian),[406] for was it not the sign of the heavenly banquet to which they already felt themselves so close? Two brief references to martyrs' visions will suffice to evoke the atmosphere in which this view of the eucharist was bound to thrive.[407] The first comes from the time of Marcus Aurelius.

A certain Agathonica was standing by [at the martyrdom of Papylus and Carpus]; and seeing the glory of the Lord which Carpus said he had seen, and perceiving the invitation to be a heavenly one, she at once lifted up her voice: 'For me too this dinner (ἄριστον) has been prepared, I too must eat my share of the glorious dinner.'[408]

The second example dates from the persecution of Valerian. James, who was to undergo martyrdom with Marianus, recounts a similar vision just before his death.

'Good,' said James, 'I am on my way to the banquet (*convivium*) of Agapius and the other blessed martyrs. Last night, brethren, I saw Agapius happy amid all the others who had been in prison along with us at Cirta, sitting at a solemn and joyful banquet (*convivium*). When Marianus and I hurried there in the spirit of love and charity, as if to a lovefeast, there ran up to meet us a boy, who was clearly one of the twins who had suffered martyrdom with their mother three days ago. He was wearing a garland of roses round his neck and held a green palm-branch in his right hand. "Why do you rush?" he said, "Rejoice and be glad, for tomorrow you also will dine (*cenabitis*) with us." '[409]

Without endorsing the now largely discredited theory that the catacombs were ever regular places of worship, I would hold that the practice of celebrating the eucharist at martyrs' tombs (as was done especially on the anniversary of their martyrdom) must have contributed, for as long as persecution and martyrdom remained fresh in the memory and might be renewed, to keeping the eschatological dimension of the eucharist vividly present to the church's mind.[410] But with the peace of the church things began to change, at least within the bounds of the Empire.

For, in the third place, the recognition of Christianity by Constantine and its establishment by Theodosius led to a more positive evaluation of the present age. It was undoubtedly right that the church should seek to permeate the structures of society with Christian values; but day to day absorption in political, economic and social tasks seems unfortunately to have led to a loss of awareness of the fact that the church's action in the world has value *in so far as it is a witness to the coming kingdom*.

Fourth (and no doubt due to the recognized and established church's sense of being more at home in the world), it was from the fourth century onwards, and beginning from the Jerusalem to which Etheria's *Travel Diary* bears witness,[411] that a historicizing interest started to gain hold on the liturgy. To re-enact the events of Jesus's life round the holy sites in Palestine was a first step towards seeing the mass as a dramatic biography of the earthly life of the Lord. Looking upon the liturgical action in this way is not necessarily reprehensible, provided it is not considered necessary to give every minor detail of the liturgy its biographical significance, and provided also that the first coming of the Lord therein represented is understood as the promise of His final advent. Theodore of Mopsuestia, whose writings are the first evidence we have for this way of looking on the regular course of the eucharistic liturgy, met these requirements; but his successors in this line of interpretation, with few exceptions, did so less and less.[412]

Fifth, we note the increasing influence of a 'vertical' and individualized eschatology dressed in the colours of a platonizing mysticism. The main vehicle of the spreading influence, first in the Greek world but already from the seventh century in the West also, was the literary production of the pseudo-Areopagite, which dated from around 500 but was believed to come from the pen of Paul's Athenian convert, Dionysius (Acts 17:34). The vertical and the individual references of eschatology are not to be denied, and they are clearly present in the New Testament witness; but the exaggerated development of a combination of the vertical and the individual references to the detriment of both the futurist and the corporate references could only lead to an impoverishment in the understanding of the eucharistic meal as the sign of the kingdom. If the Fourth Gospel speaks of the individual already having eternal life, it also speaks of a common abiding in the Vine and of a future resurrection. If Hebrews uses the scheme of 'above' and 'below', it knows that Christ is the *fore*-runner and that the end is still to come; and the epistle is exceedingly strong on the corporate nature of salvation (2:17; 3:6; 4:9; 8:9–13; 10:19–25; 12:22–24; 13:1–17). If the synoptic gospels know of an existing kingdom waiting to be entered by individuals (Mark 12:34; Mark 10:14f = Luke 18:16f; Matt. 6:33 = Luke 12:31; Matt. 16:19; 21:31b; 23:13/14), they can hardly be accused of neglecting either the communal or the still-to-come dimensions of the kingdom. It was only by selective use of New Testament material, and by the subtle distortion of certain expressions innocuous enough in themselves,[413] that the unilateral development of the individual and 'vertical' themes of eschatology could take place. It is understandable that such a development should take place in areas where the thought pattern owed much to Greek philosophy; but we must regret the absence of Semitic counter-influence to safeguard the view of the eucharist as the common meal of the people of God in the last days before the parousia and the consequent transformation of heaven and earth in the unequivocal establishment of the divine kingdom. Maximus the Confessor was able to hold together in his conception of the eucharist *both* an eschatology with churchly and futurist dimensions[414] *and* (for he was a confessed admirer of the Areopagite) an interpretation of the liturgical action in terms of its meaning for the individual soul's present experience. In this second style of interpretation, the priest's descent from the throne after the reading of the gospel represents the descent of the Logos to sift the thoughts of the soul, while the subsequent closing of the outer doors and the entry of the gifts represent the exclusion of worldly and material thoughts and the translation of the soul to contemplation of ineffable spiritual things, and the holy communion itself effects union with God through faith and by participation.[415] But what Maximus could join together, others put asunder: and the distant inheritors of a unilateral interpretation in the vertical and individualist line are those pietists of Western catholicism who even today speak of 'making my communion'.

Sixth, we note the long neglect of the doctrine of the Holy Spirit in the Western church. Some have argued that the Johannine doctrine of the Paraclete, and the early church's insistence on the Holy Spirit's presence in the liturgy (typified by the pneumatological epiclesis), are to be understood as compensations for the failure of a quick parousia.[416] It seems more important to call attention to the fact that at least from the days of Paul there has existed a doctrine of the Holy Spirit which expresses the relation between the 'already' and the 'not yet' of the kingdom in a way which is quite independent of the *length* of the interval between the first coming of Christ and the second. The Holy Spirit is the firstfruits (Rom. 8:23) and earnest (II Cor. 1:22; 5:5; Eph. 1:13f) of final salvation. We have noticed in the course of our study that the same two terms, firstfruits and earnest, may also appropriately be used to express the relation between the eucharist and the final kingdom. Was the loss of the full eschatological perspective by Western theologians in their treatment of the eucharist due at least in part to an inadequate pneumatology? Did the understanding of the eschatological scope of the eucharist fare considerably better in the East because of the more developed doctrine of the Holy Spirit which found eucharistic expression in the pneumatological epiclesis? It seems highly likely that there is some connection between pneumatology and an eschatological eucharist, though the detection and apportionment of cause and effect are probably more complex than my two questions suggest.

Last, we remark on the manner in which the eucharist has long been celebrated in both East and West. In comparison with table customs in everyday life a certain stylization is probably inevitable in a ritual meal; but in both East and West the resemblance of the Lord's supper to a meal was reduced to a minimum.[417] It is correspondingly difficult to see in it the sign of the banquet in the final kingdom. It is not, I think, without significance that in our century which has witnessed the rediscovery of eschatology and of the church as the people of the last days, there should be serious theological proposals for restoring to the eucharist something of its character as a meal: so, for instance, M. Barth, *Das Abendmahl* (1945), pp. 54–63 and W. Marxsen, *Das Abendmahl als christologisches Problem* (1965[2]), pp. 31f.[418]

It is clear that these factors which contributed towards, or at least accompanied, the earlier restriction in the church's awareness of the eschatological content and import of the eucharist no longer apply to the same extent: (1) It is better realized, among the theologians at any rate, that the nearness of the parousia is much more a question of quality, whatever conceptual scheme they employ to express this, than of chronological quantity. (2) Christians again suffer various kinds of persecution, in different Asian, African and East European countries. (3) The minority position of the eucharistic community in areas of new missionary outreach is a reminder of the church's distinction from this world and its passing form; and the dissolution of Western christendom should eventually bring home to the most 'secular' of theologians who would remain a Christian that it is because Christians are citizens of heaven that they are able to love the world and work for its salvation. (4) In Western catholicism there is a revulsion from the anecdotal style of interpreting the course of the liturgical action. (5) Ecclesiology has come into its own in the last two or three generations; and we now know that the church is not simply a collection of individual souls but the company of God's people in the last days, and the eucharist is seen as what a recent Orthodox theologian has called 'le sacrement de l'assemblée'.[419] (6) Western theology has seen something of a blossoming of studies on the doctrine of the Holy Spirit, of which we may mention particularly the quite remarkable 'pneumatological ecclesiology' put forward by the Roman Catholic scholar Heribert Mühlen in *Una Mystica Persona—Die Kirche als das Mysterium der Identität des*

*Heiligen Geistes in Christus und den Christen: Eine Person in vielen Personen*, München/Paderborn/Wien, 1967².[420] (7) The liturgical movement has been rather timid in the matter of giving to the eucharistic celebration its character as a meal; but in various quarters recently there have been proposals to re-study the relation between eucharist and agape,[421] and some practical experiments have taken place.[422] In the light of this changed situation, and at a time when there has been a recovery of the eschatological dimension in the whole range of academic theology, it is hardly surprising that such recent liturgical compositions as the eucharistic texts of the Church of South India,[423] and of the monastic community of Taizé,[424] should have taken on a noticeable eschatological colouring. Our task now, however, is to look at what bearing a full recovery of the eschatological understanding of the eucharist would have on the theological and practical issues involved (first) in the mission of the church in the world and (second) in the search for Christian unity.

## 2. An eschatological eucharist and an eschatological mission

To put the matter in one sentence: the eucharist has an inescapable missionary significance in so far as it is the sign of the great feast which God will offer in the final kingdom to express for ever the universal triumph of His saving will and purpose. The following four points may be seen as elucidating and developing that general thesis.

(a) The Isaianic apocalypse had looked forward to a feast which God would offer for the nations 'on this mountain' (that is, mount Zion), when death would be swallowed up for ever and there would be rejoicing in the salvation wrought by the Lord (Isa. 25:6–9). Jesus looked forward to the feast in the final kingdom of God when many will come from east and west, and from north and south, and sit at table with Abraham, Isaac and Jacob (Matt. 8:11; Luke 13:29). Before going out to the death by which He conquered death and gave men to rejoice in the salvation wrought by the Lord, Jesus gave to His disciples, on mount Zion, a feast which they would continue to celebrate among the nations as they went to the farthest bounds of the earth dispreading the gospel which must needs be preached before the end. No longer tied to the earthly Jerusalem, the church has come close to the heavenly; Christians have no abiding city on earth but seek the one which is to come: and this eschatological journey of the church is seen to have missionary dimensions in the fact that the apostles *went out from* Jerusalem, and that the church has continued to celebrate wherever it has gone the meal which is the sign of that final kingdom in which the salvation effectively promised by Jesus's resurrection and ascension will have attained the scope which God intends. The sign of the eucharist is enacted among the nations so that many may grasp the promise in hope and already taste the feast of the kingdom which is being projected into the present in sacramental mode. The Wesleys called the eucharist 'the banquet for all He so freely did make' and set its celebration in the universal context of the ends of the earth and the end of time, thus:

*O that all men would haste*
*To the spiritual feast,*
*At Jesus's word*
Do this, *and be fed with the love of our Lord!*

*Bring near the glad day*
*When all shall obey*
*Thy dying request,*
*And eat of Thy supper, and lean on Thy breast.*

*Then, then let us see*
*Thy glory, and be*
*Caught up in the air,*
*This heavenly supper in heaven to share.*
(Hymns on the Lord's Supper, no. 92, vv. 8, 10, 12)

**(b)** On several occasions already I have called attention to the way in which eucharistic implications are to be found in the feeding miracles recorded in the gospels (see pp. 28f, 35f, 42f). Here we simply note that in enacting these messianic signs of the divine largesse in salvation, Jesus apparently provided food for as many as came to hear Him, without inquiring into their credentials. The Fourth Gospel makes it clear that not all who ate their fill of the loaves understood the real significance of the meal (John 6:26ff); indeed the intimate disciples apparently did not do so at first (Mark 8:14–21, Matt. 16:5–12).[425]

**(c)** We saw in the second chapter (p. 28) how Jesus ate with sinners and how sinners sought His company at table. By and at and in the eucharist Christ continues to draw sinners into His transforming presence that they may pass from death to life. This is how Julius Firmicus Maternus about the year 347 presents the eucharist to those who remain dead in sin because they are attached to a pagan religion which does not know the life-giving presence of Christ:

O wretched men subject to death! Seek the grace of the food of salvation, and drink the cup of immortality. By his feast Christ calls you to the light, and gives life to limbs and joints made numb and putrid by a strong poison. By this heavenly food renew the man of perdition, so that what is dead in you may be reborn thanks to the divine favours. You have been told what you should do: now make your choice. There it is death that results: but here immortal life is given. (*De errore profanorum religionum*, 19, PL 12, 1024f)

The Wesleys expressed the general invitation to sinners in this way:

*Come, to the supper come,*
*Sinners, there still is room;*
*Every soul may be His guest,*
*Jesus gives the general word;*
*Share the monumental feast,*
*Eat the supper of your Lord.* (*Hymns on the Lord's Supper*, no. 8, v. 1)

To His feast in the final kingdom God is inviting all men, for He has willed to have mercy on all (Rom. 11:32); and the invitation to the sacramental meal which is the sign of that final feast is therefore likewise universal.⁴²⁶ The universality of the invitation makes of every celebration of the eucharist a missionary event. For it is an offer of salvation through the transforming presence of Christ to all who will accept; and on the shadow side, those who will not yet, or who will no longer, accept the invitation are choosing death rather than life, are excluding themselves from salvation.

**(d)** Knowing that God is inviting all men to the feasting in the final kingdom, the church may be confident that it is the divine will that as many as possible should be brought to enjoy already the meal which is the sign of that feasting. It is strange that though the 'Compel them to come in' of Luke 14:23 has often inspired the church in its missionary task,⁴²⁷ yet the church in all its denominations has shown itself loth to accept the implications of the fact that ἀνάγκασον εἰσελθεῖν is not an isolated expression but part of the parable of the great supper. We have pressed men to come in . . . and then left them without food and drink at the meal which is the sign of the great supper of the final kingdom, telling them rather that they must wait several years until by their acquired knowledge and virtues they have earned the right (we do not use quite those words, of course) to baptism and, after a further interval, 'confirmation' (by whatever name), and only then will they be admitted to the Lord's table.⁴²⁸ Having made this criticism, I am committed to examine the question of the conditions of admission to the Lord's supper: and we may hope that the question will be illuminated by the adoption of an eschatological perspective.

\*     \*     \*

We begin with Paul's shipwreck. Acts 27:33–38 reads thus:

³³As day was about to dawn, Paul urged them all to take some food, saying, 'Today is the fourteenth day that you have continued in suspense and without food, having taken nothing. ³⁴Therefore I urge you to take some food; it will give you strength [τοῦτο γὰρ πρὸς τῆς ὑμετέρας σωτηρίας ὑπάρχει: *it will be seen that the R.S.V. hardly does justice to the Greek*], since not a hair is to perish from the head of any of you.' ³⁵And when he had said this, he took bread, and giving thanks to God in the presence of all he broke it and began to eat. ³⁶Then they all were encouraged and ate some food themselves. ³⁷(We were in all two hundred and seventy-six persons in the ship.) ³⁸And when they had eaten enough, they lightened the ship, throwing out the wheat into the sea.

Now there is little doubt that if verse 35 occurred in almost any other context, the theologians would fasten with glee upon the 'eucharistic' vocabulary: καὶ λαβὼν ἄρτον εὐχαρίστησεν τῷ Θεῷ ἐνώπιον πάντων καὶ κλάσας ἤρξατο ἐσθίειν. We have in fact a perfect correspondence with what Dom Gregory Dix taught us to recognize as 'the "four-action" shape of the eucharist'.⁴²⁹ Paul took bread (='offertory'), he gave thanks (=great eucharistic prayer), he broke the bread (=fraction), he ate (=communion).⁴³⁰ But because Paul was in this way presiding over a meal shared by a whole boatload of presumably heathen sailors and passengers (for there is no indication of two separate meals, one for Paul, Aristarchus and 'the travel-diarist', and another for the heathen), it is usually said that this *cannot have been a eucharist* but was rather a case of Paul observing the Jewish custom of grace before meat.[431] Some years ago Bo Reicke tried to do more justice to the eucharistic tone of Acts 27:35 than is done by interpreting the verse in terms of a Jewish grace, but even he stopped short of saying that Paul actually celebrated the eucharist.[432] It was Reicke's argument that Acts 27:33–38 is a further stylized account of an incident upon which Paul himself had already put a quasi-eucharistic stamp at the time of its happening: Paul had let the people on board participate in 'a prefiguration of the Christian eucharist as a potential preparation for later discipleship', and the author of Acts, understanding the episode in the same way, had used the story of what happened on the voyage to open up also the prospect of the work that Paul would do in the wider context of the mission when he reached Rome (cf. Acts 28:28, 30). The missionary significance of Acts 27:33–38 I am glad to admit, but is it not a case of Reicke being driven by dogmatic considerations to unjustified hair-splitting when he maintains that Paul could have presided only at a *prefiguration* of the eucharist?[433] For it is not history but dogma which informs us that in A.D. 61 Paul *could not* have presided at a eucharist for unbaptized sailors and passengers. Those on board a ship running on the rocks (Acts 27:29) were confronted by 'the last things': it was a matter of life and death, both physically and, for the heathen, spiritually. Must we exclude the possibility that when Paul proposed to them all that they should take food, telling them that this was for their salvation (τοῦτο γὰρ πρὸς τῆς ὑμετέρας σωτηρίας ὑπάρχει, v. 34; cf. σωθῆναι at v. 31), and having already announced to them that their destiny was in the hands of his God whose will it was that there should be no loss of life among them (vv. 21–26; cf. v. 34c), he then celebrated for them the very meal which is life to all who will choose life?

Whether Paul did or not, it seems clear that J. C. Hoekendijk would have celebrated precisely *the eucharist* for them. In characteristically bold style the Dutch missiologist has proposed that there should be absolutely no conditions set upon eucharistic communion, for every celebration of the Lord's supper is a sign erected of the coming great banquet, and God wishes His house to be full. The offer of communion is as open and free as the offer of the gospel: Whosoever will may come![434] Hoekendijk has developed a little more fully in another place his conception of the eschato-logical nature of the eucharist against the background of which his proposal of a globally open communion is to be seen,[435] and so we are able to piece his ideas together. He writes, for instance: 'Communion as an eschatological sacrament is the representation of the Kingdom in the *world*; it is impossible to lock up the Kingdom in the Church, it is equally impossible to make this sacrament of the Kingdom a purely churchly event.' For Hoekendijk, eschatology means that 'the new overpowers the old'. At the Lord's table the new order is present because Jesus Christ is present: communion is the 'first fulfilment' of the promised feast for the nations 'to which already now the guests are on their way from far and wide', and they must be welcomed 'from wherever they come'. Hoekendijk's position, so far as one is able to piece it together from his tantalizingly fragmentary comments, is so close to the view that has been presented at length in the present study that I am reluctant to offer criticism; but at one point criticism must be made. The first sacramental moment of response to the preaching of the gospel is normally *baptism*. Hoekendijk passes this over in silence in his two articles on the eucharist (to the extent even of misquoting the Augsburg Confession in the form 'to preach the gospel in concord and to administer the sacrament [*singular*] according to the Word of God'). But a brief discussion will show that the church has not been without its reasons in insisting, as it has done in the overwhelming part of its history, that only the baptized may communicate.

I do not say that baptism was a condition of communion from the very beginning. The parable of the man without the wedding garment in Matt. 22:11–13 reflects, I would suggest, a *controversy* in the primitive church as to whether baptism was required for admission to the Lord's supper.

[The parable of the man without the wedding garment was probably told by Jesus with reference to the unexpected crisis that had come upon Israel through His own coming. But it has been fused by Matthew (or his source) with the parable of the great supper which, in its present Matthaean and Lucan forms, is clearly meant to apply to the situation of the church before the End. From the rabbinic parallel (b. Shab. 153a) and the O.T. text (Isa. 61:10) to which J. Jeremias calls attention (*Die Gleichnisse Jesu*, 1952², pp. 134f, and 1956⁴, pp. 154–57), it appears that the festal garment means both repentance and salvation. Whereas Jeremias takes Matthew to be combating antinomianism *within the church* (1956⁴, pp. 37–40), C. H. Dodd prefers to see the 'Judaistic' Matthew intending 'to guard against the reception of the Gentiles into the Church on too easy terms' (*The Parables of the Kingdom*, 1961 paperback edition, p. 91). I agree with Dodd that the parable has to do with *initial reception into the church*, and with Jeremias that the garment means *repentance and salvation*. Matthew is saying that only the repentant are to be admitted to the church, which is the present sign of the saved community of the final kingdom. But in sacramental terms this means that only the baptized (for baptism is the sacrament of μετάνοια, e.g. Acts 2:38, and of salvation, e.g. Titus 3:5) are to be admitted to the Lord's supper (for the Lord's supper is the focus of the congregation's life, being itself the sign of the great supper of the end). If Matthew needed to state this in such grave terms, it is highly likely that the question was controversial, and it is for this reason that I would wish to leave open the possibility that Paul, particularly in the circumstances of an imminently threatened death for all by drowning, should have celebrated the eucharist for all: for to the repentant, whether or not they had been baptized, it would have been πρὸς τῆς σωτηρίας [αὐτῶν]. Certainly the patristic church took the view that only the baptized might participate in the eucharist, and there are occasional hints that Matthew's wedding garment was interpreted in this sense. Narsai is quite explicit in his appeal to Matt. 22:11-13 for the church's practice of expelling the unbaptized (and indeed those also who by heresy, apostasy or some sin meriting discipline had gone back on their baptism) before the beginning of the strictly eucharistic part of the liturgy: 'By her expulsion (of these) Holy Church depicts typically those that go forth into that darkness which is in Gehenna. The king saw a man not clad in the garments of glory, and he commanded and they bound him and cast him forth into that outer darkness. So the Church scans her congregations at the time of the Mysteries, and every one that is not adorned with clean garments she casts forth without' (Hom. 17, ed. R. H. Connolly, p. 3). The thought of Matt. 22:11-13 cannot be far from Cyril of Jerusalem's mind in the eucharistic context of the fourth of the Mystagogical Catecheses, for he refers to the white raiment which the neophytes have put on in place of their old garments (§8), and he calls them the children of the bride-chamber (§2). In his letter to Charlemagne, Maxentius of Aquileia referred to the neophytes who, 'clothed in white robes, that is, wedding garments, come to the table of the heavenly kingdom' (Ep. ad Carolum, 3, PL 106, 52f). When the Anglican Prayer Book of 1549, and in a slightly different wording the 1552 Book also, exhorts the people to come to communion repentant, 'as they whiche shoulde come to a moste Godly and heavenly Banket, not to come but in the marriage garment required of God in scripture, that you may (so muche as lieth in you) be founde worthie to come to suche a table': then, though in a *corpus christianum* situation it is hardly envisaging any unbaptized persons presenting themselves for communion, it is certainly saying that only those who show the repentance *of which baptism is the sacrament* should come to communion. A confirmatory hint of liturgical interest on the part of Matthew (or his source) in his presentation of the parable of the man without the wedding garment is to be found in the use of οἱ διάκονοι in v. 13, for 'the deacons' were early associated with the agape-cum-eucharist of the church (Acts 6; Justin, *Apol. I*, 65 and 67); whereas in the originally separate (and not *directly* eucharistic) parable of the great supper the servants are called οἱ δοῦλοι (verses 3, 4, 6, 8, 10).]

But it is beyond doubt that from an early date the baptized alone might communicate,[436] and two points in particular may be urged in favour of this practice. First, it is to *the church* that the task has been entrusted of erecting the sign of the banquet of the future kingdom by eating bread and drinking wine together in the name of Christ: and entry into the sign-erecting community of the church is by baptism. For, second, it is only as a man has himself been brought by the preaching of the gospel of the kingdom to *repentance and faith* in Jesus Christ who is 'the kingdom in person (αὐτοβασιλεία)' that he can bear witness to the kingdom: and baptism is the sacrament of such repentance and faith, for in it the old man dies to sin and is reborn, a new creation, to life in Christ. These two connected points may be seen as safeguarding the *distinctiveness* of the church which is necessary even, or rather precisely, in the missionary perspective which is so much a concern of Hoekendijk's and which I share; for every blurring of the church's edges is a threat, sometimes more serious than others,[437] to its continuing existence as a covenant group[438] able to celebrate the signs that summon the world to that kingdom of God which is, for men who freely accept it, salvation.[439]

In the light of these remarks it is now possible to set out a number of principles which could profitably inform the church's practice as it celebrates the eucharist as the sign of the coming great banquet, an action ordered in hope of the future kingdom:

(i) The Lord's supper should be celebrated *in public*, because it is a sign of the kingdom of God to which the whole world is being summoned. The gospels make it clear that Jesus's signs were usually performed in the open, for they were part of a ministry that was the announcement of the kingdom of God and an invitation to men to enter that kingdom; and those who would not read the signs aright were *excluding themselves* from the kingdom. So also with the eucharist: far from making of the eucharist a private celebration behind closed doors (as the early church long did, with its *disciplina arcani*, and as is still technically the case in those Eastern rites which retain the expulsion of the unbaptized), the church should seek, by whatever means climate and social custom make appropriate, to celebrate the Lord's supper *coram publico*, so that as many as possible may be drawn towards the Christ who is present through the sign He ordained. The more the sign takes on the form of a *meal*, the better will it show forth to 'outsiders or unbelievers'[440] who witness it the qualities of the kingdom (see pp. 58f).

(ii) The Lord's supper is the meal in which the baptized and believing church enjoys already the taste of what the final kingdom will bring in its fulness. But the church is no more than the firstfruits of God's creatures, chosen by God according to the principle of representative election and meant by Him to be an instrument in bringing all mankind to salvation: and so the church must hope and expect that through the words and actions of the eucharistic sign which it performs before the world, God will arouse in those who have not so far committed themselves to His kingdom the desire to share in the blessings of salvation. *No one should be refused communion who has been moved by the celebration of the sign then in progress to seek saving fellowship with the Lord through eating the bread and drinking the wine.*

(iii) But then he should be brought to *baptism*, and *soon*. For if he has on this first and exceptional occasion been drawn to the Lord's table as the recipient of a salvation to which he was hitherto a stranger, he has by the very reception of salvation been constituted a witness to the saving work of God: and the company of those who actively proclaim for others the salvation which they themselves receive is the church, to which the normal rite of admission, administered even, or rather precisely, in the case of Cornelius (Acts 10:47f), is baptism. A man who then refuses baptism is not in earnest about his desire to enter the kingdom, and he will not be admitted to the Lord's table again until he has been so persuaded; but he must know that salvation scorned turns to judgement.

(iv) It is obviously of a piece with the preceding principles to urge that *all* who have been brought to repentance and faith, by whatever instance of the church's missionary witness, should be brought to baptism and communion as soon as possible, so that they may already taste the feast of the future kingdom and share in celebrating the sign of the meal before the world.[441]

## 3. An eschatological eucharist and the search for Christian unity

Throughout the present study I have spoken of 'the church' as though the term could be used unequivocally. The reader will have understood the word according to his own definition, and I hope that he will have found something of value for his understanding of the eucharist within the context of his own ecclesiology. But 'the church' is not an unequivocal term, for definitions and ecclesiologies vary. It would be both a shirking of the theological and practical problems posed by Christian disunity and also a failure to exploit the results of our study of *eucharist and eschatology*, if we omitted to ask what contribution an understanding of the eucharist in its eschatological content and import might make to the solution of the theological and practical difficulties in which ecclesiology finds itself as a result of division among Christians. In the modern ecumenical movement the problem, which must always emerge in one form or another where there is disunity among Christians, of the relations between sacraments and church has taken the form of *the intercommunion question*, and it is this question which I shall seek to illuminate from an eschatological perspective.

As is well known,[442] there have been two main attitudes towards the question of intercommunion. The one was defined at the Fourth World Conference on Faith and Order at Montreal in 1963 in this way:

Some Christians believe that the degree of ecclesial communion which we have in the body of Christ, through baptism and through our fundamental faith, although we are still divided on some points, urges us to celebrate Holy Communion together and to promote intercommunion between the churches. It is Christ, present in the Eucharist, who invites all Christians to his table: this direct invitation of Christ cannot be thwarted by ecclesiastical discipline. In the communion at the same holy table, divided Christians are committed in a decisive way to make manifest their total, visible and organic unity.[443]

It is on these lines that especially Congregationalists, Methodists, Presbyterians, and open Baptists (most of whom would of course want to omit the words 'through baptism and', as far as their relations with paedo-

baptists were concerned), have practised intercommunion among themselves and have sought it with others. Not all in those denominations would
place such stress on the need 'to make manifest their total, visible and
organic unity' as the Montreal paragraph does, whereas others among
them would wish to make clearer than Montreal does that it is to Christ
Himself, as He is met at His table, that they look for the gracious building
up of their unity into total unity.

The other main attitude was described at Montreal as follows:

Some Christians believe that eucharistic communion, being an expression of
acceptance of the whole Christ, implies full unity in the wholeness of his truth;
that there cannot be any 'intercommunion' between otherwise separated
Christians; that communion in the sacraments therefore implies a pattern of
doctrine and ministry, which is indivisible; and that 'intercommunion' cannot
presume upon the union in faith that we still seek.[444]

On the whole, this has been the attitude of Eastern Orthodoxy,[445] Roman
Catholicism,[446] many Lutherans,[447] and some Anglicans.[448] It was
particularly the need, felt more perhaps by Lutherans than by Reformed,
for agreement in the doctrine of the eucharist itself that promoted the
discussions leading to the Dutch Consensus between Lutherans and
Reformed in 1956,[449] and to the publication of the Arnoldshain Theses in
Germany in 1957 (though the German churches have been slow to approve
the agreements reached by their theologians).[450]

But there have been in very recent years some small but important shifts
in position on the question of intercommunion. Among the Orthodox N.
Zernov was already proposing in 1952 that 'pioneering groups' of 'workers
for reconciliation' should be allowed to practise intercommunion, sanctioned by the presidents of their respective eucharistic communities and
in the context of corporate penance for the sin of disunity;[451] more
recently N. Afanassieff has put forward an argument whose consequences
for intercommunion between Orthodoxy and Roman Catholicism are not
far to seek, arguing namely that the separation between the churches is
*merely canonical* and that they have always remained united at a deeper
level by the celebration of the one and the same eucharist;[452] and H.
Symeon has advanced some carefully guarded suggestions that Orthodox should practise a limited intercommunion with others in furtherance
of the mutual love which will put an end to division.[453] The Second Vatican
Council did in fact, from the Roman Catholic side though apparently
without consultation with the Orthodox, declare that in certain circumstances Orthodox might be admitted to communion at Catholic altars and
that Catholics might communicate at Orthodox eucharists.[454] Among
Anglicans, who from the early days of the modern ecumenical movement
have been generous in their invitations to others to communicate at
eucharists presided over by Anglicans in the framework of ecumenical
conferences, we now find in the 1968 report of the English Archbishops'
commission on intercommunion a firmer encouragement to Anglicans to

accept others' invitations to communion in similar circumstances.[455] At a less official level it appears, if newspaper reports are to be trusted, that a good deal of occasional intercommunion, and that reciprocal, is being practised between Roman Catholics and Protestants. I believe that these are tendencies in the right direction, for I hold that the eschatological nature of the eucharist impels divided Christians towards the practice of intercommunion. The justification of this view has to be made in two stages: first, and negatively, it must be shown that there is *no* satisfactory doctrine of the relation between sacraments and church when Christians are divided; second, and positively, it must be seen that the eschatological character of the eucharist drives us towards one particular term of each of a series of alternatives that would be *false* alternatives *if there were no division among Christians.*

Broadly one may distinguish five positions on the question which division among Christians poses concerning the relation between sacraments and church. In the main, it has been baptism,[456] and to a less extent ordination, which have been at issue in the past, but the same five attempted solutions may be applied to the eucharist.[457]

(a) The first position to be mentioned was already that of Tertullian, but it is chiefly associated with the name of Cyprian who expounded it in the controversy over the need to (re)baptize those who had already been baptized at Novatianist hands when they came over to what won through as 'the Catholic Church'.[458] The Cyprianic position is unambiguous. The church is a single indivisible institution. A dissident group does not possess the Holy Spirit, and its sacraments are charades. When Novatianists joined the Catholic church, it was not a question of *re*baptizing them but quite simply of baptizing them. According to the Cyprianic view, the eucharist celebrated by a dissident group is valueless. Objections can be made to this position, as follows.

First, hindsight often shows that there were rights and wrongs on both sides at any rupture. Love was lacking in the two camps, and each side was so anxious to preserve one aspect or implication of revealed truth that it seized on that alone, without paying heed to what the other was fighting for. How then is it possible to determine which group is the continuing church and which the non-church? J. H. Newman ruled out finally any simplistic appeal to the Vincentian canon of *quod semper, quod ubique, quod ab omnibus*;[459] and in any case, divisions usually arise over what are to some extent new issues and in what are certainly fresh circumstances, so that no exact precedent can be cited.

Second, the 'sacraments' of the allegedly non-church group seem in practice to be experienced by those who participate as moments of encounter between a gracious God and the community, and seem to bear fruit in the lives of the individual dissidents. It would seem that the Lord is not ashamed to own their charades as sacraments.

Third, we note that even the Eastern Orthodox churches, which hold closest to the Cyprianic position, have not maintained it in all its strictness.

They have made distinctions in the way in which they have received into communion converts from various dissident groups: whereas of some baptism itself has been required, for others chrismation has sufficed, and yet others have been received simply on profession of faith.[460] And modern Orthodox theologians have put forward an albeit variously defined principle of 'economy' to justify the fact that Orthodox baptism has sometimes not been required of converts already baptized in heterodoxy.[461] It seems therefore that even the Eastern churches, whether of charity for dissident Christians (though it should be noted that saving value has been attributed to sacraments received in dissidence, only when the heretic has been converted to Orthodoxy) or out of respect for the sacraments as being somehow greater than the circumstances of their performance, have not been willing to regard sacraments celebrated by dissident groups as completely without value.

The Catholic church of the West settled the dispute between Cyprianic Carthage and Rome (for Rome maintained that converted Novatianists should not be *re*baptized on entry into the Catholic church) in the following way, at the Council of Arles (314):

Concerning the Africans who use their own laws and rebaptize, the decision is that if anyone should come to the Church from heresy, they should ask him the creed and if they see that he was baptized in the Father, and the Son and the Holy Spirit, let a hand only be imposed upon him so that he may receive the Holy Spirit. But if he should respond negatively to the question about the Trinity, let him be baptized.   (Denzinger-Schönmetzer, §123)

This canon of Arles raises various intricate questions, but it is enough for our purpose to note that such value was attached to dissident baptism administered in the trinitarian faith that no repeated baptism was required of converts to the Catholic church. There are, however, two different theological justifications which must be reckoned with as possibly lying behind this decision; and I shall now expound them as the second and third positions that have been adopted on the question posed by Christian disunity concerning the relation between sacraments and church.

(b) The second position was classically argued by Augustine. Faced with the decision of how to receive converted Donatists into Catholic communion, Augustine elaborated a theological principle which amounts to a distinction between the validity of a sacrament and its efficaciousness. He allowed that the dissidents' sacraments are still the sacraments of Christ. By virtue of this, the baptism and the ordination that were received at Donatist hands were *valid* (and not to be repeated in the case of a convert joining the Catholic church), but were not *fruitful* unless and until their recipients joined the Catholic church in which alone the Holy Spirit dwelt.[462] Even though Augustine himself was not concerned with the Donatists' *eucharist* (the eucharist being in any case a repeatable sacrament), it would be quite in line with Augustine's thought to make the same distinction between validity and utility in its case also.

Just as to the Cyprianic position, so also to the Augustinian the objections may be made that it is difficult to make any clear-cut decision as to which is the continuing church and which the dissident group, and that the sacraments of the allegedly dissident group seem to be experienced as the Lord's sacraments and to bear fruit in the life of the recipients. And, although the Augustinian position is rather more positive than the Cyprianic towards the dissidents' sacraments, it faces even more objections. For, first, if the dissidents' eucharist is a valid sacrament, then Christ is present, and it is difficult to think that when believers gather to meet Him His presence will avail only to condemnatory judgement and not to their profit. And second, the notion of a valid sacrament whose beneficial effect can somehow be stored up until such time as the recipient joins the catholic church seems far removed from the conception of the sacraments as instances of gracious personal encounter between God and man, a conception which is happily being recovered in modern sacramental theology.[463]

It may be that the Council of Arles was already working with an 'Augustinian' distinction between validity and fruitfulness. On the other hand, it is possible that the Council was basing its decision on a different principle, the one that marks the third position which I am about to outline.

(c) As reported by Firmilian of Cappadocia in a letter to Cyprian, Stephen of Rome had argued that the African Catholics should not re-baptize, for 'whoever is baptized in the name of Christ, no matter where, immediately obtains the grace of Christ' (apud Cyprian, Ep. 75, 18). It has been suggested that this is a misrepresentation of Stephen's view due to the fact that Cyprian and Firmilian had failed to understand that Stephen's refusal to (re)baptize converted dissidents was already based on an 'Augustinian' distinction between validity and utility.[464] However that may be, the fact remains that the Latin church eventually came to regard all baptism administered with water and in the threefold Name as both valid and efficacious.[465] These same values are attached to the eucharist of the Eastern Orthodox churches, which is presided over by a minister in valid orders.[466] The ground on which the validity and fruitfulness of sacraments administered by dissidents is allowed by the Roman Catholic Church is this: the sacraments really belong to the (Roman) Catholic Church, and it is thence that they draw their beneficial effects.

This position is no more satisfactory than the two already mentioned. Roman Catholic theologians themselves recognize that an anomaly is involved:[467] dissidents receive benefit from participation in Catholic sacraments without being in ecclesiastical communion with the Catholic church. To the alleged dissidents themselves the artificiality of the Roman Catholic position is entirely apparent: they see the Lord acting through His sacraments in their own community which they know to be at least part of the Church universal, without need of the Roman church as an intermediary in any way.

(d) The fourth position is a reversal of the Augustinian: it allows the spiritual efficacy of dissident sacraments without admitting their validity. It has been particularly characteristic of ecumenically-minded members of the Catholic wing of the Anglican communion in their attitude to the eucharist celebrated in Protestant churches which do not possess a valid ministry because they lack bishops in the apostolic succession. The same thinking seems to underlie the rather reticently worded statement in the decree *On Ecumenism* of Vatican II: 'We believe that the churchly communities separated from us [in the West], chiefly on account of their lack of the sacrament of order, have not preserved the whole reality of the eucharistic mystery. Nevertheless in celebrating at the Holy Supper the memorial of the death and resurrection of the Lord, they profess that life consists in communion with Christ and they await his return in glory.'

The objection to this view can be succinctly stated. Of validity and fruitfulness the greater is fruitfulness, and the greater either includes the less or outweighs it in importance. By its own logic the fourth position should lead to complete recognition of dissident eucharists.[468]

(e) The fifth position depends on the view that schism takes place, and separated groups continue to live, *within the one church*. This view characterizes those Anglicans who hold to a branch-theory of the church, the Church Catholic being considered to embrace, in Lancelot Andrewes's phrase, 'Eastern, Western, our own'; it is also characteristic of perhaps the great majority of Protestants, who would draw the boundaries of the Church Catholic rather more widely. A eucharist celebrated in any group considered to be within the Church Catholic will be regarded as a true eucharist, even though there will be differences among the denominations as to its theology and the manner of its celebration. It is adherence to the Lord which constitutes the church, and He may be trusted to visit an assembly of His people when they enact the sacraments He Himself has instituted.

The objection to this position is obvious. How can it simultaneously be true that we are members of one Body and that we live in separation from one another? How, on the one hand, can it be claimed that it is the one eucharist that is being celebrated throughout the Church Catholic and yet, on the other hand, the denominational groups be out of eucharistic fellowship with one another? It is not enough to say, as is said by one Orthodox theologian who inclines to this position, that the separation of 'the churches' is *merely canonical*.[469] No separation among Christians may be thought of as merely superficial: all separation among Christians is in contradiction with the deepest nature of the church. In short, the fifth position acquiesces too readily in a situation of disunity which constitutes a betrayal of the eschatological vocation of the church to unity (Eph. 4:1-6, 13-16).

*          *          *

Our review of the five positions has made it clear that none of them is satisfactory. There *can* be no satisfactory account of the relation between sacraments and church as long as there is disunity among Christians. It will now be my positive contention that in the ecclesiologically abnormal situation of disunity we are driven by the eschatological content and import of the eucharist to choose one particular term in each of a series of alternatives that would not be conflicting alternatives but rather complementary pairs in a situation of Christian unity.

### (i) Lord's supper and church's supper[470]

In an 'ideal' theology which takes no account of the fact of Christian disunity, there is of course no problem: it is the Lord's supper in His church, and all His people gather together round His table. Some modern Catholic theologians have made impressive presentations of sacramental theology in this perspective: one thinks at once of E. Schillebeeckx, *Christus, Sacrament van de Godsontmoeting* (1957), O. Semmelroth, *Die Kirche als Ursakrament* (1953), and K. Rahner, *Kirche und Sakramente* (1960). But in a state of affairs marred by human sin (and Christian disunity is such a state), we may be obliged to choose between the order Christ-church-sacraments and the order Christ-sacraments-church. In that case the choice must fall in favour of the second, and not the first as it would with Schillebeeckx, Semmelroth and Rahner.[471] The need to choose, and then this positive choice, are forced upon us by the fact that human sin may cause a degree of separation between the church and its Lord (and result in a division among Christians and in faulty performance of the sacraments which the Lord has given His church to perform as signs by which to enjoy and proclaim the kingdom of God) but that the sacraments remain the Lord's entirely, and may be used by Him, even when (at the purely human level) defectively performed, as the vehicles of His presence to bring His church to a more obedient acknowledgement (and therefore greater enjoyment and more faithful proclamation) of the kingdom of God. In the light of this eschatological purpose, no obstacle of ecclesiastical discipline dependent on a sinful state of Christian disunity must be allowed to block the Lord's invitation to *all* penitents among His sinning people to gather round His table wherever it is set up and receive His forgiveness for sins that have led to disunity and be filled through His transforming presence with the love that unites. Those who then, like the renegers in the parable of the Great Supper, refuse his invitation are *excluding themselves*, and may be pre-enacting their own final judgement at the hands of a Lord whose offer of salvation they spurned (see pp. 130, 134f).

When a state of Christian disunity obliges us to choose between Lord's supper and church's supper, eschatology then impels us to choose *the Lord's* supper, and that means intercommunion.

### (ii) The eucharist as expressive of unity and as creative of unity

Again there is in principle no problem. As we saw (pp. 115–17), the eucharist both *expresses* an already existing unity among the Lord's people and also *increases and deepens* their love for one another until such time as it will have borne its full fruit in the perfect peace and unity of heaven.

But this twofold pattern is spoilt when Christian fellowship is disrupted through dispute. In the past, it has almost always been the case that a serious disagreement over a question of doctrine or practice has entailed a break in eucharistic fellowship, each group believing that the eucharist should be celebrated together only by those in harmony with one another, and therefore excluding members of the opposed group from its own celebration and not itself expecting to be invited to the eucharistic celebration of that other group.[472] The sentiment that only those who are already at peace with one another may gather together round the Lord's table is thoroughly respectable, since it depends on a dominically confirmed principle that only those reconciled with one another should appear before God:

If you are offering your gift at the altar, and there remember that your brother has something against you, leave your gift there before the altar and go; first be reconciled to your brother, and then come and offer your gift;  (Matt. 5:23f)

and with this we may compare the saying of John:

If any one says, I love God, and hates his brother, he is a liar; for he who does not love his brother whom he has seen, how can he love God whom he has not seen?  (I John 4:20)

It might be in better agreement with this principle if *neither* of the disputing groups celebrated the eucharist until such time as they were reconciled to one another and able to meet round the Lord's table *together*.[473] In fact, however, the disputing groups have always continued to celebrate a eucharist, in isolation from each other. Each separate eucharist may have expressed the unity of the group that celebrated it, but the continuing celebration of the eucharist in mutual isolation has become a mark of the *dis*unity of the Lord's people. Thus the eucharist's value as an expression of unity, though it has not entirely disappeared, has certainly been much reduced in a divided Christendom.

All the more reason, therefore, that the eucharist's *causative* value should be allowed to have the upper hand over its expressive value. Even in 'ideal' circumstances of an undivided Christendom, it might be argued from the eschatological perspective that the eucharist is more important for *what it makes of us* than for what it expresses as being already true of us, for our love for one another is certainly to be increased and deepened in the coming and final kingdom in comparison with what it is already. But in circumstances of Christian disunity it becomes, if possible, even clearer that the greater weight must be placed on the eucharist as a *creative sign*. Common participation in the one eucharist must be allowed to promote reconciliation among the opposing groups. The eucharist's value as expression will not be entirely lost, for it will express both the measure of unity that still holds the two parties together and also the will to reconciliation that already exists in those who seek fellowship at the Lord's table even with their temporary adversaries. But more important will be the fact that common participation in the one eucharist will allow the Lord creatively to bring us closer to the perfect peace and unity that will mark the final kingdom; for such a eucharist will be the occasion for Him to exercise the three eschatological functions of casting out from us in judgement what is amiss in us, of uniting us closer to Himself in divine fellowship, and of joining us together in common enjoyment of His presence and gifts.

When a state of Christian disunity obliges us to choose between the eucharist's value as expressive of existing unity and its value as creative of deeper unity, eschatology then impels us to choose the eucharist's *creative value*, and that means intercommunion.

### (iii) Truth and love

'Speaking the truth in love' (Eph. 4:15) is obviously a correct description of the relation between truth and love, and the First Letter of John also makes clear the fact of perfect complementarity between professing the right belief and loving the brethren. If God is both ultimate truth and perfect love, then clearly there can be no final opposition between truth and love.

But before the final coming of the kingdom we may sometimes be faced with an apparent choice between truth and love, and this is particularly true when a doctrinal or practical dispute threatens to disrupt the community of love, or when the two sides are seeking reconciliation after such a disruption. There are at least three factors suggesting that, though a line must somewhere be drawn beyond which our respect for truth will not allow us to go, the primacy of love should be exercised as generously as possible to preserve or restore the churchly fellowship that is expressed around the eucharistic table, and that the demarcation against heresy which renders eucharistic fellowship impossible should be drawn as reluctantly as possible. For apart from the fact that there is an orthodoxy which even devils may share (Jas. 2:19), we note, first, that human reception is an integral part of the revelatory event or word—and here eschatology enters again, this time with a reminder that all is 'not yet' accomplished, to warn us that our human apprehension of the divine communication is still imperfect because sin has not yet disappeared; and so we must beware of pointing out the heretical speck in our brother's eye without noticing that there is a log in our own eye (cf. Matt. 7:3). Second, we remark that according to Paul in I Cor. 13, even the eschatological gifts of prophecy, understanding of mysteries, and knowledge are nothing without love (v. 2). Present prophecy and knowledge are imperfect, and will pass away when the perfect comes (vv. 8–10). 'For now we see in a mirror dimly, but then face to face. Now I know in part; then I shall understand fully . . .' (v. 12). But love never ends (v. 8), and of the three that remain, faith, hope, love, the greatest is love (v. 13). And third, our apprehension of final truth itself will benefit from our living together in one fellowship; for in the first place, love for the brethren leaves less room for the sin which distorts our understanding of the truth, and in the second place we shall more readily profit from our brother's understanding of the truth when we live at peace with him.

When a state of Christian disunity obliges us to choose between truth as we may at present apprehend it and love as we are commanded to practise it, eschatology then impels us to choose *love*, and that means inter-communion.[474]

### (iv) Order and mission

Again there is no necessary opposition between the church as a society with its own internal structures and the church as the instrument of God's mission reaching out to the world in proclamation of the gospel. The aim of the mission is to bring men to acknowledge the rule of God, and the purpose of the inner ministries of the church is to deepen men's obedience to their acknowledged King.

But Christian disunity has often brought in its wake disputes on the internal ordering of the church and on the competence to perform their task of those charged by a different Christian group than one's own to preside at the eucharist. Disagreement on these matters has constituted one of the chief reasons for refusing to resume eucharistic fellowship even when a sufficient measure of doctrinal agreement has otherwise been achieved.[475] But if one is compelled to choose between ministerial order and missionary witness, two or three arguments at least speak strongly in favour of missionary witness. Since (first) the goal of God's mission is to sum up all things in Christ (Eph. 1:10), the church as the sign of that eschatological condition must already display its unity in Christ as part of its witness before the world to God's purpose. Jesus prayed 'that they may all be one . . ., so that ($\"\iota\nu\alpha$) the world may believe that thou hast sent me' (John 17:21). In the light of this ultimate purpose, ministerial order must be seen as purely ancillary, and Christians of differently ordered bodies should be prepared, for the sake of the role that unity among Christians is given to play in the church's witness to the world, to receive the bread and wine from the hands of all whose ministry of presidency at the eucharist God Himself has not been ashamed to use in arousing and deepening men's obedience to His rule. Second (unless this is the same point in different guise), the eucharistic celebration is part of that preaching of the gospel of the kingdom after which the End will come (Matt. 24:14); and as the dramatic embodiment of the kerygma, it must show forth clearly and urgently the human unity which is the entail of Christ's giving of His flesh 'for the life of the world' (John 6:51) and His outpouring of His blood 'for the many' unto remission of sins (Matt. 26:28; cf. Mark 14:24). And third, the life of the kingdom is not a life unto self, but a life unto God and for others. More important than the church's in-turned preservation of particular structures in its own midst is its self-spending in the mission of God to the world for the world's salvation; and if in certain circumstances the better prosecution of the mission by the Christian community as a whole demands the surrender by one group of Christians of its view that its own pattern of internal order is the exclusively right one for the church, then they may hope that God will use the common participation in His mission in order to perfect the obedience of all Christians to His kingly rule in ways which will more than compensate for the contribution that one particular pattern of internal ministries might make to that end.

When a state of Christian disunity obliges us to choose between a particular pattern of internal order and the missionary witness to the kingdom to be made before the world, eschatology then impels us to choose *missionary witness*, and that means intercommunion.

### (v) *Institution and event*

If with a little artificiality in its way of presenting the evidence, J. L. Leuba's study *L'institution et l'événement* (1950) made it abundantly clear that according to the New Testament the church partakes of the nature both of an institution and of an event. The church is neither simply a continuing institution in which God does nothing new once Christ has founded it, nor simply a momentaneous event which happens ever anew when a group of Christians meet and act together under the inspiration of a fresh influx of the Holy Spirit. The church is rather a *continuing institution* created by the Christ-*event* and *repeatedly visited* by the Lord in an action of judgement (I Cor. 11:32; cf. I Pet. 4:17) and renewal (cf. II Cor. 4:16; Eph. 4:23; Col. 3:10).

But in the time before the final kingdom, which will itself be an 'eventful institution' since (it is commonly supposed) the life of heaven is both rest and motion,[476] we may sometimes find ourselves compelled to choose between the church as institution and the church as event. For it is of the nature of an institution to *have been* founded, and sinful man's tendency to cling to the *past* may so attach him to the institutional forms which the past has bequeathed to the present that he becomes insensitive to the Lord's active visitation of His people in judgement and renewal. This institutional blindness has been an important factor in the origin and persistence of divisions among Christians, and therefore in the severance of eucharistic fellowship and the continued celebration of the eucharist in mutual isolation. Where such division has taken place, it is particularly important that the separated groups should in fact meet together, despite the *institutional* impossibility of their meeting, in order that the Lord's people may together await the *event* of His visitation in judgement and renewal;[477] and an occasion of that visitation in judgement and renewal is certainly the eucharist. The precise contribution which eschatology makes to the choice of event in preference to institution may be expressed so: the final kingdom will be instituted only by the divine *event* of the universal judgement and renewal; and the eucharist, as event, is a projection into the present of that final parousia when Christ will *come* to judge the quick and the dead (which includes the church) and inaugurate the renewed creation which is entirely obedient to His Father's royal will.

When a state of Christian disunity obliges us to choose between the church as institution and the church as event, eschatology then impels us to choose *event*, and that means intercommunion.

Provided its practice is consciously governed by the motives which have encouraged us in the five choices we have just made, intercommunion will not appear as static acquiescence in a continuing situation of disunity among Christians, or as an imperfect unity to be enjoyed on the cheap. It will rather work dynamically in favour of the deliberate goal of full communion in a church which by its unity is true to its eschatological vocation (Eph. 4).

# Conclusion

THIS SHORT conclusion will draw together some of the threads that have run all through the foregoing study. The aim of the main study was to demonstrate the eschatological dimension attaching to the eucharist, and to make clear how an awareness of that dimension assists our understanding and practice of the sacrament. The purpose of the conclusion is twofold: first, to show where the eucharist in its eschatological content and import may either confirm or challenge existing conceptual schemes proposed by the theologians to express the pattern of eschatology in general; and second, to show what the eucharist may itself contribute in the way of concepts and images to express the eschatological relation between present and future, time and eternity, below and above, provisional and ultimate reality.

To put things briefly: the eucharist confirms a particular eschatological schema in so far as that schema takes account of the following points, and calls it into question in so far as it neglects them.

## 1. Eschatology contains a polarity of the 'already' and the 'not yet'

The eucharist is already a meal, and the Bible's favourite picture for the final kingdom is that of feasting. At the eucharist Christ is present to the eyes of faith: at His table in the final kingdom we shall see Him face to face (cf. I Cor. 13:12a). The eucharist is a periodic celebration: in the final kingdom the worship and rejoicing, as in the life of heaven, will be perpetual. In the eucharist a part of mankind and a part of the world serve the glory of God: in the final kingdom God will be all in all. The people who celebrate the eucharist are imperfect in their obedience: in the final kingdom their submission to the rule of God will be total. Eucharistic joy is marred by our persistence in sin: the joy of the final kingdom will be full. No schema of general eschatology is acceptable which fails to take into account the constitutive relation between the 'now' and the 'then', the 'here' and the 'there', and within that relation the polarities of hiddenness and visibility (contestability and incontestability), interruption and permanence, limited extension and universal scope, incomplete obedience and complete service, spoilt joy and perfect bliss.

## 2. Eschatology concerns the individual in community

The eucharist is the celebration of Christians in assembly, and the Book of Revelation pictures the final kingdom as a *civitas* of obedient subjects.

At the eucharist, Christians 'come together to eat' (I Cor. 11:33), and the Lord confronts each individual (ἄνθρωπος, *ibid.*, v. 28) in judgement and salvation: so will every man be judged as part of the universal last assize. At the eucharist, each individual (ὁ τρώγων μου τὴν σάρκα, John 6:54) eats the flesh and drinks the blood of the Son of Man within the context of the common meal: so will he be raised up at the last day (*ibid.*) as part of the general resurrection. Common participation in the eucharistic loaf unites the many into one body (I Cor. 10:17), the body of Christ: so will the final kingdom be the summing up of all things ἐν τῷ Χριστῷ (Eph. 1:10), when we shall all have attained to the measure of the stature of the fulness of Christ, whose body we are (4:11–16). The eucharistic cup is, according to the institution narratives, the cup of the (new) covenant, and the new covenant is made with the disciples as a group (Luke 22:20) and with the many (Mark 14:24; Matt. 26:28): so in the final kingdom will the disciples share the table of Christ as a group (Matt. 26:29; Luke 22:30), and many will come from east and west, from north and south, to sit at table in the final kingdom (Matt. 8:11; Luke 13:29). It is clear that no atomistic eschatology of the sort that threatens mysticism, pietism and Protestant existentialism alike, can be allowed to stand. Nor, it is equally clear, may any eschatology of totalitarian optimism which removes the factor of individual responsibility in the process of sweeping all into the church and the final kingdom.

### 3. Eschatology implies both a divine gift and its human appropriation

In the eucharist, man's dependence on the transcendent Creator for his life is made clear by the fact that we are there fed on the divine gifts of bread and wine: and in the final kingdom we shall continue to be entirely dependent on God for our preservation. In the eucharist, the divine gift is also more intimate than an external provision for physical needs; it is the Lord Himself who comes and bestows the gift of His own presence on His people, a presence so intimate that we may be said to feed on Christ: and to inaugurate the final kingdom the Lord Himself will come, and the life of that kingdom will consist in the permanent enjoyment of the inexhaustible gift of His presence. As the eucharist, so also the final kingdom which it promises: both are first and foremost a divine gift. But the divine gift is to be appropriated by men, to be received and actively displayed to the glory of God. In the eucharist, we are given a promise of the righteousness, peace and joy that are the marks of the kingdom (see p. 59), being consequences of the active presence of God for men; and it is our business to grasp what is there given us in promise, and to order all our actions in hope of its final fulfilment. The eucharistic community will act in the world in such ways as to display the righteousness, peace and joy of the kingdom, and so it will bear witness to the giver of these gifts, co-operating in the establishment of the kingdom without ever a thought of denying that the work is entirely God's and will be drastically completed by Him.[478] We may thus think of the church as reproducing in its everyday life in witness before the world the pattern of the kingdom which it itself receives and learns in entire dependence on the Lord present at the eucharist—and this conception is sufficient to· dispel the false alternative between an eschatology in which men may contribute not at all to the coming of a kingdom which will impose itself by force from above and beyond, and an eschatology in which men may build up the divine kingdom on earth by their own moral and spiritual efforts based on the Master's teaching. A eucharist rightly understood and practised in its eschatological content and import would powerfully confirm a general eschatology of the sort proposed by J. Moltmann in his widely influential *Theologie der Hoffnung* (1964), an eschatology which strives to ride between the two alternatives that were only slightly caricatured at the end of the last sentence.

### 4. Eschatology embraces the material as well as the spiritual

As Irenaeus well realized, the eucharist gives the lie to any kind of gnosticizing eschatology which sees man's ultimate destiny to consist in the release of his soul from the evil prison of his material body in order that it may regain its native spirit-realm.[479] For the use of bread and wine at the eucharist confirms the picture that emerges from the opening chapters of Genesis of a material creation that is destined to be the scene and vehicle of the communion God intends between Himself and the human creature who is both the crown of creation and the image of God.[480]

If the Old Testament may picture the mountains and hills breaking forth into song and the trees of the field clapping their hands together because they are the scene of the salvation God gives to Israel,[481] then we may consider that in becoming the vehicle of saving fellowship between God and man the bread and wine of the eucharist are granted, at least in a hidden way, fulfilment of the destiny after which the whole material creation groans (cf. Rom. 8:19–23). What is true of the inanimate creatures of bread and wine cannot be less true of the body of the man who consumes them at the eucharist, and so we may be confident that the human body shares, and will continue to share, in an appropriate way in that personal obedience to a loving King in which the highest and ultimate destiny of man consists. The eschatological condition in which God will be all in all (I Cor. 15:28) is envisaged by the New Testament as new heavens and a new earth (II Pet. 3:13), peopled by men and women in their risen and glorified *bodies* (I Cor. 15:35–58; Phil. 3:21): any eschatology which reduces the cosmic reference to anthropology, and the anthropology to 'spiritualism', is guilty simply of ignoring the bread and wine of the eucharist.[482]

### 5. Eschatology is universal in scope

The eucharistic celebration and the eucharistic community are instances of the principle of representative election at work (see pp. 119f). From the whole of humanity God chooses the eucharistic community, and from the whole of the rest of creation this bread and this wine, in order to show forth His purpose for the whole universe. At the eucharist men and matter receive and render the divine glory in token of the fact that God's glory will fill the whole universe when God is everywhere actively present and all His creation bows the knee in obedience to His royal will (cf. Phil. 2:10f.). To obviate the charge of universalist heresy, though I would prefer to risk that charge if the alternative was to give up hope that all men will be saved (Rom. 11:32; I Tim. 2:4), it may be said that it is indeed just conceivable that the glorification of God by complete obedience to His sovereign will might bring no joy to some. In the eucharist the accent certainly falls on the *gracious* will of God to give Himself to men in a way which makes free human obedience both possible and a joy.

## 6. Eschatology allows progress in the establishment of the kingdom

At the eucharist, the future is invading the present to fill the moment with a content that is part of God's eternal purpose but which is still future in His dealings with men. At the eucharist, deepest reality is breaking through to the surface to give superficiality its truer meaning. At the eucharist, men and nature are being lifted by their Creator to their highest destiny, which is to serve the will and purpose of God in openness to His presence. In more biblical terms, the Lord's supper is the occasion of God's granting to men the righteousness, the peace, and the joy in the Holy Spirit which are the kingdom of God (Rom. 14:17; see p. 59). The eucharistic celebration does not leave the world unchanged. The future has occupied the present for a moment at least, and that moment is henceforth an ineradicable part of the experience of those who lived it. Where the surface has been broken from below, the ripples spread in ever-broadening circles. What has been raised to its highest destiny will not readily be content to relapse to a lower level of existence. When God has visited a receptive people in the eucharist, men have been made more righteous, the peace of God has been more firmly established among them, and the Holy Spirit has brought an ineffaceable experience of joy to their hearts. At the risk of falling into a facile doctrine of progress, it must be said that if the history of the individual, of the church, of the human race, and of the world bears in any way a cumulative character so that each moment of the past may become part of acquired and permanent experience, then the kingdom of God has come closer with each eucharistic celebration. There is no denial here that it will be a final and drastic event that brings in the universal kingdom. But an eschatology which denies historical progress in the kingdom's establishment is not doing justice to the present activity of the (re)creative Word and the (re)creative Spirit in the eucharist (see pp. 95–102).

## 7. Eschatology includes a moment of judgement and renewal

The risk of a facile doctrine of progress is removed if it is remembered that eschatology includes a moment of judgement and renewal. According to

II Pet. 3:13f, at the day of the coming of the Lord the heavens will be kindled and dissolved and the elements will melt with fire, and there will be new heavens and a new earth in which righteousness dwells. But in the eucharist we have precisely a projection, from the future and in terms of a set of comprehensible symbols, of the coming of the Lord. In the eucharist the Lord comes to judge and to recreate; to cast out what remains of unrighteousness in His people, and to continue the work of renewal begun in baptism; to threaten the world with an end to its old existence, and to give it the promise, through the new use to which bread and wine is put, of attaining its true destiny. No general eschatology will have done justice to the evidence of the eucharist unless it includes a present moment of judgement and renewal which is the projection of the cataclysm that will inaugurate the universal and incontestable reign of God.[483]

*     *     *

Our final task is to indicate what concepts or images the eucharist may offer as particularly characteristic contributions to the description of the polarity between the 'already' and the 'not yet' which marks the structure of eschatology. Four may be mentioned:

## 1. The eucharist is a taste of the kingdom

It may be that in general usage the word taste has lost some of its evocative power through being used as a practically dead metaphor both in highly abstract contexts and also in the often trivially employed expressions 'good taste' and 'bad taste'. But the Lord's supper, in which bread is eaten and wine is drunk, should keep the word, as far as the church is concerned, firmly rooted in elementary physiological sensation, and that as experienced at moments of high religious awareness—and therefore allow it to retain its poetical potentialities in theological use.[484] These potentialities are apparent from biblical use of טָעַם (to taste), חֵךְ (palate, taste), and γεύσεσθαι (to taste).

> O taste and see that the Lord is good!
> Happy is the man who takes refuge in him!
> O fear the Lord, you his saints,
> for those who fear him have no want!
> The young lions suffer want and hunger;
> but those who seek the Lord lack no good thing.   (Ps. 34:8–10)

> How sweet are thy words to my taste,
> sweeter than honey to my mouth.   (Ps. 119:103)

> My son, eat honey, for it is good, and the drippings of the honeycomb are sweet to your taste. Know that wisdom is such to your soul.   (Prov. 24:13)

> As an apple tree among the trees of the wood,
> so is my beloved among young men.
> With great delight I sat in his shadow,
> and his fruit was sweet to my taste.
> He brought me to the banqueting house,

and his banner over me was love.
Sustain me with raisins,
refresh me with apples;
for I am sick with love.   (Cant. 2:3–5)

When the steward of the feast tasted the water now become wine . . . he called the bridegroom and said to him, Every man serves the good wine first; and when men have drunk freely, then the poor wine; but you have kept the good wine until now. This, the first of his signs, Jesus did at Cana in Galilee, and manifested his glory. . . .   (John 2:9–11)

For it is impossible to restore again to repentance those who have once been enlightened, who have tasted the heavenly gift, and have become partakers of the Holy Spirit, and have tasted the goodness of the word of God and the powers of the age to come . . .   (Heb. 6:4f)

Like newborn babes, long for the pure spiritual milk, that by it you may grow up to salvation; for you have tasted the kindness of the Lord.   (I Pet. 2:2f)[485]

To taste is to try the relish; and to say that the eucharist provides a taste of the kingdom therefore allows us to express both the provisionality and yet the genuineness of the kingdom as it flavours the present. We recall what Peter Chrysologus, in the fifth century, had said in his eucharistic interpretation of the fourth petition of the Lord's prayer: Christ gave us the eucharist 'that we might by it attain unto endless day and the very table of Christ, and there receive in fulness and unto all satiety that of which we have here been given the taste (*ut unde hic gustum sumpsimus, inde ibi plenitudinem totasque satietates capiamus*).'[486] Charles Wesley could sing:

> Yet onward I haste
>   To the heavenly feast:
> That, that is the fulness; but this is the taste;
>   And this I shall prove,
>   Till with joy I remove
> To the heaven of heavens in Jesus's love.[487]

And in the *Hymns on the Lord's Supper* the Wesleys repeat the theme:

> How glorious is the life above,
>   Which in this ordinance we taste;
> That fulness of celestial love,
>   That joy which shall for ever last!   (Hymn 101)

> Here He gives our souls a taste,
>   Heaven into our heart He pours . . .   (Hymn 103)[488]

This use of *taste* is much rarer in the eucharistic liturgies and theologians than one might have expected; but its value as an expression for the relation between the 'already' and the 'not yet' is undeniable.

## 2. The eucharist is a sign of the kingdom

As we saw (pp. 29f, 41), the eucharist has much in common with the category of phenomena to which belong the prophetic אֹת and the

Johannine σημεῖον. In view of what has been said, we need not spend long on this point here. Suffice it to recall that the eucharist *announces* and *initiates*, or (as we should rather say in the case of the eucharist) *furthers*, the coming of the kingdom of God. The eucharist proclaims God's will to bring all men and all nature into His service, and already He puts that will into practice in a representative way at the eucharist. The eucharist proclaims that for men the kingdom of God means righteousness, peace, and joy in openness to the divine presence, and already the Lord is establishing these things by His coming at the eucharist.

Again we find that the eucharist, by its character as *sign*, forms a valuable expression for the relation between the 'already' and the 'not yet' of eschatology.

### 3. The eucharist is an image of the kingdom

We discovered above that Theodore of Mopsuestia and Maximus the Confessor considered the eucharist as an εἰκών of the heavenly kingdom.[489] There is no need to scent here an unsatisfactory Greek notion of the world of the phenomena as a pale and perpetual reflection of the eternal world of the noumena. Both Theodore and Maximus show that the eucharist is firmly anchored in the real events of earthly history, and that it is for men but the *prefiguration* of the life of a kingdom still to come. With these safeguards, the notion of image may usefully express the relation between a kingdom that belongs to God's eternal purpose and the form which that kingdom may at present take on earth. In human portraiture, the important thing about an 'image' is that it should capture the qualities of the person portrayed; clearly it is not identical with the subject himself, and yet it may convey his personality to the beholder. The eucharist is not identical with the kingdom of God itself, and yet it shares the nature of that kingdom (even more intimately than a portrait or statue shares the nature of its subject), in such a way that it may communicate the qualities of the kingdom to the spectator and, *a fortiori*, to the participants (whose existential engagement is even deeper than that of the most aesthetically sensitive person standing before a painting or a sculpture). We recall the prayer from the Leonine Sacramentary 'ut ... quod in imagine gerimus sacramenti, manifesta perceptione sumamus', and the prayer from the Roman Missal 'ut quae nunc specie gerimus rerum veritate capiamus'.[490] Or as Ambrose has it: The events under the Law were the *shadow*, the sacraments of the Gospel are the *image*, while perfect *truth* belongs to heaven where Christ already is and where one day we shall be.[491]

Such a use of *image* is capable of extension beyond the directly eucharistic domain, and it may make a valuable contribution to the general question of the relation between the kingdom as eternally purposed by God and the present form of that kingdom.

### 4. The eucharist as mystery of the kingdom

As is well known, from the third and fourth centuries onwards the Greek

Fathers spoke of the eucharist as μυστήριον. Without at all going into the question of the relation between the Christian sacraments and the Hellenistic mystery-cults, we may nevertheless ask whether this designation, in the light of the New Testament use of μυστήριον, may not serve to sum up the eucharist's role in that state of eschatological tension between hiddenness and visibility which marks 'the time of the church' and which we have often seen reflected in the eucharistic liturgies and in eucharistic theology in the course of our study.[492]

According to the New Testament, the Mystery is primarily the secret counsel of God, fixed before all ages, to bring men (and not Israel alone) to salvation in Jesus Christ (Rom. 16:25–27; I Cor. 2:6–10; Eph. 1:9f; 3:1–12; 6:19; Col. 1:24–29; 4:3; I Tim. 3:16). But the revelation of the Mystery in Jesus Christ has taken place in such a manner that it can be understood only by those to whom the grace is given, whereas for 'those outside' it remains *mere παραβολαί*, i.e. enigmatic (Mark 4:10–13). To those that are perishing in their unbelief the gospel remains veiled (II Cor. 4:3f).

The eucharist epitomizes the divine Mystery. To the eyes of faith it is the revelation of God's design for man's salvation in Jesus Christ; for in the eucharist the Lord receives men in fellowship at His table. But it remains a sign that can be contradicted (cf. Luke 2:34). It exemplifies the *clair-obscur* of 'the time of the church'. When the Mystery of God has been completed (Rev. 10:7), sacraments will cease and the eucharist will give way to the vision of God in His incontestable kingdom.

# Notes

1 See for instance the *Heidelberg Catechism* (1563), questions 75–80.
2 See the survey of post-Tridentine theologians on this point in T. Fitzgerald, *The Influence of the Holy Eucharist on Bodily Resurrection*, pp. 63–93.
3 In the series *Le Mystère chrétien*, section *Théologie sacramentaire*.
4 Typical would be this statement of the Anglican A. J. B. Higgins, formerly a Congregationalist: 'Thus the Church's Eucharist is at one and the same time a remembrance of the death of Christ, and an expectation of perfect joy with him in the Kingdom, which is already in a measure anticipated at each celebration by the experience of his risen living presence' (*The Lord's Supper in the New Testament*, 1952, p. 54).
5 Ignatius of Antioch, *Eph.* 20:2: φάρμακον ἀθανασίας.
6 Apart from his *Geschichte der Leben-Jesu-Forschung* ( = *The Quest of the Historical Jesus*, 1910), there is the earlier *Das Messianitäts- und Leidensgeheimnis* (1901), the later *Die Mystik des Apostels Paulus* (1930), and the posthumous *Reich Gottes und Urchristentum* (1967).
7 The classic expression of Dodd's 'realized eschatology' is found in his book *The Parables of the Kingdom*, 1935.
8 T. F. Glasson, *The Second Advent: The Origin of the New Testament Doctrine*, 1945, especially pp. 63–105, 162–79, 185–87, 194, 202–5.
9 J. Jeremias, *Die Gleichnisse Jesu*, 1956⁴, e.g. pp. 42f., 127–48, 186–91, 194. See also I. H. Marshall, *Eschatology and the Parables*, 1963.
10 To say that these parables were *inventions* of the primitive church designed to keep up flagging spirits in face of the delay of a mistakenly awaited second advent begs too many questions.
11 G. R. Beasley-Murray (*Jesus and the Future*, 1954) can hardly be said to have vindicated the authenticity of Mark 13 as far as he would like, but he makes some acute remarks on the prophecies of tribulation for the disciples (vv. 9, 11, 13) which may also improve the credit of predictions of future persecutions before the end elsewhere in the gospels (pp. 192–94).
12 Dodd's treatment of ἐληλυθυῖαν in *The Parables of the Kingdom*¹, pp. 53f, is a good example of over-subtle interpretation: 'The bystanders are not promised that they shall see the Kingdom of God *coming*, but that they shall come to see that the Kingdom of God *has already come*, at some point before they became aware of it'—and that point was the ministry of Jesus. See the criticisms made by W. G. Kümmel, *Verheissung und Erfüllung*, 1945, pp. 13–16, and by R. H. Fuller, *The Mission and Achievement of Jesus*, 1954, pp. 27f. Dodd himself later modified this interpretation of Mark 9:1 to the extent of taking the coming of the kingdom '*in power*' as referring to the Resurrection, Pentecost and the beginning of a new era, 'the kingdom of Christ on earth' (*The Coming of Christ*, 1951, pp. 13f.; he had already seen the possibility of this later interpretation in *Parables*¹, p. 54).

13 A strong statement of this view is found in W. G. Kümmel, *Verheissung und Erfüllung*, 1945[1] [1953[2]]. After his careful and detailed survey of twentieth-century writing on the subject, N. Perrin concludes that 'it may be said to be established that the Kingdom is both present and future in the teaching of Jesus' (*The Kingdom of God in the Teaching of Jesus*, 1963, p. 159). A similar survey leads to a similar conclusion in G. Lundström's book of identical title (1963; the Swedish original dates from 1947).

14 R. H. Fuller, *The Mission and Achievement of Jesus*, pp. 27f, 118–20.

15 *In the End, God . . .*, 1950, especially pp. 56–70, and *Jesus and His Coming*, 1957, especially pp. 38f, 87, 100f, 180–85. According to Robinson, the New Testament never pictures the parousia as 'Jesus coming again within the sequence and boundaries of history as we know it' (*In the End, God . . .*, 1950, p. 67).

16 On Luke–Acts see especially H. Conzelmann, *Die Mitte der Zeit*, 1954.

17 R. Bultmann, *History and Eschatology*, p. 43.

18 See G. Bornkamm, 'Enderwartung und Kirche im Matthäusevangelium' in W. D. Davies and D. Daube (edd.), *The Background of the New Testament and its Eschatology*, 1956, in particular pp. 254f.; and cf. E. Grässer, *Das Problem der Parusieverzögerung in den synoptischen Evangelien und in der Apostelgeschichte*, 1957, pp. 200–4.

19 Thus R. Bultmann: 'His going away is salutary for them; for else He could not send the Paraclete, the Spirit (John 16:7). But not otherwise than in the Spirit will He return; the old, primitive-Christian conception of His parousia has been given up; the world will perceive nothing of His coming (14:21f)' (*Theologie des Neuen Testaments*, 1958[3], p. 437, cf. pp. 410f). Compare C. H. Dodd, *The Interpretation of the Fourth Gospel*, 1953, pp. 403–6, 414f.

20 See R. Bultmann, *Das Evangelium des Johannes* (Meyer commentary), 1941, e.g., pp. 193–97, and *Theologie des Neuen Testaments*[3], pp. 389–92. Bultmann claims the support of Paul, though not quite so absolutely perhaps, for the same view. See 'History and Eschatology in the N.T.' in *NTS* 1 (1954–55), pp. 5–16, and *History and Eschatology*, 1957, pp. 40–49.

21 See R. Schnackenburg, *Gottes Herrschaft und Reich*, 1959, pp. 226–29. C. K. Barrett points out that the 'platonizing' or 'alexandrian' eschatology of Hebrews may have other and more direct roots in a Palestinian rabbinism which knew a 'new Jerusalem' that was both a 'Jerusalem above' and a 'Jerusalem of the age to come' ('The Eschatology of the Epistle to the Hebrews' in W. D. Davies and D. Daube (edd.), *The Background of the N.T. and its Eschatology*, pp. 363–93). Barrett passes the following favourable comment: 'The most significant contribution of Hebrews to the growing problem of N.T. eschatology [posed by the delay in the parousia] lies in the author's use of philosophical and liturgical language. By means of this terminology it is possible to impress upon believers the nearness of the invisible world without insisting upon the nearness of the *parousia*. The author of Hebrews did believe that the *parousia* was near (10:25: *we may add 9:28*), but lays no stress on this conviction' (p. 391).

22 Quoted from the earlier Althaus by J. Moltmann, *Theologie der Hoffnung*, p. 33.

23 R. Bultmann, *History and Eschatology*, pp. 149–55.

24 Some of the criticisms made in an article by K. G. Steck are pertinent here: 'Eschatologie und Ekklesiologie in der römisch-katholischen Theologie von

heute' in *Materialdienst des Konfessionskundlichen Instituts* 9 (1958), pp. 81–90.

25 See the bibliographical references above, p. 9.

26 *Le retour du Christ*, 1945², p. 14.

27 True, Cullmann devotes a chapter of *Christus und die Zeit* to 'the sovereignty of God over time'; but this is hard to square with the preceding chapter in which he seems to conceive of time as equally increate with God or as part of God's nature. In upholding the eternity of God, I do not mean that He is altogether unaffected by what happens in time. Every human act affects thenceforth the form concretely taken by God's realization in history, and (definitively) in the final kingdom, of His constant and eternal purpose for creation.

28 *Gottes Herrschaft und Reich*, pp. 147f.

29 *Gottes Herrschaft und Reich*, pp. 224–29.

30 Clément also speaks of time being *porous* to eternity ('Le dimanche et le Jour éternel' in *Verbum Caro* no. 79 (1966), in particular p. 112).

31 See the much altered fourth (1933) or especially the fifth (1949) editions of his *Die letzten Dinge: Lehrbuch der Eschatologie*, first published in 1922.

32 A similar view to Althaus's is presented by P. Maury, *L'Eschatologie*, 1959, *in nuce*, pp. 57f.

33 R. Bultmann, *History and Eschatology*, pp. 150–52; F. Gogarten, *Verhängnis und Hoffnung der Neuzeit*, 1953 (ch. 11: 'Die neutestamentliche Eschatologie').

34 See especially pp. 66–70, 86–96, of the first edition.

35 G. von Rad, 'Typologische Auslegung des Alten Testaments' in *Evangelische Theologie* 12 (1952/53), pp. 17–33, and *Theologie des Alten Testaments* II, 1960, pp. 329–31, 384f, 386f, 397f; also W. Zimmerli, 'Verheissung und Erfüllung' in *Evangelische Theologie* 12 (1952/53), pp. 34–59. And see now H. D. Preuss, *Jahweglaube und Zukunftserwartung*, 1968.

36 John Chrysostom's attitude of fear and trembling is still alive in Orthodoxy. See E. Bishop's appendix on 'Fear and awe attaching to the eucharistic service' in R. H. Connolly, *The Liturgical Homilies of Narsai*, pp. 92–97.

37 Thus Pascher: 'Das Mahl [ist] die Grundsymbolik der Eucharistie' (p. 149); and 'Die Kirche ist die eine grosse Mahlgemeinschaft der Getauften' (p. 375). See also A. Verheul, 'De gestalte van de Eucharistieviering Maaltijd of Offer?' in *Tijdschrift voor Liturgie* 45 (1961), pp. 39–59.

38 E. Lohmeyer, 'Vom urchristlichen Abendmahl' in *Theologische Rundschau* n.F.9 (1937), pp. 168–227, 273–312, and n.F. 10 (1938), pp. 81–99; and 'Das Abendmahl in der Urgemeinde' in *Journal of Biblical Literature* 56 (1937), pp. 217–52.

39 See F. Bammel, *Das heilige Mahl im Glauben der Völker*, 1950.

40 Many scholars have taken J. Jeremias's word for the fact that 'my blood of the covenant' is a grammatical impossibility in Semitic languages (*Die Abendmahlsworte Jesu*, 1949², p. 99); but J. A. Emerton seems, on the basis of Semitic parallels, to have established the contrary ('The Aramaic underlying τὸ αἷμά μου τῆς διαθήκης in Mk. XIV 24' in *JTS* n.s. 6 (1955), pp. 238–40, and 'τὸ αἷμά μου τῆς διαθήκης: the evidence of the Syrian versions' in *JTS* n.s. 13 (1962), pp. 111–17; in any case, Jeremias has now, on other grounds, withdrawn his objections to the expression (*Abendmahlsworte³*, pp. 186–88). Jesus declares that He ('my') is inaugurating a *new* covenant,

even though the word 'new' does not appear in Mark (the reading of A f1 f13 700 lat sy being secondary).

41 Most scholars consider that the allusion here is to Jer. 31:31–34; but any reference to a *new* covenant implies also a reference back to the *old*.

42 On the importance of the notion of the event of Exod. 24:9–11 for the eucharist, see already the work of the Old Catholic scholar E. Gaugler, 'La sainte cène' (1945), pp. 78f; also E. Schweizer's article, 'Das Herrenmahl im Neuen Testament' reprinted in his *Neotestamentica*, 1963, in particular pp. 350f.

43 See A. Feuillet, 'Les thèmes bibliques majeurs du discours sur le pain de vie' in *NRTh* 82 (1960), in particular pp. 817f.

44 H. H. Rowley (*Worship in Ancient Israel*, London, 1967, pp. 122–25) rather dampens the theory that the sharing of the beast between God and the worshippers in the זִבְחֵי שְׁלָמִים expresses and strengthens the communion between the Lord and His people *because they are eating the same beast.*

45 A. Feuillet, *art. cit.*, pp. 918–22.

46 Other references to the feast offered by Wisdom may be found in Ecclus. 6:19; 15:3; 24:19–21.

47 R. H. Charles (ed.), *The Apocrypha and Pseudepigrapha of the O.T.* II, Oxford, 1913, pp. 497f. See further Strack-Billerbeck IV, pp. 888–90 (with supporting references on pp. 949–55).

48 Because of the later transference of ideas associated with the manna to the eucharist, we may here cite the names given to the manna in the Jewish tradition. It is most frequently called 'bread from heaven' (Exod. 16:4; Ps. 105:40; Neh. 9:15; Wisd. 16:20; cf. Ps. 78:24). In Ps. 78:25 it is called 'the bread of the strong' (לֶחֶם אַבִּירִים), which the LXX correctly interprets as ἄρτος ἀγγέλων. A similar Greek expression appears at Wisd. 16:20 (ἀγγέλων τροφή); and cf. 4 Ezra. 1:19. If angels do not need food (cf. Tobit 12:19), the expression may mean 'bread *brought by angels*' (so A. Feuillet, *art. cit.*, p. 808, n. 7). Otherwise it may refer to the supernatural quality of the food or to its excellencies on which Wisd. 16:20f dwells: 'Thou didst give thy people the food of angels, and without their toil thou didst supply them from heaven with bread ready to eat, providing every pleasure, and suited to every taste. For thy sustenance (ἡ ὑπόστασίς σου, *substantia tua*) manifested thy sweetness toward thy children; and it, ministering to the desire of the one who took it, was changed to suit every one's liking.'

49 R. H. Charles, *Apocrypha and Pseudepigrapha* II, p. 498.

50 Strack-Billerbeck II, p. 481, where reference is also made to Midr Cant 2, 9f and NuR 11.

51 Whether the Last Supper was *as a matter of historical fact* a passover meal, is a much debated question. Many scholars consider that its being a regular passover meal is excluded by the Johannine fixing of the moment of the *crucifixion* as the time of the killing of the paschal lambs (John 19:14, cf. 18:28); but the Johannine chronology itself may be theological rather than historical (cf. also the theological motif of John 19:36 referring back to Exod. 12:46 and Num. 9:12). The indispensable guide to the debate is J. Jeremias, *Die Abendmahlsworte Jesu*, 1960[3], which tries to meet the various objections that have been made to the synoptic chronology. It is only a pity that Jeremias tends to treat in rather a cavalier manner objections that have

been made to his own arguments as they have appeared in previous editions of his book (1935[1]; 1949[2]). This is especially true of his treatment (3rd ed., pp. 18f.) of the brilliant thesis of A. Jaubert (*La Date de la Cène*, 1957) which seeks to reconcile the synoptic presentation of the Last Supper as a passover meal with the Johannine chronology of the crucifixion by placing the Last Supper on the *Tuesday evening* as a passover meal celebrated according to a calendar (found in Jubilees and Qumran) other than the official one.

52 The two most recent studies are A. Strobel, 'Die Passa-Erwartung als urchristliches Problem in Lc 17:20f' in *ZNW* 49 (1958), pp. 157–96, and R. Le Déaut, *La Nuit Pascale*, 1963.

53 R. Le Déaut, *op. cit.*, p. 283.

54 *Bell. Jud.* V, 98ff; VI, 290–95.

55 See J. Jeremias, *Abendmahlsworte*[3], p. 199, n. 4.

56 Rabbinic sources make great play with the לֵיל שִׁמֻּרִים (or לֵיל נְטִיר in some rabbinic texts) of Exod. 12:42. In the 'poem of the four nights', the Targum (on the various traditions of the text see R. Le Déaut, pp. 264–79) makes it clear that the night of 14/15 Nisan was the night of creation, the night of the covenant with Abraham, the night of the deliverance from Egypt—and 'the fourth night will be when the world reaches its end and is delivered [*or* dissolved]. The yokes of iron will be broken and the generations [דרי, Codex Neofiti] of iniquity will be destroyed. Moses will come forth from the desert, and king Messiah will come forth from on high [accepting M. Black's suggestion, considered probable by Le Déaut pp. 359–69, of ממרומא instead of מרומה, "from Rome": *An Aramaic Approach to the Gospels and Acts*, Oxford, 1954[2], pp. 172–74].' (The reference to the messiah is missing from Codex Neofiti, but Le Déaut, pp. 271f, gives good grounds for thinking that the omission was accidental.) The Midrash Mechiltha testifies to the same expectation of deliverance: 'In this night they were redeemed (from Egypt), and in this night they will be redeemed. These are the words of Rabbi Joshua [ben Hananya, *fl. c.* 90 A.D.]' (Mekh Ex 12, 42, Strack-Billerbeck I, p. 85). The Midrash Rabba looks for the coming of 'the messiah who is called the first (cf. Isa. 41:27)' in 'the first month', that is Nisan, the month of passover (Ex R 15, 2 on Ex 12:2; see J. Jeremias, *Abendmahlsworte*[3], p. 198, n. 4). See also Ex R 18 in Strack-Billerbeck IV, p. 55.

57 The hymn which the company sang at the end of the meal (Mark 14:26; Matt. 26:30) was the second part of the passover hallel (J. Jeremias, *Abendmahlsworte*[3], p. 49). The messianic interpretation of the hallel (Pss. 113–18), and particularly of Ps. 118:24–29, to which rabbinic sources testify, seems confirmed for the time of Jesus by Mark 11:9, Matt. 21:9, John 12:13 (J. Jeremias, *op. cit.*, pp. 246–52). On the eschatological associations of the passover cups see F. J. Leenhardt, *Le sacrement de la sainte cène*, pp. 20f (cf. pp. 39–48); J. Jeremias, *op. cit.*, p. 53; and P. Lebeau, *Le vin nouveau du royaume*, pp. 35–45.

58 A. Strobel, *art. cit.* as in n. 52.

59 B. Lohse, *Das Passafest der Quartadecimaner*, especially pp. 78–84. Though accepting Lohse's positive evidence for the advent expectations of the Quartadecimans at the paschal festival, I am inclined to think that he overplays the contrast (see especially p. 121) between a Quartadeciman passover

governed by eschatological expectations and a 'Roman' Easter understood as a commemoration of the death and resurrection of Jesus Christ. On the one hand, Lohse underestimates the importance of the death and resurrection of Christ in the Quartadeciman festival:

1.) The *Epistola Apostolorum* (a Quartadeciman document, *circa* 150–160 A.D.), besides providing evidence for a hope of the parousia at passover tide, speaks also of a 'remembrance of my death' in association with the passover (edd. C. Schmidt and I. Wajnberg, in *Texte und Untersuchungen*, vol. 43, Leipzig, 1919, pp. 52–59).

2.) The paschal sermon of the Quartadeciman bishop Melito of Sardis, though it contains hints of the eschatological expectation, is principally an interpretation of Christ's saving death (and resurrection).

3.) The *Epistola Apostolorum* indicates that the Quartadecimans closed their paschal vigil with a eucharist at *cockcrow*, which was precisely a traditional timing of the resurrection of Christ (cf. *Didascalia Apostolorum*, 21, ed. R. H. Connolly, Oxford, 1929, p. 192; *Apost. Const.* V, 19, 3 & 6f; Denys of Alexandria, *ep. ad Basilidem*, PG 10, 1272f).

4.) If the mention of the hope of the resurrection of Asian worthies at the return of the Lord in Polycrates's letter to Victor of Rome (*apud* Eusebius, *H.E.* V. 24. 2–5) is taken as a hint that the Quartadecimans attached the importance they did to the right dating of the paschal festival on account of the parousia hope they associated with the festival, then it must also be said that Polycrates's hope for the *final* resurrection must, theologically (I Cor. 15), have been grounded in Christ's resurrection.

On the other hand, it is a quite gratuitous assumption of Lohse's that the catholic church's paschal expectation (evidences of which we are about to give in the text above) was a borrowing from the Quartadecimans rather than a continuation, equally with the Quartadecimans', of a primitive Christian hope.

60 R. H. Charles, *Apocrypha and Pseudepigrapha of the O.T.* II, pp. 228f (the importance of the mention of *glory* in this text will be clear after my pp. 102–4). Other examples of the future feasting are: *Pirkē Aboth* 3:20, '. . . and everything is prepared for the banquet' (Charles, *op. cit.* II, p. 702 and note); Slavonic Enoch 42:5; Ex R 25, with appeal to Isa. 65:13 (Strack-Billerbeck IV, p. 1148); and many references in Strack-Billerbeck IV, pp. 1154–65.

61 In J. Carmignac, E. Cothenet & H. Lignée, *Les Textes de Qumran* II, Paris, 1963, pp. 124f.

62 'Feast' may be finding too much in מוֹעֵד. Cross admits that the precise meaning of the word, found in Num. 16:2 (whence the whole expression within quotation marks is drawn), is not clear. D. Barthélemy renders more generally: '*Voici* (*l'ordre de*) session des hommes de renom invités aux convocations pour les délibérations communes, au cas où Dieu *mènerait* le Messie avec eux' (D. Barthélemy & J. T. Milik, *Discoveries in the Judaean Desert. I: Qumran Cave I*, Oxford, 1955, p. 117).

63 Isa. 2:2–4 (Micah 4:1–3); 25:6–9; 55:4f; 56:6–8; 60; 66:19–24; Hag. 2:6–9; Zech. 2:11; 8:20–23; 14; Tobit 13:11; 14:5–7. See for instance J. Jeremias, *Jesu Verheissung für die Völker*, 1956, pp. 47–58; and R. Martin-Achard, *Israël et les Nations: La perspective missionnaire de l'A.T.*, 1959.

64 See pp. 128f.

65 The rich find it hard to enter the kingdom: Mark 4:19 (and pars.); 10:17–27

(and pars.); Luke 1:53; 6:24; 12:13–21; 16:19–31; cf. Mark 12:41–44 (=Luke 21:1–4).

66 See Strack-Billerbeck I, pp. 972f.

67 But what then is the marriage-feast from which the master comes? Intratrinitarian bliss?

68 For bridegroom as a messianic title see (despite J. Jeremias, *art.* νύμφη, νυμφίος in *TWNT* IV, pp. 1092–99) Matt. 25:1–13; John 3:29; II Cor. 11:2; Eph. 5:22–33; Rev. 19:7–9.

69 H. Lietzmann saw his 'Jerusalem type' of eucharist as a continuation of the daily meals of Jesus and His disciples during His ministry.

70 Cf. Ecclus. 51:23–27. Ἀναπαύσω naturally suggests the idea of refreshment with food and drink: cf. Luke 12:19.

71 At John 6:27 the text has variant forms. 'The food . . . which the Son of man *will give* (δώσει) you' is read by most witnesses, whereas ℵ D e ff² j syr cur read *gives* (δίδωσιν). Jesus Himself, the bread of heaven, is already present, and it seems that one may already eat of Him (vv. 32–35); yet the giving still has a future reference also, at this point in the ministry (v. 51c). On the feeding miracles of Jesus as the eschatological counterpart of Moses and the manna, see A. Heising, *Die Botschaft der Brotvermehrung*, 1966.

72 G. H. Boobyer, 'The Miracles of the Loaves and the Gentiles in St Mark's Gospel' in *Scottish Journal of Theology* 6 (1953), pp. 77–87.

73 It is noteworthy that the early church took up the Matthaean saying 'Do not give dogs what is holy' (7:6) and used it in *excluding* the unbaptized and heretics from the eucharist (*Didache*, 9; Athanasius, *Apol. contra Arianos*, 11 PG 25, 268; pseudo-Basil, PG 31, 1688; John Damascene, *de fid. orth.* IV, 13, PG 94, 1153)—and left alone the *generous* approval given by Jesus to the Syrophoenician woman's reply to an equally canine saying ('Yes, Lord, yet even the dogs eat the crumbs that fall from their master's table'). On the question of qualifications for receiving communion see pp. 128–35.

74 H. Riesenfeld, *Jésus transfiguré*, pp. 318–24.

75 On p. 322 Riesenfeld speaks of it being 'l'aube des temps messianiques'. On p. 319 he had said that the conduct of the disciples on the sabbath 'prefigures' the great sabbath of messianic times, and on p. 320 that the symbolic act shows that the time of the messianic sabbath 'has arrived'. His overall position seems therefore to be one of *inaugurated* eschatology.

76 On the association between wine and eschatological salvation in the Jewish tradition, see P. Lebeau, *Le vin nouveau du royaume*, pp. 33–52.

77 Dating perhaps from H. W. Robinson, 'Prophetic Symbolism' in *Old Testament Essays*, 1927, pp. 1–17. See G. Fohrer, *Die symbolischen Handlungen der Propheten*, and literature there cited.

78 Other examples are: Exod. 9:8–12; Josh. 8:18–26; I Kings 11:23–29; II Kings 13:13–19; Isa. 8:1–14; 20; Jer. 13:1–11; 16:1–9; Ezek. *passim*.

79 See for example E. C. Hoskyns, *The Fourth Gospel*, 1947², p. 190; C. K. Barrett, *The Gospel according to St John*, 1955, pp. 63–65; C. H. Dodd, *The Interpretation of the Fourth Gospel*, 1954, pp. 141–43; R. Schnackenburg, *Das Johannesevangelium* I, 1965, pp. 344–56 (with references to other literature).

80 In view of what we know about the Jewish ברכה form which the use of εὐλογεῖν and εὐχαριστεῖν in eucharistic or quasi-eucharistic contexts in the New Testament implies (see G. A. Michell, *Eucharistic Consecration in the*

*Primitive Church*, 1948, and J. P. Audet, 'Esquisse historique du genre littéraire de la "Bénédiction" juive et de l'"Eucharistie" chrétienne' in *Revue Biblique* 65 (1958), pp. 371–99), we must probably reject the thesis of J. Schousboe ('La messe la plus ancienne' in *Revue de l'Histoire des Religions* 96 (1927), pp. 193–256) and A. Schweitzer (*Die Mystik des Apostels Paulus*, p. 268) that the Lord's prayer was used as a eucharistic consecration prayer. On the place of the Our Father in the preparatory part of the communion cycle see J. A. Jungmann, *Missarum sollemnia*, II, pp. 343–63. The earliest evidences for its use before communion are: Cyril of Jerusalem, *Myst. Cat.* V, 11 (ed. Cross, p. 34); Ambrose, *de sacramentis* VI, 24; Jerome, *adv. Pelag.* III, 15, PL 23, 585; John Chrysostom, *In cap. IX Gen. hom. XXVII* PG 53, 251; Augustine, e.g. *Ep.* 149, 16, PL 33, 636. It does not occur in the eucharistic liturgy of *Apost. Const. VIII*, nor in that reflected in Theodore of Mopsuestia's catecheses. On the date of its introduction at Rome see Jungmann, pp. 343–46. The Reformers retained the Lord's prayer in their eucharistic liturgies but often shifted it from its traditional place between the great prayer and the communion (e.g. the Anglican rite of 1552 and 1662 puts it *after* communion).

81 The only known instance of secular use appears to be in a list of expenses in an Egyptian papyrus (F. Preisigke, *Sammelbuch griechischer Urkunden aus Ägypten* I, 5224, 20), where the incomplete word ἐπιουσι . . . probably represents a neuter plural meaning 'a day's ration'; but this in itself would give no help as to whether ἐπιούσιος meant 'for today', 'for tomorrow', 'for each day' or even 'the needed (amount)' (on all of which see later). Leaving aside the twisted history of the Codices Sergii (see D. Y. Hadidian, 'The meaning of ἐπιούσιος and the Codices Sergii' in *NTS* 5 (1958–59), pp. 75–81), I have found only two instances of the use of ἐπιούσιος not in connection with the Lord's prayer. In his *Life of Chrysostom* Palladius clearly understands it, like Chrysostom himself, of food for the body, for he says of Elijah the Tishbite: οὐχὶ διὰ κοράκων τὴν ἐπιούσιον ἐδέχετο μᾶζαν (*vita Chrys.*, 12, PG 47, 43). In the tenth century, Nicephorus uses it outside the Lord's prayer and with a similar meaning of bodily food: ἔργῳ χειρῶν κοπιῶντας τὸν ἐπιούσιον πορίζεσθαι ἄρτον (*vita Sym.*, 14, 116, PG 86, 3096).

82 Here is a list, by no means exhaustive, of fairly recent treatments of the word: Eb. Nestle, 'Unser täglich Brot' in *ZNW* 1 (1900), pp. 250–52, *art.* 'Lord's Prayer' in T. K. Cheyne & J. S. Black (edd.), *Encyclopaedia Biblica* III, London, 1902, col. 2819–21, and 'ἐπιούσιος in Hebrew and Aramaic' in *Expository Times* 21 (1909–10), p. 43; R. Eisler, in 'Das letzte Abendmahl' in *ZNW* 24 (1925), in particular pp. 190–92; J. Schousboe, in 'La messe la plus ancienne' in *Revue de l'Histoire des Religions* 96 (1927), pp. 193–256; G. Dalman, *Die Worte Jesu*, 1930², pp. 321–34; J. Jeremias, *Jesus als Weltvollender*, 1930, pp. 52f, and 'Das Vater-Unser im Lichte der neueren Forschung' in *Abba*, 1966, pp. 165–67; A. Schweitzer, *Die Mystik des Apostels Paulus*, 1930, pp. 233–35; F. Hauck, 'ἄρτος ἐπιούσιος' in *ZNW* 33 (1934), pp. 199–202; W. Foerster, *art.* ἐπιούσιος in *TWNT* II (1935), pp. 587–95; J. Henning, 'Our daily bread' in *Theological Studies* 4 (1943), pp. 445–54; E. Lohmeyer, *Das Vater-Unser*, 1947², pp. 92–110, 176–78; H. Pétré, 'Les Leçons du *Panem Nostrum Quotidianum*' in *Recherches de Science Religieuse* 40 (1951–52), pp. 63–79; T. W. Manson, in 'The Lord's Prayer' in *Bulletin of the John Rylands Library* 38 (1955–56),

pp. 110–12; D. Y. Hadidian, 'The meaning of ἐπιούσιος and the Codices Sergii' in *NTS* 5 (1958–59), pp. 75–81; C. Vona, 'La quarta petitio dell'oratio dominica nell'interpretazione di antichi scrittori cristiani' in *Convivium Dominicum*, 1959, pp. 215–55; R. F. Cyster, 'The Lord's Prayer and the Exodus Tradition' in *Theology* 64 (1961), pp. 377–81; J. Carmignac, *Recherches sur le 'Notre Père'*, 1969, pp. 118–221. It may be said already at this point that putative back-translations into Hebrew or Aramaic are not much use: for any theory at all may find a Semitic scholar to concoct the lost original. The following may be cited as examples: (1.) A. Meyer (*Jesu Muttersprache*, 1896, pp. 107f.) proposed an Aramaic לַחְמָא דְמִיסַתְנָא (bread which is sufficient for us) on the analogy of the Targum interpretation of לֶחֶם חֻקִּי (my apportioned bread) at Prov. 30:8 as לַחְמָא מִסְתִּי (bread which is sufficient for me), the evangelists' ἐπιούσιος probably being derived from ἐπὶ τὴν οὐσίαν (meaning: *zum Dasein gehörig*, necessary, needful). (2.) Eb. Nestle favoured a Hebrew לֶחֶם הַתָּמִיד on the basis of the shewbread at Num. 4:7, 'the bread of continuity'; and he translated as 'continual, constant' in the Lord's Prayer. (3.) In his Hebrew N.T. Delitzsch had translated as לֶחֶם חֻקֵּנוּ (cf. Gen. 47:22; Prov. 30:8; Ezek. 16:27). (4.) M. J. Lagrange (*Matthieu*, 1923², p. 129f) favoured 'bread for the day (just beginning)' on the basis of Prov. 27:1, where לֶחֶם הַיּוֹם is translated ἡ ἐπιοῦσα by the LXX [and is apparently distinguished from יוֹם מָחָר (αὔριον)]. (5.) F. Hauck put forward the root צרך to give a rough meaning of 'bread of our need', this root being often used in the Talmud in contexts of necessary and daily provision. (6.) According to M. Black (*An Aramaic Approach to the Gospels and Acts*, Oxford, 1946, pp. 149–53), the Greek ἐπιούσιον (connected with ἐπιέναι) was introduced because of a misunderstanding of an Aramaic idiom *yoma den wᵉyomaḥra* (lit. = today and tomorrow) meaning 'day by day'. Matthew has preserved the mistranslation: σήμερον is *yoma* (*den*), and τὸν ἐπιούσιον corresponds to (*den*) *wᵉyomaḥra* (דין ויומחרא having been misread as דין דיומחרא, τὸν ἐπιούσιον); Luke retains τὸν ἐπιούσιον but combines it with a true version of the idiom, τὸ καθ' ἡμέραν. The original meaning was 'Give us our bread day by day'. (7.) Jeremias gives the rhythmic Aramaic *laḥmán dᵉlimḥár/hab lán joma dén*, 'Our bread of tomorrow give us today'.

83 *De oratione*, 27, PG 11, 505–21; cf. PG 17, 145.
84 *Myst. Cat.* V. 15, ed. Cross, p. 35.
85 Augustine, *De serm. Dom. in monte* II, 7, 27, PL 34, 1280f, and *Serm.* 56–59, PL 38, 381, 389f, 395, 401. On the whole, the Latin tradition has considered the petition to include both a material (*carnaliter, simpliciter*) and a spiritual (*spiritaliter*) sense, the latter being usually interpreted of the eucharist. See Tertullian, *de or.*, 6, PL 1, 1160f; Cyprian, *de or. dom.*, 18–21, PL 4, 531–34; Chromatius, *In Matt. tr.* 14, 5, PL 20, 360f.; Ps-Augustine, *Serm.* 64, 8, PL 39, 1868; Catechism of Trent, Part IV, ch. 13.
86 Jerome's Vulgate has *quotidianum* at Luke 11:3 (though *supersubstantialem* at Matt. 6:11; but even here codices C D E Ep ᵐᵍ L T W have *quotidianum*). *Quotidianum* is used by many old Latin authors, e.g. Tertullian, *de or.*, 6, PL 1, 1160; Cyprian, *de or. dom.* 7 & 18, PL 4, 523 & 531; Ambrose, *de sacr.* V, 4, 18 and VI, 5, 24, PL 16, 450 and 460; Chromatius, *In Mt. tr.* 14, 5, PL 20, 360f; Augustine, *de Serm. Dom. in monte* II, 4, 15, and II,

7, 25–27, PL 34, 1275 and 1279–81, *Serm.* 56–59, PL 38, 377–402, *Ep.* 130, PL 33, 502, *Enchir.* 115, PL 40, 286. *Quotidianum* is also used in the ordinary of the Roman mass.

87 Theodore of Mopsuestia (*Hom. Cat.* XI, 14f, edd. Tonneau and Devreesse, pp. 309–15) and the Peshitta have *lahma desunqanan*, 'the bread of our necessity', 'our necessary bread'.

88 The following instances may be given of commentators in this tradition. John Chrysostom: ἄρτον . . . ἐπιούσιον, οὐ τρυφήν, ἀλλὰ τροφήν, τὴν τὸ ἐλλεῖπον ἀναπληροῦσαν τοῦ σώματος . . . ἐπὶ τὴν οὐσίαν τοῦ σώματος διαβαίνοντα, καὶ συγκροτῆσαι ταύτην δυνάμενον (*hom. de angusta porta et in orat. dom.* 5, PG 51, 46); τὸν ἄρτον τὸν ἐπιούσιον, τουτέστι τὸν ἐφήμερον (*In Mt. hom.* 19, 5, PG 57, 280); τὸν ἄρτον . . . τὸν ἐπιούσιον, ἀντὶ τοῦ, τὴν τῆς ἡμέρας τροφήν (*In Gen. hom.* 54, 5, PG 54, 478); μηδὲν πλέον τοῦ ἄρτου τοῦ ἐπιουσίου, τουτέστι, τοῦ καθημερινοῦ (*In Jo. hom.* 43, 2, PG 59, 247f.). Basil the Great: τὸν ἐπιούσιον ἄρτον, τουτέστι, τὸν πρὸς τὴν ἐφήμερον ζωὴν τῇ οὐσίᾳ ἡμῶν χρησιμεύοντα (*reg. brev.* 252, PG 31, 1252). Gregory of Nyssa (*De orat. dom.*, IV, PG 44, 1168–77) interprets it as what is necessary for the temperate needs of the body a day at a time (τὸν ἐφήμερον ἄρτον). Cyril of Alexandria also could explain it as the daily food needed by the body—though he connects ἐπιούσιον linguistically with περιούσιον, which he sees in Titus 2:14 as meaning τὸν ἀρκοῦντα (PG 72, 692f., PG 69, 452). Euthymius Zigabenus explicitly follows Chrysostom (PG 129, 237), though in MS A he has suffered a marginal addition calling attention to the need of the soul for divine knowledge. The thirteenth-century Jacobite Syrian Bar-Hebraeus reads 'bread of our need' and adds the comment 'and not of superfluity' (so Hauck, *art. cit.*, p. 200). The meaning of food for our daily physical needs is one of the various known to 'Peter of Laodicaea': ἄρτον δὲ ἐπιούσιον, ἢ τὸν συνιστῶντα τὸ σῶμα ἡμῶν φησι, τουτέστι τὸν ἐφήμερον . . . (PG 86, 3333); and to Theophylact: Ἐπιούσιον, τὸν ἐπὶ τῇ οὐσίᾳ καὶ συστάσει ἡμῶν αὐτάρκη, φησίν. ἀναιρεῖ δὲ τὴν περὶ τῆς αὔριον μέριμναν (*Enarr. in Ev. Mt.* 6:11, PG 123, 205, cf. 856). When the Latins mention the 'material' sense they usually, like Chrysostom and the rest, make the points of necessity and not luxury, and of restriction to a day at a time: see e.g. Tertullian, *de or.*, 6, PL 1, 1161; Cyprian, *de or. dom.*, 19–21, PL 4, 532–34; Chromatius, *In Mt. tr.* 14, PL 20, 360f. Jerome (PL 26, 43) knows that some interpret it *simpliciter* of material provision (with appeal to I Tim. 6:8 and Matt. 6:34), but he himself scorns this interpretation (PL 26, 588).

89 *Quotidianum, supersubstantialem, substantivum, praecipuum, superventurum, crastinum.*

90 ' "Give us this day our supersubstantial bread" . . . Where we have translated by supersubstantial, the Greek has *epiousios*. This word the Septuagint very often gives as *periousios*. We have examined the Hebrew of the passages where the Seventy have translated by *periousios*, and we have always found *segullah*, which Symmachus translated as *exairetos*, that is superior (*praecipuus*) or excellent (*egregius*), though in one place he rendered it special (*peculiaris*). So when we pray God to give us the special or superior bread, we are asking for him who said: I am the living bread which came down from heaven' (*In Mt.* I, ad 6:11, PL 26, 43); 'What is written in the Latin translation of the Gospel as "Give us this day our daily bread (*quotidianum*)", is rather in the Greek: our *epiousion* bread, that is superior (*praecipuum*),

excellent (*egregium*), special (*peculiarem*), which is obviously the one who came down from heaven and said: I am the bread which came down from heaven' (*In Tit.* ad 2:12ff, PL 26, 588). We are justified in seeing a eucharistic reference because Jerome elsewhere interprets the same phrase 'the bread come down from heaven' expressly of the eucharistic body of Christ (*Ep.* 120, 2, PL 22, 986).

91 'We can also understand supersubstantial bread in another way: which is above (*super*) all substances and surpasses all creatures' (*In Mt.* I ad 6:11, PL 26, 43); 'The apostles pray for the coming of daily bread, or the bread that is above all substances, that they may be worthy to receive the body of Christ' (*Dial. adv. Pelag.* III, 15, PL 23, 585); 'Some consider that the bread is called *epiousios* in the Lord's prayer because it is above all *ousias*, substances. If accepted, this meaning is not much different from the one we have expounded [i.e. *epiousios* = *periousios* = *egregius, praecipuus*]. For whatever is excellent and superior is beyond (*extra*) all things, and above (*super*) all things' (*In Tit.* ad 2:12ff, PL 26, 589). John Cassian gives a similar meaning: 'Give us this day our *epiousios*, that is supersubstantial, bread. . . . It signifies that quality of nobility and substance (*substantiae*) by which it is above all substances, surpassing all creatures in its sublime magnificence and sanctification' (*de or.*, 21, PL 49, 794f).

92 In G. Morin, *Anecdota Maredsolana*, vol. III pars 2: Sancti Hieronymi presbyteri tractatus sive homiliae, Maredsoli/Oxoniae, 1897, p. 262. There may be a verbal echo here of Wisd. 16:20f, where the meaning is no more than 'thy sustenance' (see my n. 48); but the meaning of the expression for Jerome must be seen in the light of his other references to the supersubstantial bread as the eucharistic body of Christ. The thought of Victorinus the African moves in similar, 'ontological' paths (*Adv. Arium* II, 8, PL 8, 1094): 'We Christians, that is we who believe in Christ, are taught in the Gospel how we should pray to God the Father. In that prayer, we pray among other things for bread. This bread is life, for thus it is said: This is the bread which comes down from heaven. This life, which is the life of Christ and of God, that is eternal life, what name does he give it? *Epiousios artos*, bread of (*ex*) the same *ousia*, that is consubstantial life coming from (*de*) the life of God. For whence shall we become sons of God except by participation in eternal life which Christ brought from the Father and gave us? That, then, is the meaning of Give us our *epiousios* bread; that is: life of (*ex*) the same substance. And if what we receive is the body of Christ, and if Christ himself is life, then we are asking for *epiousios* bread. For deity dwells in Christ bodily. . . . Whether because they did not understand it, or because they could not express it in their language, the Latins were not able to say this, and they simply put daily (*quotidianus*) and did not translate *epiousios*' (translation from the text in the edition by P. Henry and P. Hadot in Sources chrétiennes, vol. 68). Similarly Ambrose, also arguing against the Arians (*de fid.* III, 15, 127, PL 16, 614): 'Can they deny that *ousia* is read in Scripture when the Lord spoke of *epiousios* bread and when Moses wrote: You shall be to me a *periousios* people (Exod. 19:5)? And what is *ousia*, or whence is it derived, except from *ousa aei*, that which remains for ever? He who is, and is for ever, is God; and so, since it remains for ever, the divine substance is called *ousia*. The bread is called *epiousios* because it ministers out of the substance

of the Word a substance of lasting power to the heart and soul; for it is written: Bread strengthens the heart of man (Ps. 104:15).'

93 אֲמִינָא. Apart from being found in the Sinaitic and Curetonian versions of the N.T. and in *Acts of Thomas*, 144, this version is also known to James of Sarugh ( + 521) in his homily on the Lord's prayer (P. Bedjan (ed.), *Homiliae selectae Mar Jacobi Sarugensis* vol. I, Parisiis, 1905, e.g. p. 234, line 15, and p. 235, line 17).

94 This range of meaning is illustrated by the word employed in the Gothic version of the N.T.: 'hlaif unsarana thana *sinteinan* gif uns himma daga'. The same word is used at II Cor. 11:28 for καθ' ἡμέραν; while the adverb *sinteino* is used for διὰ παντός, πάντοτε, ἀεί.

95 A German translation is given by S. Weber in vol. 58 of the *Bibliothek der Kirchenväter: Ausgewählte Schriften der armenischen Kirchenväter*, II, München, 1927, pp. 282f. The petition cannot, says St Elisha, be for earthly bread, for God gives that to all without their asking (Ps. 36:6), and in any case it is not everlasting. The 'everlasting bread' is the Lord Himself, the living bread who came down from heaven and who gives Himself at the altar in the sacrament which communicates immortality. Elisha appeals chiefly to John 6:49–51; we may compare also John 6:27: 'the food which *remains* (μένουσαν) unto eternal life'.

96 One might perhaps have expected the present participle: τὸν ἐπιόντα. But the adjectival form ἐπιούσιος corresponds to the participle ἐπιών as ἑκούσιος corresponds to ἑκών, and ἐθελούσιος to ἐθέλων.

97 *In Ev. Mt.* I ad 6:11, PL 26, 43; see also the text quoted on my p. 33, for which the reference is given in n. 103.

98 Ambrose believed that the Greek word ἐπιούσιος contained both the notion of feeding the 'substance' of our soul, and also the notion of 'the next day'. In the course of explaining why the Lord's prayer and its mention of 'bread' can still be used even after the words of eucharistic consecration, Ambrose says: 'He did indeed say bread, but he said *epiousios*, that is supersubstantial. This is not the bread which goes into the body, but rather the bread of eternal life which sustains the substance of our soul. That is why it is called *epiousios* in Greek. The Latin called daily (*quotidianum*) this bread which the Greek called coming (*advenientem*), because the Greeks call the coming day *ten epiousan hemeran*. So what the Latin said and what the Greek said both seems useful. The Greek signified the two meanings by a single word, the Latin said daily' (*De sacramentis* V, 24, PL 16, 452; the Migne reading of *supersubstantialem* is rejected in favour of *substantialem* in B. Botte's edition of the treatise in Sources chrétiennes, 1961²).

99 This is the meaning preferred by T. W. Manson: 'rations given on one day for use on the following day', and so 'Give us this day our bread for the coming day' (*Bulletin of the John Rylands Library* 38 (1955–56), in particular pp. 110–12, 436).

100 W. Foerster, *art.* ἐπιούσιος, in *TWNT* II, p. 589.

101 Matthew's σήμερον falls in an emphatic end-position. Luke's τὸ καθ' ἡμέραν (and present imperative δίδου, instead of Matthew's δός) may not accord so well with this understanding, but does not exclude it.

102 Among the moderns who favour this eschatological meaning are: R. Eisler, J. Schousboe, J. Jeremias and A. Schweitzer (in the places mentioned,

p. 162, n. 82), H. Riesenfeld, *Jésus transfiguré*, p. 320, n. 11, and N. Perrin, *The Kingdom of God in the Teaching of Jesus*, pp. 193f. J. Jeremias points to 'tomorrow' as a rabbinic synonym for the age to come (*Abba*, p. 166).

103 *Apud* G. Morin (as in n. 92), p. 262.

104 *Comm. in Ezek.* VI, ad 18:7, PL 25, 175. John Cassian makes a similar point, attaching his remarks to the word *hodie*; 'It is also possible to understand the word "today" as referring to the present life. That is: While we live in this world, give us this bread. For we know that thou wilt also give it in the future age to those who have merited it, but we ask thee to give us it today, for unless one has been worthy to receive it in this life, one will not be able to have a share in it in that' (*de or.* 21, PL 49, 795f).

105 *In Luc.* 11:3, PG 72, 693.

106 PL 52, 395, 400, 402, & 406.

107 Since the four brief passages from Peter Chrysologus express succinctly several of the major themes of the present study, I feel justified in reproducing them here. It is only a matter of regret that he thought it necessary to make an *opposition* between eucharistic-eschatological bread and 'temporal' bread.

*Sermon 68:* 'After the heavenly kingdom, who could ask for temporal bread? But He wishes us to ask for that daily viaticum of bread which is day by day in the sacrament of His body, in order that by it we may attain to endless day and the very table of Christ, and there receive in fulness and unto all satiety that of which we have here been given the taste.'

*Sermon 70:* 'After the heavenly kingdom, we are not ordered to ask for earthly bread, for He himself forbids it when He says: Do not be anxious about your life, what you shall eat or what you shall drink. But because He himself is the bread which came down from heaven, we beg and pray that this very bread by which we shall be fed daily, that is without end (*jugiter*), in eternity—we may receive it today, that is in the present life, from the banquet of the holy altar for the strengthening of our body and soul.'

*Sermon 71:* 'After the fatherhood of God, after the hallowing of the divine name, after the heavenly kingdom, we are ordered to pray for our daily bread. Christ is not being forgetful, Christ is not demanding things contrary to His own commandments. He himself said: Do not be anxious about your life, what you shall eat or what you shall drink. But He himself is the bread which came down from heaven. He was ground into flour by the mill of law and grace. He was kneaded by the suffering of the Cross. He was fermented by a mystery of great love . . . In being baked by the heat of His own divinity, He melted the oven of hell. He is brought daily to the table of the church as a heavenly food. He is broken for the remission of sins. He feeds and nourishes unto everlasting life those who eat Him. This is why we ask that this bread be given us daily until we enjoy it to the full in the day that knows no end.'

*Sermon 72:* 'By "daily" we mean "everlasting (*jugem*)". This everlasting bread is He who came down from heaven: I am the bread which came down from heaven. This is therefore the bread of perfect bliss. Today, that is in the present age, we begin already to live on the food of that bread by which we shall never cease to be filled, every day, in the future age.'

108 PG 86, 3333.

109 *De fid. orth.* IV, 13, PG, 94, 1152.

110 Negatively it is to be noticed that Ambrose does not seem to exploit his

knowledge that in Greek ἐπιούσιος has in part to do with the coming *day* in order to interpret the eucharist in terms of the bread of the coming *age* (though he does call the eucharist *panis vitae aeternae*). In *de sacramentis* V, 24–26 (ed. Botte, pp. 132ff), he is much more concerned to use the *quotidianum* of the Lord's prayer to argue in favour of a *daily communion*. In this passage he unites most of the themes which recur in eucharistic applications of the fourth petition throughout Latin theology; the indifferent are warned, in contradistinction to the Eastern practice of infrequent communion, of the need to communicate daily for the forgiveness of sins and for perseverance in communion with the life-giving Christ: cf. Tertullian, *de or.*, 6, PL 1, 1160f; Cyprian, *de or. dom.*, 18, PL 4, 531f; Hilary, *frag.* 7, PL 10, 725; Chromatius, *In Ev. Mt.* tr. 14, 5, PL 20, 360f; Augustine, e.g. *de perserv.*, 4, 7, PL 45, 998; Isidore of Seville, *de off. eccl.* I, 18, 7f, PL 83, 756; Catechism of Trent, Part IV, ch. 13, q. 21.

111 *Die Mystik des Apostels Paulus*, pp. 233–35.

112 *Das Vater-Unser*², pp. 92–110, 176–78.

113 Rather similarly: J. Jeremias, *Abba*, pp. 165–67.

114 *Op. cit.*, p. 109.

115 Though only Paul and Luke (longer text) give the 'command to repeat', Mark 14:22–25 and Matt. 26:26–29 clearly mean to be 'institution narratives' also. In this sense the synoptic and Pauline texts are aetiological. But we remain unimpressed by the latest assertion (it can hardly be called an argument, where so many questions are begged) that they are merely aetiological *fabrications* intended to fix a moment of institution for the phenomenon of the sacrament which in reality simply grew out of the meals of Jesus during His ministry and the meals after Easter in which the community felt the 'presence' of the Lord: so W. Marxsen, *Das Abendmahl als christologisches Problem* [1963], 1965². If, however, Marxsen is right, the argument we are about to present will still show the particular relation which *the primitive church*, if not Jesus Himself, saw between its eucharist and the meals of Jesus's ministry. I would myself certainly not wish to discount the influence exercised by primitive liturgical practice on the 'institution narratives' in the period between the first accounts given by the apostles of what happened at the Last Supper and the final redactions of Paul and the Synoptists (see for instance H. Schürmann, *Der Einsetzungsbericht Lk 22, 19–20*, not omitting the critical question raised on pp. 142–50). For arguments that there existed an original 'historical' account of the institution before liturgical practice began its work of moulding, see J. Jeremias, *Abendmahlsworte*³, pp. 100–31, 183–85.

116 The presence of a reference to the covenant in the earliest attainable form of the institution narrative is accepted for instance by J. Jeremias (*Abendmahlsworte*³, pp. 161–65, 185–88), E. Schweizer (in *Neotestamentica*, pp. 347–51), and H. Schürmann (*Der Einsetzungsbericht Lk 22, 19–20*, pp. 129–31, 151–53), among those who have recently engaged in detailed study of the institution narratives from the point of view of *Traditionsgeschichte* and *Redaktionsgeschichte*. The importance of the notion of (new) covenant to Jesus's actions at the Last Supper, and indeed to much of His entire ministry, is brought out by B. Cooke in 'Synoptic Presentation of the Eucharist as Covenant Sacrifice' in *Theological Studies* 21 (1960), pp. 1–44, and by J. Lécuyer, *Le sacrifice de la Nouvelle Alliance*, 1962. For W. Marxsen

the primitive church's understanding of itself as the community of the new covenant was the chief factor in its shaping of the eucharist.

117 J. Jeremias considers John 6:51c to be a Johannine version of the eucharistic bread-word (*Abendmahlsworte*³, pp. 101f, 192f, 221).

118 See J. Jeremias, *Abendmahlsworte*³, pp. 171–74, 218–23, on the scope of (οἱ) πολλοί.

119 The objections made by the Quaker G. H. Boobyer are quite unconvincing: 'The Eucharistic Interpretation of the Miracles of the Loaves in St Mark's Gospel' in *JTS* n.s.3 (1952), pp. 161–71.

120 Several liturgies insert a reference to Christ's 'looking up to heaven' in the institution narrative of their great eucharistic prayer: so *Apostolic Constitutions VIII* (Brightman, p. 20), Greek *St James* (p. 51), Alexandrian *St Mark* (p. 132), Coptic *St Cyril* (p. 176), Ethiopian *Anaphora of the Apostles* (p. 232), Ambrose *de sacramentis* IV, 5, 21f (ed. Botte, p. 114), and the Roman canon.

121 Cf. John 6:23: 'near the place where they ate bread after the Lord had given thanks' (though εὐχαριστήσαντος τοῦ Κυρίου is omitted by D 13 a e syr^sin/cur arm).

122 *Die Botschaft der Brotvermehrung*, 1966, pp. 61–80.

123 His argument (pp. 61–68) for the pre-Marcan use is as follows. The second Marcan feeding is a doublet of the first. How then did εὐλόγησεν καὶ κατέκλασεν of Mark 6:41 become εὐχαριστήσας ἔκλασεν of Mark 8:6b, which is exactly the same as I Cor. 11:24 whereas Mark 14:22 has εὐλογήσας ἔκλασεν? The form used in the doublet is not Mark's doing, and is therefore a pre-Marcan *Hellenistic* version standing close to the account of the eucharistic institution given at I Cor. 11:24 (cf. ἀπὸ μακρόθεν at Mark 8:3b, a phrase used of the *Gentiles* at Acts 2:39; 22:21; Eph. 2:11–22).

124 Καὶ ἔδωκεν αὐτῷ 'Αβιμέλεχ ὁ ἱερεὺς τοὺς ἄρτους τῆς προθέσεως, ὅτι οὐκ ἦν ἐκεῖ ἄρτος ὅτι ἀλλ' ἢ ἄρτοι τοῦ προσώπου οἱ ἀρῃρημένοι ἐκ προσώπου Κυρίου παρατεθῆναι ἄρτον θερμὸν ᾗ ἡμέρα ἔλαβεν αὐτούς (1 Regn. 21:7).

125 For varied arguments in its favour see for example: P. Benoit, 'Le récit de la Cène dans Lc. XXII, 15–20. Etude de critique textuelle et littéraire' in *Revue Biblique* 48 (1939), pp. 357–93; J. Jeremias, *Abendmahlsworte* [² pp. 67–79], ³pp. 133–53; H. Schürmann, 'Lk. 22, 19b–20 als ursprüngliche Textüberlieferung' in *Biblica* 32 (1951), pp. 364–92, 522–41.

126 Οὐκέτι is read by D W Γ Δ Ψ 700.

127 Ephraim the Syrian, *Evangelii concordantis expositio*, 19 (ed. L. Leloir, in Sources chrétiennes, vol. 121, Paris, 1966, p. 334); John Chrysostom, *In Mt. hom.* 82, 2, PG 58, 739f; Euthymius Zigabenus, PG 129, 669 (so, at least, on Matt. 26:29 = Mark 14:25 = Luke 22:18; but he places the fulfilment of Luke 22:16 in the kingdom of God τῇ κατὰ τὸν αἰῶνα τὸν μέλλοντα); M. Barth, *Das Abendmahl*, pp. 42–44. On the history of this and other interpretations of the 'eschatological prospect' see H. Vogels, 'Mk 14, 25 und Parallelen' in N. Adler (ed.), *Vom Wort des Lebens*, 1951, pp. 93–104; and P. Lebeau, *Le vin nouveau du royaume: Etude exégétique et patristique sur la parole eschatologique de Jésus à la cène*, 1966.

128 O. Cullmann points out (*RHPhR* 16 (1936), pp. 8f) that in the Pseudo-Clementines μεταλαβεῖν τῶν ἁλῶν is a technical term for 'to celebrate the Lord's supper'.

129 In the *TWNT* article κλάω (vol. III, p. 728, n. 13), J. Behm adduces two

other instances of post-Resurrection meals: In the Gospel according to the
Hebrews the risen Jesus appears to James [cf. I Cor. 15:7] who had sworn
to eat no bread after his last meal with Jesus until the Resurrection, and
*tulit panem et benedixit, ac fregit et dedit Jacobo iusto et dixit ei: frater mi,
comede panem tuum, quia resurrexit filius hominis a dormentibus* (*apud*
Jerome, *de vir. illust.*, 2); and an epistolary fragment of Epiphanius records
a meal of Jesus with the disciples in prison: ἔκλασεν ἄρτον ψιλὸν καὶ
συνεγεύσατο μετ' αὐτῶν ἐν τῇ φυλακῇ. See also Ignatius of Antioch,
*Smyrn.*, 3.

130 'La signification de la Sainte Cène dans le christianisme primitif' in *RHPhR*
16 (1936), pp. 1–22. Cullmann stresses particularly the first meal with the
assembled disciples in Jerusalem on Easter Sunday evening. He calls it
(p. 20) 'un accomplissement anticipé' of the Last Supper prophecy that
Jesus would next drink wine with His disciples in the kingdom of God. (In
*Urchristentum und Gottesdienst*[2], pp. 18f, he speaks of the 'Ostermahlzeiten,
in denen das von Jesu beim letzten Abendmahl verheissene messianische
Mahl schon *teilweise vorweggenommen* wurde'.) The joy of the primitive
Jerusalem-type eucharist (Acts 2:42, 46) springs from the memory of the
meal-appearances of the risen Jesus, and from the renewed experience of
His presence, now invisible, at the community's common meals.

131 J. Jeremias (*Abendmahlsworte*[3], pp. 113f) stresses that 'the breaking of bread'
was *not* a Jewish name for a full meal. The Christian use of it as a *terminus
technicus* implies a self-sufficient rite, which is the sacramental eucharist.
This overrules J. P. Audet's attempted distinction between the breaking of
bread ( =agape) and the eucharist proper at Did. 14:1 (*La Didachè*, pp. 415,
461).

132 Cf. J. Dupont, 'Le repas d'Emmaüs' in *Lumière et Vie*, no. 31 (1957),
pp. 77–92.

133 E. C. Hoskyns, *The Fourth Gospel*, 1947[2], p. 188; O. Cullmann, *Urchristentum und Gottesdienst*, 1950[2], pp. 67–72; J. Daniélou, *Bible et Liturgie*,
1958[2], pp. 296–98; C. H. Dodd, *The Interpretation of the Fourth Gospel*,
1953, pp. 297f, and more decisively, *Historical Tradition in the Fourth Gospel*,
1963, p. 224; A. Feuillet, 'L'heure de Jésus et le signe de Cana' in *Ephemerides Theologicae Lovanienses* 36 (1960), pp. 5–22. Among the patristic and
liturgical evidences adduced by A. Smitmans, *Das Weinwunder von Kana:
Die Auslegung von Jo 2, 1–11 bei den Vätern und heute*, one may mention the
following: Irenaeus, *A.H.* III, 11, 5, PG 7, 883, where the expressions
*benedictio escae* and *gratia potus* seem to ensure a eucharist reference;
*A.H.* III, 16, 7, PG 7, 926, where Irenaeus explains that Mary wanted the
*compendii poculum* (the cup that recapitulates) too soon (*intempestiva
festinatio*); Cyprian *Ep.* 63, 12, *CSEL*, pp. 710f, arguing against the aquarians; Maximus of Turin, *Hom.* 23, PL 57, 273; Peter Chrysologus, *Serm.*
160, PL 52, 622, cf. *Serm.* 137, PL 52, 569; and compare the use of John
2:7a, 9a, 10c, 11 as the communion verse on Epiphany II in the Roman rite.

134 So lately O. Cullmann, *Urchristentum und Gottesdienst*[2], pp. 110–13, and
even R. Bultmann, *Johannesevangelium*, p. 525 (as a redactional inter-
polation, of course).

135 On this interpretation of Luke 17:21 see W. G. Kümmel, *Verheissung und
Erfüllung*, 1945, pp. 17–19, and N. Perrin, *The Kingdom of God in the
Teaching of Jesus*, pp. 174–76.

136 I am inclined to favour a eucharistic reference at 16:34, with P. H. Menoud, 'Les Actes des Apôtres et l'Eucharistie' in *RHPhR* 33 (1953), pp. 21–36.

137 See A. Schweitzer, *Die Mystik des Apostels Paulus*, pp. 245f, who refers also to I Pet. 4:13, Jude 24, Rev. 19:7 for eschatological rejoicing; R. Bultmann, *art.* ἀγαλλιάομαι, ἀγαλλίασις in *TWNT* I, pp. 18–20; and A. B. du Toit, *Der Aspekt der Freude im urchristlichen Abendmahl*, 1965.

138 See, for instance, O. Cullmann, *RHPhR* 16 (1936), pp. 14f; E. Käsemann, 'Anliegen und Eigenart des paulinischen Abendmahls', now in *Exegetische Versuche und Besinnungen* I, p. 23; B. Reicke, *Diakonia, Festfreude und Zelos in Verbindung mit der altchristlichen Agapenfeier*, 1951, pp. 252–93; P. Neuenzeit, *Das Herrenmahl: Studien zur paulinischen Eucharistie-auffassung*, 1960, pp. 170–72, 221–25; and cf. G. Bornkamm, 'Herrenmahl und Kirche bei Paulus' in *ZThK* 53 (1956), pp. 312–49, in particular pp. 344–46.

139 P. Benoit, *art. cit.*, p. 390, n. 3; M. Barth, *Das Abendmahl*, pp. 50f; B. Cooke, 'Synoptic Presentation of the Eucharist as Covenant Sacrifice' in *Theological Studies* 21 (1960), in particular pp. 23f.

140 O. Cullmann, in *RHPhR* 16 (1936), pp. 10–12, 22, and *Urchristentum und Gottesdienst*², pp. 16–21; and P. Lebeau, *Le vin nouveau du royaume* (1966), with somewhat more emphasis than Cullmann on the 'already' and somewhat less on the 'not yet'.

141 See my pp. 132f.

142 E. Käsemann, 'Anliegen und Eigenart des paulinischen Abendmahls', now in *Exegetische Versuche und Besinnungen* I, pp. 28–31.

143 R. Schnackenburg, *Gottes Herrschaft und Reich*, pp. 173–80, and *Die Kirche im Neuen Testament*, pp. 165–72.

144 J(oseph) Wilpert, *Fractio Panis: die älteste Darstellung des eucharistischen Opfers in der 'Cappella Graeca'*, 1895; *Die Malereien der Sakraments-kapellen in der Katakombe des hl. Callistus*, 1897; G(iuseppe) Wilpert, *Roma Sotterranea: Le pitture delle catacombe romane*, 1903 (one vol. of commentary, one of plates). F. J. Dölger, *Die Fisch-Denkmäler in der frühchristlichen Plastik, Malerei und Kleinkunst = ΙΧΘΥΣ*, vol. V, Münster, 1943, especially pp. 503–40.

145 A eucharistic interpretation of John 21:9–14 is known among the Fathers: Augustine, *In Jo. tract.* 123, PL 35, 1966; 'Prosper' ( = Quodvultdeus), *de promissionibus et praedicationibus Dei*, II, 39, PL 51, 816; Sedulius, *pasch* V, PL 19, 747f (*CSEL* vol. 10, pp. 143f, 300f). At John 21:13 εὐχαριστήσας is inserted by D d f r¹ syrˢⁱⁿ.

146 Of baptism (see J. Daniélou, *Sacramentum futuri*, pp. 170–73): Tertullian, *de bapt.*, 9, PL 1, 1209f; Cyprian, *ep.* 63, 8, *CSEL*, pp. 706f; Gregory of Elvira, *Tract.* XV, 10, in *Corpus Christianorum*, series latina, vol. 69, Turnholti, 1967, p. 114. Of the eucharist (see J. Daniélou, *Bible et Liturgie*², pp. 201–8): John Chrysostom, *In apost. dictum, I Cor 10:1*, PG 51, 248f, and *Hom. in II Cor.*, XI, 2, PG 61, 476; Theodoret, *Quaest. in Exod.*, XXVII, PG 80, 257; Ambrose, *de sacr.* V, 3, ed. Botte, pp. 120f (cf. *de myst.*, 48, ed. Botte, p. 182); Augustine, *In Jo. tract.* XXVI, 12, PL 35, 1612.

147 Of baptism: Irenaeus, *A.H.*, III, 17, 2, PG 7, 930; and Cyprian, *ep.* 63, 8, *CSEL*, pp. 706f. Of the eucharist: 'Prosper' ( = Quodvultdeus), *de prom. et praed.*, I, 39, PL 51, 765f; Caesarius of Arles, PL 39, 2279; cf. Primasius of Hadrumetum, *Comm. in Apoc.* II, 7, PL 68, 854.

148 For a picture and interpretation see G. Agnello, 'Motivi Eucaristici nella

Iconografia paleocristiana della Sicilia' in *Convivium Dominicum*, 1959, pp. 15–34, in particular pp. 32f.

149 See L. Fonck, *Die Wunder des Herrn im Evangelium*, Innsbruck, 1907², pp. 172–74; also H. Leclercq, in the article 'Alexandrie' in *DACL*, vol. I, cols. 1125–33.

150 P. Lebeau, *Le vin nouveau du royaume*, pp. 38–41, 142–84.

151 I am indebted for some of the following references to the article by Vogels and the book by Lebeau, details of which are given in n. 127. In reading Lebeau allowance must be made for the way in which he presses doubtful patristic texts into the service of his own strong emphasis on the fact that the eucharist *already* belongs to the (ecclesiastical) kingdom.

152 Irenaeus, *A.H.* V, 33, 1f, & 36, 3, PG 7, 1212 & 1224; cf. Victorinus of Pettau, *Comm. in Apoc.* XXI, 6, *CSEL* vol. 49, p. 154.

153 *Quaestiones Evangelorum* I, 43, PL 35, 1331f.

154 'How, then, do they say that the flesh passes into corruption and does not partake of life, that flesh which is fed by the body and blood of the Lord? Let them either change their opinion, or else decline to make the offerings of which I have spoken [i.e. the eucharist]. But our opinion is in agreement with the eucharist, and the eucharist in turn confirms our opinion. For we offer to him the things which are his own, [*here there is a textual difficulty*] proclaiming thereby a union and communion of flesh and spirit and confessing a resurrection of flesh and spirit. For as the bread from the earth, receiving the *invocationem Dei*, is no longer common bread but a eucharist composed of two things, an earthly and a heavenly: so also our bodies, partaking of the eucharist, are no longer corruptible, having the hope of eternal resurrection' (*A.H.* IV, 18, 5, PG 7, 1027–29). See also V. 2, 3, quoted n. 344.

155 *GCS*, vol. 1 of Origen, 1899, p. 38.

156 In J. Sickenberger, *Titus von Bostra: Studien zu dessen Lukashomilien* in Texte und Untersuchungen, 21, I, Leipzig, 1901, p. 242.

157 From the German translation by P. S. Langersdorfer in *Ausgewählte Schriften der syrischen Dichter*, vol. 6 of *Bibliothek der Kirchenväter*, 1913, p. 13 (67).

158 Apart from the *de sacramentis* and the *de mysteriis*, see also e.g. *De Cain et Abel* I, 5, 19, PL 14, 326f.

159 See, for example, H. R. Schlette, 'Die Eucharistielehre Hugos von St Viktor' in *Zeitschrift für katholische Theologie* 81 (1959), pp. 67–100, 163–210. According to Hugh of St Victor, whose general position combines a light-mysticism learnt from the Areopagite with a view of the *Heilsgeschichte* as *opus restaurationis*, communion at the altar is for the worthy recipient the *imago et forma* of that transforming participation in the divine Christ which may already be spiritually enjoyed *per dilectionem* and which will finally be fully enjoyed in glory directly *per contemplationem*. Thomas Aquinas also shows himself rather more aware than most of the medievals of the eschatological scope of the eucharist: see, for example, J. M. R. Tillard, 'La triple dimension du signe sacramental (A propos de *Sum. Theol.* III, 60, 3)' in *NRTh* 83 (1961), pp. 225–54. In a further article Tillard shows that though St Thomas has much to say on churchly unity and love as the *res* of the eucharist, he usually remains at the individual level when he sets the eucharist in the perspective of the hope of glory; it is more rarely that

he puts the two notions together, as when, quoting Augustine, Thomas says that the eucharist is the food 'qui eos a quibus sumitur immortales et incorruptibiles facit in societate sanctorum, ubi pax erit et unitas plena atque perfecta', S.T. III, 79, 2 ('L'Eucharistie, sacrement de l'espérance ecclésiale' in *NRTh* 83 (1961), in particular pp. 561–67).

160 Though the quotation is called forth by the occurrence of *ointment* in the LXX text of Isaiah and is made with special reference to the candidate's anointing with chrism, the prophecy of Isa. 25:6 is seen by Cyril as fulfilled in the rites of Christian initiation (which included first communion): 'Of this (chrism) the blessed Isaiah in olden times prophesied and said: "And on this mountain (now he calls the church a mountain elsewhere also, as when he says: And in the last days the mountain of the Lord shall be manifest, Isa. 2:2) the Lord will make (a feast) for all the nations, they shall drink wine, they shall drink gladness, they shall be anointed with ointment." ' (*Myst. Cat.* III, 7, ed. Cross, p. 25).

161 R. Tonneau and R. Devreesse, *Les Homélies Catéchétiques de Théodore de Mopsueste* in *Studi e Testi*, vol. 145, 1949, gives a facsimile of the fifth-century Syriac translation (based on a lost Greek original) and a French translation. Our interest lies in Hom. XII, 5–7, XV and XVI.

162 There are several other ways in which τύπος is used by Theodore of the eucharist: chiefly, the course of the liturgy is a τύπος of the liturgy offered by Christ in His death, resurrection, ascension and heavenly work.

163 R. H. Connolly, *The Liturgical Homilies of Narsai*, p. 17.

164 'Ἑρμηνεία τῆς θείας λειτουργίας, PG 150, 368–492. Edition and French translation by S. Salaville, *Nicolas Cabasilas: Explication de la Divine Liturgie*, in *Sources chrétiennes*, vol. 4, 1967². English translation by J. M. Hussey and P. A. McNulty, *Nicholas Cabasilas: A commentary on the divine liturgy*, 1960.

165 PG 150, 493–725. French translation by S. Broussaleux, *Nicolas Cabasilas: La Vie en Jésus-Christ*, 1960².

166 The same use is made of Luke 12:37 in *De vita in Christo* IV, PG 150, 620 (*La Vie en Jésus-Christ*, p. 132).

167 PG 150, 461f. Similar ideas were already expressed by Athanasius, *Ep. Fest.* 7, 8 (E.T. from the Syriac, in *Nicene and Post-Nicene Fathers*, vol. 4, London/New York, 1892, p. 526).

168 PG 150, 625 (*La Vie en Jésus-Christ*, pp. 137f).

169 Τράπεζα βασιλική was a favourite expression of John Chrysostom: *In I Cor. Hom.* 27, 5, PG 61, 232; *In Eph. Hom.* 3, 5, PG 62, 29; *In Hebr. Hom.* 17, 4 & 5, PG 63, 132 & 133; cf. his *Huit catéchèses baptismales* (ed. A. Wenger, *Sources chrétiennes*, vol. 50, 1957), II, 27, and IV, 6. *Apostolic Constitutions* VI, 30, 2 speaks of 'an acceptable eucharist, the antitype of the royal body of Christ' (ed. Funk I, p. 381).

170 Ed. M. Bonnet, in *Acta Apostolorum Apocrypha*, Lipsiae, 1903, p. 166.

171 So at least the *Syro-Malabar Missal: A new English translation* [by G. Kandathil, s.j.] *of the restored Kurbana with the first anaphora, namely the anaphora of the blessed apostles Mar Addai and Mar Mari, doctors of the East*, Ernakulam (India), 1963.

172 Brightman, pp. 21, 25, 54, 65f, 104, 134, 180, 287, 302; cf. 338, 390.

173 An old fragmentary text of the Syriac Anaphora of St James places a prayer between the 'oblation' and the 'epiclesis' which speaks of being grieved and

filled with trembling by the thought 'that we should fall (away) from [Thy] praise and be rejected of Thy love: [that we should be stripped] of Thy grace and should see [them that come] from the East and from the West and recline [with Thee] together with the fathers, but we [ourselves] go forth without and hear the bitter word: Amen, amen, I say unto you, I know you not' (*apud* R. H. Connolly & H. W. Codrington, *Two Commentaries on the Jacobite Liturgy*, p. 96). Narsai reports the following summons to prayer, after the Creed: '. . . Pray, brethren, over the oblation which we offer, that it may be acceptable before God to whom it is offered; and that by the brooding of the Holy Spirit, it may be consecrated, *that it may become unto us a cause of life in the Kingdom on high*' (*Liturgical Homilies of Narsai*, ed. Connolly, p. 6).

174 So the edition cited in n. 171. Cf. Brightman, p. 298.

175 B. Botte, 'Fragments d'une anaphore inconnue attribuée à S. Epiphane' in *Le Muséon* 73 (1960), pp. 311–15.

176 Already in the Gelasian Sacramentary (St Gall manuscript), ed. Mohlberg, 1939², no. 348. In translating the lapidary Latin of the Western, and especially the Roman, liturgies, my aim has been to achieve accuracy of sense, itself no easy matter, rather than to furnish a version that reads well.

177 *An Early Euchologion: The Dêr-Balizeh Papyrus* enlarged and re-edited by C. H. Roberts and B. Capelle, Bibliothèque du *Muséon* 23, Louvain, 1949, pp. 30, 54–56.

178 *The Order of the Holy Qurbana of the Syro-Malankara Rite* (*The Anaphora of St Xystus*), with an introduction and a short commentary, Trivandrum (India), 1964.

179 *Corpus Reformatorum*, vol. 89 ( =vol. 2 of Zwingli), p. 607. The value of Zwingli's use of the expression is unfortunately attenuated by his general refusal to allow any *constitutive* relation between eating and drinking the bread and wine and being fed by Christ.

180 Quoted by Y. Brilioth, *Nattvarden i evangeliskt gudstjänstliv*, 1951², p. 262, from the *Forma ac ratio tota ecclesiastici ministerii*.

181 E.g. Hymn 158:

> *O what a taste is this,*
> *Which now in Christ we know,*
> *An earnest of our glorious bliss,*
> *Our heaven begun below!*
> *When He the table spreads,*
> *How royal is the cheer!*
> *With rapture we lift up our heads,*
> *And own that God is here.*

182 *Hymns on the Lord's Supper*, 93.

183 This has been stressed by S. McCormick Jr, in *The Lord's Supper: a Biblical interpretation*, 1966, pp. 99f, 105f. He notes particularly the apparently permanent sitting at table in Matt. 8:11 =Luke 13:29 and the statement 'That you may *be eating* and *be drinking* at my table in my kingdom' (Luke 22:30), calling attention to the *present* subjunctives (ἵνα ἔσθητε καὶ πίνητε), not aorist.

184 Ardent opponents of any constitutive connection between eating and drinking the elements at the eucharist and 'feeding on God' are referred to further discussion; see pp. 105–10.

185 For its ultimate worthlessness otherwise (and still in terms of food and drink), cf. Luke 13:25–27; 16:19–31.

186 Some ancient commentators on the liturgy give this interpretation to the president's salutation 'Peace be with you' (which is a declaration of the divine peace with man), and to the kiss of peace which all the members of the assembly exchange among themselves (a sign of peace among men). Thus Theodore of Mopsuestia in commenting on the pontiff's prayer 'Peace be with you' refers to the peace from death, corruption, sin, passion and the vexation of demons which Christ won for us by his 'economy', and says that the salutation is also an announcement of the magnificent blessings which have been promised and of which the liturgy is already a sign and type (XV, 34f); and in commenting on the kiss of peace which all exchange, Theodore appeals to Matt. 5:22–24 and I Cor. 10:17 and explains the kiss as a profession of the union of the baptized in mutual love which is necessary before partaking of the one bread (XV, 39–41). In explanation of the priest's salutation 'Peace be with you' before the *Sursum corda*, Narsai mentions the reconciliation wrought by Christ's death and the fact that Christians 'have been summoned to the Kingdom aloft by Him who entered first to prepare a place for us all' (ed. Connolly, p. 8); and in connection with the priest's same salutation before communion, Narsai refers to the Lord's use of those very words after His Resurrection: ' "Peace be with you," said our Lord to His familiars; "for lo, I am risen, and I raise up the whole nature." "Peace be with you," said He to His brethren, His intimates, "for lo, I am ascending and preparing a place for you all." "Peace be with you," said our Lord to His twelve, "for I am with you for ever without end." And this peace the priest gives to the sons of the Church; and he confirms them in love and hope and faith' (p. 26). According to Maximus the Confessor the kiss of peace prefigures the concord that will reign in the age to come among all who are united in Christ: 'Ὁ δὲ πᾶσι προσφωνούμενος πνευματικὸς ἀσπασμός, τὴν ἐσομένην πάντων πρὸς ἀλλήλους ἐν τῷ καιρῷ τῆς τῶν μελλόντων ἀρρήτων ἀγαθῶν ἀποκαλύψεως, κατὰ πίστιν τε καὶ ἀγάπην, ὁμόνοιάν τε καὶ ὁμογνωμοσύνην, καὶ ταυτότητα λογικήν, δι' ἣν τὴν πρὸς τὸν Λόγον καὶ Θεὸν οἰκείωσιν οἱ ἄξιοι δέχονται, προτυποῖ καὶ προδιαγράφει (*Myst.*, 17, PG 91, 693f).

187 "Ἄχρι(s) οὗ followed by aorist subjunctive opens up an eschatological goal elsewhere in the N.T.: Luke 21:24, Rom. 11:25, I Cor. 15:25.

188 Mark 8:38 = Matt. 16:27f = Luke 9:26; Mark 13:26f = Matt. 24:30f = Luke 21:27; Mark 13:33–37 = Matt. 24:42–44 = Luke 12:35–40; Matt. 24:27 = Luke 17:24; Matt. 10:23; Matt. 25:1–13; Matt. 25:31; Luke 17:28–30; Luke 18:8b; John 5:25–29; 6:39, 40, 44, 54; Acts 1:11; I Cor. 1:7f; 15:23; Phil. 1:6, 10; 2:16; 3:20f; 4:5; Col. 3:4; I Thess. 2:19; 3:13; 4:13–17; 5:2, 23; II Thess. 2:1–12; I Tim. 6:14; II Tim. 4:1; Heb. 9:28; 10:37; Jas. 5:7–9; I Pet. 1:13; II Pet. 3; I John 2:28; 3:1; Rev. 3:11; 22:7, 12, 20. I would not deny that some of the gospel sayings ascribed to Jesus may be ecclesiastical re-applications to the second coming of sayings which He originally meant to refer to present or future events in His first coming; nor that the apocalyptic colouring may have been heightened in some cases.

189 On this ancient anaphora see E. C. Ratcliff, 'The Original Form of the Anaphora of Addai and Mari: A Suggestion' in *JTS* 30 (1928–29), pp. 23–32; G. Dix, *The Shape of the Liturgy*, pp. 177–87; and, most important,

B. Botte, 'L'Anaphore Chaldéenne des Apôtres' in *Orientalia Christiana Periodica* 15 (1949), pp. 259–76. Also L. Bouyer, *Eucharistie*, 1966, pp. 146–58.

190 *Das Abendmahl . . .*, p. 49.

191 J. Hamer, *L'Eglise est une communion*, Paris, 1962, pp. 213–17, with philological appeal to H. Bietenhard, *art. ὄνομα* in *TWNT*, vol. V, p. 267, lines 28ff.

192 The Greek word παρουσία reflects this humanly indispensable relation between a presence and a coming, since it is used for both. Its use in the liturgies and in eucharistic theology probably helped the Greeks to keep a rather better hold than the Latins did on the fact that the eucharist is the moment of the Lord's *visitation* of His people, not allowing the more *static* question of the mode in which the presence was attached to the elements to dominate. It is interesting that in secular Greek παρουσία was the word used for the arrival of a king.

193 J. Doresse and E. Lanne, *Un temoin archaïque de la liturgie copte de S. Basile*, Louvain, 1960 (with an appendix by B. Capelle, 'Les liturgies "basiliennes" et saint Basile'), p. 18. See also the Byzantine *St Basil* (Brightman, p. 328), and the later Alexandrian Greek *St Basil* (Renaudot I, p. 68)—though these add also a mention of the resurrection and, in the second case, the ascension. The Byzantine oddly drops the final 'till I come'.

194 See A. Wilmart, 'Une exposition de la messe ambrosienne' in *Jahrbuch für Liturgiewissenschaft* 2 (1922), pp. 47–67; the tenth-century Sacramentary of Biasca, quoted by J. H. Srawley, *The Early History of the Liturgy*, 1947², p. 158, n. 3; and A. Ratti and M. Magistretti, *Missale Ambrosianum*, 1913, p. 243. In the Stowe Missal Moelcaich's hand adds: *passionem meam predicabitis, resurrectionem meam adnuntiabitis, adventum meum sperabitis donec iterum veniam ad vos de caelis* (ed. Warner, p. 13).

195 Already in its early Egyptian form (J. Doresse, E. Lanne and B. Capelle, *op. cit.*, pp. 18f), and also in its later Alexandrian Greek form (Renaudot I, p. 68).

196 The Alexandrian *St Mark* does not use a verb of remembering in its 'annesis' at all, but 'proclaims' the death, 'confesses' the resurrection, ascension and heavenly session and 'awaits' the second coming (Brightman, p. 133; similarly the Coptic *St Cyril*, Brightman, p. 178).

197 W. J. Grisbrooke, *Anglican Liturgies of the seventeenth and eighteenth centuries*, 1958, p. 289. Similarly in the Non-Jurors' Liturgy of 1734, though in the form 'Therefore in commemoration of . . .' (*ibid.*, p. 310).

198 See B. Wigan (ed.), *The Liturgy in English*, [1962¹] 1964².

199 E. T. from A. Linton, *Twenty-five Consecration Prayers*, pp. 52f.

200 For a theological statement of Casel's position see the writings contained in the fourth edition (posthumous, edited by E. Neunheuser) of his *Das christliche Kultmysterium*, 1960. For Casel's method of dealing with liturgical history see his article, 'Das Mysteriengedächtnis der Messliturgie im Lichte der Tradition' in *Jahrbuch für Liturgiewissenschaft* 6 (1926), pp. 113–204.

201 M. Thurian, *L'Eucharistie: Mémorial du Seigneur, Sacrifice d'action de grâce et d'intercession*, 1959.

202 Thus D. R. Jones, 'ἀνάμνησις in the LXX and the Interpretation of I Cor. XI. 25' in *JTS* n.s.6 (1955), pp. 183–91, makes a linguistic attack which is very narrowly based on the five occurrences of ἀνάμνησις in the LXX (Lev.

24:7 and Num. 10:10, where Jones seems not averse to seeing a Godward reference; the headings of Pss. 38(37) and 70(69), which he rightly regards as too obscure to be used in the argument; Wisd. 16:6, where the reference is unambiguously manward), arguing that since ἀνάμνησις does not of itself contain a *certain* implication of memorial *before God* the Godward reference would have been made clearer if it had been intended in the 'command to repeat'. A similar objection is found also in W. C. van Unnik, 'Kanttekeningen bij een nieuwe verklaring van de anamnese-woorden' in *Nederlands Theologisch Tijdschrift* 4 (1949–50), pp. 369–77, and in H. Kosmala, ' "Das tut zu meinem Gedächtnis" ' in *Novum Testamentum* 4 (1960), pp. 81–94.

203 D. R. Jones, *art. cit.*; H. Kosmala, *art. cit.*; G. D. Kilpatrick, 'L'eucharistie dans le Nouveau Testament' in *Revue de Théologie et de Philosophie* 97 (1964), in particular pp. 196–98.

204 H. Gross, 'Zur Wurzel *zkr*' in *Biblische Zeitschrift* n.F.4 (1960), pp. 227–37; B. S. Childs, *Memory and Tradition in Israel*, London, 1962; P. A. H. de Boer, *Gedenken und Gedächtnis in der Welt des A.T.*, Stuttgart, 1962; W. Schottroff, '*Gedenken' im Alten Orient und im Alten Testament*, Neukirchen, 1964. Closely related is recent work on the *Vergegenwärtigung* of the saving events of the past in Israel's worship: see, for instance, also S. Mowinckel, *Psalmenstudien II*, Kristiania, 1922, e.g. pp. 54–65; M. Noth, 'Die Vergegenwärtigung des A.T. in der Verkündigung' in *Evangelische Theologie* 12 (1952–53), pp. 6–17; H. J. Kraus, *Gottesdienst in Israel*, München, 1954[1], pp. 125–28; G. von Rad, *Theologie des Alten Testaments*, II, 1960, pp. 112–25; H. Zirker, *Die kultische Vergegenwärtigung der Vergangenheit in den Psalmen*, Bonn, 1964; and cf. W. Eichrodt, 'Heilserfahrung und Zeitverständnis im A.T.' in *Theologische Zeitschrift* 12 (1956), pp. 103–25. M. Thurian must be given credit for his detailed examination of *zkr* in the O.T. before the major monographs of Childs, de Boer and Schottroff had appeared; since his exegesis is at times strained in the interests of his liturgical thesis, it is as well to state that many other of his points are confirmed by these O.T. specialists.

205 The fact that other Greek words than ἀνάμνησις, e.g. μνημόσυνον, were frequently used in the LXX to translate זכר and its derivatives is neither here nor there, as is shown for instance by the equivalence of μνημόσυνον and ἀνάμνησις as translations for זִכָּרוֹן (Lev. 23:24; Num. 10:10) or for אַזְכָּרָה (Lev. 2:2; 24:7).

206 *Theologie des Alten Testaments*, I, 1957, p. 241.

207 On this psalm see A. R. Johnson, *Sacral Kingship in Ancient Israel*, Cardiff, 1955 [1967²], pp. 17–22 [19–25].

208 G. von Rad, *Theologie des Alten Testaments*, I, p. 255. After an exhaustive examination W. Schottroff accepts this as the eventual though not the original meaning of אַזְכָּרָה (*op. cit.*, pp. 328–38). In the case of the poor man's sin-offering (Lev. 5:12) and the cereal offering of jealousy (Num. 5:15, 18, 26) the purpose of the אַזְכָּרָה is probably to *remind God* so that, in the first case, he may pardon the sin and, in the second, he may give judgement on the alleged offence.

209 *Das formgeschichtliche Problem des Hexateuch*, Stuttgart, 1938, pp. 23–30, now in his *Gesammelte Studien zum A.T.*, München, 1958, pp. 33–41.

210 For Theodore of Mopsuestia Christ's *death*, resurrection, ascension and *continuing high-priestly work in heaven* constitute a single movement, of which the eucharist is the present earthly τύπος. Not dissimilar is the Wesleys' vision, as in *Hymns on the Lord's Supper*, no. 116:

### 1

*Victim divine, Thy grace we claim*
*While thus Thy precious death we show;*
*Once offer'd up, a spotless Lamb,*
*In Thy great temple here below,*
*Thou didst for all mankind atone,*
*And standest now before the throne.*

### 2

*Thou standest in the holiest place,*
*As now for guilty sinners slain;*
*Thy blood of sprinkling speaks, and prays,*
*All-prevalent for helpless man;*
*Thy blood is still our ransom found,*
*And spreads salvation all around.*

### 3

*The smoke of Thy atonement here*
*Darken'd the sun and rent the veil,*
*Made the new way to heaven appear,*
*And show'd the great Invisible;*
*Well pleased in Thee our God looked down,*
*And call'd His rebels to a crown.*

### 4

*He still respects Thy sacrifice,*
*Its savour sweet doth always please;*
*The offering smokes through earth and skies,*
*Diffusing life, and joy, and peace;*
*To these Thy lower courts it comes,*
*And fills them with divine perfumes.*

Compare the whole section 'The Holy Eucharist as it implies a sacrifice' (nos. 116–127).

211 It is generally recognized that ἐμός represents an objective genitive. See for instance J. Jeremias, *Abendmahlsworte*[3], p. 242.

212 In his commentary on the liturgy (PG 140, 417–68), the eleventh- or twelfth-century Theodore of Andida also sees the eucharist as a memorial of *Christ and all his work*. Basing himself on the words of Christ 'This is my body' where 'body' means His whole body and not only part, Theodore begins his commentary by arguing that the eucharistic liturgy as the memorial of Christ must symbolically depict the whole of the christological economy of salvation. Besides appealing to the example of an ordinary biography which tries to portray the whole life of the person concerned, Theodore further justifies his view of the eucharistic memorial as the memorial of Christ and all His work by mentioning the fact that the gospels give a complete picture of Christ's life 'from His conception to His final ascension into heaven and His second coming thence', and by comparing the liturgy to the icons, in which may be seen 'all the mysteries of the human life of Christ our God, from the archangel Gabriel's visit to the Virgin to the Lord's ascension into heaven and His second coming'. He then goes on in fact to review the course of the liturgy and to indicate the symbolic christological significance of the various ceremonies, moving between the annunciation and, finally (ch. 38, PG 140, 465), the ascension with its promise of the return. On Theodore's commentary see H. J. Schulz, *Die byzantinische Liturgie*, 1964, pp. 149–62.

213 The Greek reads τῷ Θεῷ Δαυίδ, but Lietzmann takes the form υἱῷ given in the revision of the Didache in *Apostolic Constitutions* VII, 26, 5 and found at Matt. 21:9, 15.

214 'Die Mahlgebete der Didache' in *ZNW* 37 (1938), pp. 32–41.

215 10:5 is considered a separate prayer.

216 J. P. Audet, *La Didachè: Instruction des Apôtres*, Paris, 1958, pp. 410–24.

217 G. Bornkamm, *Das Ende des Gesetzes*, München, 1952, pp. 123–32, a revision of his article in *Theologische Literaturzeitung* 75 (1950), cols. 227–30. A not dissimilar argument was put forward almost simultaneously by J. A. T. Robinson, 'Traces of a liturgical sequence in I Cor. 16:20–24' in *JTS* n.s.4 (1953), pp. 38–41.

218 C. F. D. Moule, 'A reconsideration of the context of *Maranatha*' in *New Testament Studies* 6 (1959–60), pp. 307–10, has not done enough to necessitate any great change in this interpretation.

219 See, above all, the art. μαραναθά by K. G. Kuhn in *TWNT* IV (?1942), pp. 470–75, which shows that the question is linguistically far more complicated than is commonly assumed.

220 In the East: John Chrysostom, *In I Cor. hom.* 44, 3, PG 61, 377; Theodoret, *In I Cor.* 16:21, PG 82, 373; John Damascene, *In I Cor.* 16:22, PG 95, 705; Theophylact, *In I Cor.* 16:22, PG 124, 793. So also in the West, as Ambrosiaster shows, *In I Cor.* 16:22, PL 17, 276; though the ambivalent form of *venit* allows the Westerners to take it as a present (with future meaning) also. See F. Vigouroux, art. *Maranatha* in F. Vigouroux (ed.), *Dictionnaire de la Bible*, vol. IV, Paris, 1908, cols. 712–14.

221 So also O. Cullmann, *Urchristentum und Gottesdienst*, 1950², pp. 16f, and *Die Christologie des N.T.*, Tübingen, 1957, pp. 217f.

222 If Dibelius's repartition of the dialogue in Did. 10:6 is correct, then 'Hosanna to the Son of David' and 'Maranatha' follow as successive responses by the *people*, and this would bear a particularly close resemblance to the *people's* cry in Matt. 21:9: Ὡσαννὰ τῷ υἱῷ Δαυίδ. Εὐλογημένος ὁ ἐρχόμενος ἐν ὀνόματι Κυρίου.

223 J. A. Jungmann, *Missarum Sollemnia*, II, pp. 170f, says that this is first attested by Caesarius of Arles ( + 540), PL 39, 2277. That it was a common feature in Gallican masses is shown by the frequency with which the *Post-sanctus* prayer begins 'Vere sanctus, vere benedictus . . .'. The *Benedictus qui venit* was customary at Rome at least from the seventh century, for it appears in most, though not all, of the manuscripts of the Roman canon (see B. Botte, *Le canon de la messe romaine*, Louvain, 1935, p. 30).

224 J. Cooper and A. J. Maclean (edd.), *The Testament of our Lord*, Edinburgh, 1902, p. 75 [I. 23].

225 Brightman, p. 24. This strengthens my suggestion that the 'Blessed is he that comes' replaced the *Maranatha*, for the Didache's 'If any one is holy . . .' may well be a predecessor of Τὰ ἅγια τοῖς ἁγίοις. It may also strengthen Lietzmann's position that Did. 10:6 came immediately before communion rather than in a more distant position at the beginning of the eucharistic liturgy; support for this immediately pre-communion position would not commit us to Lietzmann's awkward theory of the displacement of Did. 10:6, since he is driven to this conjecture only by his (mistaken, as I consider) belief that the prayers of 9:2, 3 are properly eucharistic and do not merely belong to an agape.

226 The present Byzantine liturgy of *St Chrysostom* makes a similar use of the 'Blessed is he that comes' as *Apostolic Constitutions VIII* (Brightman, pp. 393–96).

227 Brightman, p. 432. Brightman indicates that it occurs at this point 'in some

churches and on some days'. It occurs there in the *Divine Liturgy of the Armenian Apostolic Orthodox Church*, New York, 1950, pp. 58f.

228  In *Apostolic Constitutions* VII, 26 *maranatha* had come at the end of a prayer *after* communion. This was because in its revision of Did. 9–10 *Apostolic Constitutions* VII, 25f turned chapter 9 into an undeniably eucharistic prayer and chapter 10, necessarily, into a *post-communion* prayer (μετὰ δὲ τὸ ἐμπλησθῆναι of 10:1 becoming μετὰ δὲ τὴν μετάληψιν).

229  *Abendmahlsworte*[3], pp. 247–50.

230  Moses bār Kēphā comments thus on the West Syrian rite's 'Blessed is he that came and cometh in the name of the Lord': 'That is: *He came*, in that his first coming, and redeemed us; *He cometh* again, in that second coming, for the judging and rewarding of all . . .' (R. H. Connolly & H. W. Codrington, *Two Commentaries on the Jacobite Liturgy*, p. 51). A similar form is found also in the East Syrian *Addai and Mari* (Brightman, p. 284). In the Armenian liturgy the form after the *Sanctus* is 'Blessed art thou who didst come and comest in the name of the Lord' (Brightman, p. 436; cf. J. M. Hanssens, *Institutiones Liturgicae de ritibus orientalibus* III, p. 394: 'qui venisti et venturus es . . .').

231  Byzantine liturgy of *St Chrysostom* (Brightman, p. 379); the Greek *St Mark*, from Alexandria (Brightman, p. 122); the Armenian liturgy (Brightman, p. 432).

232  So in the Greek *St James*, where the Cherubic Hymn begins Σιγησάτω πᾶσα σάρξ and goes on: . . . ὁ γὰρ βασιλεὺς τῶν βασιλευόντων Χριστὸς ὁ Θεὸς ἡμῶν προέρχεται (Brightman, p. 41), thus making explicit (as the Armenian liturgy does also) the *christological* reference.

233  Brightman, pp. 430–34. Cf. *The Divine Liturgy of the Armenian Apostolic Orthodox Church*, New York, 1950, pp. 54–63.

234  We may date the introduction of the Great Entry in the Greek rites, at least in its solemn form, in the sixth century, for it is probably as to a novelty that Eutychius of Constantinople (+582) objects to the hailing of the elements as 'the king of glory' already at that point and therefore before the epiclesis (*de pasch. et sacrosancta euch.*, 8, PG 86, 2400f; see Brightman, p. 532, n. 9). The phrase Ἰδοὺ γὰρ εἰσπορεύται ὁ βασιλεὺς τῆς δόξης is now found, in the Byzantine liturgy, only in the hymn that accompanies the Great Entry in the Liturgy of the *Presanctified*—a hymn whose introduction seems to date from the year 615 (so H. J. Schulz, *Die byzantinische Liturgie*, pp. 73f, with reference to the *Chronicon Paschale*, PG 92, 989). H. J. Schulz, *op. cit.*, pp. 69–75, may well be right that at the time of Eutychius's objections to 'the king of glory' it was Ps. 24 itself which was used at the Great Entry in the regular liturgy, the Cherubic Hymn with its 'king of all' not being introduced till 573/4 (cf. PG 121, 748); we ourselves have noted that Ps. 24 is used by the Armenian liturgy at the Great Entry, and this could be a relic of ancient use. The expression 'king of glory' occurs in *prayers* at the time of the entrance of the 'unconsecrated' gifts in the Greek *St James* (Brightman, p. 41), the ninth-century Byzantine *St Basil* (Brightman, p. 318) and the modern *St Chrysostom* (Brightman, p. 377). It is remarkable that all the liturgies mentioned use the expression 'king of glory' *only in connection with the great entry*. On the iconographic development of the theme see R. Bauerreiss, 'ΒΑΣΙΛΕΥΣ ΤΗΣ ΔΟΞΗΣ: ein frühes eucharistisches Bild und seine Auswirkung' in *Pro Mundi Vita*, pp. 49–67.

235 Ἄνω τὸν νοῦν (*Apost. Const. VIII*, Brightman, p. 14); Ἄνω τὰς καρδίας (so Cyril of Jerusalem, *Myst. Cat.* V, 4, ed. Cross, p. 31); Ἄνω σχῶμεν τὰς καρδίας (Byzantine *St Basil* and *St Chrysostom*); Ἄνω σχῶμεν τὸν νοῦν καὶ τὰς καρδίας (Greek *St James*; cf. Syriac also); Ἄνω ἡμῶν τὰς καρδίας (Greek *St Mark* and Coptic *St Cyril*).

236 Cyprian, *de or. dom.*, 31, PL 4, 539; Cyril of Jerusalem, *Myst. Cat.*, V, 4, ed. Cross, pp. 31f.

237 G. P. Wetter, *Altchristliche Liturgien: Das christliche Mysterium*, 1921, p. 12.

238 In D. Baillie & J. Marsh (edd.), *Intercommunion*, 1952, p. 337.

239 Was this perhaps the original sense of the deacon's warning Ὄρθοι πρὸς Κύριον . . . before the introductory dialogue to the anaphora in *Apost. Const. VIII*? But even in *Apost. Const VIII* (and certainly in its variant forms in later liturgies: Στῶμεν καλῶς . . . etc.) it is connected with the fact that the eucharistic *sacrifice* is about to take place. We notice all the same that Moses bār Kēphā gives the following reasons for the deacon's admonition 'Let us stand well, let us stand in fear': 'because the holy and divine mysteries are about to be revealed (and stripped) of the covering that is placed over them' and 'because in this hour the doors of heaven are opened, and the heavenly hosts and "the spirits of the righteous made perfect" come down to meet and honour the holy mysteries' (R. H. Connolly & H. W. Codrington, *Two Commentaries on the Jacobite Liturgy*, p. 44). Is there an echo here of, among other things, I Thess. 3:13b?

240 *The Order of the Holy Qurbana of the Syro-Malankarese Rite* (*The Anaphora of St Xystus*) with an introduction and a short commentary, Trivandrum (India), 1964, pp. 90f.

241 W. Rordorf, *Der Sonntag*, 1962, pp. 218, 270.

242 On the expression 'the breaking of bread' or 'to break bread' see n. 131.

243 H. Riesenfeld, 'Sabbat et jour du Seigneur' in A. J. B. Higgins (ed.), *New Testament Essays*, 1959, pp. 210–17.

244 So W. Rordorf, *Der Sonntag*, pp. 193–202, 213–33.

245 Cf. J. A. Jungmann, *Missarum Sollemnia*, I, pp. 23f.

246 What Pliny says is: 'Adfirmabant autem hanc fuisse summam vel culpae suae vel erroris, quod essent soliti stato die ante lucem convenire carmenque Christo quasi deo dicere secum in vicem seque sacramento non in scelus aliquod obstringere, sed ne furta, ne latrocinia, ne adulteria, committerent, ne fidem fallerent, ne depositum appellati abnegarent: quibus peractis morem sibi discedendi fuisse rursusque coeundi ad capiendum cibum, promiscuum tamen et innoxium; quod ipsum facere desisse post edictum meum, quo secundum mandata tua hetaerias esse vetueram' (*Epp.* X, 96). The baptismal interpretation, *sacramentum* being understood as the baptismal vow, is made by H. Lietzmann, 'Die liturgischen Angaben des Pliniusbriefes' in *Geschichtliche Studien für A. Hauck zum 70. Geburtstag*, 1916, pp. 34–38, and is accepted in a modified form by W. Rordorf, *Der Sonntag*, pp. 249–57.

247 W. Rordorf, *Der Sonntag*, pp. 246–48. We note that a *morning* eucharist is probably implied by Justin (*Apol.* I, 67) and certainly by Cyprian (*Ep.* 63, 16).

248 As part of his unconvincing attempt to cast doubt on Sunday's being the day of the weekly eucharistic assembly before the middle of the second

century, C. W. Dugmore takes the admittedly curious phrase κατὰ κυριακὴν δὲ Κυρίου of the Didache MS Hierosolymitanus 54 as meaning '*the* Sunday of the Lord . . . the Sunday on which he rose from the dead . . . i.e. Easter Sunday' ('Lord's Day and Easter' in *Neotestamentica et Patristica*, Supplements to *Novum Testamentum*, vol. VI (Leiden, 1962), pp. 272–81); but his claim that the phrase τὴν ἀναστάσιμον τοῦ Κυρίου ἡμέραν, τὴν κυριακὴν φαμεν of *Ap. Const.* VII, 30, 1 (where Did. 14 is worked over) supports the interpretation '*Easter* Sunday' is contradicted by the evidence of *Ap. Const.* II, 59, where καὶ ἐν τῇ τοῦ Κυρίου ἀναστασίμῳ, τῇ κυριακῇ clearly means '*every* Sunday', Sunday's eucharistic assembly being contrasted with the weekday gatherings for psalms and prayers. J. P. Audet has suggested how the text of Hier. 54 may have arisen from a marginal gloss explaining the archaic expression ἡμέρα Κυρίου (*La Didachè*, pp. 72f., 460).

249  *Apol.*, 16, PL 1, 371; *Ad nat.* I, 13, PL 1, 579.

250  Ignatius, *Magn.*, 9; *Ep. Barn.*, 15, 8f; Justin, *Apol.* I, 67 (PG 6, 432) and *Dial.* 41 & 138 (PG 6, 564f & 793); Tertullian, *de or.*, 23, PL 1, 1191; Eusebius, *H.E.* III, 27, 5; *Apost. Const.* II, 59, V, 20, 19, VII, 23, 3, VII, 30, 1, VIII, 33, 2; Basil, *de spir.s.*, 27, 66, PG 32, 192; Jerome, *apud* G. Morin, *Anecdota Maredsolana* III, 2 (1897), p. 418; Augustine, *Ep.* 55, 23, PL 33, 215. The Russian name for Sunday is still воскресенье.

251  *Ep. Barn.* 15:8f; Justin, *Dial.* 138, PG 6, 793; Clem. Alex., *Strom.* V, 14, 106, in *GCS*, vol. 15 ( =vol. 2 of Clement), 1906, p. 397; Basil, *de spir.s.* 27, 66 (PG 32, 192); Augustine, Serm. 94 in A. Mai's *Bibliotheca Nova*, vol. I, pp. 184f, and *Ep.* 55, 23 (PL 33, 215), *De civ. Dei*, XXII, 30, 4, PL 41, 803f. In the doubtfully Athanasian *De sabbatis et circumcisione* Sunday appears, by virtue of the Lord's resurrection, as the 'memorial' of the renewed creation which Christ has begun: . . . Τέλος μὲν οὖν τῆς προτέρας κτίσεως ἦν τὸ Σάββατον, ἀρχὴ δὲ τῆς δευτέρας, ἡ Κυριακή, ἐν ᾗ τὴν παλαιὰν ἀνενεώσατο καὶ ἀνεκαίνισεν. Ὥσπερ οὖν ἐντείλατο φυλάττειν πρότερον τοῦ Σαββάτου τὴν ἡμέραν, μνήμην οὖσαν τοῦ τέλους τῶν προτέρων, οὕτως τὴν Κυριακὴν τιμῶμεν μνήμην οὖσαν ἀρχῆς δευτέρας ἀνακτίσεως. Οὐ γὰρ ἄλλην ἐπέκτισεν, ἀλλὰ τὴν παλαιὰν ἀνεκαίνισε . . . (PG 28, 137f).

252  Justin writes that the eight people saved in the ark were 'a symbol of the eighth day (forever first in power) in which Christ appeared when he rose from the dead. For Christ, being the firstborn of every creature, became again *the head of another race which he himself regenerated* . . .' (*Dial.*, 138, PG 6, 793).

253  Luke 24:51, as read by A B W Θ fl f13 *pl* lat; Mark 16:19, apparently; *Gospel of Peter*, 13 (56), where the 'young man' at the tomb says ἀνέστη γὰρ καὶ ἀπῆλθεν ἐκεῖ ὅθεν ἀπεστάλη; *Ep. Barn.* 15:9, if we do not read a comma after νεκρῶν: '. . . the eighth day, ἐν ᾗ καὶ ὁ Ἰησοῦς ἀνέστη ἐκ νεκρῶν [,] καὶ φανερωθεὶς ἀνέβη εἰς οὐρανούς'; Jerome: 'unde et dominica dicitur quia Dominus in ea victor ascendit ad Patrem' (*In dom. paschae*, in G. Morin, *Anecdota Maredsolana* III, 2 (1897), p. 418); and for evidence of the Ascension as an Easter lesson see F. C. Conybeare, *Rituale Armenorum*, Oxford, 1905, p. 523.

254  Eusebius of Caesarea speaks of 'a most important festival, the august and holy solemnity of Pentecost, which is distinguished by a period of seven weeks and sealed with that one day on which the Divine Oracles attest the ascension of our common Saviour into heaven and the descent of the Holy

Spirit among men' (de vit. Const. IV, 64, PG 20, 1220; cf. PG 24, 700). Etheria describes a service (including the reading of Acts 2) which took place on the fiftieth day after Easter at the traditional site of the descent of the Holy Spirit on the apostles, the church on Mount Sion, at the third hour; then just after mid-day there was a service (including the reading of the Ascension passages) at the Imbomon, the sanctuary on the traditional site of the Ascension (§43, ed. Pétré, pp. 246ff). The earliest evidence for a separate feast of the Ascension forty days after Easter (in accordance with the inference drawn from Acts 1: 9, 13) is *Apost. Const.* V, 20, 2, cf. VIII, 33, 4. On the association between Ascension and Pentecost see A. A. McArthur, *The Evolution of the Christian Year*, London, 1953, pp. 141–57; G. Kretschmar, 'Himmelfahrt und Pfingsten' in *Zeitschrift für Kirchenge-schichte* 66 (1954–55), pp. 209–53; J. Boekh, 'Die Entwicklung der alt-kirchlichen Pentekoste' in *Jahrbuch für Liturgik und Hymnologie* 5 (1960), pp. 1–45.

255 How readily the Fathers find themselves called to mention the parousia by a mention of the ascension will be seen in the following texts: Tertullian, *de bapt.*, 19 (PL 1, 1222); *Apost. Const.* V, 20, 2 (ed. Funk, I, pp. 293f).

256 E.g. in the Discourse of St John the Divine concerning the falling asleep of the Holy Mother of God, §37, in M. R. James, *The Apocryphal New Testament*, Oxford, 1953 (reprint), pp. 206f.

257 Translated by B. P. Pratten in *Syriac Documents attributed to the first three centuries* (in the Anie-Nicene Christian Library), Edinburgh, 1871, pp. 35–49, from three manuscripts in the British Museum, Cod. Add. 14, 644, fol. 10, Cod. Add. 14, 531, fol. 109, and Cod. Add. 14, 173, fol. 37.

258 Nor should the eschatological connotation of the very name 'Lord's day (ἡ ἡμέρα κυριακή)' be missed. In the LXX ἡ ἡμέρα τοῦ Κυρίου is used for 'that day' on which Yahweh will visit in judgement: the Christians' exalted Lord is expected to return in judgement at the end ἐν τῇ ἡμέρᾳ τοῦ Κυρίου ἡμῶν Ἰησοῦ (I Cor. 1:8; 5:5; II Cor. 1:14; cf. ἡμέρα Χριστοῦ Ἰησοῦ Phil 1:6, 10; 2:16; ἡμέρα Κυρίου I Thess. 5:2; ἐκείνη ἡ ἡμέρα II Tim. 1:12), and already He comes in the weekly eucharist.

259 Zwingli deliberately decreed four celebrations a year (*Action oder Bruch des Nachtmahls*, April 1525). There is no doubt that in the Lutheran and Calvinist traditions the Lord's supper was celebrated less often than either Luther or Calvin would have liked (see W. D. Maxwell, *An Outline of Christian Worship*, 1936, pp. 74; 112–19), but there is no indication that these two Reformers seized the *theological* connection between Sunday and Eucharist. In the Church of England the 1662 extension to Sundays (as well as 'holy days') of the rubric providing for *ante*-communion alone if there were not sufficient communicants sanctioned the use of ante-communion as the principal Sunday service in most parishes, communion being celebrated only a few times annually; and so it remained until the nineteenth-century Oxford movement. When John Wesley sent *The Sunday Service of the Methodists* to North America in 1784, he advised an administration of 'the Supper of the Lord on every Lord's day' (*Letters*, ed. J. Telford, vol. VII, London, 1931, p. 239), but the weekly eucharist has been rare in Methodism anywhere in the world.

260 So already Dom L. Beauduin in his address to the liturgical congress at Malines in 1909.

261 *Der Gottesdienst im Neuen Testament*, 1952, p. 147.

262 *Worship: its Theology and Practice*, 1965, pp. 213–27, 237–39.

263 *De fid. orth.* IV, 12, PG 94, 1133f. The major monograph on orientation is F. J. Dölger, *Sol Salutis: Gebet und Gesang im christlichen Altertum mit besonderer Rücksicht auf die Ostung in Gebet und Liturgie*, Münster i.W., 1920 (1925²). Like much else of Dölger's, this work is unfortunately marred by forced interpretations of evidence.

264 E.g. Jerome, *apud* G. Morin, *Anecdota Maredsolana* III, 2 (1897), p. 418; Maximus of Turin, *Hom.* 61, PL 57, 371.

265 Tertullian says that *Oriens* was a 'figure of Christ' (*Adv. Valent.*, 3, PL 2, 545). Apart from Luke 1:78, the LXX reads 'Ἀνατολή and the Vulgate *Oriens* for צמח in the messianic texts of Zech. 3:8 and 6:12.

266 The parousia is compared with daybreak at Rom. 13:12; II Pet. 1:19; cf. I John 2:8. Note also the possibilities left open by the variant reading 'shall visit' (so p⁴ א* B W Θ sy co arm) at Luke 1:78.

267 *Didascalia* II, 57, 5 (ed. Funk, I, pp. 160f); *Apost. Const.* II, 57, 14 (ed. Funk, I, p. 165); Germanos of Constantinople, PG 98, 392; Thomas Aquinas, S.T.II.2.84.3.

268 'For the sign of the cross shall arise from the east even unto the west, with a brightness exceeding the sun's, and shall announce the advent and manifestation of the Judge to give to everyone according to his works' (*de consumm. mundi*, 36, PG 10, 940).

269 Thomas Aquinas also adopts the use of Matt. 24:27 with similar intent, S.T.II.2.84.3. Cf. also Germanos of Constantinople: 'We pray towards the east . . . because we expect the rising of the lightning of the second coming of the Lord and the re-birth [ =resurrection]' (PG 98, 392).

270 *Apost. Const.* II,57,14; Basil, *de spir.s.*, 27, 66, PG 32, 189f; pseudo-Athanasius, PG 28, 620; Greg. Nyss., *de or. dom.* V, PG 44, 1184; Chrysostom, *In Dan.* VI, 10, PG 56, 226f; Germanos of Constantinople, PG 98, 392; pseudo-George of Arbela, Corpus Scriptorum Christianorum Orientalium, Scriptores Syri, series secunda, t.91, Romae, 1913, pp. 88–90; Thomas Aquinas, S.T.II.2.84.3.

271 The widespread custom of burying the dead feet eastwards belongs to the same realm of associations: at the resurrection the dead are to stand upright to meet the coming Lord. See Durandus ( +1296): 'Debet autem quis sic sepeliri, ut capite ad occidentem posito, pedes dirigat ad orientem, in quo quasi ipsa positione orat, et innuit, quod promptus est, ut de occasu festinet at ortum, de mundo ad saeculum' *Rat. div. off.* VII, 35, 39, cited by F. J. Dölger, *Sol Salutis*, p. 199, n. 2 (1925², p. 264, n. 1).

272 Apart from texts already mentioned, see Tertullian, *Ad Nat.* I, 13, PL 1, 579; *Apol.* 16, PL 1, 370f; Clem. Alex., *Strom.* VII, 7, 43, in *GCS*, vol. 17 ( =vol. 3 of Clement), 1909, pp. 32f.

273 It is probable that this style of orienting church buildings started in the East and only later became the rule in the West. The architectural question is complicated, but a glimpse of the factors involved can be gained from J. G. Davies, *The Origin and Development of Early Christian Church Architecture*, London, 1952, pp. 81–83.

274 Ed. F. X. Funk, I, pp. 159f, 165.

275 Canon 97, *apud* W. Riedel, *Die Kirchenrechtsquellen des Patriarchats Alexandrien*, Leipzig, 1900, p. 274.

276 Rom. 6; 8:1–4; II Cor. 5:21; Gal. 3:10–14; Col. 2:12–14. See C. F. D. Moule, 'The Judgment Theme in the Sacraments' in W. D. Davies and D. Daube (edd.), *The Background of the New Testament and its Eschatology*, 1956, pp. 464–81, in particular 464–68.

277 Exegetical help is found in E. Käsemann, 'Anliegen und Eigenart der paulinischen Abendmahlslehre' in his *Exegetische Versuche und Besinnungen*, I, 1960, pp. 11–34, in particular pp. 21–34 (the whole essay was first published in *Evangelische Theologie* 7 (1947–48), pp. 263–83); and in C. F. D. Moule, *art. cit.*, pp. 468–76. Moule's article does not bring out clearly enough the fact that, whereas baptism is participation in the judgement which Christ bore, in the eucharist it is Christ Himself who now (after His exaltation) and already (in anticipation of His coming to judge the quick and the dead) is the *judge*; Käsemann provides a useful corrective at this point.

278 Συνέρχεσθαι (vv. 18, 20, 33, 34), often with ἐπὶ τὸ αὐτό (v. 20), seems to be almost a technical term for liturgical assembling: cf. I Cor. 14:23; Ignatius, *Eph.* 13:1; *Did.* 14:2.

279 So taken, for instance, by W. G. Kümmel, in H. Lietzmann-W. G. Kümmel, *An die Korinther I. II*, Tübingen, 1949⁴, p. 186; A. J. B. Higgins, *The Lord's Supper in the N.T.*, 1952, pp. 72f.; and E. Best, *One Body in Christ*, London, 1955, pp. 107–10.

280 The difficulty with regard to interpreting σῶμα in v. 29 of the eucharistic element lies in the fact that though the rest of the passage always works in couples (eats/drinks, bread/cup, body/blood), there is mention here only of 'discerning the body', and not 'the blood'. Nor does Käsemann do more than mitigate this difficulty when, in arguing in favour of 'the body' as the sacramental element, he explains its being mentioned alone here in part by the fact that for Paul it was the more important of the two sacramental elements (p. 27). When in fact we remember the reason which Käsemann has earlier (pp. 12f) given for thinking that the body was the more important of the eucharistic elements for Paul, namely that it provides the foundation for the apostle's conception of the supper as effecting incorporation into the *body* of Christ (I Cor. 10:16f): then we are pointed towards a *dual* understanding of σῶμα in v. 29, both the *eucharistic* and the *ecclesial* body being intended (so taken by P. Neuenzeit, *Das Herrenmahl*, pp. 38f, who considers σῶμα to be chiefly eucharistic, with an ecclesiological undertone). C. F. D. Moule (*art. cit.*, pp. 471–74) proposes a solution which, he claims, transcends the alternative: ecclesial *or* eucharistic, and embraces both. He takes the σῶμα of v. 29 as a reference back to the body of Christ *on the cross*. Remarking that Paul insists to the Corinthians that the Lord's supper is a memorial of Christ's *death*, Moule draws a parallel between μὴ διακρίνων τὸ σῶμα in I Cor. 11:29 and κοινὸν ἡγησάμενος τὸ αἷμα in Heb. 10:29: both represent 'a culpable failure to recognize, to discern, that the life which was surrendered [on the Cross] was that of the Lord himself', and in a eucharistic context this means failure to be 'alert to the meaning with which the bread and wine are charged both in regard to the incarnate Christ given for us and in regard to the fellow members of the Body which that surrender created'. Cf. G. Bornkamm, 'Herrenmahl und Kirche bei Paulus' in *Zeitschrift für Theologie und Kirche*, 53 (1956), pp. 312–49: '. . . den Leib unterscheiden, Christi Leib in seiner Besonderheit achten, das heisst verstehen, dass der für uns hingegebene und im Sakrament empfangene Leib Christi die Emp-

fangenden zum "Leib" der Gemeinde zusammenschliesst und sie in der Liebe für einander verantwortlich macht' (p. 342).

281 With ἁμαρτημάτων in the cup-word. See J. Wordsworth, *Bishop Sarapion's Prayer-Book: an Egyptian Sacramentary dated probably about* A.D. 350–356, 1910², pp. 62f.

282 It is present in the early Egyptian *St Basil* (Doresse-Lanne-Capelle, pp. 16ff), in the Alexandrian Greek *St Basil* (Renaudot, I, pp. 67f), in the 9th-century Byzantine *St Basil* (Brightman, p. 328, where it is absent from the parallel text of *Chrysostom*), and in the modern Greek *St Chrysostom* (Brightman, pp. 385f).

283 G. Kandathil (ed.), *Syro-Malabar Missal*, Ernakulam (India), 1963.

284 A corresponding prayer follows communion: 'And, O my Lord, may this earnest which we have received and are receiving be to us for . . . (and so on as above)' (Brightman, p. 302).

285 Except, of course, in the Creed and in the Advent preface. The new eucharistic prayers introduced after Vatican II have changed the situation.

286 The value of this way of presenting things lies in its stress on salvation as a continuing process: but the absence of reference to the coming universal crisis at Christ's parousia means a shortening of the New Testament witness.

287 The merest echo of it is found again in the 1662 form of the prayer 'for the church militant here in earth'.

288 Cranmer, like Luther in particular among the other Reformers, continued to place the heaviest stress here, as the medieval West had done.

289 *De fid. orth.* IV, 13, PG 94, 1145f; and a little later on: ἂν μὲν χρυσὸν λάβῃ κίβδηλον, διὰ τῆς κριτικῆς πυρώσεως καθαίρει, ἵνα μὴ ἐν τῷ μέλλοντι σὺν τῷ κόσμῳ κατακριθῶμεν (PG 94, 1152). In this chapter John Damascene cites the 'till he come' on two occasions without, however, developing it.

290 Ἑρμηνεία περὶ τοῦ θείου ναοῦ, PG 155, 697–749. Some guidance, though incomplete, in the field of Byzantine commentaries on the course of the liturgy and the events represented therein may be found in H. J. Schulz, *Die byzantinische Liturgie* (1964): on Maximus the Confessor see pp. 81–90, on Germanos of Constantinople (+733), pp. 118–30, on Theodore of Andida (11th or 12th century) pp. 149–62, on Nicholas Cabasilas (+1363), pp. 202–12, and on Symeon of Thessalonica (+1429), pp. 187–202.

291 Apart from the difficulties entailed in this twofold interpretation we may note that his compendious borrowing from various systems of interpretation leads him, purely at the level of the depiction of the events of the *Heilsgeschichte*, to play strange tricks with chronological sequence. The bishop's first descent from his throne represents the descent of the Logos and his incarnation. His walking through the church represents Christ's life among men. Christ's death and descent into Hades are represented by the bishop's walking as far as the west doors of the church. The Resurrection is shown both by the bishop's bowing and raising of his head in association with the prayers said while he remains outside the sanctuary and also by the deacon's elevation of the gospel-book with the cry 'Wisdom! Upright!' The bishop's entry into the sanctuary represents the ascension of the risen Lord. The lections signify the apostles' missionary preaching after the Lord's ascension, and the gospel in particular prepares for the coming of the End. The deacons' dismissal of the catechumens and the excommunicate represents the angels' work of separation at the End. The great entry signifies the parousia and

the coming of the kingdom. So far so good, but then chronological complications arise. When Symeon, now drawing on other systems of interpretation which saw the liturgy from the great entry onwards as representing the events associated with the passion and resurrection, views the liturgical representation of these last events of the Lord's earthly life as a kind of flash-back seen from the vantage-point of the final kingdom which has been entered (for this may be inferred from what he says about the kingdom of God consisting in the contemplation of Christ's saving work), we may admire his clever use of a cinematographic technique: but unfortunately confusion arises as to chronological sequence *within* the flash-back. For the start of the flash-back is the great entry and the deposition of the elements on the altar representing the bringing in of the dead body of Christ and its burial (presupposing the *proskomide* which had taken place before the start of the public liturgy and which Symeon had left out of account because, whether its incarnation-symbolism or its passion-symbolism had been developed [see the end of this note], it would have queered his pitch as far as starting the *public* liturgy with the descent of the Logos and the incarnation was concerned)—and yet, after the epiclesis has intervened to make the elements into 'the living Jesus' (Q. 86), there is a further manifestation of the lifting up of Jesus on the cross by the elevation of the bread, and then also of the crucified Jesus by the placing of four pieces of broken bread in the shape of a cross after the fraction. Symeon's difficulty arises, first, from his unwillingness to omit the long-traditional interpretation of the placing of the gifts on the altar as the burial of Christ (it is already found in Theodore of Mopsuestia, and in the Byzantine liturgy the troparion of the Noble Joseph of Arimathaea was sung at this point), whereas Theodore of Andida had included this interpretation only in a secondary way and with an embarrassed apology and Nicholas Cabasilas had simply left it out, because it did not fit into their respective (and similar) schemes; and second, from his desire to retain as far as possible the resurrection-symbolism of the epiclesis (already in Theodore of Mopsuestia) and at the same time to keep the crucifixion-symbolism of the elevation which is found in Theodore of Andida (who, however, gives *no* symbolic significance to the epiclesis and makes the elevation signify both crucifixion *and* resurrection). As to the proskomide: we note that in the time of Germanos of Constantinople the preparation of the elements took place just before the great entry; by the end of the eighth century, however, it had been transposed to precede the public liturgy; its most obvious symbolic potentialities lay in the realm of sacrifice, and the theme of the passion at first predominated, but Theodore of Andida was able to elaborate a detailed incarnation-symbolism for it, and Nicholas Cabasilas (PG 150, 376–91) and Symeon of Thessalonica himself (in another work, Κατὰ πασῶν τῶν αἱρέσεων, of which chapters 79–100 are on the liturgy, PG 155, 253–304) were able to combine the incarnation-symbolism and the passion-symbolism by making play with the notion that Jesus was from birth dedicated to God and destined to offer himself in sacrifice.

292 St Thomas, S.T.III.79.3; III.80.4. For Trent see Denzinger-Schönmetzer, §§ 1647, 1655, 1661, cf. 1465.

293 Apart from the central and essential symbolism of bread eaten and wine drunk, there is of course a whole range of secondary symbolism attaching

to the eucharist which, though ecclesiastically rather than dominically instituted and though bearing a less intimate relation to the reality symbolized, has at the very least the value of dramatizing in a potentially gripping way the realities of the kingdom to be finally brought about by a Christ who at His first coming did not spurn parables and acted signs in His proclamation. It is in this light that a positive value may be ascribed to the *Sunday* celebration of the eucharist, to *orientation*, to *processions* and *gestures* as depicting the saving events (though there is a danger here of anecdotalism), and to liturgical *vestments* (provided the raiment is not thought to be more than the body).

294  See *de mysteriis*, IX, 52–54 (ed. Botte, pp. 186f): 'For this sacrament which you receive is "confected" by the word (*sermone*) of Christ. . . . Concerning all the works of the universe you have read: He spoke and they were made, he commanded and they were created [Ps. 32:9; 148:5]. Cannot therefore the word of Christ, which could make from nothing that which was not, also change the things that are into what they were not? For it is not less difficult to bring new things into being than to change their natures. . . . The Lord Jesus himself declares: This is my body. Before the benediction of the heavenly words, another kind of thing is named; after the consecration it is designated the body. He himself says that it is his blood. Before the consecration it is called otherwise; after the consecration it is named the blood. . . .' (cf. *de sacr.* IV, 4, 13 to 5, 26, ed. Botte, pp. 108–16).

295  In the *Decretum pro Armeniis*: 'The form of this sacrament is the words (*verba*) of the Saviour, by which he "confected" this sacrament; for the priest, speaking *in persona Christi*, "confects" the sacrament. By the power of these very words the substance of the bread is converted into the body of Christ, and the substance of the wine is converted into his blood—but this in such wise that the whole Christ is contained under the appearance of the bread and the whole Christ under the appearance of the wine' (Denzinger-Schönmetzer, *Enchiridion Symbolorum*, §1321). What the precise words of Christ are, is spelt out in the *Decretum pro Jacobitis* (*ib*. §1352).

296  *Myst. cat.* V, 7, ed. Cross, pp. 32f.

297  See the most important essay of G. A. 'Michell, *Eucharistic Consecration in the Primitive Church*, 1948, which called attention particularly to the significance of the Jewish *berakah* form, and to the text of I Tim. 4:3–5 (see my n. 301). J. A. Jungmann, *Missarum sollemnia*, II, p. 254, n. 9, declares that the primitive conception of consecration through the whole eucharistic prayer persisted in many cases into the middle ages.

298  So, for instance, it is surely an indication of his own objectivist approach when E. L. Mascall, *Corpus Christi*, 1953, pp. 73f, complains that to view the whole prayer as consecrating implies a view of consecration analogous to the change effected by the gradual melting of wax.

299  G. Dix, *The Shape of the Liturgy*, 1945, pp. 275–92 (cf. pp. 183f, 253, 301).

300  S. Salaville gives abundant historical evidence from East and West in his article 'Epiclèse eucharistique' in *Dictionnaire de Théologie Catholique*, vol. V, col. 194–300. A short and less technical treatment from the same irenical viewpoint is found in E. Jeauneau, 'L'Esprit et l'Eucharistie' in *La Vie Spirituelle* 100 (1959), pp. 655–69. And more lately, J. M. R. Tillard, 'L'Eucharistie et le Saint-Esprit' in *NRTh* 90 (1968), pp. 363–87.

301  I. Tim. 4:3–5 must be mentioned at this point (see n. 297). Verses 4 and 5

read: ὅτι πᾶν κτίσμα Θεοῦ καλόν, καὶ οὐδὲν ἀπόβλητον μετὰ εὐχαριστίας λαμβανόμενον. ἁγιάζεται γὰρ διὰ λόγου Θεοῦ καὶ ἐντεύξεως. Now there is certainly a dependence here on the Jewish *berakah*, of which G. A. Michell (*op. cit.*, p. 4) says: 'By the first century A.D. at latest it was obligatory for faithful Jews to "bless" food and certain observances by formulas (*berakoth*) in which God was blessed (i.e. thanked) for having created the food or commanded the observance as the case might be. These *berakoth* consisted of (a) an invariable first clause: "Blessed art Thou, O Lord our God, King of the Universe", followed by (b) a relative clause referring to the particular divine word (creative word or command) which was relevant to whatever was being blest.' If, as seems likely, this is the clue to how the earliest church thought of the eucharist as being consecrated, then it is clear that Christ plays a prominent part in the consecration since He spoke the *words* of the original ordinance and is indeed Himself (as the Logos-doctrine of John 1:1–14, Heb. 1:1–3a, the second-century Apologists, and the Alexandrians Clement and Origen presented him) the creative *Word* of God. This is the certain background to a number of early passages whose detailed interpretation is controversial. Justin: 'For as through the Word of God (διὰ λόγου Θεοῦ) Jesus Christ our Saviour became incarnate and assumed flesh and blood for our salvation, so also we have been taught that the food which has been eucharistized δι' εὐχῆς λόγου τοῦ παρ' αὐτοῦ [either "by the word of (the) prayer which came from him" *or* "by the prayer of the word which came from him" *or*, as is perhaps most probable in view of the parallelism apparently intended between the role of the Logos in the incarnation and his role in the eucharist, "by the prayer of the Word which is from him (i.e. from God)"], by which our flesh and blood are nourished by assimilation, is the flesh and blood of that Jesus who became incarnate. For the apostles in their memoirs, which are called gospels, transmitted as follows what was enjoined upon them: Jesus, having taken bread and given thanks, said *Do this in memory of me, this is my body*, and likewise having taken the cup and given thanks he said *This is my blood*' (*Apol.* I, 66, PG 6, 428f). Irenaeus says that the bread and wine 'receive the Word of God' and become εὐχαριστία (*A.H.* V. 2.3, PG 7, 1125 & 1127), and we incline to write a capital W in the light of this statement in *A.H.* IV.18.5 (PG 7, 1028): ὡς γὰρ ὁ ἀπὸ τῆς γῆς ἄρτος προσλαβόμενος τὴν ἐπίκλησιν τοῦ Θεοῦ οὐκέτι κοινὸς ἄρτος ἐστὶν ἀλλ' εὐχαριστία ἐκ δύο πραγμάτων συνεστηκυῖα, ἐπιγείου τε καὶ οὐρανίου.... Origen refers to the eucharistic bread as being sanctified 'by the Word (*or* word) of God and prayer' (*In Matt.* XI, 14, PG 13, 948f). On all this see the essay by E. Bishop, 'The Moment of Consecration', in R. H. Connolly, *The Liturgical Homilies of Narsai*, pp. 126–63. None of it *excludes* the activity of the Holy Spirit also.

302 J. Wordsworth, *Bishop Sarapion's Prayer-Book*, 1910², p. 63.

303 PG 26, 1325 and PG 86, 2401. Hints of a role ascribed to the Logos in the eucharistic consecration are to be found in the Cappadocian Fathers: Gregory of Nyssa, *or. cat.*, 37, PG 45, 96f (in *Hom. de bapt. Christi*, PG 46, 581, he associates consecration with the work of the Spirit); Gregory Nazianzen, *ep.* 171, PG 37, 280f. Later Egyptian writers than Serapion and Athanasius ascribe a role to the Holy Spirit in the eucharistic consecration (so already, Peter II of Alexandria, 373–80, *apud* Theodoret, *H.E.* IV, 19, PG 82, 1169; and the Paschal letter of Theophilus of Alexandria for 402,

*apud* Jerome, *Ep.* 98, 13, PL 22, 801); and the extant Alexandrian liturgies have a 'Syrian'-style epiclesis for the descent of the Holy Spirit to consecrate the elements.

304 At the time of the Reformation, note the English Prayer Book of 1549: '... and with thy holy spirite and worde, vouchsafe to bl + esse and sanc + tifie these thy gyftes, and creatures of bread and wyne, that they maie be unto us the bodye and bloude of thy moste derely beloued sonne Jesus Christe.'

305 F. J. Leenhardt, *Ceci est mon corps*, 1955, in particular pp. 15–40. Among Catholics J. de Baciocchi's article 'Présence eucharistique et transsubstantiation' in *Irénikon* 32 (1959), pp. 139–61, shows positive indebtedness to Leenhardt, though he is developing hints contained in his own article 'Le Mystère eucharistique dans les perspectives de la Bible' in *NRTh* 77 (1955), pp. 561–80; but charges of 'extrinsicality' and 'extreme nominalism' are levelled against Leenhardt's view by A. M. Henry in 'Un débat sur l'Eucharistie' in *Istina* 3 (1956), pp. 215–28, and by V. Larrañaga in *Estudios Ecclesiásticos* (Madrid) 32 (1958), pp. 86–92. Some recent Dutch Catholic attempts at a terminology of 'transsignification' and 'transfinalization' seem to be indebted to Leenhardt as well as to Baciocchi, to judge by the criticism directed at Leenhardt in the rather cool and conservative article by E. Schillebeeckx, 'Christus' tegenwoordigheid in de Eucharistie' in *Tijdschrift voor theologie* 5 (1965), pp. 136–73, in particular pp. 167–72. A curious anticipation of the notions of transfinalization and transsignification is found in the still noteworthy study by the Anglican theologian O. C. Quick, *The Christian Sacraments*, 1932²: 'The change wrought in the bread and wine is sufficiently represented as a change in use and meaning, and is not a change in the physical objects as such' (p. 227).

306 Or quite as he stood in 1955. For in an article entitled 'La présence eucharistique' in *Irénikon* 33 (1960), pp. 146–72, and in his book, *La Parole et le Buisson de Feu*, Neuchâtel, 1962, pp. 68f, 134f, Leenhardt seems to put a view close to the one we shall eventually propose: he argues that 'transsubstantiation' goes between ultra-symbolism and ultra-realism, allows room for both symbol and reality, 'les limite l'un par l'autre'--like the bush which burned but was not consumed.

307 Cf. R. H. Connolly, 'Sixth-Century Fragments of an East Syrian Anaphora' in *Oriens Christianus* 12–14 (1925), pp. 99–128, in particular pp. 112f.

308 Irenaeus pictures the Word and the Spirit as God's two 'hands' in creation (*A.H.* IV, praef. 4; IV.20.1; V.1.3; V.5.1; V.6.1).

309 See later, pp. 115f.

310 Though see Ambrose (*de myst.*, IX, 58, ed. Botte, p. 190).

311 E. Käsemann, 'Anliegen und Eigenart . . .' in *EVuB*, pp. 15–17; J. Betz, *Die Eucharistie in der Zeit der griechischen Väter*, II/1, 1961, pp. 118–21; P. Lebeau, *Le vin nouveau du royaume*, 1966, pp. 115–17; J. J. von Allmen, *Essai sur le repas du Seigneur*, 1966, p. 33. When E. Schweizer (art. πνεῦμα, in *TWNT* VI, pp. 435f) rejects any idea of 'Spirit-bearing' elements, we may applaud his desire to avoid objectivism but may suspect the Zwinglianism which is never far from the surface in the Zürich professor's writings on the eucharist.

312 The quotation follows B. Botte, *La Tradition apostolique de saint Hippolyte; essai de reconstitution*, 1963. It is well known that *Apostolic Tradition* poses

many problems of text and authorship: see, for instance, L. Bouyer, *Eucharistie*, 1966, pp. 158–81.

313 On the epiclesis in *Addai and Mari* the most important articles are that of E. C. Ratcliff, 'The Original Form of the Anaphora of Addai and Mari: a suggestion' in *JTS* 30 (1928–29), pp. 23–32; and three by B. Botte: 'L'Anaphore chaldéenne des Apôtres' in *Orientalia christiana periodica* 15 (1949), pp. 259–76; 'L'Epiclèse dans les liturgies syriennes orientales' in *Sacris Eruditi* 6 (1954), pp. 48–72; and 'Problèmes de l'anaphore syrienne des apôtres Addaï et Mari' in *L'Orient Syrien* 10 (1965), pp. 89–106.

314 The 'upon us' is present, for instance, in the East Syrian *Theodore* (Renaudot, II, p. 621), but not in *Nestorius* (Renaudot, II p. 633); the West Syrian evidence is also mixed. The verbs used in the East to express the change in the elements are many and various: ἁγιάζειν, ἀναδεικνύναι, ἀποφαίνειν, γίνεσθαι, μεθιστάναι, μεταβάλλειν, μεταπλάσσειν, μεταποιεῖν, μεταρρυθμίζειν, μεταστοιχειοῦν, ποιεῖν; and in the West: commutare, conficere, consecrare, convertere, efficere, facere, mutare, sanctificare, transferre, transfigurare, transformare, transire, transmutare. This ought to be a warning against any single theoretical explanation of the mode of the presence. On the value of variety in eucharistic vocabulary in general, see some remarks by J. J. von Allmen, *Essai sur le repas du Seigneur*, 1966, pp. 15–17.

315 Cf. the following fragment of a popular poem dated by its editor in the third or fourth century:

> τῆς ἁγίας σου τραπέζης προκειμένης,
> καὶ ἀχράντων μυστηρίων μελιζομένων,
> ἐνετείλω τοῖς ἁγίοις μαθηταῖς.
> λάβετε (πάντες) φάγετέ μου τὸ σῶμα.
> γεύσαθε (πάντες) πίετέ μου τὸ αἷμα.
> χαρᾶς εμπλήσθητε, λάβετε πνεῦμ' ἅγιον.

In N. Borgia, *Frammenti eucaristici antichissimi: saggio di poesia sacra popolare bizantina*, p. 60.

316 H. J. Schulz, *Die byzantinische Liturgie*, pp. 75–81, argues convincingly that the symbolism here has to do with the work of the Holy Spirit in the Resurrection of Christ (cf. Rom. 8:11). J. M. R. Tillard has recently assembled the traditional evidence for the view that it is the risen body of Christ, glorified by the Holy Spirit, which is received in communion (*L'Eucharistie, pâque de l'Eglise*, 1964, pp. 59–105).

317 Just one outlandish quotation from Ephraim the Syrian may be given as a reminder that the Graeco-Roman is not the only style of doing theology: 'Jesus took into his hands plain bread, and blessed, signed and hallowed it in the name of the Father and in the name of the Holy Spirit, and broke it and distributed it piecemeal to his disciples in his good favour. He called the bread his living body and he filled it with himself and the Spirit. Stretching out his hand he gave them the bread which his own right hand had hallowed: "Take and eat, all of you, of this which my word has hallowed. . . . Take, eat in faith, nothing doubting that this is my body, and whoever eats it in faith eats in it fire and Spirit. . . . Take of it, all of you eat, and in it eat the Holy Spirit; for it is truly my body. . . ." ' (T. J. Lamy (ed.), *Sancti Ephraem Syri hymni et sermones* I, Mechliniae, 1882, cols. 416f).

318 For the biblical theology of glory see the following works: G. Kittel & G.

von Rad, art. δόξα in *TWNT*, II, pp. 235–58; A. M. Ramsey, *The Glory of God and the Transfiguration of Christ*, London, 1949; R. Schnackenburg, art. 'Doxa', in *Lexikon für Theologie und Kirche* III, 1959, cols. 532–34; E. Pax, art. 'Herrlichkeit' in *Handbuch Theologischer Grundbegriffe* (ed. H. Fries), I, 1962, pp. 680–85.

319 See pp. 117f.

320 A eucharistic interpretation of this verse is favoured by Hilary, *de trin.*, VIII, 12–17, PL 10, 244–49, and by Cyril of Alexandria, *In Jn ev.*, XI, 12, PG 74, 561–65. Compare the passage from the Syrian Balai quoted above, p. 47.

321 That our apprehension of the divine glory may involve the sense of touch as well as the sense of sight is suggested by the root כבד, whose meaning of weight II Cor. 4:17 shows not to have been lost.

322 A hymn, by C. W. Humphries, based on Ἀπὸ δόξης εἰς δόξαν πορευόμενοι is found in several modern English hymnbooks.

323 See the discussion in H. Lietzmann, *Messe und Herrenmahl*, pp. 74–81.

324 A 6th-century Coptic fragment picks up in this way from the *Sanctus*: 'Full are the heaven and the earth with this glory with which thou hast glorified us through thy only Son Jesus Christ, the firstborn of all creation, who sits at the right hand of thy majesty in the heavens, who will come to judge the living and the dead, of whose death we make memorial, offering to thee these thy creatures, thy bread and this cup. And we pray and beseech thee to send forth upon them thy Holy and Comforting Spirit from the heavens . . . hal[low] . . . the bread the body of Christ, &c' (L. Th. Lefort, 'Coptica Lovaniensia: no. 27' in *Le Muséon* 53 (1940), pp. 22–24).

325 Since writing the text I have discovered one Roman Catholic theologian who is clearly aware of the problem, though it can hardly be said that he solves it: V. Warnach, 'Symbolwirklichkeit der Eucharistie' in *Concilium* 4 (1968), in particular pp. 760ff.

326 The strong whiff of pantheism attaching to Teilhard de Chardin's eschatology is not unconnected with his penchant for using the doctrine of transubstantiation as a more general theological model.

327 It will be clear from the passages about to be quoted that there can be no thought of an easy escape by saying that there is a merely 'analogical' relation intended between the consecrated eucharistic elements and the final condition of creation.

328 First quotation from 'Messe et eschatologie' in *La Maison-Dieu* no. 24 (1950), in particular pp. 57f. Second quotation from *L'eucharistie, pâque de l'univers*, 1966 [a work which apparently came out in some form in 1947], in particular p. 109.

329 P. de Haes, 'Eucharistie en Eschatologie' in *Praesentia Realis* (Verslagboek van de studiedagen gewijd aan 'De moderne problematiek betreffende de Praesentia Realis' Nijmegen, 18–19 April 1963), which is the July–August 1963 issue of *Sanctissima Eucharistia* (Nijmegen), pp. 37–54, in particular p. 53. In a much more finely nuanced essay, L. Scheffczyk ('Die materielle Welt im Lichte der Eucharistie' in M. Schmaus, ed., *Aktuelle Fragen zur Eucharistie*, 1960, pp. 156–79) considers the eucharistic consecration as an illustration, an index (*Hinweis*), a pledge (*Unterpfand*) and even an earnest (*Angeld*) of the destiny of matter in God's plan; but it is only by tacitly refusing to draw the full consequences from his starting-point dictated by

the dogma of transubstantiation (he says that 'brute matter' is here in the Mass claimed by God in its deepest being, substantially therefore and not merely functionally, and transformed into Christ's glorified body) that he stops short of saying that the whole material creation is destined to become substantially the body of Christ and inclines rather to the view (which we could share and which does not presuppose transubstantiation) that the eucharistic consecration effects a *consecratio mundi* in that it glorifies one part of an inter-connected whole as a representative and veiled anticipation of the finally transfigured creation.

330 See pp. 25–42.

331 Modern exegetes are practically unanimous in allowing that John 6:51c–58 is eucharistic in reference. (The issue was not so clear cut in medieval and Reformation times—and Luther, for instance, refused all eucharistic reference to John 6, as is apparent already in his *Babylonish Captivity*.) But just as striking as the moral unanimity of modern exegetes in allowing the eucharistic reference is their wide diversity as to its interpretation. Roman Catholics see the passage as a proof-text for the *real* presence (e.g. D. Mollat, 'Le chapitre VIe de Saint Jean' in *Lumière et Vie* no. 31 (1957), pp. 107–19); while Zwinglians cannot get beyond their master's interpretation of John 6:63, which, no matter how much the fact is denied or disguised, really makes the eucharistic eating and drinking superfluous provided one has faith (see, for instance, E. Schweizer, 'Das johanneische Zeugnis vom Herrenmahl' in his *Neotestamentica*, 1963, pp. 371–96). Believing a Zwinglian exegesis of John 6:63 to be not the only possible one, I would rather endorse the remarks made on this explanatory verse by C. K. Barrett, who accepts the eucharistic reference of the principal text, vv. 51–58: 'It is important to note the standpoint which is established by this reference to the Spirit. John is writing with the completed work of Christ (7:39) in mind, including his ascension and the gift of the Spirit, and the discourse of this chapter is incomprehensible except from this standpoint; otherwise the words of Jesus could have led only to a crude cannibalism. Moreover it was necessary that Jesus himself should be understood as the bearer of the Holy Spirit (cf. 1:32f); otherwise his flesh and blood would lose all meaning . . . There is no *opposition* between the lifegiving flesh and the lifegiving words . . . [my italics]' (*The Gospel according to St John*, 1955, *ad loc.*). Cf. also E. C. Hoskyns, *The Fourth Gospel*, 1947², pp. 283–86, 297–301, 304–7.

332 Cf. Col. 3:4: ὁ Χριστὸς . . ., ἡ ζωὴ ἡμῶν.

333 Cf. Eph. 3:14–19.

334 'Until . . . I drink . . .', 'new', 'with you', 'at my table'.

335 The distinction which Eastern Orthodox theology makes between the divine 'essence' and the divine 'energies' is one attempt to conceptualize this truth.

336 I take this to be fundamental to any sound doctrine of God. See, e.g., E. L. Mascall, *He Who Is*, London, [1943¹] 1966², and *Existence and Analogy*, London, [1949¹] 1966².

337 See R. Mehl, 'Structure philosophique de la notion de présence' in *RHPhR* 38 (1958), pp. 171–76, who makes interesting play with the relationship between 'a present' and 'presence'. A similar notion is employed by L. Smits, *Actuele vragen rondom de transsubstantiatie en de tegenwoordigheid des Heren in de eucharistie*, 1965; but at this point he is accused by other

Catholic theologians of not doing justice to the full ontological content of
the doctrine of transubstantiation.

338 See St Thomas, S.T. III.81.1.

339 See, e.g., L. Bouyer, 'La première eucharistie dans la dernière cène' in
*La Maison-Dieu* no. 18 (1949), pp. 34–47.

340 The problem which even, or especially, Catholic theologians find (most
obviously in connection with the Last Supper) in the 'double presence' of
Christ as both host and food is heightened, and their embarrassment
increased, when they face the question of whether or not Jesus drank of the
sacramental cup at the Last Supper. L. Tondelli (*op. cit.*, pp. 27–31) and
H. Vogels ('Mk. 14, 25 und Parallelen' in N. Adler, ed., *Vom Wort des
Lebens*, 1951, pp. 93–104) have had the courage to make clear that there is
some patristic tradition that Jesus *did* drink of the sacramental cup: so
Irenaeus, *A.H.* V.33.1 (PG 7, 1212), Chrysostom, *In Mt. hom.* 82, 1 (PG 58,
739), and Jerome ('Dominus Jesus ipse conviva et convivium, ipse comedens
et qui comeditur'), *Ep.* 120 (PL 22, 986); so also the Gospel of the Hebrews,
*apud* Jerome, *de vir. ill.*, 2 (PL 23, 613) if we read . . . *qua biberat calicem
dominus* and not *domini*, and Augustine, *de doctr. christ.* II.3.4 (PL 34, 37)
if we read *sacramento corporis et sanguinis sui praegustato* [and not: *per
gustatum*] *significavit quod voluit*; and later on, Theophylact (PG 123, 445),
Euthymius Zigabenus (PG 129, 669) and Thomas Aquinas, S.T. III.81.1,
cf. III.84.7. We may note also that some liturgical institution narratives
insert 'he drank' or 'he tasted': so the Armenian liturgy (Brightman,
p. 437), and in Egypt the Dêr-Balizeh papyrus (edd. Roberts and Capelle,
p. 28), *St Cyril* (Brightman, p. 177), the Alexandrian Greek *St Basil* (Renaudot I, p. 67), and the Coptic form of *St Gregory* (Renaudot I, p. 31).

341 For the full form of these two prayers see p. 100. If we thought in Western
scholastic terms, we might say that the thought moves straight from the
*sacramentum tantum* to the *res tantum*, though no doubt the *res et sacramentum* is implied.

342 The ecclesiological reference of the epiclesis has been strongly emphasized
by N. A. Nissiotis, 'Worship, Eucharist and "Intercommunion": an Orthodox reflection' in *Studia Liturgica* 2 (1963), pp. 193–222.

343 *Hymns on the Lord's Supper*, no. 60, v. 1.

344 Here surely Irenaeus is right, against the 'spiritualizing' Gnostics: 'Giving
counsel to his disciples to offer to God the firstfruits from his creatures (not
as though God were in want, but in order that they themselves might be
neither unfruitful nor ungrateful), the Lord took bread which is part of
creation, and gave thanks, and said "This is my body". And likewise the
cup, which is part of that creation to which we belong, he professed
to be his own blood, and taught the new oblation of the new covenant;
which the church, receiving from the apostles, offers throughout the
whole world to the God who provides us with food, the firstfruits of his
own gifts, in the new covenant' (*A.H.* IV. 17.5, PG 7, 1023). 'Since,
then, the cup which is mixed and the bread which is made receive the
Word of God and become the eucharist of the body and blood of Christ,
and of them the substance of our flesh grows and subsists: how can they
deny that the flesh is capable of the gift of God which is eternal life, that
flesh which is fed by the body and blood of the Lord and is a member of
him? For blessed Paul says in his Letter to the Ephesians: "We are members

of his body, of his flesh and of his bones." He does not say this of a spiritual and invisible sort of man (for spirit has no flesh and bones), but of man in his real constitution of flesh and nerves and blood. It is this which receives nourishment from the cup which is his blood, and growth from the bread which is his body. And as the wood of the vine planted into the ground bears fruit in its season, and the grain of wheat falls into the ground and moulders and is raised manifold by the Spirit of God who upholds all things; and afterwards through the wisdom of God they come to be used by men, and having received the Word of God become the eucharist which is the body and blood of Christ: so also our bodies, nourished by the eucharist, and put into the ground, and dissolved therein, will rise in their season, the Word of God giving them resurrection to the glory of God the Father' (*A.H.* V.2.3, PG 7, 1126f). See also *A.H.* IV.18.4, quoted later, n. 392.

345 B. A. Gerrish, among others, has argued ('The Lord's Supper in the Reformed Confessions' in *Theology Today* 23 (1966–67), pp. 224–43) that Calvin held the view that the eating and drinking of the bread and wine in the supper is *instrumental* in our feeding on Christ—whereas the Second Helvetic Confession and the Heidelberg Catechism see no more than a *parallel* relation between feeding in the earthly supper and feeding by faith on the heavenly Christ. On Calvin see also M. Thurian, *L'Eucharistie* . . . pp. 258–67, and F. J. Leenhardt in *Irénikon* 33 (1960), pp. 146–57. I must, however, confess that their arguments do not quite convince me that Calvin was *consistently* an 'instrumentalist', for many of his texts are, to say the least, compatible with 'mere parallelism'.

346 The Synoptists and Paul have σῶμα, whereas John 6 has σάρξ and this form is known also to Ignatius of Antioch (*Philad.*, 4:1; *Rom.*, 7:3; *Smyrn.*, 7:1) and Justin, *Apol.* I, 66 (also σῶμα). Hebrew and Aramaic specialists vary, of course, as to the original words used.

347 This view finds strongest support in Mark/Matt. with the parallel words 'This is my body . . .' and 'This is my blood . . .', and in John 6:51c–58. It is strongly represented by J. Dupont, ' "Ceci est mon corps", "Ceci est mon sang" ' in *NRTh* 80 (1958), pp. 1025–41; cf. J. Jeremias, *Abendmahlsworte³*, pp. 211–16, who insists on flesh/blood as a sacrificial pair.

348 See, for instance, E. Käsemann, 'Anliegen und Eigenart . . .' in *EVuB*, pp. 28–34; G. Bornkamm, 'Herrenmahl und Kirche bei Paulus' in *ZThK* 53 (1956), in particular pp. 334–37. In *Le sacrement de la Sainte Cène*, 1948, and in 'Le pain et la coupe' (*Foi et Vie* 46 (1948), pp. 509–26), F. J. Leenhardt made a clear distinction between, on the one hand, the eucharistic *bread* as signifying Jesus's body given in sacrificial death and the present benefits of that death to each faithful communicant (and in *Ceci est mon corps*, 1955, it will be in connection with the bread alone that Leenhardt develops the thought of the instrument of Christ's presence) and, on the other hand, the eucharistic *cup* as giving rendez-vous with Christ at the messianic feast in the final kingdom (to share a cup is, in Hebrew idiom, to share a destiny).

349 See, e.g., A. R. Johnson, *The One and the Many in the Israelite Conception of God*, Cardiff, 1942¹ [1961²], and *The Vitality of the Individual in the Thought of Ancient Israel*, Cardiff, [1949¹] 1964², pp. 2f.

350 Gen. 16:7–14; 18; 32:22–32; Exod. 3:1–6; Judg. 6:11–24; 13; Hos. 12:4f (EVV 3f).

351 And a person's shadow (Acts 5:15)? or his handkerchief (Acts 19:12)? If

someone should put these questions with irony in his voice, I think I would
reply No. But that does not affect my argument. For the thing which makes
us sceptical in the case of the shadow and the handkerchief, namely the
lack of any deliberate personal intention on the part of the owner to be
present and operative by these means, does not apply when a man sends his
word or his messenger or his servant, nor when a man says 'This is my
body, this is my blood, do this as my memorial'.

352 I had not long struggled through to the view presented in the text when I
received an essay on the eucharistic presence from a pupil, Mr Zachary Talla
Kengne (a Bamileke, from Cameroon), which showed how much easier it
all is for an African: 'L'âme africaine se nourrit quotidiennement du
mystère de "la présence" et du "sang" personnels. Nos disparus ne sont
pas morts. Seuls ceux qui meurent "sans verser une goutte de sang" (i.e.
sans laisser une descendance) sont réellement morts. Nos disparus sont
toujours présents au sein de la famille qu'ils protègent et bénissent. Ils sont
présents par leur "sang" (i.e. leurs descendants, prolongation de l'incarnation), par leur "crâne" (d'où la vénération des crânes d'ancêtres, dialogue
avec les ancêtres au moyen de leur crâne, prières et sacrifices aux ancêtres
par l'intermédiaire de leur crâne). Tout objet laissé par nos disparus, ayant
appartenu à eux, continue leur présence auprès de ceux qui vivent encore:
photo, siège, pipe, réserves alimentaires, propriété foncière, arbres fruitiers,
coupes de vin (corne de la vache pour les nobles Bamiléké), ustensiles de
cuisine, tout cela donne un certain apaisement, une certaine consolation à
ceux qui s'en servent. . . . Les rites africains traditionnels n'associent pas la
présence personnelle seulement au sang. Ils lient également la présence
d'une personne à sa voix, à sa parole, à sa descendance, à ses effets (vête-
ments, cheveu, ongle, ombre, trace du pied, etc. . . . peuvent être identifiés
à la personne même). L'Africain non-chrétien croit à tout cela. C'est
pourquoi, lorsqu'il se convertit à la foi chrétienne, il accueille sans aucun
doute la présence du Christ sous les espèces du pain et du vin.'

353 See pp. 52–57, 84–89.

354 The most important recent studies here are all by Roman Catholics. They
are: M. Schmaus, 'Die Eucharistie als Bürgin der Auferstehung' in *Pro
Mundi Vita*, 1960, pp. 256–79; J. Pascher, 'Heilsmittel der Unsterblichkeit'
in *Pro Mundi Vita*, pp. 280–93; A. García Vieyra, 'La Eucaristía, sacramento
de la gloria' in *Estudios teológicos y filosóficos* (Buenos Aires) 3 (1961),
pp. 9–25; and two doctoral theses defended at the Angelicum in Rome:
W. B. McGrory, *The Mass and the Resurrection*, 1964, which is chiefly a
study of how *Christ's* resurrection is 'signified' in the Mass and may be
considered as being complemented by T. Fitzgerald, *The Influence of the
Holy Eucharist on Bodily Resurrection*, 1965, which deals with the relation
between communion and the *general* resurrection.

355 Already in the Gelasian, for Lent II (L. C. Mohlberg, *Liber Sacramentorum
Romanae Aeclesiae Ordinis anni circuli*, 1960, no. 166).

356 L. C. Mohlberg, *Sacramentarium Veronese*, 1956, no. 507.

357 L. C. Mohlberg, *Liber Sacramentorum Romanae Aeclesiae . . .*, 1960. no. 76.

358 Already in the Gregorian, ed. H. Lietzmann, 1921, nos. 44[10] and 75[3].

359 Already in the Leonine (ed. Mohlberg, 1956, no. 1314), Gelasian (ed.
Mohlberg, 1960, no. 117), and Gregorian (ed. Lietzmann, 1921, no. 156[8])
sacramentaries.

360 Already in the Gregorian, ed. Lietzmann, 1921, nos. 191[8] and 27[4].

361 Already in the Leonine (ed. Mohlberg, 1956, no. 531) and Gelasian (ed. Mohlberg, 1960, no. 223).

362 *Cat. Or.*, 37 (PG 45, 93). See also Cyril of Alexandria: *de ador. in spir. et ver.*, XII, PG 68, 793; *In Luc.* 4:38ff, PG 72, 552, and *ibid.*, 22:19, PG 72, 908–12; *In Jo. ev.* IV, 2 (ad 6:54–57), PG 73, 576–85. (Cf. J. Mahé, 'L'eucharistie d'après Saint Cyrille d'Alexandrie' in *Revue d'Histoire ecclésiastique* 8 (1907), pp. 677–96).

363 Σπέρμα ζωοποιόν (PG 72, 912), σπέρμα τῆς ἀθανασίας (PG 73, 581).

364 This lack of 'automatic' effect is well expressed by the Gelasian (St Gall manuscript) post-communion prayer: 'Fac nos, Domine quaesimus, accepto pignore salutis aeternae sic tendere congruenter ut ad eam pervenire possimus' (ed. K. Mohlberg, *Das fränkische sacramentarium gelasianum in alamannischer Überlieferung*, 1939[2], no. 348). (The prayer figures in the *Missale Romanum* on the Friday after Lent II.)

365 A. García Vieyra has stressed (*art. cit.*) that it was the doctrine of Thomas Aquinas that communion effected *directly* the beginnings of the 'adeptio gloriae', both in virtue of the fact that the eucharist represented Christ's passion which is the source of our glory, and also in virtue of the fact that it is the glorious Christ who is received (see S.T. III.79.1–2). Thomas taught a direct effect of communion on the soul, and an indirect effect on the body by redundancy (see T. Fitzgerald, *op. cit.*, pp. 43–54).

366 'Die Eucharistie als Bürgin der Auferstehung' in *Pro Mundi Vita*, pp. 256–79. Unfortunately some textual omission or dislocation seems to have taken place in pages 273–79.

367 Hom. XXI, ed. Connolly, pp. 60f. The summons to communicate runs: 'Come, ye mortals, let us aim at the mark that is hidden in our Mystery; and let us not relinquish the expectation of the life that is promised' (*ibid.* p. 61).

368 *Serm.* 63, 7, PL 54, 357; cf. *ep.* 59, 2: '. . . ut accipientes virtutem coelestis cibi, in carnem ipsius qui caro nostra factus est transeamus' (PL 54, 868). Augustine hears Christ say to him, 'You will not change me into yourself as you do the food of your flesh, but you will be changed into me' (*Conf.*, VII, 10, PL 32, 742)—and though the meaning is not explicitly eucharistic in Augustine, Thomas Aquinas adopts the text and sees the eucharist as conforming to the principle that whereas ordinary food is changed by the eater into his own substance, spiritual food changes the eater into *its* substance (S.T.III.73.3). We find this grotesque.

369 Among the liturgical texts we note: 'Quaesumus, omnipotens Deus, ut inter ejus membra numeremur cujus corpori communicamus et sanguini' (*Missale Romanum*, post-communion, Saturday after Lent III; already in the Leonine Sacramentary, ed. Mohlberg, 1956, no. 1116).

370 *Myst. Cat. IV*, 1 & 3, ed. Cross, pp. 26 & 27.

371 *In Jo. Ev.* XI, 11, PG 74, 560. Translation from the relevant volume in A Library of Fathers, London, 1885, pp. 549f, slightly altered.

372 Tertullian and Cyprian had spoken in these terms of the necessity of receiving the eucharistic body of Christ for present and lasting salvation: 'However, we may rather understand "Give us this day our daily bread" in a spiritual sense. For Christ is our bread, because Christ is life, and bread is life. I am the bread of life, he says. And just before: The bread is the Word

of the living God which came down from heaven. Then also his body is reckoned to be bread: This is my body. And so, in asking for daily bread, we are asking for perpetuity in Christ, and indivisibility from his body' (Tertullian, *de or.*, 6, PL 1, 1160f); 'Just as we say "Our Father" because He is the Father of those who understand and believe, so also we say "our bread", because Christ is the bread of those who, like us, come in contact with his body (*contingimus*). We ask that this bread be given us daily, that we who are in Christ and daily receive his eucharist as the food of salvation may not be separated from Christ's body by some more serious sin coming to oblige abstinence from communion and so deprive us of the heavenly bread; for he himself proclaimed: I am the bread of life which came down from heaven; if anyone shall eat of my bread, he will live for ever; the bread which I shall give is my flesh for the life of the world. When, therefore, he says that whoever shall eat of his bread will live for ever, then just as it is clear that those who touch (*attingunt*) his body and receive the eucharist by the means of communion are living, so on the other hand we must fear and pray lest anyone should remain far from salvation by being separated, by abstinence, from the body of Christ; for he himself warned: Unless you eat the flesh of the Son of man and drink his blood, you will have no life in you. And so we pray that our bread—that is, Christ—may be given us daily, so that we who abide and live in Christ may not depart from his sanctification and body' (Cyprian, *de or. dom.*, 18, PL 4, 531f).

373 See my article, 'Scripture and tradition: a systematic sketch' in *Church Quarterly* 3 (1970–71), in particular pp. 25f.

374 An early study, to which much recent French writing is indebted, is found in H. de Lubac, *Corpus mysticum: l'eucharistie et l'Eglise au moyen âge*, Paris, [1944¹] 1949². Among the articles in other languages we may mention the following: F. Puzo, 'La unidad de la Iglesia en función de la Eucaristía (estudio de teología bíblica)' in *Gregorianum* 34 (1953), pp. 145–86; P. Bläser, 'Eucharistie und Einheit der Kirche in der Verkündigung des Neuen Testaments' in *Theologie und Glaube* 50 (1960), pp. 419–32; E. Stakmeier, 'Die Eucharistie, die Einheit der Kirche und die Wiedervereinigung der Getrennten' in *Theologie und Glaube* 50 (1960), pp. 241–62; H. Fries, 'Die Eucharistie und die Einheit der Kirche' in *Pro Mundi Vita*, 1960, pp. 165–80; and, particularly valuable, J. Lescrauwaert, 'Eucharistische Eredienst en kerkelijke eenheid' in *Bijdragen* 25 (1964), pp. 117–41.

375 T. Schmidt, *Der Leib Christi: eine Untersuchung zum urchristlichen Gemeindegedanke*, Leipzig, 1919, pp. 206–9; F. Kattenbusch, 'Der Spruch über Petrus und die Kirche bei Matthäus' in *Theologische Studien und Kritiken*, 1922, p. 114; A. E. J. Rawlinson, in G. K. A. Bell & A. Deissmann (edd.), *Mysterium Christi*, London, 1930, pp. 227f. It is accepted as a partial explanation by L. Cerfaux, *La Théologie de L'Eglise suivant Saint Paul*, Paris, 1942, pp. 213–25, and by L. Malevez, 'L'Eglise, corps du Christ: sens et provenance de l'expression chez saint Paul' in *Recherches de Science Religieuse* 32 (1944), pp. 27–94, in particular pp. 74–77. So also J. A. T. Robinson, *The Body*, London, 1952, pp. 55–58.

376 See P. Neuenzeit, *Das Herrenmahl*, pp. 199f.

377 See E. Käsemann, 'Angliegen und Eigenart . . .', pp. 12–15; P. Neuenzeit, *Das Herrenmahl*, pp. 59–62, 201–19.

378 Clement of Alexandria, *Paed.*, I, 6, PG 8, 288, which reads καὶ πάντες ἑνὶ

πόματι ἐπίομεν. Chrysostom, *In ep. ad Cor. hom.*, 30, 2, PG 61, 251. Thomas, *In I Cor. XII, lect.* 3 (*Opera omnia*, t.XIII (Expositio in omnes S. Pauli Epistolas), Parmae, 1862, p. 255). Calvin, in *Corpus Reformatorum*, vol. 77 (=*Opera Calvini*, vol. 49), Brunsvigae, 1892, col. 502. A. Osiander, *Biblia Sacra*, Tubingae, 1600, N.T. p. 65 verso. (Augustine and Luther must be taken on trust: consultation of a score of commentaries on I Corinthians reveals that it is scholarly practice to relay these names without giving the original references; and my own consultation of the voluminous writings of the Father and the Reformer has not yet been successful.) Among modern champions of a eucharistic interpretation are E. Käsemann, 'Anliegen und Eigenart . . .' in *EVuB*, p. 15; L. Goppelt, in *TWNT*, vol. VI, pp. 147 (n. 18), 160; M. E. Boismard, 'L'eucharistie selon Saint Paul' in *Lumière et Vie*, no. 31 (1957), in particular p. 103; J. Betz, *Die Eucharistie in der Zeit der griechischen Väter*, II/1, pp. 121f; P. Lebeau, *Le vin nouveau du royaume*, pp. 118f; and Th. Süss, *La communion au corps du Christ*, pp. 12f.

379 The prayer is already in the Leonine (ed. Mohlberg, 1956, no. 1049) and Gelasian (ed. Mohlberg, 1960, no. 1330) sacramentaries. See also, in *Missale Romanum*, the post-communion of Pentecost IX: 'Tui nobis, quaesumus Domine, communio sacramenti, et purificationem conferat, *et tribuat unitatem*'; and the secret of Corpus Christi: 'Ecclesiae tuae, quaesumus Domine, unitatis et pacis propitius dona concede: quae sub oblatis muneribus mystice designantur.'

380 S.T.III.73.1 & 3. J. M. R. Tillard has shown how St Thomas sets the final realization of the eucharistic *res* in heaven: see 'L'Eucharistie, sacrement de l'espérance ecclésiale' in *NRTh* 83 (1961), in particular, pp. 561–67.

381 'As this broken bread was scattered on the mountains and then being gathered together became one, so may thy church be gathered together from the ends of the earth into thy kingdom.' See also the anaphora of Serapion, where the theme is also used as a prayer for the gathering of the church into unity (though with no explicit eschatological reference): '. . . and as this bread has been scattered on the top of the mountains and gathered together came to be one, so also gather thy holy church out of every nation and every country and every city and village and house and make one living catholic church' (ed. J. Wordsworth, pp. 62f.).

382 See *serm.* 57, 7, PL 38, 389; *serm.* 227, PL 38, 1099–1101; *serm.* 272, PL 38, 1247f. Cyprian also had seen the grains and the bread, the grapes and the wine, as an illustration of the existing unity of the church (*Ep.* 69, 5, *CSEL*, pp. 753f; cf. *Ep.* 63, 13, *CSEL*, p. 712).

383 See (sometimes with explicit mention of the kiss of peace): Did. 14:2; Cyril of Jerusalem, *Myst. Cat.*, V, 3, ed. Cross, p. 31; John Chrysostom, *Adv. Jud.* III, 5 (PG 48, 869f), *Ad pop. Ant. hom.* XX, 1 & 7 (PG 49, 198 & 207f), *De prod. Jud. hom.* I, 6 & *hom.* II, 6, PG 49, 381f & 390–92), *In I Cor. hom.* XXIV, 3 (PG 61, 203); *Apost. Const.* II, 57, 16f; Jerome, *ep.* 82, 2, PL 22, 736f; Theodore of Mopsuestia, *Hom. Cat.* XV, 39–41; Augustine, *contra ep. Parm.* II, 6, 11, PL 43, 57; Caesarius of Arles, PL 39, 2024; Gregory of Tours, *Hist. franc.*, VI, 40, PL 71, 406; Isidore of Seville, *de off. eccl.* I, 15, 2, PL 83, 752f.

384 The phrase dates perhaps from Innocent III: 'significat et efficit unitatem ecclesiasticam' (*de sacro altaris mysterio* IV, 36, PL 217, 879).

385 See pp. 29f.

386 Cf. Rev. 4:8 and Isa. 6:3. The fullest theological study of the *Sanctus* is
E. Peterson, *Das Buch von den Engeln: Stellung und Bedeutung der heiligen
Engel im Kultus* (1935), which deals particularly with the Book of Revelation
and the *Sanctus* of the Alexandrian liturgy of *St Mark*. The *Sanctus* is found
in all extant classical anaphoras except those of *Apostolic Tradition* (though
E. C. Ratcliff has ingeniously argued that it belonged to the original form of
the prayer even there, and indeed that it formed the concluding climax of
the prayer: see 'The Sanctus and the Pattern of the Early Anaphora' in
*Journal of Ecclesiastical History* 1 (1950), pp. 29–36, 125–34), the *Testamentum Domini*, and a fragmentary anaphora of St Epiphanius (see B.
Botte, 'Fragments d'une anaphore inconnue attribuée à S. Epiphane' in
*Le Muséon* 73 (1960), pp. 311–15).

387 Notice the expressions: ἀκαταπαύστως καὶ ἀσιγήτως (*Apost. Const. VIII*,
Brightman, p. 18), ἀκαταπαύστοις στόμασιν, ἀσιγήτοις δοξολογίαις (Greek
*St James*, Alexandrian *St Mark*, Byzantine *St Basil*, Brightman, pp. 50, 131,
323).

388 The West Syrian liturgy of *Severus of Antioch* also mentions 'the spirits of
just men' and 'the church of the firstborn written in heaven' at the *Sanctus*
(Renaudot, II, pp. 322f). In the Mozarabic Easter mass 'all the angels and
saints do not cease to shout. . . .' (M. Férotin, *Liber Mozarabicus Sacramentorum*, col. 256). On the participation of the saints in the eucharistic
worship see, e.g., P. Y. Eméry, *L'unité des croyants au ciel et sur la terre*,
Taizé, 1962, pp. 197–240. Note the way in which the particles of bread in the
Byzantine *proskomide* are associated with the Virgin Mary, John the Baptist,
the prophets, apostles, saints, the faithful departed, and the whole church
on earth.

389 Writing on the *Sanctus* (*Hom. XVI*, 6–9), Theodore will stress that it is
with the worship offered by 'the invisible powers' that we are associating
ourselves: and he will see this as an anticipation of our final destiny, for at
the resurrection we shall be 'like the angels of God' (Luke 20:36), 'when we
shall be caught up in the clouds to meet our Lord in the air, and so we shall
be forever with our Lord' (I Thess. 4:17).

390 See also H. J. Schulz, *Die byzantinische Liturgie*, 1964, pp. 62–69, 82–86,
cf. pp. 182–86.

391 N. Maurice-Denis-Boulet, 'La leçon des églises de l'antiquité' in *La Maison-
Dieu* no. 63 (1960), pp. 24–40, in particular pp. 31–35: Une salle diffé-
renciée: le *bêma* et l'autel.

392 Thus Irenaeus on the firstfruits of creation: 'For we must make our oblation
to God and in all things be found grateful to God the creator, offering the
firstfruits of his own creatures (*primitias earum, quae sunt eius, creaturarum*)
with a pure mind and faith unfeigned, with firm hope and fervent love.
And this oblation the church alone offers pure to the creator, offering to
him, with thanksgiving, from his creation. . . . How will they [the Gnostics]
allow that the bread over which thanksgiving has been said is the body of
their Lord, and that the chalice is the chalice of his blood, if they do not say
that he is the Son of the creator of the world; that is to say, his Word
through whom the tree bears fruit and the fountains flow and the earth
yields first the blade, then the ear, then the full corn in the ear?' (*A.H. IV.
18.4*, PG 7, 1026f; see also IV.17.5, quoted above, n. 344). It is to be noted
that the Syrian traditions call the eucharistic bread the *firstborn* (*būchro* in

the West Syrian, and *būchra* in the East: so Brightman, pp. 571f), and that the Copts call the wine for the eucharist *abarkâ* (from ἀπαρχή, firstfruits: so O. H. E. Burmester, 'Rites and Ceremonies of the Coptic Church' in *Eastern Churches Quarterly* 8 (1949), in particular p. 32).

393 The twin ideas of *election* and *representation* may be said to give the *Covenant* its meaning. So, *in nuce*, these words of the Lord to the Servant: 'I am the Lord, I have called you in righteousness, I have taken you by the hand and kept you; I have given you as a covenant to the people, a light to the nations . . .' (Isa. 42:6, RSV). Note the reference to *the (new) covenant* at the cup-word in the eucharist.

394 See *The Order of the Holy Qurbana of the Syro-Malankara Rite* (*The Anaphora of St Xystus*), with an introduction and a short commentary, Trivandrum (India), 1964, pp. i and 14f. I do not think a scornful smile would have appeared on the lips of the Anglican systematician, O. C. Quick, for that is precisely what he himself was saying in terms of his own philosophical system in his now neglected book, *The Christian Sacraments* (1927¹, 1932²).

395 It is on these lines that J. M. R. Tillard has written an impressive theology of the eucharist as the *passover* of the church, the *transitus* from sin to life: *L'Eucharistie, pâque de l'Eglise* (1964). See also A. Winklhofer, *Eucharistie als Osterfeier* (1964).

396 Apart from the evidence of the O.T., we may call attention in the N.T. to the striking frequency with which words of vision and visibility (ὁρᾶν, θεωρεῖν, βλέπειν, φανεροῦν, ἀποκαλύπτειν, ἀποκάλυψις, ἐπιφάνεια) occur in connection with δόξα (Matt. 24:30 = Mark 13:26 = Luke 21:27; John 17:24; Rom. 8:18; Col. 3:4; Titus 2:13; I Pet. 4:13) and with the final coming of the Son of Man and the kingdom (Matt. 16:28 = Mark 9:1 = Luke 9:27; Matt. 26:64 = Mark 14:62; Matt. 23:39 = Luke 13:35; Luke 17:22; Luke 19:11; Acts 1:11; Rom. 2:5; I Cor. 1:7; 3:13; 13:12; II Thess. 1:7; I Tim. 6:14f; II Tim. 4:1; Heb. 9:28; I Pet. 1:5, 7; 5:4; I John 2:28; 3:2).

397 H. J. Schultz, *Die byzantinische Liturgie*, p. 122, n. 15, calls attention to the frequent use by Germanos of Constantinople, in his commentary on the liturgy, of the verb ἐμφαίνει in connection with the liturgical symbols and the realities they represent, which would suggest that the liturgical form is conceived as 'völlig transparentes Erscheinungsmedium höherer (heilsgeschichtlicher und himmlischer) Wirklichkeit'—at least for the faithful. Compare the following passage from M. Bucer's *Confession concerning the Holy Eucharist* (1550): '. . . we through faith are raised to heaven and placed there together with Christ, and lay hold of him in his heavenly majesty and embrace him as he is shown and offered to us by the mirror and riddle of words and sacraments discernible by sense' (*Scripta Anglicana*, Basileae, 1577, p. 540, cited by D. Stone, *A History of the Doctrine of the Holy Eucharist*, vol. II, p. 47).

398 Priest's prayer before the elevation in the liturgy of *St Chrysostom*, Brightman, pp. 392f. Compare also Leo, 'Quod itaque Redemptoris nostri conspicuum fuit, in sacramenta transivit' (*Serm.* 74, 2, PL 54, 398).

399 Thus at the Transfiguration there broke through into visibility the glory of the one who was the kingdom personified (αὐτοβασιλεία, Origen, PG 13, 1197) but who presented Himself at His first coming as a sign that could be contradicted (cf. Luke 2:34).

400 It may not be until II Peter that we find the withholding of the parousia ascribed to the loving forbearance of God (3:9, 15); but it has been well argued, for instance by A. L. Moore in *The Parousia in the N.T.* (1966), especially pp. 191–218, that the whole ministry of Jesus as well as the time of the church may be seen in terms of the tension between, in Moore's terminology, the eschatological motif (i.e. the 'threat' of God's rule to manifest itself unambiguously) and the grace motif (i.e. the veiling of God's sovereignty so that men may have time and opportunity and freedom to repent).

401 Note especially the influential commentaries of Amalarius: on which see J. A. Jungmann, *Missarum Sollemnia*, I, pp. 115–20.

402 This is not the place to enter into the question of whether late medieval theologians considered the sacrifice offered in the mass as a repetition of Calvary or rather as in some sense identical with Calvary. The interested reader will find a useful collection of evidence, together with one well-argued interpretation, in the work of the Jesuit scholar, F. Clark, *Eucharistic Sacrifice and the Reformation*, 1960[1], 1967[2].

403 See for instance the Florentine *Decretum pro Armeniis*, in Denzinger-Schönmetzer, §1322; and the book on holy communion in *The Imitation of Christ*.

404 For example, E. Grässer, *Das Problem der Parusieverzögerung in den synoptischen Evangelien und in der Apostelgeschichte*, 1957, and (with extension into the early church) M. Werner, *Die Entstehung des christlichen Dogmas*, 1941[1], 1953[2].

405 I think that A. L. Moore, *The Parousia in the N.T.*, does not quite succeed in his attempt to remove all mention of a temporal delimitation of the parousia from the N.T.: Matt. 10:23, Mark 9:1 and 13:30 hold out against him (on these texts see W. G. Kümmel, *Verheissung und Erfüllung*, 1945, pp. 35–37, 13–16, 33–35, and 91). I agree with Moore that the important thing is the *nearness* of the final kingdom rather than the exact temporal delimitation of its coming.

406 *Acta Saturnini, Dativi et al.*, 11, in Th. Ruinart, *Acta primorum martyrum sincera et selecta*, Parisiis, 1689 (Amstelaedami, 1713), p. 414 (p. 387); cf. 'Intermitti Dominicum non potest', *ibid.*, 9 & 10, pp. 413f (p. 386). It was while he was himself being transported towards Rome and martyrdom that Ignatius of Antioch could write of the eucharist as 'the medicine of immortality, the antidote against dying, but rather that one may live forever in Jesus Christ' (Eph. 20:2).

407 I was first pointed to these examples by G. Wilpert, *Roma sotterranea: Le pitture delle catacombe romane*, Roma, 1903, p. 432.

408 A. von Harnack (ed.), Die Akten des Karpus, des Papylus und der Agathonike, in *Texte und Untersuchungen*, vol. III (3/4), Leipzig, 1888, pp. 451f (§42).

409 *Passio Ss. Mariani et Iacobi*, ed. P. Franchi de' Cavalieri, in *Studi e Testi*, vol. 3, Roma, 1900, p. 60 (§11).

410 See J. A. Jungmann, *The Early Liturgy to the time of Gregory the Great*, 1963 paperback edition, pp. 175–87. When, from the fourth century onwards, persecution no longer threatened, the eschatological significance of martyrdom tended to disappear, at least in the West (though the Roman canon did have the *Nobis quoque*, and a genuine eschatological note is struck in some of the relevant post-communions); and into the company of

martyrs were admitted holy men who had died in their beds: to leave us with a cult of the saints that was triply characterized by a backward-looking historical commemoration, a theologically dubious appeal to have our prayers heard in virtue of the saints' merits, and an unedifying scramble for relics (relics which, even when placed under the eucharistic altar in dependence on Rev. 6:9–11, were popularly more valued for their thaumaturgical properties than as a concretion of the impatient cry 'How long?').

411 Latin text, French translation, and notes, by H. Pétré, *Ethérie: Journal de Voyage*, in 'Sources chrétiennes', vol. 21, Paris, 1948.

412 Some understanding of the factors which contributed to the historicizing interpretation of the liturgical action may be gained from G. Dix, *The Shape of the Liturgy*, pp. 303–96.

413 E.g. ἡ αἰώνιος βασιλεία II Pet. 1:11; ἡ βασιλεία αὐτοῦ ἡ ἐπουράνιος II Tim. 4:18; θείας κοινωνοὶ φύσεως II Pet. 1:4; ἡ σωτηρία ψυχῶν I Pet. 1:9; as well as the Matthaean ἡ βασιλεία τῶν οὐρανῶν and the Johannine ζωὴ αἰώνιος.

414 See pp. 73, 117 and n. 186.

415 See *Mystagogia*, in particular chs. 13 & 22–24, PG 91, 692, & 697–709.

416 Above all, M. Werner, *Die Entstehung des christlichen Dogmas* (1953²), especially pp. 447–67.

417 A recent archaeological study has argued that in some parts of the Roman Empire agape and eucharist were held in a combined celebration up to the fifth century, all participants sitting at a sigma-shaped table: K. Gamber, *Domus Ecclesiae: Die ältesten Kirchenbauten Aquilejas sowie im Alpen- und Donaugebiet bis zum Beginn des 5. Jh. liturgiegeschichtlich untersucht*, Regensburg, 1968.

418 This would also be in accordance with the main thrust of P. Philippi, *Abendmahlsfeier und Wirklichkeit der Gemeinde*, 1960.

419 N. Afanassieff, 'Le sacrement de l'assemblée' in *Internationale kirchliche Zeitschrift* 46 (1956), pp. 200–13.

420 See also K. Barth, *The Holy Ghost and the Christian Life*, London, 1938 [E.T. of a lecture given in 1929]; C. K. Barrett, *The Holy Spirit and the Gospel Tradition*, London, 1947 [1966²]; J. E. Fison, *The Blessing of the Holy Spirit*, London, 1950; J. G. Davies, *The Spirit, the Church and the Sacraments*, London, 1954; G. S. Hendry, *The Holy Spirit in Christian Theology*, London, 1957; L. Dewar, *The Holy Spirit and Modern Thought: an inquiry into the historical, theological, and psychological aspects of the Christian doctrine of the Holy Spirit*, London, 1959; H. P. van Dusen, *Spirit, Son and Father*, London, 1960; J. E. Yates, *The Spirit and the Kingdom*, London, 1963; F. J. Leenhardt *et al.*, *Le Saint-Esprit*, Genève, 1963; H. Berkhof, *The Doctrine of the Holy Spirit*, London, 1965; J. H. E. Hull, *The Holy Spirit in the Acts of the Apostles*, London, 1967.

421 See the documents of the W.C.C. Commission on Faith and Order, Aarhus 1964 (Faith and Order Paper no. 44, p. 55), and Bristol 1967 (Faith and Order Paper no. 50, p. 142); L. Vischer, 'Questions on the Eucharist, its past and future celebration' in *Studia Liturgica* 5 (1966), in particular pp. 78–81; J. J. von Allmen, *Essai sur le repas du Seigneur*, 1966, pp. 65–70.

422 Particularly in Holland, in Catholic-Protestant encounter.

423 *An Order for the Lord's Supper or the Holy Eucharist*, 1950¹, 1954², 1962³, now printed in *The Church of South India: The Book of Common Worship, as authorised by the Synod of 1962*, Oxford University Press, 1963.

424 *Eucharistie à Taizé.*

425 These last two passages seem to suggest that the two evangelists (or more probably their predecessors in one strand of the traditionary process) may not have understood either. For why is the saying 'Beware of the leaven of the Pharisees &c.' introduced here? Luke puts this (obviously floating) saying in a totally different context (12:1). What the disciples failed to understand straight after the feeding miracles was not, surely, the saying about the leaven but . . . the significance of the feeding miracles! The saying 'Beware of the leaven &c.' probably belongs to a different occasion altogether. The eucharistic vocabulary in the accounts of the feedings themselves was no doubt already present in the traditional material before the evangelists used it, but it seems highly probable that the evangelists endorsed the eucharistic connection (see pp. 35f); and Mark's comment about the 'one loaf' (8:14b, Mark only) may therefore indicate that Mark suspected also that the subsequent discussion between Jesus and the disciples had really turned on the messianic (and therefore, from Mark's point of view if not already Jesus's, also eucharistic; see p. 36) significance of the feeding of the crowds, but since the saying 'Beware of the leaven &c' had already become attached to the discussion incident in the strand of the *Traditionsgeschichte* which reached him he kept the saying in that place. Matthew obviously considered Mark 8:14–21 confused enough to demand some straightening out: in particular he omitted Mark's (christological and eucharistic) comment on the 'one loaf' and spelt out that the leaven-saying (a single verse in Mark but thrice mentioned in Matthew's version) referred to 'the teaching of the Pharisees and Sadducees' (16:12); but this 'clarification' only makes it more obvious that we have to do with two originally unrelated elements: the discussion on the significance of the feedings, and the leaven-saying. The reason for their junction in the earlier course of tradition was probably no more than the association of ideas between bread and leaven.

426 Consider the universal scope both of the saying that introduces the most explicitly eucharistic part of the discourse of John 6: 'The bread which I shall give *for the life of the world* is my flesh' (v. 51c), and also of the expression 'for the many' in the cup-word in the institution narratives (on the inclusive meaning of ὑπὲρ πολλῶν see J. Jeremias, *Abendmahlsworte*[3], pp. 171–74, 218–23).

427 It must be admitted that the *compelle intrare* has sometimes been used to justify physical coercion (as with Augustine and the Donatists, for example) rather than urgent advocacy of the gospel.

428 My criticism has been worded to aim at this abuse particularly as it has appeared in much 19th and 20th century 'overseas missionary' work done by Anglicans, Methodists, Lutherans and Reformed. But the same reluctance to be anywhere near as generous as the Lord who ate with sinners and who liberally fed the crowds who came to hear Him is to be found in the church at many periods and in many settings. Hippolytus reveals that there was a three-year catechumenate before baptism in the Roman church at the beginning of the 3rd century (*Apostolic Tradition*, 17). How long did the Philippian jailor have to wait before he was baptized . . . and the (eucharistic) table was spread (Acts 16:25–34)?

429 G. Dix, *The Shape of the Liturgy*, 1945, *in nuce*, pp. 48f. I think this point of Dix's still stands, despite disfavour in certain quarters.

430 More precisely, Acts 27:35 says that 'he began to eat', and this may be compared with the practice at the eucharist, according to which the president himself communicates first, before the distribution. Certain manuscripts and versions of Acts make the *rapprochement* even more obvious, for they add ἐπιδιδούς (*part. praes.*) καὶ ἡμῖν (so 614 and a few minuscules, the Harclean Syriac and the Sahidic).

431 So among recent commentators on Acts F. F. Bruce (1951), E. Hänchen (1956), C. S. C. Williams (1957). Tertullian does not seem to have seen any difficulty in a eucharistic interpretation. Explaining how the injunction of I Tim. 2:8 on prayer *omni loco* is to be squared with the dominical command to pray 'in secret' (Matt. 6:5f), Tertullian appeals to apostolic precedent for praying in public when opportunity or necessity demanded, and he refers to Acts 16:25 and 27:35, using the technical word *eucharistia* in the latter case: . . . *apud Paulum, qui in navi coram omnibus eucharistiam fecit* (*de or.*, 24, PL 1, 1192).

432 B. Reicke, 'Die Mahlzeit mit Paulus auf den Wellen des Mittelmeers Act. 27, 33-38' in *Theologische Zeitschrift* 4 (1948), pp. 401–10.

433 Even Ph. H. Menoud ('Les Actes des Apôtres et l'Eucharistie' in *RHPhR* 33 (1953), pp. 21–36), who accepts a strictly eucharistic sense at Acts 2:42, 46; 16:34; 20:7–11, seems not to intend going beyond Reicke's thesis when he calls the episode of Acts 27:33ff 'l'eucharistie prophétique célébrée par Paul'.

434 Briefly, as part of an article reprinted in J. C. Hoekendijk, *The Church Inside Out*, London, 1967, pp. 89–107. It is unfortunately pretty clear that the English translation is poor; but I think I have not misrepresented Hoekendijk's position. I have not found access to the original Dutch, which appeared obscurely in 1959 and is presumably reprinted in *De Kerk Binneste Buiten*, Amsterdam, 1964.

435 English original: 'Exceptions, Eschatology and Our Common Practices' in *Youth* (W.C.C., Youth Department) no. 6 (December 1962), pp. 63–77. Reprinted in *The Church Inside Out*, pp. 148–66, under the title 'Safety Last'. The German version bears the title 'Weltoffenes Abendmahl', in J. C. Hoekendijk, *Die Zukunft der Kirche und die Kirche der Zukunft*, Stuttgart/ Berlin, 1964, pp. 58–81.

436 The Didache contains the injunction: 'None is to eat and drink of your εὐχαριστία but they that have been baptized in the name of the Lord' (9:5). The *Apostolic Tradition* of Hippolytus directs that 'a catechumen shall not recline together [with the faithful] *in cena dominica*' (27, ed. Botte, 1963, pp. 68f). If these two texts apply simply to the agape, they are in any case sufficient basis for an *a fortiori* argument with respect to the eucharist. But the direct evidence of Justin is good enough by itself: 'We call this food εὐχαριστία [the context makes clear that it can only be a question of the sacramental eucharist here], and no one is allowed to share in it apart from the man who believes our teaching to be true, who has been washed with the laver of remission of sins and regeneration, and who lives as Christ taught' (*Apol. I*, 66). Cf. 'Let everyone hurry, that an unbeliever may not taste of the eucharist, or a mouse or any other animal, or lest any of it fall and be lost. For the body of Christ is meant to be eaten by the faithful, and not to be treated with contempt' (*Apostolic Tradition*, 37, ed. Botte, 1963, p. 84).

437 I think, for instance, of the effect that the admission of pious Hindus to communion would have on the church in India. It would not be long before Christianity was seen simply (as some Hindu intellectuals see it already) as one permissible form of an all-accommodating Hinduism, and the scandal of particularity would be lost.

438 See above, pp. 119f and n. 393.

439 I realize that the more widespread the practice of infant baptism (where there can hardly be question of repentance and faith in the subject), the less force the above two arguments have. But then, precisely, I am not at all convinced that the practice of infant baptism, except perhaps where baptized, believing and communicant parents ask for it for their children, is a desirable or even tolerable thing. See my *Christian Initiation*, London, 1969, and 'The Need for a Methodist Service for the Admission of Infants to the Catechumenate' in *London Quarterly and Holborn Review*, 191 (1968), pp. 51–60. People who dispense baptism to those without repentance and faith should, by their own logic, show equal lack of discrimination in dispensing the bread and wine of the eucharist. If the Western paedobaptist churches nevertheless do not usually admit those baptized as infants to communion before some form of profession of personal faith, we would admire their wisdom in so far as their practice now depends on the sense that the human side of the sacrament of baptism is a condition of admission to the Lord's table; and we would only hope that they may be persuaded *from their own communion practice* that it would be better if repentance and faith were also present in those who meet with God in baptism.

440 Ἰδιῶται ἢ ἄπιστοι, I Cor. 14:23f. Were those who strayed into glossalalia sessions turned out when it came to meal time? Or did they stay to watch? Or were they even allowed to share in the meal?

441 A Methodist feels himself constrained to add a word on John Wesley's view of the holy communion as a 'converting ordinance'. Particularly in the years directly after his own 'evangelical conversion' in 1738, Wesley urged that 'unbelievers', by which he meant those who had not yet enjoyed an experience of conversion like his own, should communicate regularly if they were earnest 'seekers' (see J. C. Bowmer, *The Sacrament of the Lord's Supper in Early Methodism*, 1951, pp. 103–22). I myself would not use quite the same criterion of belief and unbelief; nor is our situation the same as Wesley's, for in the *corpus christianum* of 18th-century England he could presuppose *baptism*, in infancy, on the part of his seekers: but the views expressed in the text above spring from a belief in the converting power of the eucharist that is not, I think, totally dissimilar to Wesley's.

442 The fullest guide to the attitudes of the denominations to the question of intercommunion is still the report and related essays presented to the Third World Conference on Faith and Order at Lund in 1952: D. Baillie & J. Marsh (edd.), *Intercommunion*, 1952. There is also a useful study paper by M. Thurian, 'Intercommunion' in *Verbum Caro* no. 66 (1963), pp. 199–213.

443 *The Fourth World Conference on Faith and Order, Montreal 1963*, the Report edited by P. C. Rodger and L. Vischer, London, 1964 ( =Faith and Order Paper No. 42), p. 78, §138.

444 *Op. cit., loc. cit.*, §139.

445 So for instance N. A. Nissiotis, 'Worship, Eucharist and "Intercommunion": an Orthodox reflection' in *Studia Liturgica* 2 (1963), pp. 193–222.

446 Y. M. J. Congar, 'Amica Contestatio' in D. Baillie and J. Marsh (edd.), *Intercommunion*, 1952, pp. 141–51; E. Stakmeier, 'Die Eucharistie, die Einheit der Kirche und die Wiedervereinigung der Getrennten' in *Theologie und Glaube* 50 (1960), pp. 241–62.

447 So for instance W. Elert, *Abendmahlsgemeinschaft in der alten Kirche*, 1954, and 'Abendmahl und Kirchengemeinschaft in der alten Kirche' in *Koinonia*, 1957, pp. 57–78. The Lutherans are more concerned with a single pattern of doctrine (the required extent of which they do not often define) than with a single pattern of ministry. See *Koinonia: Arbeiten des Oekumenischen Ausschusses der Vereinigten Evangelisch-Lutherischen Kirche Deutschlands zur Frage der Kirchen- und Abendmahlsgemeinschaft*, 1957, and V. Vajta (ed.), *Kirche und Abendmahl: Studien und Dokumente zur Frage der Abendmahlsgemeinschaft im Luthertum*, 1963.

448 For a description of the view of some Anglicans on the necessity of a single pattern of ministry as well as of doctrine, see *Intercommunion Today, being the Report of the Archbishops' Commission on Intercommunion*, London, 1968, pp. 46–54.

449 The sixth of the ten points reads as follows: 'Both churches confess that in and through the sacrament of the holy supper the promise is given and confirmed of the great supper of the marriage of the Lamb, when the congregation of Christ will drink the wine new with him in the kingdom that has then come.'

450 A detailed study of the Arnoldshain Theses by a Jesuit will be found in W. L. Boelens, *Die Arnoldshainer Abendmahlsthesen: Die Suche nach einem Abendmahlskonsens in der Evangelischen Kirche in Deutschland 1947–1957 und eine Würdigung aus katholischer Sicht*, 1964. Here we note particularly Thesis 1, sentence 2: 'In the supper the exalted Lord invites his people to his table and grants them already now a share in the future fellowship (*Gemeinschaft*) in the kingdom of God.'

451 N. Zernov, *The Reintegration of the Church—a study in intercommunion*, 1952, pp. 51–75. On p. 75 Zernov wrote: 'Confidence in intercommunion as a method of reconciliation arises from the belief that God, the author of the Church, wants Christians to be united, and that He will help them to attain this goal when they ask him to bring them into one fold. The true oneness of the Church depends neither on its doctrinal system, nor on its hierarchical organization, but springs out of communion with the incarnate Lord, and is safeguarded by the action of the Holy Spirit.'

452 N. Afanassieff, 'L'Eucharistie, principal lien entre les Catholiques et les Orthodoxes' in *Irénikon* 38 (1965), pp. 337–39.

453 H. Symeon, 'De l'eucharistie comme sacrement de l'unité' in *Contacts* 16 (1964), pp. 126–46 = 'The Eucharist as the Sacrament of Unity' in *Sobornost* 4 (1964), pp. 637–50.

454 So the decree *Orientalium Ecclesiarum*.

455 *Intercommunion Today* (1968), §§155–72, 186–91, 224 (iv & v). In the 16th, 17th and 18th centuries the weight of Anglican opinion fell in favour of reciprocal intercommunion with the classical Protestant churches of the continent of Europe whenever circumstances of travel occasioned it (see N. Sykes, *The Church of England and Non-episcopal Churches in the Sixteenth and Seventeenth Centuries*, London, 1949, and *Old priest and new presbyter*, Cambridge, 1956). The heavy emphasis put by the Oxford

Movement on 'apostolic succession' (as the Movement understood it) was later influential in making many Anglicans much more reluctant to receive communion from ministers whose ministry was invalidated by their lack of 'episcopal ordination'.

456 See the chapter on baptism and unity in my book, *Christian Initiation*, London, 1969, pp. 57–70.

457 On the question in ancient Christendom, and for some pertinent remarks on our own situation (though he seems to come to rest in the fifth position outlined soon, which also must be regarded as unsatisfactory), see S. L. Greenslade, *Schism in the Early Church*, London, 1964², pp. x–xii, xviii–xxi, 168–221.

458 Tertullian, *de bapt.*, 15, PL 1, 1216. Cyprian, *epp.* 69–75 (Vienna corpus numbering).

459 *Essay on the Development of Christian Doctrine*, 1845¹, pp. 7–24; 1878², pp. 9–27.

460 Basil, *ep.* 188, 1, PG 32, 664–72; Timothy of Constantinople, *de receptione haereticorum*, PG 86, 10–74; Council in Trullo, canon 95, on which see C. J. von Hefele, *Conciliengeschichte*, vol. 3 (1877²), p. 342. See further G. Wainwright, *Christian Initiation*, 1969, pp. 60f.

461 See F. J. Thompson, 'Economy. An examination of the various theories of Economy held within the Orthodox Church, with special reference to the economical recognition of the validity of non-Orthodox sacraments' in *JTS* n.s. 16 (1965), pp. 368–420.

462 On Augustine's position see the detailed note in G. Wainwright, *Christian Initiation*, 1969, p. 99.

463 See above all E. Schillebeeckx, *Christus, Sacrament van de Godsontmoeting*.

464 So B. Leeming, *Principles of Sacramental Theology*, 1960², pp. 189–93.

465 The Council of Trent calls it *verum baptismum* (Denzinger-Schönmetzer §1617). See G. Baum, *That they may be one: a study of papal doctrine* (*Leo XIII–Pius XII*), London, 1958, pp. 38–40, 59–64.

466 G. Baum, *op. cit.*, pp. 36f, 131. See now the Vatican II decrees *On Ecumenism* and *On the Eastern Churches*.

467 G. Baum, *op. cit.*, pp. 39, 59–64.

468 Should any be tempted to justify his refusal to go beyond the unstable fourth position by talking of 'uncovenanted mercies' or by misapplying the tag *Deus non alligatur sacramentis sed nos*, let him read L. Newbigin, *The Household of God*, London, 1953, pp. 78f. Two recent Roman Catholic writers have maximized the statement from *De oecumenismo* just quoted in the text, but, in order to avoid toppling into the fifth position, have combined the fourth position with elements from the third that have already been criticized above: see J. M. R. Tillard, 'Le *Votum Eucharistiae*: l'eucharistie dans la rencontre des chrétiens' in *Miscellanea Liturgica*, vol. 2, 1967, pp. 143–94, and P. Lebeau, 'Vatican II et l'espérance d'une eucharistie oecuménique' in B. Bobrinskoy *et al.*, *Intercommunion*, 1969, pp. 117–54.

469 N. Afanassieff, 'L'Eucharistie, principal lien entre les Catholiques et les Orthodoxes' in *Irénikon* 38 (1965), pp. 337–39.

470 E. Schlink gave the title 'Lord's supper or church's supper' to his essay in D. Baillie & J. Marsh (edd.), *Intercommunion*, 1952, pp. 296–302.

471 A similar point is made by P. Brunner in his comments on Rahner's book, but with the important difference that he believes such a choice must be

made in principle, and not just (as I believe) when circumstances force on us what is in principle a *false* alternative: 'The chief difference between the Protestant doctrine and Rahner's conception may perhaps be indicated by the following question: Is the church the subject which bears the word of God and the sacraments, or is the church rather borne by them? Of course, Protestant doctrine knows the church also as the bearer of word and sacrament. But the church is such, only because and in so far as she herself has her existence through the word of God and the sacraments instituted by Christ. Significant in many respects is the way in which Rahner can pass directly from the Christ-event to the church that Christ founded, the church clearly being thought of as existing immediately—and only then, from the standpoint of this existing church, does he catch sight of the sacraments. . . . By contrast, Protestant theology will pinpoint the fact that the church which Christ willed to be the people of God of the last days becomes a historically tangible reality only when the chosen witnesses of the Risen One comply with the charge of preaching given them by Christ, and when the sacraments instituted by Christ are administered to those who come to faith in the gospel. Must not therefore the relation between church and gospel, and accordingly also the relation between church and sacraments, basically be seen as the exact reverse of Rahner's view of the matter?' (in *Theologische Literaturzeitung* 88 (1963), col. 176).

472 A partial exception may be found in the case of those English Dissenters who, after 1662, continued to practise 'occasional conformity' at the eucharist of the Established Church. It is also true that for centuries after the official rupture between East and West, the faithful of the two camps continued, where geography favoured it, occasionally to practise *communicatio in sacris*.

473 It is interesting to note that the Kirdis of North Cameroon, when they have been converted to the Christian faith, have brought with them from their family sacrifices a notion that prevents the Lord's supper from being celebrated unless every member of the community is present to enjoy it. What an encouragement to reconciliation! See H. Eichenberger, 'Le chemin nouveau: évangélisation parmi les Kirdis du Cameroun' in *Flambeau* (Yaoundé) no. 19 (1968), pp. 160–69.

474 Support for the primacy of love over doctrine in certain circumstances comes now from the quarter of Orthodoxy in N. A. Nissiotis, *Die Theologie der Ostkirche im ökumenischen Dialog*, Stuttgart, 1968, pp. 137–39 (in material that represents an addition to an essay which originally appeared under the title 'Worship, Eucharist and "Intercommunion": an Orthodox reflection' in *Studia Liturgica* 2 (1963), pp. 193–222).

475 Emphasis on ministerial order has been a characteristic Anglican contribution to modern discussions on intercommunion.

476 See already the Gospel of Thomas, saying 51: '. . . If they ask you, What is the sign of your Father who is within you? say to them, It is a movement and a rest' (R. M. Grant and D. N. Freedman, *The Secret Sayings of Jesus*, London, 1960, p. 152).

477 It is because the institutional church, though itself a sign of the kingdom, will be included in the universal scope of the final judgement and renewal that H. Küng can speak of the 'provisional' church awaiting the definitive revelation of the divine kingdom 'als die kritische Vollendung ihres Auf-

trages' (*Wahrhaftigkeit: Zur Zukunft der Kirche*, Freiburg i.B., 1968, pp. 48f).

478 Paul, the apostle of grace, is not afraid of the word συνεργός (I Cor. 3:9; cf. II Cor. 6:1).

479 See the passages quoted, nn. 154 & 344.

480 See some fine remarks in the study of the sacraments by the Orthodox theologian, A. Schmemann, *For the Life of the World*, 1963, pp. 1–10. E.g.: 'In the Bible the food that man eats, the world of which he must partake in order to live, is given to him by God, and it is given as *communion with God*. . . . All that exists is God's gift to man, and it all exists to make God known to man, to make man's life communion with God. . . . The unique position of man in the universe is that he alone is to *bless* God for the food and the life he receives from Him' (pp. 3f).

481 Isa. 55:12; cf. Isa. 44:23; 49:13; 52:9; Pss. 65:12; 69:34–36; 89:12; 96:10–13; 98:7–9; 148; I Chron. 16:31–34.

482 For a justification which makes an 'embodied' view of the eschatological condition as philosophically respectable as (or for the unbeliever, no more unconvincing than) the 'spiritualist' view, see J. Hick, *Christianity at the Centre*, London, 1968, pp. 107–12.

483 For an essay on judgement and renewal as constituent parts of the sacramental event, see J. J. von Allmen, 'Pour un prophétisme sacramentel' in his *Prophétisme sacramentel*, 1964, pp. 9–53.

484 At the level of secular art, one thinks of the use made of taste imagery by the Symbolist poets of the nineteenth century.

485 Does this mean that the newly-baptized tasted already in New Testament times the cup of milk and honey that was certainly given in some later rites in token of the promised land? So at least F. L. Cross, *I Peter: A paschal liturgy*, London, 1954, pp. 32f. See Tertullian (*de cor. mil.*, 3; *adv. Marc.*, I, 14), Hippolytus, *Apostolic Tradition* 23, 2, and Clement of Alexandria (*Paed.* I, 6 & 34ff).

486 *Serm.* 68, PL 52, 395. See my n. 107.

487 *Methodist Hymn Book* (London, 1933), no. 406, v. 3.

488 See also Hymn 108 (quoted p. 57) and Hymn 158 (quoted in n. 181).

489 See pp. 73, 117f.

490 See p. 54, for these two texts. Compare also the Gelasian: 'ut . . . quod imaginem contingimus sacramenti manifesta percepcione sumamus' (ed. Mohlberg, 1960, no. 949; H. A. Wilson, *The Gelasian Sacramentary*, Oxford, 1894, p. 186, reads *imagine*).

491 'The shadow came first, the image followed, the truth is still to be. The shadow was in the law; the image in the gospel; the truth will be in the heavenly places. The law was the shadow of the gospel and the church; the gospel is the image of future truth; and the truth will be in the divine judgement. So the things which are now celebrated in the church had their shadow in the prophetic writings: in the Flood, in the Red Sea when our fathers were baptized in the cloud and the sea, and in the rock which spouted water and followed the people. For was that not in shadow a sacrament of this most holy mystery? In shadow, was not the water from the rock as it were the blood which flowed from Christ and which followed the people who fled from it, so that they might drink and not thirst, be redeemed and not perish? But now the shadow of the Jews' night and gloom is dispersed, the day of the church has come. We now see the good things in an

image, and we possess the good things of the image itself. We have seen the prince of priests come to us, we have seen and heard him offering his blood for us. We, as priests, follow as we are able, that we may offer a sacrifice for the people. Though feeble in our own merit, yet we are honourable in the sacrifice we offer. For although Christ is not now seen to offer, yet it is he himself who is offered on earth, when the body of Christ is offered. Or rather he himself is seen to offer in us, for it is his word which hallows the sacrifice that is offered. He himself assists us as an advocate before the Father. Now we do not see him, but one day we shall see, when the image has passed away and the truth come. Then it will be no longer in a mirror, but face to face, that the perfect is seen' (*In Ps.* 38, 25, PL 14, 1051f); and: 'So we are to seek those things in which perfection is, and truth. First the shadow, then the image, and finally the truth. The law was the shadow; the gospel the image; and truth is in the heavenly places. Before it was a lamb that was offered, and a calf; now it is Christ who is offered. But he is offered as a man, as one suffering the passion; and as a priest he offers himself, to do away with our sins. Here it is in an image, there it is in truth where he intercedes as an advocate for us with the Father. Here, therefore, we walk in an image, we see in an image; but there face to face, where there is full perfection; for all perfection is found in the truth' (*de off.* I, 48, 238, PL 16, 94).

492 For the N.T. evidence see G. Bornkamm, art. μυστήριον, in *TWNT* IV (1942), pp. 809–34, and G. Richter, art. 'Geheimnis', in H. Fries (ed.), *Handbuch Theologischer Grundbegriffe*, vol. I, München, 1962, pp. 442–47.

# Bibliography

This list includes only items which, in whole or in substantial part, have to do with either the eucharist or eschatology. Other works referred to incidentally may be traced through the index to their mention in the text or in the notes, where details of publication are given. A separate index is given for patristic, scholastic and Reformation references, though the present list includes, under the name of the editor, a number of convenient modern editions of some outstanding patristic texts. Square brackets contain information about other editions of a work than the edition consulted.

Afanassieff, N., 'Le sacrement de l'assemblée' in *Internationale kirchliche Zeitschrift* 46 (1956), pp. 200–13.

— 'L'eucharistie, principal lien entre les Catholiques et les Orthodoxes' in *Irénikon* 38 (1965), pp. 337–39.

Agnello, G., 'Motivi eucaristici nella iconografia paleocristiana della Sicilia' in *Convivium Dominicum*, Catania, 1959, pp. 15–34.

Allmen, J. J. von, 'Pour un prophétisme sacramentel' in his *Prophétisme sacramentel*, Neuchâtel, 1964, pp. 9–53.

— *Worship: its Theology and Practice*, London, 1965.

— *Essai sur le Repas du Seigneur*, Neuchâtel, 1966.

— 'Les conditions d'une intercommunion acceptable' in *Concilium* no. 44 (1969), pp. 13–19.

Althaus, P., *Die letzten Dinge: Lehrbuch der Eschatologie*, Gütersloh, 1922[1], 1949[5].

Armenian Apostolic Orthodox Church, Divine Liturgy of the, New York, 1950.

Atchley, E. G. C. F., *On the Epiclesis of the Eucharistic Liturgy*, London, 1935.

Audet, J. P., *La Didachè: Instruction des Apôtres*, Paris, 1958.

— 'Esquisse historique du genre littéraire de la "Bénédiction" juive et de l' "Eucharistie" chrétienne' in *Revue Biblique* 65 (1958), pp. 371–99.

Baciocchi, J. de, 'Le Mystère eucharistique dans les perspectives de la Bible' in *NRTh* 77 (1955), pp. 561–80.

— 'Présence eucharistique et transsubstantiation' in *Irénikon* 32 (1959), pp. 139–61.

— *L'Eucharistie*, Tournai, 1964.

— 'Eglise et Trinité dans le Mystère eucharistique' in *L'Evangile, hier et aujourd'hui: Mélanges offerts au Professeur F. J. Leenhardt*, Genève, 1968, pp. 241–49.

Baillie, D., and Marsh, J., *Intercommunion: The report of the theological commission appointed by the Continuation Committee of the World Conference on Faith and Order together with a selection from the material presented to the commission*, London, 1952.

Baillie, J., *And the Life everlasting*, London, 1934.

Bammel, F., *Das heilige Mahl im Glauben der Völker*, Gütersloh, 1950.

Bannister, H. M., *Missale Gothicum* (*MS. Vatican. regin. lat. 317*), *text and introduction*, London, 1917.

Barrett, C. K., 'The Holy Spirit in the Fourth Gospel' in *JTS* n.s.1 (1950), pp. 1–15.

— 'New Testament Eschatology' in *Scottish Journal of Theology* 6 (1953), pp. 136–55, 225–43.

— *The Gospel according to Saint John*, London, 1955.

— 'The Eschatology of the Epistle to the Hebrews' in W. D. Davies and D. Daube (edd.), *The Background of the New Testament and its Eschatology*, Cambridge, 1956, pp. 363–93.

Barth, M., *Das Abendmahl: Passamahl, Opfermahl, Messiasmahl*, Zürich, 1945.

Beasley-Murray, G. R., *Jesus and the Future*, London, 1954.

Behm, J., *art. κλάω* in *TWNT*, vol. III, pp. 726–43.

Benoit, P., 'Le récit de la Cène dans Lc. xxii, 15–20. Etude de critique textuelle et littéraire' in *Revue Biblique* 48 (1939), pp. 357–93.

— 'Les récits de l'institution et leur portée' in *Lumière et Vie* no. 31 (1957), pp. 49–76.

Berkhof, H., *Gegronde verwachting: Schets van een christelijke toekomstleer*, Nijkerk, 1967.

Betz, J., *Die Eucharistie in der Zeit der griechischen Väter*, vol. I/1 (*Die Aktualpräsenz der Person und des Heilswerkes Jesu im Abendmahl nach der vorephesinischen griechischen Patristik*), Freiburg i.B., 1955; vol. II/1 (*Die Realpräsenz des Leibes und Blutes Jesu im Abendmahl nach dem Neuen Testament*), Freiburg i.B., 1961.

— 'Eucharistie' in H. Fries (ed.), *Handbuch Theologischer Grundbegriffe*, vol. I, München, 1962, pp. 336–55.

Bishop, E., 'Fear and awe attaching to the eucharistic service' in R. H. Connolly, *The Liturgical Homilies of Narsai*, Cambridge, 1909, pp. 92–97.

— 'The moment of consecration' in R. H. Connolly, *The Liturgical Homilies of Narsai*, Cambridge, 1909, pp. 126–63.

Bläser, P., 'Eucharistie und Einheit der Kirche in der Verkündigung des Neuen Testaments' in *Theologie und Glaube* 50 (1960), pp. 419–32.

Bobrinskoy, B., 'Ascension et liturgie' in *Contacts* 11 (1959), pp. 166–84.

— 'Le Saint-Esprit dans la liturgie' in *Studia Liturgica* 1 (1962), pp. 47–59.

Bobrinskoy, B., Heitz, J. J., and Lebeau, P., *Intercommunion*, Tours (?), 1969.

Boelens, W. L., *Die Arnoldshainer Abendmahlsthesen: Die Suche nach einem Abendmahlskonsens in der Evangelischen Kirche in Deutschland 1947–1957 und eine Würdigung aus katholischer Sicht*, Assen, 1964.

Boismard, M. E., 'L'Eucharistie selon saint Paul' in *Lumière et Vie* no. 31 (1957), pp. 93–106.

Boobyer, G. H., 'The Eucharistic Interpretation of the Miracles of the Loaves in St Mark's Gospel' in *JTS* n.s.3 (1952), pp. 161–71.

— 'The Miracles of the Loaves and the Gentiles in St Mark's Gospel' in *Scottish Journal of Theology* 6 (1953), pp. 77–87.

Borgia, N., *Frammenti eucaristici antichissimi: saggio di poesia sacra popolare bizantina*, Grottaferrata, 1932.

Bornkamm, G., 'Enderwartung und Kirche im Matthäusevangelium' in W. D. Davies and D. Daube (edd.), *The Background of the New Testament and its Eschatology*, Cambridge, 1956, pp. 222–60.

Bornkamm, G., 'Die eucharistische Rede im Johannesevangelium' in *ZNW* 47 (1956), pp. 161–69.

— 'Herrenmahl und Kirche bei Paulus' in *Zeitschrift für Theologie und Kirche* 53 (1956), pp. 312–49.

Botte, B., *Le canon de la messe romaine*, Louvain, 1935.

— 'L'Anaphore Chaldéenne des Apôtres' in *Orientalia Christiana Periodica* 15 (1949), pp. 259–76.

— 'L'épiclèse dans les liturgies syriennes orientales' in *Sacris Erudiri* 6 (1954), pp. 48–72.

— 'Fragments d'une anaphore inconnue attribuée à S. Epiphane' in *Le Muséon* 73 (1960), pp. 311–15.

— *Ambroise de Milan: Des sacrements; Des mystères*, in the series *Sources chrétiennes*, vol. 25, Paris, 1961².

— *La Tradition apostolique de saint Hippolyte: essai de reconstitution*, Münster i.W., 1963.

— 'Problèmes de l'anaphore syrienne des apôtres Addaï et Mari' in *L'Orient Syrien* 10 (1965), pp. 89–106.

Bouyer, L., 'La première eucharistie dans la dernière cène' in *La Maison-Dieu* no. 18 (1949), pp. 34–47.

— *La Vie de la Liturgie*, Paris, 1956.

— *Eucharistie: théologie et spiritualité de la prière eucharistique*, Tournai, 1966.

Bowmer, J. C., *The Sacrament of the Lord's Supper in Early Methodism*, London, 1951.

Brightman, F. E., *Liturgies Eastern and Western*, vol. I (*Eastern Liturgies*), Oxford, 1896.

Brilioth, Y., *Nattvarden i evangeliskt gudstjänstliv*, Stockholm, [1926¹], 1951² (*Eucharistic Faith and Practice: Evangelical and Catholic*, London, 1930).

Broglie, G. de, 'Pour une théologie du festin eucharistique' in *Doctor Communis* 2 (1949), pp. 3–36, and 3 (1950), pp. 16–42.

Broussaleux, S., *Nicolas Cabasilas: La Vie en Jésus-Christ*, Chevetogne, 1960².

Brunner, E., *Das Ewige als Zukunft und Gegenwart*, Zürich, 1953.

Brunner, P., 'Zur Lehre vom Gottesdienst der im Namen Jesu versammelten Gemeinde' in K. F. Müller and W. Blankenburg (edd.), *Leiturgia: Handbuch des evangelischen Gottesdienstes*, vol. I, Kassel, 1952, pp. 83–364.

— 'Zur katholischen Sakramenten- und Eucharistielehre' in *Theologische Literaturzeitung* 88 (1963), cols. 169–86.

Buchanan, C. O., *Modern Anglican Liturgies 1958–1968*, London, 1968.

Bultmann, R., art. ἀγαλλιάομαι, ἀγαλλίασις, in *TWNT*, vol. I, pp. 18–20.

— *Das Evangelium des Johannes*, Göttingen, 1941.

— 'History and Eschatology in the New Testament' in *NTS* 1 (1954–55), pp. 5–16.

— *History and Eschatology*, Edinburgh, 1957.

— *Theologie des Neuen Testaments*, Tübingen, 1958³.

Buri, F., *Die Bedeutung der neutestamentlichen Eschatologie für die neuere protestantische Theologie*, Zürich/Leipzig, 1935.

Carmignac, J., *Recherches sur le 'Notre Père'*, Paris, 1969, pp. 118–221 ('Notre Pain').

Casel, O., 'Das Mysteriengedächtnis der Messliturgie im Lichte der Tradition' in *Jahrbuch für Liturgiewissenschaft* 6 (1926), pp. 113–204.

— *Das christliche Kultmysterium*, Regensburg, 1960.

Clark, F., *Eucharistic Sacrifice and the Reformation*, London, 1960 [Oxford, 1967²].

Clark, N., *An Approach to the Theology of the Sacraments*, London, 1956.

Clavier, H., 'L'accès au Royaume de Dieu' in *RHPhR* 22 (1942), pp. 1–29, 215–39, and 23 (1943), pp. 185–236.

Clément, O., *Transfigurer le Temps: notes sur le temps à la lumière de la tradition orthodoxe*, Neuchâtel, 1959.

— 'Le dimanche et le Jour éternel' in *Verbum Caro* no. 79 (1966), pp. 99–124.

Connolly, R. H., *The Liturgical Homilies of Narsai*, Cambridge, 1909.

— and Codrington, H. W., *Two Commentaries on the Jacobite Liturgy by George Bishop of the Arab Tribes and Moses bār Kēphā, together with the Syriac Anaphora of St James and a document entitled 'The Book of Life'*, London/Oxford, 1913.

— 'Sixth Century Fragments of an East Syrian Anaphora' in *Oriens Christianus* 12–14 (1925), pp. 99–128.

*Convivium Dominicum: Studi sull'Eucaristia nei Padri della Chiesa e miscellenea patristica*, Catania, 1959.

Conzelmann, H., *Die Mitte der Zeit: Studien zur Theologie des Lukas*, Tübingen, 1954.

— 'Gegenwart und Zukunft in der synoptischen Tradition' in *Zeitschrift für Theologie und Kirche* 54 (1957), pp. 277–96.

Cooke, B., 'Synoptic Presentation of the Eucharist as Covenant Sacrifice' in *Theological Studies* 21 (1960), pp. 1–44.

Cooper, J., and Maclean, A. J., *The Testament of Our Lord*, Edinburgh, 1902.

Cross, F. L., *St Cyril of Jerusalem's Lectures on the Christian Sacraments*, London, [1951] 1960.

Cross, F. M., *The Ancient Library of Qumran and Modern Biblical Studies*, New York, 1958, pp. 62–67.

Cullmann, O., 'La signification de la Sainte Cène dans le christianisme primitif' in *RHPhR* 16 (1936), pp. 1–22.

— *Le Retour du Christ, espérance de l'Eglise, selon le Nouveau Testament*, Neuchâtel, [1943] 1945².

— *Christus und die Zeit: die urchristliche Zeit- und Geschichtsauffassung*, Zürich, 1946¹, 1962³.

— *Urchristentum und Gottesdienst*, Zürich, 1950².

— 'Parusieverzögerung und Urchristentum: der gegenwärtige Stand der Diskussion' in *Theologische Literaturzeitung* 83 (1958), cols. 1–12.

— *Heil als Geschichte*, Tübingen, 1965.

Cyster, R. F., 'The Lord's Prayer and the Exodus Tradition' in *Theology* 64 (1961), pp. 377–81.

Dahl, N. A., 'Anamnesis. Mémoire et Commémoration dans le christianisme primitif' in *Studia Theologica* 1 (1947 =Lund, 1948), pp. 69–95.

Daniélou, J., 'Les repas de la Bible et leur signification' in *La Maison-Dieu* no. 18 (1949), pp. 7–33.

— *Sacramentum futuri: études sur les origines de la typologie biblique*, Paris, 1950.

— *Bible et Liturgie: la théologie biblique des sacrements et des fêtes d'après les Pères de l'Eglise*, Paris, 1958².

Davies, J. G., *The Spirit, the Church and the Sacraments*, London, 1954.

— *Worship and Mission*, London, 1966.

Delling, G., *Der Gottesdienst im Neuen Testament*, Göttingen, 1952.

Denzinger, H., and Schönmetzer, A., *Enchiridion Symbolorum*, Freiburg i.B., 1965[33].

Dewick, E. C., 'A Review of Attitudes towards the Problem of Inter-Communion' in *Modern Churchman* 40 (1950), pp. 36–47.

Dibelius, M., 'Die Mahlgebete der Didache' in *ZNW* 37 (1938), pp. 32–41.

Dix, G., *The Shape of the Liturgy*, Westminster, 1945.

Dodd, C. H., *The Parables of the Kingdom*, London, 1935[1], 1961 (paperback).

— *The Apostolic Preaching and its Developments*, London, 1936 (appendix on 'Eschatology and History').

— 'The Sacrament of the Lord's Supper in the New Testament' in N. Micklem (ed.), *Christian Worship*, Oxford, 1936, pp. 68–82.

— *The Coming of Christ*, Cambridge, 1951.

— *The Interpretation of the Fourth Gospel*, Cambridge, 1953.

— *Historical Tradition in the Fourth Gospel*, Cambridge, 1963.

Dölger, F. J., *Die Fischdenkmaler in der frühchristlichen Plastik, Malerei und Kleinkunst* ( =*ΙΧΘΥΣ*, vol. V), Münster, 1943.

Doresse, J., and Lanne, E., *Un témoin archaïque de la liturgie copte de S. Basile. En annexe: Les liturgies 'basiliennes' et saint Basile, par B. Capelle* (Bibliothèque du *Muséon*, vol. 47), Louvain, 1960.

Dufort, J. M., ' "Coeleste convivium" dans la symbolique des premiers Pères' in *Sciences ecclésiastiques* 14 (1962), pp. 31–56.

Dugmore, C. W., 'Lord's Day and Easter' in *Neotestamentica et Patristica*, Supplements to *Novum Testamentum*, vol. VI, Leiden, 1962, pp. 272–81.

Dupont, J., 'Le repas d'Emmaüs' in *Lumière et Vie* no. 31 (1957), pp. 77–92.

— ' "Ceci est mon corps", "Ceci est mon sang" ' in *NRTh* 80 (1958), pp. 1025–41.

du Toit, A.B., *Der Aspekt der Freude im urchristlichen Abendmahl*, Winterthur, 1965.

Eichrodt, W., 'Heilserfahrung und Zeitverständnis im Alten Testament' in *Theologische Zeitschrift* 12 (1956), pp. 103–25.

Eisler, R., 'Das letzte Abendmahl' in *ZNW* 24 (1925), in particular pp. 190–92.

Elert, W., *Abendmahlsgemeinschaft in der alten Kirche*, Berlin, 1954.

— 'Abendmahl und Kirchengemeinschaft in der alten Kirche' in *Koinonia*, Berlin, 1957, pp. 57–78.

Emerton, J. A., 'The Aramaic underlying τὸ αἷμά μου τῆς διαθήκης in Mk. xiv, 24' in *JTS* n.s. 6 (1955), pp. 238–40.

— 'τὸ αἷμά μου τῆς διαθήκης: the evidence of the Syriac versions' in *JTS* n.s. 13 (1962), pp. 111–17.

Eméry, P. Y., *L'unité des croyants au ciel et sur la terre*, Taizé, 1962.

Evdokimov, P., *L'Orthodoxie*, Neuchâtel, 1959.

Every, G., *Basic Liturgy: a study in the structure of the eucharistic prayer*, London, 1961.

Féret, H. M., 'Messe et eschatologie' in *La Maison-Dieu* no. 24 (1950), pp. 46–62.

— *L'eucharistie, pâque de l'univers*, Paris, 1966.

Férotin, M., *Liber Mozarabicus Sacramentorum*, Paris, 1912.

Feuillet, A., 'L'heure de Jésus et le signe de Cana' in *Ephemerides Theologicae Lovanienses* 36 (1960), pp. 5–22.

— 'Les themes bibliques majeurs du discours sur le pain de vie' in *NRTh* 82 (1960), pp. 803–22, 918–39, 1040–62.

Fison, J. E., *The Christian Hope: the Presence and the Parousia*, London, 1954.

Fitzgerald, T., *The Influence of the Holy Eucharist on Bodily Resurrection*, Romae, 1965.

Flender, H., *Heil und Geschichte in der Theologie des Lukas*, München, 1965.

— *Die Botschaft Jesu von der Herrschaft Gottes*, München, 1968.

Foerster, W., art. ἐπιούσιος in *TWNT*, vol. II, pp. 587–95.

Fohrer, G., *Die symbolischen Handlungen der Propheten*, Zürich, 1953[1], 1968[2].

Frere, W. H., *The Anaphora or great eucharistic prayer*, London, 1938.

Fridrichsen, A., 'Eglise et sacrement dans le Nouveau Testament' in *RHPhR* 17 (1937), pp. 337–56.

Fries, H., 'Die Eucharistie und die Einheit der Kirche' in *Pro Mundi Vita*, München, 1960, pp. 165–80.

Fuchs, E., *Das urchristliche Sakramentsverständnis*, Bad Cannstadt, n.d. (1958 ?).

Fuller, R. H., *The Mission and Achievement of Jesus*, London, 1954.

Funk, F. X., *Didascalia et Constitutiones Apostolorum*, vol. I, Paderbornae, 1905.

García Vieyra, A., 'La Eucaristía, sacramento de la gloria' in *Estudios teológicos y filosóficos*, Buenos Aires, 3 (1961), pp. 9–25.

Gaugler, E., *Das Abendmahl im Neuen Testament*, Basel, 1943.

— 'La Sainte Cène' in G. Deluz, J. P. Ramseyer and E. Gaugler, *La Sainte Cène*, Neuchâtel, 1945, pp. 53–89.

George, A., 'Le Jugement de Dieu: essai d'interprétation d'un thème eschatologique' in *Concilium* no. 41 (1969), pp. 13–23.

George, A. R., *Communion with God in the New Testament*, London, 1953.

Gerrish, B. A., 'The Lord's Supper in the Reformed Confessions' in *Theology Today* 23 (1966–67), pp. 224–43.

Glasson, T. F., *The Second Advent: The Origin of the New Testament Doctrine*, London, 1945.

— *His Appearing and His Kingdom: The Christian Hope in the Light of its History*, London, 1953.

Gloege, G., *Reich Gottes und Kirche im Neuen Testament* [Gütersloh, 1929], Darmstadt, 1968.

Gogarten, F., *Verhängnis und Hoffnung der Neuzeit*, Stuttgart, 1953 (pp. 169–88, 'Die neutestamentliche Eschatologie').

Grabner-Haider, A., *Paraklese und Eschatologie bei Paulus: Mensch und Welt im Anspruch der Zukunft Gottes*, Münster, 1968.

Grässer, E., *Das Problem der Parusieverzögerung in den synoptischen Evangelien und in der Apostelgeschichte*, Berlin, 1957[1], 1960[2].

Greenslade, S. L., *Schism in the Early Church*, London, 1964[2].

Grisbrooke, W. J., *Anglican Liturgies of the Seventeenth and Eighteenth Centuries*, London, 1958.

Groot, J. C., 'Reformiert-Lutherischer "Consensus über das Abendmahl" in Holland' in *Catholica* 13 (1959), pp. 212–26.

Haes, P. de, 'Eucharistie en Eschatologie' in *Praesentia Realis*, the July–August 1963 issue of *Sanctissima Eucharistia*, Nijmegen, pp. 37–54.

Hageman, H. G., *Pulpit and Table*, Richmond, Va., 1962.

Hahn, F., 'Die alttestamentlichen Motive in der urchristlichen Abendmahlsüberlieferung' in *Evangelische Theologie* 27 (1967), pp. 337–74.

Hanssens, J. M., *Institutiones Liturgicae de ritibus orientalibus*, vols. II & III, Romae, 1930–32.

Hartingsveld, L. van, *Die Eschatologie des Johannesevangeliums: eine Auseinandersetzung mit Rudolf Bultmann*, Assen, 1962.

Hayek, M., *Liturgie maronite: histoire et textes eucharistiques*, Tours (?), 1964.

Heising, A., *Die Botschaft der Brotvermehrung*, Stuttgart, 1966.

Henning, J., 'Our daily bread' in *Theological Studies* 4 (1943), pp. 445–54.

Higgins, A. J. B., *The Lord's Supper in the New Testament*, London, 1952.

Hodgson, L., *Church and Sacraments in divided Christendom*, London, 1959.

Hoekendijk, J. C., 'Exceptions, Eschatology and our common practices' in *Youth* (World Council of Churches Youth Department) no. 6 (December 1962), pp. 63–77 [now in his *The Church Inside Out*, London, 1967, pp. 148–66].

Hook, N., *The Eucharist in the New Testament*, London, 1964.

Hoskyns, E. C., *The Fourth Gospel*, London, 1947².

Hussey, J. M., and McNulty, P. A., *Nicholas Cabasilas: A commentary on the Divine Liturgy*, London, 1960.

Iersel, B. van, 'Die wunderbare Speisung und das Abendmahl in der synoptischen Tradition (Mk. vi, 35–44 par., viii, 1–20 par.)' in *Novum Testamentum* 7 (1964–65), pp. 167–94.

India, Church of South, *Book of Common Worship*, London, 1963.

*Intercommunion Today, being the Report of the Archbishops' Commission on Intercommunion*, London, 1968.

Janot, E., 'L'Eucharistie dans les sacramentaires occidentaux' in *Recherches de Science Religieuse* 17 (1927), pp. 5–24.

Jaubert, A., *La date de la Cène*, Paris, 1957.

Jeauneau, E., 'L'Esprit et l'Eucharistie' in *La Vie Spirituelle* 100 (1959), pp. 655–69.

Jeremias, J., *Jesus als Weltvollender*, Gütersloh, 1930.

— art. νύμφη, νυμφίος in *TWNT*, vol. IV (1942?), pp. 1092–99.

— *Die Abendmahlsworte Jesu*, Göttingen, [1935¹], 1949², 1960³.

— *Die Gleichnisse Jesu*, Zürich, 1947¹, Göttingen, 1956⁴.

— *Jesu Verheissung für die Völker*, Stuttgart, 1956.

— 'Das Vater-Unser im Lichte der neueren Forschung' in *Abba*, Göttingen, 1966, pp. 152–71.

Johanny, R., *L'Eucharistie, centre de l'histoire du salut chez saint Ambroise de Milan*, Paris, 1968.

Jones, D. R., 'ἀνάμνησις in the LXX and the interpretation of I Cor. xi, 25' in *JTS* n.s. 6 (1955), pp. 183–91.

Jungmann, J. A., *Missarum sollemnia: eine genetische Erklärung der römischen Messe*, vols. I and II, Wien, 1952³.

— *The Early Liturgy to the time of Gregory the Great*, London, 1963 (paperback).

Käsemann, E., 'Anliegen und Eigenart der paulinischen Abendmahlslehre' [in *Evangelische Theologie* 7 (1947–48), pp. 263–83] now in his *Exegetische Versuche und Besinnungen*, vol. I, Göttingen, 1960, pp. 11–34.

— 'Eine Apologie der urchristlichen Eschatologie' [in *Zeitschrift für Theologie und Kirche* 49 (1952), pp. 272–96] now in his *Exegetische Versuche und Besinnungen*, vol. I, Göttingen, 1960, pp. 135–57.

— 'Zum Thema der urchristlichen Apokalyptik' [in *Zeitschrift für Theologie und Kirche* 59 (1962), pp. 257–84] now in his *Exegetische Versuche und Besinnungen*, vol. II, Göttingen, 1964, pp. 105–31.

Kenny, J. P., 'Heavenly Banquet' in *American Ecclesiastical Review* 146 (1962), pp. 47–56.

Kilmartin, E. J., *The Eucharist in the Primitive Church*, Englewood Cliffs, N.J., 1965.

Kilpatrick, G. D., 'L'eucharistie dans le Nouveau Testament' in *Revue de Théologie et de Philosophie* 97 (1964), pp. 193–204.

Koinonia: *Arbeiten des Oekumenischen Ausschusses der Vereinigten Evangelisch-Lutherischen Kirche Deutschlands zur Frage der Kirchen- und Abendmahlsgemeinschaft*, Berlin, 1957.

Kosmala, H., 'Das tut zu meinem Gedächtnis' in *Novum Testamentum* 4 (1960), pp. 81–94.

Kreck, W., *Die Zukunft des Gekommenen: Grundprobleme der Eschatologie*, München, 1961.

Kümmel, W. G., 'Die Bedeutung der Enderwartung für die Lehre des Paulus' [1934] now in his *Heilsgeschehen und Geschichte*, Marburg, 1965, pp. 36–47.

— *Verheissung und Erfüllung*, Basel, 1945¹ [Zürich, 1953²].

— 'Futurische und präsentische Eschatologie im ältesten Urchristentum' [in *NTS* 5 (1958–59), pp. 113–26] now in his *Heilsgeschehen und Geschichte*, Marburg, 1965, pp. 351–63.

— 'Die Naherwartung in der Verkündigung Jesu' in *Heilsgeschehen und Geschichte*, Marburg, 1965, pp. 457–70.

Kuhn, K. G., art. μαραναθά in *TWNT*, vol. IV, pp. 470–75.

Ladd, G. E., *Jesus and the Kingdom: The Eschatology of Biblical Realism*, New York, 1964.

Langevin, P. E., *Jésus Seigneur et l'Eschatologie: exégèse de textes prépauliniens*, Bruges/Paris, 1967.

Lebeau, P., *Le Vin nouveau du Royaume: Etude exégétique et patristique sur la Parole eschatologique de Jésus à la Cène*, Paris/Bruges, 1966.

Lécuyer, J., *Le sacrifice de la Nouvelle Alliance*, Le Puy/Lyon, 1962.

Le Déaut, R., *La Nuit Pascale*, Rome, 1963.

Leeming, B., *Principles of Sacramental Theology*, London, 1960².

Leenhardt, F. J., 'Le pain et la coupe' in *Foi et Vie* 46 (1948), pp. 509–26.

— *Le Sacrement de la Sainte Cène*, Neuchâtel, 1948.

— *Ceci est mon corps: Explication de ces paroles de Jésus-Christ*, Neuchâtel, 1955.

— 'La présence eucharistique' in *Irénikon* 33 (1960), pp. 146–72.

Lescrauwaert, J., 'Eucharistische Eredienst en kerkelijke eenheid' in *Bijdragen* 25 (1964), pp. 117–41.

Leuba, J. L., *L'institution et l'événement*, Neuchâtel, 1950.

L'Huillier, P., 'Théologie de l'épiclèse' in *Verbum Caro* no. 56 (1960), pp. 307–27.

Lietzmann, H., *Das Sacramentarium Gregorianum nach dem Aachener Urexemplar*, Münster i.W., 1921.

— *Messe und Herrenmahl*, Berlin, [1926¹], 1955³.

Linton, A., *Twenty-five Consecration Prayers*, London, 1921.

Lohmeyer, E., 'Vom urchristlichen Abendmahl' in *Theologische Rundschau* n.F. 9 (1937), pp. 168–227, 273–312, and 10 (1938), pp. 81–99.

— 'Das Abendmahl in der Urgemeinde' in *Journal of Biblical Literature* 56 (1937), pp. 217–52.

— *Das Vater-Unser*, Göttingen, 1947².

Lohse, B., *Das Passafest der Quartadecimaner*, Gütersloh, 1953.

Lowe, E. A., *The Bobbio Missal (MS. Paris. lat. 13246): text*, London, 1920.

Lubac, H. de, *Corpus mysticum: l'Eucharistie et l'Eglise au moyen âge*, Paris, 1949².

Lundström, G. [*Guds Rike i Jesu Förkunnelse*, Lund, 1947, brought up to date in] *The Kingdom of God in the Teaching of Jesus: a history of the interpretation from the last decades of the nineteenth century to the present day*, Edinburgh, 1963.

Luz, U., *Das Geschichtsverständnis des Paulus*, München, 1968.

McCormick, S., *The Lord's Supper: A Biblical Interpretation*, Philadelphia, 1966.

McDonnell, K., *John Calvin, the Church, and the Eucharist*, Princeton, 1967.

McGrory, W. B., *The Mass and the Resurrection*, Romae, 1964.

Mahé, J., 'L'Eucharistie d'après Saint Cyrille d'Alexandrie' in *Revue d'Histoire Ecclésiastique* 8 (1907), pp. 677–96.

Manson, T. W., *The Teaching of Jesus*, London, 1935².

Manson, W., 'Church and Intercommunion: some considerations bearing on the present problem' in *Scottish Journal of Theology* 4 (1951), pp. 29–38.

Marshall, I. H., *Eschatology and the Parables*, London, 1963.

Martin, R. P., *Worship in the Early Church*, London, 1964.

Martin-Achard, R., *Israël et les Nations: La perspective missionnaire de l'Ancien Testament*, Neuchâtel, 1959.

Marxsen, W., *Das Abendmahl als christologisches Problem*, Gütersloh, 1965².

Mascall, E. L., *Corpus Christi: Essays on the Church and the Eucharist*, London, 1953.

Maury, P., *L'Eschatologie*, Genève, 1959.

Maxwell, W. D., *The Liturgical Portions of the Genevan Service Book 1556*, London, [1931], 1965².

— *An Outline of Christian Worship*, London, 1936.

Mehl, R., 'Structure philosophique de la notion de présence' in *RHPhR* 38 (1958), pp. 171–76.

Menoud, P. H., 'Les Actes des Apôtres et l'Eucharistie' in *RHPhR* 33 (1953), pp. 21–36.

Michell, G. A., *Eucharistic Consecration in the Primitive Church*, London, 1948.

Minear, P. S., *Christian Hope and the Second Coming*, Philadelphia, 1954.

Mohlberg, K. [=L.C.], *Das fränkische Sacramentarium Gelasianum in alamannischer Überlieferung (Codex Sangall. No. 348)*, Münster i.W., 1939².

Mohlberg, L. C. [=K.], *Sacramentarium Veronese (Cod. Bibl. Capit. Veron. LXXXV [80])*, Roma, 1956 [=The 'Leonine' Sacramentary].

— *Liber Sacramentorum Romanae Æclesiae Ordinis anni circuli (Cod. Vat. Reg. lat. 316/Paris Bibl. Nat. 7193, 41/56) (Sacramentarium gelasianum)*, Roma, 1960.

Mollat, D., 'Le chapitre VIe de Saint Jean' in *Lumière et Vie* no. 31 (1957), pp. 107–19.

Moltmann, J., *Theologie der Hoffnung*, München, [1964¹], 1966⁶.

Montcheuil, Y. de, 'Signification eschatologique du repas eucharistique' in *Recherches de Science Religieuse* 33 (1946), pp. 10–43.

Moore, A. L., *The Parousia in the New Testament*, Supplements to *Novum Testamentum*, vol. XIII, Leiden, 1966.

Moule, C. F. D., 'The Judgment Theme in the Sacraments' in W. D. Davies and D. Daube (edd.), *The Background of the New Testament and its Eschatology*, Cambridge, 1956, pp. 464–81.

— *Worship in the New Testament*, London, 1961.

Müller-Goldkuhle, P., 'Die nachbiblischen Akzentverschiebungen im historischen Entwicklungsgang des eschatologischen Denkens' in *Concilium* 5 (1969), pp. 10–17.

Neuenzeit, P., *Das Herrenmahl: Studien zur paulinischen Eucharistieauffassung*, München, 1960.

Neunheuser, B., *Eucharistie in Mittelalter und Neuzeit*, Freiburg i.B., 1963 (= M. Schmaus and A. Grillmeier (edd.), *Handbuch der Dogmengeschichte*, IV, 4b).

Nissiotis, N. A., 'Worship, Eucharist and "Intercommunion": an Orthodox reflection' in *Studia Liturgica* 2 (1963), pp. 193–222.

— 'Der pneumatologische Ansatz und die liturgische Verwirklichung des neutestamentlichen νῦν' in F. Christ (ed.), *Oikonomia*, Hamburg, 1967, pp. 302–9.

Otto, R., *Reich Gottes und Menschensohn*, München, 1934.

Oulton, J. E. L., *Holy Communion and Holy Spirit*, London, 1951.

Pannenberg, W., *et al.*, *Offenbarung als Geschichte*, Göttingen, 1963².

Paquier, R., *Traité de Liturgique: Essai sur le fondement et la structure du culte*, Neuchâtel, 1954.

Pascher, J., *Eucharistia*, Münster i.W./Freiburg i.B., [1947¹], 1953².

— 'Heilsmittel der Unsterblichkeit' in *Pro Mundi Vita*, München, 1960, pp. 280–93.

Perrin, N., *The Kingdom of God in the Teaching of Jesus*, London, 1963.

— *Rediscovering the Teaching of Jesus*, London, 1967.

Peterson, E., *Das Buch von den Engeln: Stellung und Bedeutung der heiligen Engeln im Kultus*, Leipzig, 1935.

Pétré, H., *Ethérie: Journal de Voyage*, Sources Chrétiennes, vol. 21, Paris, 1948.

— 'Les leçons du *Panem nostrum quotidianum*' in *Recherches de Science religieuse* 40 (1952), pp. 63–79.

Philippi, P., *Abendmahlsfeier und Wirklichkeit der Gemeinde*, Berlin, 1960.

Piolanti, A. (ed.), *Eucaristia: il mistero dell'altare nel pensiero e nella vita della Chiesa*, Roma, 1957.

Pousset, E., 'L'Eucharistie: présence réelle et transsubstantiation' in *Recherches de Science religieuse* 54 (1966), pp. 177–212.

Powers, J. M., *Eucharistic Theology* [1967], London, 1968.

Prenter, R., *Connaître Christ*, Neuchâtel, 1966.

Preuss, H. D., *Jahweglaube und Zukunftserwartung*, Stuttgart, 1968.

*Pro Mundi Vita: Festschrift zum eucharistischen Weltkongress 1960*, herausgegeben von der Theologischen Fakultät der Ludwig-Maximilian-Universität München, München, 1960.

Puzo, F., 'La unidad de la Iglesia en función de la Eucaristía (estudio de teología bíblica)' in *Gregorianum* 34 (1953), pp. 145–86.

Quick, O. C., *The Christian Sacraments*, London, [1927¹], 1932².

Rad, G. von, 'Typologische Auslegung des Alten Testaments' in *Evangelische Theologie* 12 (1952–53), pp. 17–33.

— *Theologie des Alten Testaments*, 2 vols., München, 1957 & 1960.

Rahner, K., 'Theologische Prinzipien der Hermeneutik eschatologischer Aussagen' in *Schriften zur Theologie*, vol. IV, Einsiedeln, 1960, pp. 401–28 [first in *Zeitschrift für katholische Theologie* 82 (1960), pp. 137–58].

— *Kirche und Sakramente*, Freiburg, i.B., 1960.

Ratcliff, E. C., 'The Original Form of the Anaphora of Addai and Mari: A Suggestion' in *JTS* 30 (1928–29), pp. 23–32.

— 'The Sanctus and the Pattern of the Early Anaphora' in *Journal of Ecclesiastical History* 1 (1950), pp. 29–36, 125–34.

Rattenbury, J. E., *The Eucharistic Hymns of John and Charles Wesley, to which is appended Wesley's Preface extracted from Brevint's 'Christian Sacrament and Sacrifice', together with 'Hymns on the Lord's Supper'*, London, 1948.

Ratti, A., and Magistretti, M., *Missale Ambrosianum*, Mediolani, 1913.

Reicke, B., 'Die Mahlzeit mit Paulus auf den Wellen des Mittelmeeres Act. 27, 33–38' in *Theologische Zeitschrift* 4 (1948), pp. 401–10.

— *Diakonia, Festfreude und Zelos in Verbindung mit der altchristlichen Agapenfeier*, Uppsala/Wiesbaden, 1951.

Renaudot, E., *Liturgiarum orientalium collectio*, vols. I and II, Parisiis, 1716.

Ricca, P., *Die Eschatologie des Vierten Evangeliums*, Zürich, 1966.

Riesenfeld, H., *Jésus transfiguré*, København, 1947.

— 'Sabbat et jour du Seigneur' in A. J. B. Higgins (ed.), *New Testament Essays*, Manchester, 1959, pp. 210–17.

Roberts, C. H., and Capelle, B., *An Early Euchologion: The Dêr Balizeh Papyrus* (Bibliothèque du *Muséon*, vol. 23), Louvain, 1949.

Roberts, H., *Jesus and the Kingdom of God*, London, 1955.

Robinson, H. W., 'Prophetic Symbolism' in *Old Testament Essays*, London, 1927, pp. 1–17.

Robinson, J. A. T., *In the End, God. . . . A Study of the Christian doctrine of the Last Things*, London, 1950, [1968²].

— 'Traces of a liturgical sequence in I Cor. 16, 20–24' in *JTS* n.s. 4 (1953), pp. 38–41.

— *Jesus and His Coming*, London, 1957.

Robinson, W., *The Administration of the Lord's Supper*, Birmingham, 1947.

Roguet, A. M., 'L'unité du Corps mystique "res sacramenti" de l'eucharistie' in *La Maison-Dieu* no. 24 (1950), pp. 20–45.

Rordorf, W., *Der Sonntag: Geschichte des Ruhe- und Gottesdiensttages im ältesten Christentum*, Zürich, 1962.

— 'La célébration dominicale de la Sainte Cène dans l'Eglise ancienne' in *Revue de Théologie et de Philosophie* 99 (1966), pp. 25–37.

Salaville, S., 'Epiclèse eucharistique' in *Dictionnaire de Théologie Catholique*, vol. V, cols. 194–300.

— *Nicolas Cabasilas: Explication de la Divine Liturgie*, Sources Chrétiennes, vol. 4, Paris, 1967².

Sauter, G., *Zukunft und Verheissung: Das Problem der Zukunft in der gegenwärtigen theologischen und philosophischen Diskussion*, Zürich/Stuttgart, 1965.

Scheffczyk, L., 'Die materielle Welt im Lichte der Eucharistie' in M. Schmaus (ed.), *Aktuelle Fragen zur Eucharistie*, München, 1960, pp. 156–79.

Schillebeeckx, E., *Christus, Sacrament van de Godsontmoeting*, Bilthoven, [1957¹], 1959³.

— 'Christus' tegenwoordigheid in de Eucharistie' in *Tijdschrift voor Theologie* 5 (1965), pp. 136–73.

— 'De eucharistische wijze van Christus' werkelijke tegenwoordigheid' in *Tijdschrift voor Theologie* 6 (1966), pp. 359–94.

— 'Enkele hermeneutische beschouwingen over de eschatologie' in *Concilium* 5 (1969), pp. 38–51.

Schlette, H. R., 'Die Eucharistielehre Hugos von St Viktor' in *Zeitschrift für katholische Theologie* 81 (1959), pp. 67–100, 163–210.

Schmaus, M., 'Die Eucharistie als Bürgin der Auferstehung' in *Pro Mundi Vita*, München, 1960, pp. 256–79.

— (ed.), *Aktuelle Fragen zur Eucharistie*, München, 1960.

Schmemann, A., *For the Life of the World*, New York, 1963 [ = *Sacraments and Orthodoxy*, New York, 1965].

Schnackenburg, R., *Gottes Herrschaft und Reich*, Freiburg i.B., 1959.

— *Die Kirche im Neuen Testament*, Freiburg i.B., 1961.

— *Das Johannesevangelium*, vol. I, Freiburg/Basel/Wien, 1965.

Schousboe, J., 'La messe la plus ancienne' in *Revue de l'Histoire des Religions* 96 (1927), pp. 193–256.

Schürmann, H., 'Lk. 22, 19b–20 als ursprüngliche Textüberlieferung' in *Biblica* 32 (1951), pp. 364–92, 522–41.

— *Der Paschamahlbericht Lk. 22, (7–14.) 15–18*, Münster, 1953.

— *Der Einsetzungsbericht Lk. 22, 19–20*, Münster, 1955.

— *Jesu Abschiedsrede Lk. 22, 21–38*, Münster, 1957.

Schulz, H. J., *Die byzantinische Liturgie: Vom Werden ihrer Symbolgestalt*, Freiburg i.B., 1964.

Schweitzer, A., *Von Reimarus zu Wrede*, Tübingen, 1906 ( = *Geschichte der Leben-Jesu-Forschung*, Tübingen, 1913²).

— *Die Mystik des Apostels Paulus*, Tübingen, 1930.

— *Reich Gottes und Urchristentum*, Tübingen, 1967.

Schweizer, E., 'Das Abendmahl eine Vergegenwärtigung des Todes Jesu oder ein eschatologisches Freudenmahl?' in *Theologische Zeitschrift* 2 (1946), pp. 81–101.

— 'Das johanneische Zeugnis vom Herrenmahl' [in *Evangelische Theologie* 12 (1952–53), pp. 341–63] now in his *Neotestamentica*, Zürich, 1963, pp. 371–96.

— 'Das Herrenmahl im Neuen Testament' [in *Theologische Literaturzeitung* 79 (1954), cols. 577–92] now in his *Neotestamentica*, Zürich, 1963, pp. 344–70.

Semmelroth, O., *Die Kirche als Ursakrament*, Frankfurt a.M., 1953.

Sloyan, G. S., 'The Holy Eucharist as an Eschatological Meal' in *Worship* 36 (1962), pp. 444–51.

Smitmans, A., *Das Weinwunder von Kana: Die Auslegung von Jo. 2, 1–11 bei den Vätern und heute*, Tübingen, 1966.

Smits, L., *Actuele vragen rondom de transsubstantiatie en de tegenwoordigheid des Heren in de eucharistie*, Roermond-Maaseik, 1965.

Solano, J., *Textos eucaristicos primitivos*, vols. I and II, Madrid, 1952 and 1954.

Srawley, J. H., *The Early History of the Liturgy*, Cambridge, 1947².

Stakmeier, E., 'Die Eucharistie, die Einheit der Kirche und die Wiedervereinigung der Getrennten' in *Theologie und Glaube* 50 (1960), pp. 241–62.

Stange, A., *Das frühchristliche Kirchengebäude als Bild des Himmels*, Köln, 1950.

Steck, K. G., 'Eschatologie und Ekklesiologie in der römisch-katholischen Theologie von heute' in *Materialdienst des Konfessionskundlichen Instituts* 9 (1958), pp. 81–90.

Stone, D., *History of the Doctrine of the Holy Eucharist*, vols. I and II, London, 1909.

Strobel, A., 'Die Passa-Erwartung als urchristliches Problem in Lc. 17:20f' in *ZNW* 49 (1958), pp. 157–96.

Stuhlmacher, P., 'Erwägungen zum Problem der Gegenwart und Zukunft in der paulinischen Eschatologie' in *Zeitschrift für Theologie und Kirche* 64 (1967), pp. 423–50.

Subilia, V., *Gesù nella più antica tradizione cristiana*, Torre Pellice, 1954 (pp. 117–219, 'La Santa Cena').

Süss, T., *La Communion au Corps du Christ: études sur les problèmes de la sainte cène et des paroles d'institution*, Neuchâtel, 1968.

Symeon, H., 'De l'eucharistie comme sacrement de l'unité' in *Contacts* 16 (1964), pp. 126–46 (= 'The Eucharist as the Sacrament of Unity' in *Sobornost* 4 (1964), pp. 637–50).

*Syro-Malabar Missal*, Ernakulam (India), 1963.

*Syro-Malankarese Rite, The Order of the Holy Qurbana of the*, Trivandrum (India), 1964.

Tanghe, D. A., 'L'eucharistie pour la rémission des péchés' in *Irénikon* 34 (1961), pp. 165–81.

Thompson, F. J., 'Economy. An examination of the various theories of Economy held within the Orthodox Church, with special reference to the economical recognition of the validity of non-Orthodox sacraments' in *JTS* n.s. 16 (1965), pp. 368–420.

Thurian, M., *L'Eucharistie: mémorial du Seigneur, sacrifice d'action de grâce et d'intercession*, Neuchâtel, 1959.

— 'Intercommunion' in *Verbum Caro* no. 66 (1963), pp. 199–213.

— 'L'anamnèse du Christ' in *L'Evangile, hier et aujourd'hui: Mélanges offerts au Professeur F.J. Leenhardt*, Genève, 1968, pp. 263–76.

Tillard, J. M. R., 'La triple dimension du signe sacramentel (A propos de *Sum. Theol.* III, 60, 3)' in *NRTh* 83 (1961), pp. 225–54.

— 'L'Eucharistie, sacrement de l'espérance ecclésiale' in *NRTh* 83 (1961), pp. 561–92, 673–95.

— *L'eucharistie, pâque de l'Eglise*, Paris, 1964.

— 'L'eucharistie et le Saint-Esprit' in *NRTh* 90 (1968), pp. 363–87.

— 'Le *Votum Eucharistiae*: l'eucharistie dans la rencontre des chrétiens' in *Miscellanea Liturgica*, vol. 2, Roma, 1967, pp. 143–94.

Tondelli, L., *L'Eucaristia vista da un esegeta*, Alba, 1951.

Tonneau, R., and Devreesse, R., *Les Homélies Catéchétiques de Théodore de Mopsueste*, Studi e Testi, vol. 145, Città del Vaticano, 1949.

Torrance, T. F., 'Eschatology and the Eucharist' in D. Baillie and J. Marsh (edd.), *Intercommunion*, London, 1952, pp. 303–50.

Unnik, W. C. van, 'Kanttekeningen bij een nieuwe verklaring van de anamnesewoorden' in *Nederlands Theologisch Tijdschrift* 4 (1949–50), pp. 369–77.

Vagaggini, C., *Il senso teologico della liturgia*, Roma, 1965[4].

Vajta, V., 'Creation and Worship' in *Studia Liturgica* 2 (1963), pp. 29–46.

— (ed.), *Kirche und Abendmahl: Studien und Dokumente zur Frage der Abendmahlsgemeinschaft im Luthertum*, Berlin/Hamburg, 1963.

Verghese, P., *The Joy of Freedom: Eastern Worship and Modern Man*, London, 1967.

Verheul, A., 'De gestalte van de Eucharistieviering Maaltijd of Offer?' in *Tijdschrift voor Liturgie* 45 (1961), pp. 39–59.

Vicedom, G. F., *Das Abendmahl in den jungen Kirchen*, München, 1960.

Vischer, L., 'Questions on the Eucharist, its past and future celebration' in *Studia Liturgica* 5 (1966), pp. 65–86.

Vogels, H., 'Mk. 14, 25 und Parallelen' in N. Adler (ed.), *Vom Wort des Lebens: Festschrift für Max Meinertz*, Münster, 1951, pp. 93–104.

Vona, C., 'La quarta petitio dell'oratio dominica nell'interpretazione di antichi scrittori cristiani' in *Convivium Dominicum*, Catania, 1959, pp. 215–55.

Warnach, V., 'Symbolwirklichkeit der Eucharistie' in *Concilium* 4 (1968), pp. 755–65.

Warner, G. F., *The Stowe Missal (MS.D.II.3 in the Library of the Royal Irish Academy, Dublin), printed text*, London, 1915.

Watteville, J. de, *Le sacrifice dans les textes eucharistiques des premiers siècles*, Neuchâtel, 1966.

Weiss, J., *Die Predigt Jesu vom Reiche Gottes* [1892¹; 1900²], Göttingen, 1964.

Wendland, H. D., *Die Eschatologie des Reiches Gottes bei Jesu*, Gütersloh, 1931.

Wenger, A., *Jean Chrysostome: Huit Catéchèses Baptismales*, Sources chrétiennes, vol. 50, Paris, 1957.

Wenz, H., *Die Ankunft unseres Herrn am Ende der Welt: Zur Überwindung des Individualismus und des blossen Aktualismus in der Eschatologie R. Bultmanns und H. Brauns*, Stuttgart, 1965.

Werner, M., *Die Entstehung des christlichen Dogmas problemgeschichtlich dargestellt*, Bern, [1941¹], 1953².

Wetter, G. P., *Altchristliche Liturgien: Das christliche Mysterium*, Göttingen, 1921.

Wigan, B., *The Liturgy in English*, London, 1964².

Wilmart, A., 'Une exposition de la messe ambrosienne' in *Jahrbuch für Liturgiewissenschaft* 2 (1922), pp. 47–67.

Wilpert, J., *Fractio Panis: die älteste Darstellung des eucharistischen Opfers in der 'Cappella Graeca'*, Freiburg i.B., 1895.

— *Die Malereien der Sakramentskapellen in der Katakombe des hl. Callistus*, Freiburg i.B., 1897.

Wilpert, G. (=J.), *Roma sotteranea: Le pitture delle catacombe romane*, vols. I and II, Roma, 1903.

Winklhofer, A., *Das Kommen seines Reiches*, Frankfurt a.M., 1959.

— *Eucharistie als Osterfeier*, Frankfurt a.M., 1964.

Wordsworth, J., *Bishop Sarapion's Prayer-Book: an Egyptian Sacramentary dated probably about A.D. 350–356*, London, 1910².

Zernov, N., *The Reintegration of the Church: a study in intercommunion*, London, 1952.

Ziegler, A. W., 'Das Brot von unseren Feldern: ein Beitrag zur Eucharistielehre des hl. Irenäus' in *Pro Mundi Vita*, München, 1960, pp. 21–43.

Zimmerli, W., 'Verheissung und Erfüllung' in *Evangelische Theologie* 12 (1952–53), pp. 34–59.

# Indexes

## SCRIPTURES AND APOCRYPHA

Only the more important references are included here

# FATHERS, REFORMERS, AND THE LIKE

# MODERN AUTHORS

# *Appendix*

NO MATERIAL change in the original edition is necessitated by any more recent or more recently discovered publications. Enrichments of detail would, however, be possible at a number of points, and the following brief book-notes are chiefly intended to indicate sources which could be drawn on.

To the 'younger systematicians' mentioned at the end of chapter I there should have been added (one cannot spot all the winners) the names of Eberhard Jüngel and Wolfhart Pannenberg. Both of them claimed exegetical bases for systematically significant interpretations of the relation between present and future. In his *Paulus und Jesus* (Tübingen, 1962), and then with precisions in his *Unterwegs zur Sache* (München, 1972, especially pp. 130-32), Jüngel argued that the future element in the preaching of Jesus did not serve to establish an interval before a divine kingdom conceived as still outstanding when measured from a present point on a merely chronological timescale. Rather, the movement was in the other direction: the eternal kingdom of God had 'come near' in the words and deeds of Jesus; the kingdom's time was coming and, by entering into our time, the kingdom was bringing our time to a critical end. During the ministry of Jesus, 'the old things were passing away, for the new had drawn near'. After the conclusive events of Jesus' cross and resurrection, the apostle could say: 'The old has passed away, behold the new has come' (II Cor. 5:17). The future has begun. Justification sets Christians free from their past deeds as they allow themselves in faith to be determined by God's gracious future.

In Pannenberg's *Grundzüge der Christologie* (Gütersloh, 1964), the resurrection of Jesus appears as the anticipation — unexpected in its singularity — of the general resurrection. The particular history of Jesus and his resurrection modifies its own hermeneutical context, that of Jewish apocalyptic. His resurrection vindicates and confirms the contested ministry, and even the person, of Jesus as Christ and Lord. There might be something to be made, for our subject, out of Pannenberg's interesting though not unproblematic notion of a certain retroaction in christology as in other matters. Its necessary background and horizon is the eternal purpose of God. In the afterword to the fifth German edition of his christology (1976), Pannenberg recognizes that his postulate of an 'eschatological ontology' requires greater elaboration in a direction that will challenge current philosophical presuppositions.

For my part, the perspectives on time and eternity first set forth in *Eucharist and Eschatology* have been extended a little in the concluding sections of my *Doxology* (New York and London, 1980, pp. 444-62; cf. pp. 118-22) and in my contribution on 'Sacramental time' to the Queen's College, Birmingham, sesquicentennial volume edited by J.M. Turner, *Queen's Essays* (Birmingham, 1980, pp. 157-73). At this stage, our thinking on time and eternity is bound to be speculative, for 'now we see through a glass darkly'. While eternity would appear to be in some senses the antithesis of time, especially when time is experienced as decay, yet eternity must relate positively to time as its creative ground. The incarnation, death and resurrection of Jesus Christ let us believe that God is not hostile to the creation of which time is the mark, but rather seeks its redemption and ultimate transformation in accordance with his own nature as love.

A German Catholic theologian, Joseph (now Cardinal) Ratzinger, has formulated the eschatological tension as that between design and reality, *Schema* and *Wirklichkeit*. In his *Eschatologie: Tod und ewiges Leben* (Regensburg, 1977), Ratzinger's main interest lies in the connections between eschatology and anthropology. Against a modern 'biblical theology' which had too easily rejected 'the soul' in the name of a certain hebraism (the word *anima* was banished from the liturgy of the dead in the Roman Missal of 1970 and from the burial ritual), and noting the embarrassment which many contemporary theologians yet feel in face of a resurrection of the body, Ratzinger had bold recourse to the distinctively Christian doctrine of the soul which came to maturity in Thomas Aquinas and which alone does justice to Scripture, early tradition and logic alike. A duality, which is not a dualism, of body and soul is needed in order to match the calling to dialogical communion addressed by the God of the living to his human creatures who are coming to their dignity as unified and total persons in the conditions of time and space. Where love is in evidence, matter is being penetrated and transformed by spirit. In communion with their fellows and with all God's creation, reconciled human beings are in Christ ripening for eternity and the vision of God.

Another comprehensive eschatological statement, sometimes in sharp conflict with Ratzinger and with a declaration on 'The Last Things' issued by the Roman Congregation for the Doctrine of the Faith on 17 May 1979, is H. Vorgrimler's *Hoffnung auf Vollendung: Aufriss der Eschatologie* (Freiburg, 1980). In the first section, the Catholic dogmatician usefully traces the work done on biblical eschatology by German-speaking exegetes in the previous decade. The second part surveys hermeneutical reflections and systematic proposals made during the last generation. Vorgrimler notes three things in particular: first, the correspondence between a theologian's eschatology and his fundamental view of the relation between God and the world; second, the widespread agreement that eschatology must inform the whole of theology and have its 'unsurpassable' centre in Christ; third, the recovery by 'political theologians' of the 'apocalyptic' thrust in biblical eschatology. In the third and final section of his book, Vorgrimler treats the special themes of death, judgment (*Rechenschaft*) and fulfilment (*Vollendung*). He outlines the traditional teachings of the Catholic magisterium; but in his own constructive and intentionally 'demythologized' statements he is much influenced by K. Rahner's 'theology of death', with its view of the 'completion' of the individual human being as a 'moment' in cosmic history, and the notion that the general 'judgment' of the world is taking place, process-wise, along the course of its history. Vorgrimler recognizes that the hope for ultimate fulfilment implies a 'radical alteration' in the present life-forms of creation. Our most trustworthy directions are to be found in Jesus' attitudes and behavior in face of the kingdom of God: 'Aware that human beings alone and in their own strength will never achieve fulfilment, and faced with the vulnerability and powerlessness of God, we are to act as if God's kingdom was to be put into practice by men and God's creation to be saved by men, until the day when God will come.'

Although eschatology has been one of the main themes of twentieth-century theology, the term itself has come under attack. J. Carmignac called the word 'confusing' ('Les dangers de l'eschatologie' in *New Testament Studies* 17, 1970-71, pp. 365-90), and 'eschatology' took pride of place in an *Expository Times* series on 'slippery words' (article by I. H. Marshall in volume 89, 1977-78, pp. 264-69). Marshall allowed the word's usefulness as well as its dangers; but Carmignac returned to the charge in an irascible book entitled *Le mirage de l'eschatologie: royauté, règne et royaume de Dieu . . . sans eschatologie* (Paris, 1979). The substantive issues are far more complex and subtle than is suggested by the apparently simple conclusion drawn by Carmignac from his examination of *basileia* and *regnum* in Scripture and tradition, namely that God's 'rule' in the soul is justification, and that God's 'kingdom' is the Church with Jesus at its head. In a sense, Carmignac thereby merely poses the real, and not just self-generating, questions which have been at stake in the 'eschatological' debate. The term eschatology was expressly defended by D. E. Aune in his materially valuable historical study which Carmignac cites without discussing, *The Cultic Setting of Realized Eschatology in Early Christianity* (Leiden, 1972). According to Aune, worship in the Spirit, the sacraments, and the liturgical assembly were from the very beginning of the Church so many instances of the 'partial', 'provisional', 'preliminary', 'anticipatory' realization of salvation and shaped its conceptualization.

The eschatological perspective was taken by R. W. Jenson as the clue to understanding Christian language in its most characteristic function. In *The Knowledge of Things Hoped For* (New York, 1969), Jenson undertook first a sympathetic and critical examination of Origen on 'image' (the 'vision' of God) and Aquinas on 'analogy' (setting the 'goal' of existence). Then, in relation to modern linguistic analysis (verification) and hermeneutical theory (historicity), he proposed that the proclamation 'Jesus is risen' be heard as a *prophecy* which will be verified, or not, eschatologically ('He will come again to judge the quick and the dead'), and which may meanwhile move us to seek in Jesus' end the conclusion of our own lives. A further linguistic study of interest to our subject is C. L. Morse's more recent *The Logic of Promise in Moltmann's Theology* (Philadelphia, 1979). J. Moltmann himself provided a concise and comprehensive statement of his eschatologically governed view on protology, history and consummation in an essay entitled 'Creation and redemption' (in R. W. A. McKinney, ed., *Creation, Christ and Culture*, Edinburgh, 1976). In *Kirche in der Kraft des Geistes* (München, 1975, pp. 268-86), Moltmann wrote more appreciatively of the eucharist than he had ever done before. Following Thomas Aquinas, he saw it as a *signum rememorativum*, a *signum demonstrativum*, and a *signum prognosticum* and characteristically called it 'a public and open meal of fellowship for the peace and the righteousness of God in the world'.

Sacraments may be considered as concrete and dramatic language. Augustine's notion of the sacraments as *verba visibilia* was taken up by F. J. Leenhardt, *Parole visible* (Neuchâtel, 1971), and by R. W. Jenson, *Visible Words* (Philadelphia, 1978). Some of the most interesting work in sacramental theology in the last fifteen years has in fact been set in the perspective of a 'phenomenology of signs', drawing help for analysis and interpretation from psychology, sociology, and cultural anthropology. Chronologically, these writings run from, say, J. P. de Jong's *De eucharistie, symbolische werkelijkheid* (Hilversum, 1966) to G. S. Worgul's *From Magic to Metaphor: A Validation of the Christian Sacraments* (New York, 1980). I will single out L. Dussaut, *L'eucharistie, pâques de toute la vie* (Paris, 1972), and G. Martelet, *Résurrection, eucharistie et genèse de l'homme* (Paris, 1972). Dussaut holds that the (pauline) emphasis on death and resurrection is too narrow: the eucharist is rather (in the perspective of the Fourth Gospel and of Hebrews) the memorial of the whole of Christ's life, with all that is thereby implied in the way of ethical example. Borrowing from structuralist analyses of ritual, Dussaut capitalizes on the bi-polar character of the Last Supper, where the action with the bread started the meal and the action with the wine took place 'after supper'. In the eucharist, the bread, sign of the body, signifies the incarnation, and the wine, sign of the blood, signifies the passion. The whole of Christ's life was a 'sacrificial meal': a sacrifice to God for humanity, a meal bringing men and women into fellowship with God. The eucharist allows people, in the time of the Church, to share the life and destiny of Christ in surrender to God. It provides a ritual focus for the personal sacrifice of Christ and of the Church. G. Martelet writes powerfully on the corporality of human existence, but his vision of the eucharistic destiny of man and the universe is marred by a deliberately teilhardian use of the transubstantiationist model (see above, pp. 104-10, especially note 326). The same criticism is made of Teilhard de Chardin by T. Runyon in an article which in many of its positive views also coincides with my chapter IV on the firstfruits of the kingdom: 'The world as original sacrament' in *Worship* 54 (1980), pp. 495-511.

The rest of my available space will be used to mention works which have brought eucharist and eschatology together in some way, though usually under a different dominant rubric. The themes of the remaining paragraphs are therefore as follows: christological, pneumatological, ecclesiological, ecumenical, liturgical, cultural, ethical and political.

Three pertinent American books on christology got lost in the North or South Atlantic. Neither in Africa nor in Europe did I come across D. Ritschl's

*Memory and Hope: An Inquiry concerning the Presence of Christ* (New York, 1967), P. C. Hodgson's *Jesus: Word and Presence* (Philadelphia, 1971), or H. W. Frei's *The Identity of Jesus Christ: The Hermeneutical Bases of Dogmatic Theology* (Philadelphia, 1975[2]). The *Christus praesens*, in whom come together the Church's memory and hope, grounds for Ritschl an ecclesiology of *ora et labora*, 'pray and work'. More attention could have been given to the Lord's supper as the gathering focus of both doxology and ethics. Hodgson, too, concentrates on 'the word', but since he allows it the density of the Hebrew *dabar*, there would have been opportunity for his treatment to be more consistently sacramental. Fortunately, the eucharist is introduced in the last two sections of the book (pp. 265-91), where present faith in the risen Jesus is taken as the mode by which we may anticipate, with ethical consequences, the eschatological love of God, who will raise us also in Christ. Hans Frei's main thesis is the inseparability of the presence and identity of Jesus Christ: 'To have Christ present is to know who he is and to be persuaded that he lives.' As yet, both Christ's presence and our grasp of it are indirect, being mysteriously mediated by the Spirit through Word and Sacrament as 'given and instituted, spatial and temporal bases'. Christ's lordship embraces both sides of the sacramental veil; in the words of George Herbert:

> Love is that liquor sweet and most divine
> Which my God feels as blood, and I as wine.

On the Roman Catholic side, F. J. van Beeck's *Christ Proclaimed: Christology as Rhetoric* (New York, 1979) treats the eucharist under the wider heading of worship and witness (*homologia*). He speaks of 'the original Christian fact' as 'the Church's self-expression in response to the presence, in the Spirit, of Jesus Christ alive', and states that 'this original fact is also future-oriented: the *actus directus* of worship and witness draws the Church into the *eschaton* with a confidence and a hope that can only come from the Father who has given the Church, in Jesus Christ, the assurance of eschatological fulfillment' (pp. 347-57). There are similarities here with the more sacramentally focused little study by the French Catholic F. X. Durrwell, *L'eucharistie, présence du Christ* (Paris, 1971). Well known for his earlier book *La Résurrection de Jésus, mystère de salut* (Le Puy/Lyon, 1950), Durrwell is guided by 'the paschal mystery' to see the eucharist as already the *parousia* of Christ, a coming which will reach its plenitude at the End when the Church is fully 'adequate' to the paschal mystery.

Concerning the pneumatological dimension of the eucharist, J. H. McKenna assembles some early and modern materials in his *Eucharist and Holy Spirit* (Great Wakering, 1975); but it is significant that this study of 'the eucharistic epiclesis in twentieth-century theology' stands 'in the shadow of "moment of consecration" problem'. It is almost exclusively in McKenna's presentation of Eastern theologians that an awareness of the eschatological import of the Spirit's role in the eucharist becomes evident. Sacramental theologians in the West have been slow to make the connections between pneumatology and eschatology (hence the importance of my chapter

IV). Even the welcome infusion of the Spirit from the charismatic movement in D. L. Gelpi's *Charism and Sacrament* (New York, 1976) leaves his chapter on 'the supper of blessing' the least excitingly renewed of the author's treatments of the various sacraments, and he fails to open up the eschatological prospect.

Ecclesiology is probably the best theme under which to mention Nicholas Lash's wide-ranging essay, *His Presence in the World: A Study in Eucharistic Worship and Theology* (London, 1968). Certainly the communitary aspect is prominent, and the whole book is marked by ecumenical openness and by sensitivity to the power of a living eucharist as witness to the gospel. In *La chiesa nell'eucaristia* (Napoli, 1975), B. Forte proposes a 'eucharistic ecclesiology' based on the documents of Vatican II. He seeks to overcome N. Afanassieff's disjunction between a eucharistic/local/Orthodox ecclesiology and a juridical/universal/Catholic view of the Church. From the eschatological angle, the author sees the eucharist as the sacrament of a Church which is still a pilgrim people in the world but is already united to Mary in heaven (cf. *Lumen Gentium*, 7 and 8, and *Gaudium et Spes*).

Ecumenically, it is good to note the recognition accorded the eschatological dimension of the sacrament in a number of recent 'agreed statements' on the eucharist. The Anglican/Roman Catholic International Commission's statement of 1971 declared: 'The Lord who thus comes to his people in the power of the Holy Spirit is the Lord of glory. In the eucharistic celebration we anticipate the joys of the age to come. By the transforming action of the Spirit of God, earthly bread and wine become the heavenly manna and the new wine, the eschatological banquet for the new man: elements of the first creation become pledges and first fruits of the new heaven and the new earth' (§ 11). In §§ 42-45 of its 1978 *Herrenmahl* text, the international Joint Roman Catholic/Lutheran Commission expounds the thesis that in the eucharist 'the future glory is promised and incipiently revealed and communicated'. The 1973/74 Leuenberg Concordat between European Lutherans and Reformed soberly stated in connection with the Supper: 'Rejoicing that the Lord has come to us, we await his future coming in glory' (§ 16). The eschatological hints in the WCC Faith and Order Commission's *One Eucharist* statement of 1974 are likely to be developed into a whole section in the revision being undertaken for the WCC Assembly in 1983. In a lecture given in Rome in 1975 I developed the Holy Year themes of reconciliation and renewal with reference to the eucharist: 'The eucharist as an ecumenical sacrament of reconciliation and renewal' in *Studia Liturgica* 11 (1976), pp. 1-18. And in a paper presented to the Conference of European Churches in Sofia in 1977 I wrote on the place of the eucharist in the development of conciliar relations among the churches: 'Conciliarity and eucharist' in *One in Christ* 14 (1978), pp. 30-49 and in *Midstream* 17 (1978), pp. 135-53. In each case I was prolonging some of the 'ecclesiological consequences' drawn in chapter V of *Eucharist and Eschatology*. In *Sakramente im Wechselspiel zwischen Ost und West* (Zürich/Güersloh, 1979), the Roman Catholic R. Hotz looked to the sense of 'mystery' in the Eastern churches — an 'eastward correction' — for a renewal of sacramental theology and practice in the West. In *Okumenische Glaubenseinheit aus eucharistischer Uberlieferung* (Paderborn, 1976), another Roman Catholic theologian, H. J. Schulz, had already argued that an adequate 'unity in faith' can be extracted from the ancient eucharistic tradition which the divided churches have retained or restored. The words, actions and celebration of the eucharistic rites, and particularly the great eucharistic prayer, provide sufficient expression of trinitarian faith, and of doctrine concerning Church, sacraments and ministry. It is to relations between the Roman and the Eastern churches that Schulz devotes most attention, but he sees positive prospects also for reconciliation with the churches of the Reformation by this route.

In liturgical studies, an eschatological awareness permeates Marianne H. Micks' presentation of 'the phenomenon of Christian worship', attractively entitled *The Future Present* (New York, 1970). Rich textual resources are assembled in 'Von der Erwartung des Kommenden', E. J. Lengeling's contribution to *Gott feiern* (ed. J. G. Plöger, Freiburg, 1980). B. Bürki's study of burial liturgies, *Im Herrn entschlafen* (Heidelberg, 1969), is specially valuable for what it says on the eucharist in connection with martyrdom and on the communion as a viaticum.

On the cultural front, we may appropriately return to Africa. In his pioneering 'study of the encounter between New Testament theology and African traditional concepts', *New Testament Eschatology in an African Background* (London, 1971), J. S. Mbiti included a long chapter on 'the eschatology of the sacraments' (pp. 91-126). He argued that magic, or the fear of it, had been responsible for an incomplete appropriation of the sacraments. Yet an opportunity was provided by 'the strong African interest in a futurist eschatology', which 'may partially be an unconscious attempt to find a spiritual homeland beginning here and now in this life; but not knowing how to find it, they revert to a largely mythical future which may be no more than a shallow veneer of escapism.' In this context, the sacraments may come into their own as 'the nexus between the physical and the spiritual worlds; and through the concrete and material realities, eschatological realities become evident and available in the temporal and physical realm': 'Jesus as the host to whom the faithful are related makes the eucharist a true messianic meal which draws them together (instead of repelling them), and through which they obtain spiritual sustenance and blessing rather than a curse.' What the largest African independent church has so far made of the eucharist can be read in M. L. Martin, *Kimbangu: An African Prophet and his Church* (Oxford, 1975, pp. 178-82).

In the absence of that part of Karl Barth's *Kirchliche Dogmatik* IV/4 which was to deal with the Lord's supper, we may mention the 'ethical and biblical inquiry', of late-barthian and neo-zwinglian inspiration, by A. C. Cochrane, *Eating and Drinking with Jesus* (Philadelphia, 1974). The author devotes long and favourable attention to the eschatological side of my *Eucharist and Eschatology* but considers the book's sacramentalism regrettable. In turn, I may heartily endorse Cochrane's ethical developments but consider that they would have been strengthened by a sacramental grounding, which is far from being an alternative to the christological base on which Cochrane rightly insists.

It is with regard to the political incidences of the Christian faith that some of the liveliest eschatological discussion took place in the past decade: eschatological, because the nature of 'the kingdom' is at stake in such debates. In his influential *Theology of Liberation* (New York, 1973), G. Gutiérrez argued against the distinction between sacred and secular history; positively, there is but 'one history', in which political liberation and the eschatological promises are continuous. Divisions between oppressors and oppressed are making eucharistic communion an impossible sham in the Latin American church (p. 137), yet the sacrament has the potential to 'build up a real human brotherhood' (pp. 262-65). In Asia, Indians will testify to the leverage supplied by equal participation at the Lord's table to the breaking up of the caste system; yet the Sri Lankan Catholic Tissa Balasuriya has argued that the eucharist itself needs liberating from its 'domestication'. In *The Eucharist and Human Liberation* (New York, 1979), he claims that the celebration of the sacrament has long served to legitimate dominant nations, classes, and males. The golden vessels are the spoils of colonialist robbery, the ecclesiastical hierarchy has allied itself with feudal lords and capitalist élites, the eucharistic presidency has been restricted to men. Freedom-seeking groups are now starting to liberate the eucharist, and the eucharist's liberating potential is beginning to be unlocked. The true eucharist is grounded in the free self-gift of Jesus Christ for the cause of 'integral human liberation': its spirituality is one of 'giving and not of grabbing'. In 'Revolution and quietism: two political attitudes in theological perspective' (in *Scottish Journal of Theology* 29, 1976, pp. 535-55), I suggested that the traditional distinction between the orders of preservation and redemption forbade any overly direct identification between present welfare and final salvation. Yet we are called to establish positive correspondences between the life of the Church, the life of the world, and the definitive divine kingdom with its values of liberty, love, justice, peace and all the rest; and particularly in chapter XII of *Doxology* I have laid down a sacramental base for personal, social and even political ethics.